THE OTHER FACE

OF

PUBLIC TELEVISION

THE OTHER FACE

OF

PUBLIC TELEVISION:

Censoring

the American Dream

ROGER P. SMITH

Algora Publishing
New York

Softcover ISBN 1-892941-82-1

Hardcover ISBN 1-892941-83-x

Library of Congress Cataloging-in-Publication Data 000904

Smith, Roger P. (Roger Phillips), 1929-
  The other face of public television : Censoring the American dream / by
Roger P. Smith.
    p. cm.
Includes index.
1. Public television—United States. I. Title.
  HE8700.79.U6 S65 1929
  384.55'4'0973—dc21

                        2002000904

Printed in the United States

Front cover: based on *TV Buddha* by Nam June Paik, 1974

To Adrian, Jean, Elsie, Ellen
and the Deans and Humanities Faculty of Yale University,
1948-1952

"Here is a tool comparable only to the invention of printing in its power to inform and to influence free thought."

U.S. Senator Clinton P. Anderson
"TV Channels for Education", 1952

"Public information and the media by which it is disseminated are the strongest possible bulwarks of the freedom we love so well."

U.S. Senator Leverett Saltonstall
"TV Channels for Education", 1952

"Nothing doth more hurt in a state than that cunning men pass for wise."

Sir Francis Bacon

"Hypocrisy is the homage that vice pays to virtue."

La Rochefoucauld

"The key to success is integrity. If you can fake that, you got it made."

Groucho Marx

"What's it all about, Alfie . . . Is it just for the moment we live?"

Popular song by Hal David & Burt Bacharach

"Creation is a patient search."

Le Corbusier

"Those who ignore history are condemned to relive it."

George Santayana

TABLE OF CONTENTS

Presumptions in this Book

- People learn from television.
- Television has become a part of the educational fabric of all Americans.
- Theater, of which television is an extension, is an art form.
- The federal government sets the rules that structure broadcasting.
- The market promulgates a philosophy of being that is reflected in our television, our education and our government.
- Public Television came into being because of commercial television's failures.
- Public Television interpenetrates a context of family, education, politics, economics, and the arts.
- The form that Public Television takes signals the course of American cultural and intellectual history.

INTRODUCTION

Shortly after World War II, a new kind of theater burst into American living rooms. Viewers were struck by its novelty. The movement and sound, and the awareness that they were witnessing happenings as they actually took place, enthralled them. "The magic of television", it was called.

The rapid and wholesale integration of this novel communication/entertainment/information medium into American culture brings into focus a question that is as yet unanswered: Can the alliance of democratic government and consumerist capitalism foster conditions that enhance a civilized society? The commercial effectiveness of television has been proven beyond a doubt, while formidable clinical, scholarly and hearsay evidence of its cultural impact has yet to receive acceptance.

The art of television began ad hoc, without much in the way of structure or rules. What television was had to be discovered in the doing. Early clues came in the form of the charm and intimacy of puppeteer Burr Tilstrom's *Kukla, Fran and Ollie*. Original drama on an intimate scale came from *Studio One*, then on a larger scale from *Playhouse 90*. Experiments in aesthetics came from *Camera Three*. How things work in science and technology came from *Adventure*. Children's curiosity about the outside world was piqued by *Let's Take a Trip*, while explorations of the arts and humanities came from *Omnibus*. Key events in current history — the riveting live coverage of the resignation of General Douglas Mac-Arthur and the Army-McCarthy hearings — established television's worthiness as an instrument of citizenship education.

Such high points were the creative achievements of pioneers exploring television's potential. The makers of these programs were people willing to experiment, willing to dare, willing to risk failure. They were exuberant, mostly young, and full of hope. Today we look at them as examples of a spirit that we think of as peculiarly American. Veterans of television production refer to that time as "the great days". For makers and viewers alike, in the years just after our victory in World War II, television was a vehicle for a hope for America's future that was nearly palpable. What these independent minds accomplished was allowable within the structure of American broadcasting as it had been established.

Broadcasting has come a long way since its beginnings in the 1920s and early 1930s. Then, the Payne Fund and the American Association of Colleges and Universities battled vainly against the specter of pitchmen being allowed to transmute the educational potential of broadcasting into a vehicle for what was seen as vulgar commercial gain. American radio was lobbied into commercialism through the resources of major American corporations, including some whose survival is testimony to the effectiveness of the tactic. The widely respected General Electric and AT&T were among them.

By edict of the federal legislature in the Communications Act of 1934, the American broadcasting industry was authorized by the Congress of the United States to be, in effect, a component of a propaganda machine for the makers of consumer products. The propaganda was called advertising. The Communications Act of 1934 invited into everybody's living room the street-hawkers who had been locked out in earlier centuries. Back then, authority for the character that radio and its successor, television, ultimately developed was negotiated by the federal legislature into the hands of the US Department of Commerce, a clear signal of its future. Television broadcasting began life under radio's regulations — its programming was legislatively subsumed by grandfathering. Picture-radio, or television, during the second half of the 20th century was supported by the State as part of the stagecraft of commerce.

It is generally acknowledged among thoughtful people that compromise is an essential element in the story of the development of commercial television in the United States. Long ago, most of us learned to expect some dissembling from commercial TV. The reason for the invention of noncommercial television was to create a medium free of some of the more egregious compromises. Developed in the shadow of England's BBC, it was thought that our television might be able to husband a standard of thought and sensibility that would outpace England's. But over time, noncommercial television in America has taken on some of the limitations of commercial television. In the areas of both authorization and management, principles that justified the creation of public television as an independent alternative have been compromised into nonexistence.

The Federal Communications Act of 1934 shrouded American commercial broadcasting behind the veil of public ownership and public service, as it laid the groundwork for the consumerism that molds the minds of our children today, and now prepares to engulf the planet. The forces that impelled commercial television have become an increasingly powerful determinant of our culture. Some of their unintended consequences, the trivialization of the culture and the waste of planetary resources, have become the stuff of common discourse.

Who is to blame? Where does the cause lie? Not with the people at the networks. What we see on American TV is the inevitable consequence of structures set by occupants of federal elective office. The interests served are two: (1) Returns on corporate debt and (2) Public revenue dependent on those returns. The mutual reinforcement of each is sanctified by governmental decree. An outcome of the Communication Act of 1934 was the development of the market culture. We can now see around us a public swayed by media tools of greater and greater sophistication toward pursuit of the single goal of the gratification of desire. The old pre-Judaic Mammon of Sumer and Akkad has returned, wearing a happyface.

During the course of its lifetime, noncommercial television has been variously called "public service" or "noncommercial" or "educational" and, now, "public". Presented to you here is the story of some of the forces involved in a half-century of the development of that part of television avowedly designated to advance the public interest.

Educational TV was initially conceived to be an example to commercial TV of potential avenues for service to the public. Educational television was meant to provide a more democratic alternative to the singular objective of commercial television, corporate enrichment through product sales. The failure of educational television was glacial and real. Within a score of years after its founding, educational television saw its mission to be unreachable. Public television, the successor to educational television has, during its over thirty years of being, been shepherded into becoming a decorous government information service. In the interest of institutional survival, America's public television bureaucracy has obeyed the dictum of Marx (Groucho), "The key to success is integrity. If you can fake that, you've got it made."

The picture is not a flattering one. If we look to history, we see ample demonstration that a group or a society is called corrupt when it allows power to devolve into the hands of people who are willing to sacrifice principle for the sake of perceived advantage. That's what Macbeth was about, after all.

Most private-sector institutions can get by for a time within an opportunistic context. But in organizations dedicated to public service, the presence of people infected with opportunism is a corruption. It was not the initiatives of people making free decisions that shaded off the promise of alternative television. People did what seemed to be required for institutional survival. They compromised. If opportunism was what they did, it was because opportunism was what the system demanded. It's what everybody else did. Why should they be different? Like the rest, they had families to support.

How does this writer know what really goes on in public television? Empirically, from day-to-day experience, from observation and inference. Not from law or science, or from *The New York Times* index, and emphatically not from press releases. Much that you will read here is otherwise undocumented. A reason is that today, clever people who may put their immediate personal advantage first avoid committing to writing anything that can harm them. One of the arts of corporate survival today is to be very careful about what gets on the record. This work presupposes that some valid truths can be uncovered inferentially. In the new market/culture, reading between the lines is perhaps a more direct route to truth than it has been.

To a person with my experience, the programs we see daily on public television advertise the story of their creation. From small clues I can see the character of the wind in the sails, when the steam pressure lessens ever so slightly in the boiler — why meritorious television programs ideas are not considered for funding.

This is a tale told by a witness. I saw the history of educational and public television as it was made, day by day. I saw hope, imagination, energy and selfless idealism succumb before the skills of the courtier. I saw administrative caution beget formula programming. I saw a dream compromised to expediency. Times have changed. New people do the jobs, but the methods and structure stand. A reading of what appears on the tube today shows that the system controls the substance. The creative community in public television that was to be the *raison d'être* of the entire enterprise has vanished. The cultural loss is significant.

This book needed to come sooner. I write it now to minimize harm to innocents. Observation of our culture's tribal mores has alerted me to the knowledge that if you rat on a going thing, some guileless people will be hurt. This angers everybody, so nobody listens to the message. The people now working in public broadcasting have the option to dismiss what I say ("Oh, he doesn't know how things are now"). But from what appears on the screen, this boulevardier can't help but recall other fresh, smiling, painted faces.

This book was written to share with you what the author has learned firsthand. In this volume I reach out toward subjects that may seem afield. That's because public television is about people in their diversity. It involves government policy. It is a form of literature, of theater, an organic part of the history of our national development. Public television as it stands today is inseparable from its context.

Eugene O'Neill's point in *The Iceman Cometh* was that the debasement of the individuals he depicted in his plays was not a cause, but an effect. The tart serves a useful social function. A modicum of style comes from second-hand finery. Techniques of beguilement are an instrument for her survival. Accommodation is her art. As a guarantee of compliance, she is supported on the edge of poverty. She never questions the sources of her beneficence. She never tells on her man. She's no threat. She is public television.

As you read, I hope you say once, "This book isn't about public television . . . it's about us."

Roger Smith
Thousand Palms, California 92276-0338

Foreword

DREAMS OF A BETTER WORLD

The development of the television medium in America during the second half of the 20th century was influence by its social, intellectual, governmental, commercial context. An understanding of the context of its development is integral to an understanding of what American television is and why it is the way it is.

One part of the context in which television has developed is its accommodation to the hopes and dreams of ordinary Americans. Americans are the recent children of the Industrial Revolution. Our parents and grandparents endured a wrenching era for the sake of a better future for us to live in. Smoky skies, greasy, noisy, noxious cities . . . there are few written records of how harsh the process of industrialization was. Some of what I know came from my mother's teaching. Some she could not or would not tell — to spare us both. Some comes from my own memory.

Ordinary Americans wanted the 20th century to be a good one. We wanted our lives to be comfortable. One way to make our lives better was through acts of sympathetic magic . . . if we pretended our lives were as they might be, they would get better. The hope was Panglossian.[1]

The hope for cures for woe made our ancestors vulnerable to patent medicine salesmen. "We're tarts, not whores", two of Eugene O'Neill's characters call out. The human tendency to put an agreeable coloration on things, as Eugene O'Neill pointed out in *The Iceman Cometh*, is, for more of us than we might care to admit, a permanent poultice. Euphemism is the neatsfoot oil on the bootstraps of self-esteem. Franz Lehar's operetta *Land of Smiles* was a hit in 1922. The song "Wishing Will Make it So" brought comfort during the Great Depression. Jerome Kern's perennial favorite, "Look for the Silver Lining", preceded it by two decades. "I'm Always Chasing Rainbows" came before that. Judy Garland's

"Somewhere, Over the Rainbow" remains a sentimental touchstone.

Industrialization's promise of the elimination of drudgery was a 19th-century dream that sustained the Western world. Everybody knew that industrialization had been an ugly process that scarred England. But the fairness and equity of its potential outcome in American democracy was thought to be worth a temporary sacrifice. The industrialization of our agrarian democracy held a promise of Arcadia that had been denied for centuries. My mother taught me that industrialization would bring some leisure, so that "People who have the desire will have the option to write, to paint, to compose music, to engage in speculative reflection, critical thought or disinterested intellectual inquiry to benefit others, instead of having to work-work-work all the time."

The process of industrialization had its down side. Its bounty included lives built around such little publicized realities as the trading in trainloads of pig snouts from Chicago's mammoth stockyards, the black lung of coal miners in West Virginia, the sweatshops of New York's Garment District, the empty drummers lives' recorded by Theodore Dreiser and Arthur Miller, and the smoky Pittsburgh steel mills that gave emphysema to my grandmother and to which my mother accommodated by equipping herself for a trip to the city with a second pair of white kid gloves. (Where the soot came from was not the affair of business.)

In the early part of the last century, American industrial efficiency became American industrial might. Talismanic imitation of models from English industrialization promised success in the development of a socio-economic system to bring a better life for more Americans. Americans compromised, sure that their sacrifice was temporary. Compromise was a way of getting along during the era of industrialization. A feudal hierarchy called "business" coexisted within a liturgical democracy. Beyond a job title, many women knew little about what their husbands "did". They didn't ask. What husbands "did" during the process of industrialization could be unpleasant unethical or brutal. It was understood that men "had to do what they had to do". "Men's work" was the euphemism women used. In business, gentility didn't count for much. A heroine of the Rodgers and Hammerstein Broadway musical *Carousel* sings, "What's the use of wondrin' if he's good or if he's bad . . . he's your honey and you love him, that's all there is to say." Mothers protected their children by looking the other way . . . they asked only for "success". Wives cultivated a world of appearances based on their interpretation of the habits of the English gentry — a world of domestic comfort, manners, etiquette. A model wife (delightfully characterized in 1930s films by the actress Billie Burke) simply didn't know about worldly matters. It was thought best not to look too closely, not to know, not to tell the children . . . they'd find out soon enough!

Accommodation became tradition. Some women made a life's work of becoming the trophy of a rich man. Politeness, courtesy, taste, charm, a large wardrobe and a cursory familiarity with the arts were requirements. In order to capture one of the better trophies, those men not overly favored by nature had to devote unremitting effort to focused acquisitiveness. A man's business success demanded willingness to sacrifice the trust and affection of colleagues and to actively repress competitive males.

Exchanges among men and women who had selected these roles took place at segregated parties, games, school events and other gatherings. These offered opportunities for their children to cultivate appropriate mating rituals. Their interrelationships were called "society". The culture of self-perpetuation among groups defined by the accumulation of vast purchasing power was known as "high society".

Aberrant children of a trophy race resisted the pressures to become contestants. Often they transferred from the role of oppressor to oppressed, joining (at least in demeanor) the underclass, the manipulated many. Before World War II, their symbol was a shirt open at the collar; after, it was long hair, jeans and a guitar. Sociologist David Reisman called their costume "proletarian drag".

In the midst of these accommodations to industrialization, the Church and the University taught ethics. These two institutions kept alive for a time the idea of mankind as a higher, thinking animal. Education in the humanities taught young Americans how wise people, intellectuals and ruling elites had thought and lived in the past; as soon as a person graduated from university tutelage, he was expected to forget this and to join the fray.

The triple-standard, one ethic for the university, one for the workplace, another quite different one for the home and family, was an accepted convention that nobody acknowledged.[2] We are as yet not liberated from this tradition.

To eschew the unattractive became an American habit, seamlessly woven into middle-class life. Institutions, like individuals, put a good face on their actions. It made life tolerable. Only after the passage of years has dulled the pain can we begin to talk of compromises made without hurting ourselves or others.

A symptom of the institutionalization of wishful thinking in America today is the upgrading of terminology. Nowadays, a part-timer at a university is "adjunct" or "visiting". Any corporate functionary not a clerk is an "executive". A person who was once a clerk is now a "representative", an "associate" or a "team member". Music that was once called "commercial" is now termed "popular". The onetime garbage collector, now "sanitary engineer", is engaged in "waste management". He uses not a dump but a "Community Collection Center". Bums are now "the homeless". What was once a peddler is now a "marketing specialist". Technology is now "science", the manufacture of armaments is "high tech industry". Exploitation is "enterprise", avarice is "The American Dream", selfishness, ambition and greed are now "individualism". A person who once may have been an acquaintance is now a "friend". What was once lust is "love". What was sensual or even lewd is "sensuous". What was "salacious" is "adult" or "mature". Once upon a time it took "a heap o' livin'" to make a house a home; today it takes only a realtor to instantly transform an empty shell into a "home", or a postage-stamp of land into an "estate". Featureless tract developments and strip-malls east of Los Angeles have been magically transformed into "The Inland Empire". Gambling has become "gaming", fake is "faux". Even the old snack bar is now billed as a "gourmet center"[3] The "tarts" of O'Neill's day are the "celebrities", "starlets" and "supermodels" of today. The creation of euphemisms has developed into a common tactic of manipulative self-interest. For this enterprise, no end is in sight.

Looking on the bright side helps to make our lives tolerable. But euphemism conceals us from ourselves. As we look for the silver lining, we signal our vulnerability to exploitation by others.

The option to use euphemism as a tool makes it easier for the so-inclined to rise to the temptation to manipulate others. The outcomes of the hopeful can be put at risk by those whose charm and wit are calculated devices to serve their own self-defined interests.

The bucolic American pastime of baseball and the sport of football were transformed into businesses by media, and became an instrument of mass marketing. Casual and bumptious game-players were metamorphosed into profit-sharing gladiators in a vast public spectacle whose justification is the selling of competitiveness and ego-enhancing perishable goods.

History is once again a worthy teacher. An examination of the fates of the ancient Athenian philosophies of Hedonism and the cult of Dionysus might prompt caution among planners in the boardrooms of America. Human history demonstrates that the antisocial consequences of those indulgent pursuits caused the ancient Greeks eventually to banish the cults that practiced them. Social consequences of the agenda offered by commercial media as the Oz of consumerism may be a repetition of historic precedent. Public egocentricity, selfishness, the dissolution of the idea of community: these lead to a disregard of the needs or desires of others. Our crime, tax revolts, educational neglect, our littered landscape are testimony to attitudes cultivated by a giddy consumerism. Mammon as a Holy of Holies was discredited in ancient times. He has appeared in a new guise, variously known today as Consumption, Ownership, The Bottom Line, or the Gross Domestic Product.

The history of American television is intimately interwoven with changes in the society at large. Some of how societal changes were both prompted and accommodated is spelled out in this volume.

Chapter 1

THE OTHER FACE OF PUBLIC TELEVISION

America has State Television. We call it public TV. Our state television acts in the interest of and selectively promulgates ideas that contribute to the perceived interest of a cadre of occupants of elective office. Through deft use of their authority, our own elected representatives, industry, and public TV itself have discreetly eased what was originally conceived and heralded as an alternative to commercial television dedicated to broadly defined enlightenment into a Federal Information Ministry paid for by "viewers like you". All the programs you watch on public TV must meet the approval of gatekeepers in the United States Congress and the Executive Branch of the Federal Government. The route is by way of the carrot-and-stick of annual funding authorization and appropriation processes. The outcome, as you might expect, is not procedural but substantive. Billed as "yours" on its station breaks, public TV is yours the way a Stealth bomber is yours . . . it's paid for largely with your tax money and made in your name according to the decisions of a few dozen men whose inclinations have led them to pursue public office as your representatives.

How did this metamorphosis happen? One cause was default, and one method was encroachment. The current procedures that determine what you see on public television are not those intended by the founders of what was meant to be an alternative to commercial television. They are instead a considerable limitation. In a maneuver not without precedent, the usurper rode under the banner of savior. Resistance was minor. You and I had other things on our minds. We were unwilling to pay for anything better. The vacuum of a stumbling democratic participation was filled by special interests. Over time, these have allowed an oligarchic control of public TV that echoes certain developments elsewhere in the democratic process. To preserve the semblance of democracy, the change has been tactically executed. In the background of public TV, the private sector discreetly

"I don't know much about art, but I know what I like."

monitors our State TV system via local, regional and national board membership and program funding, a complementary double-check on the way it leverages the behaviors of occupants of public office via legislative lobbying and campaign finance. Being of the American tradition, and therefore concerned with their own socio-economic survival, seekers of public office and public television decisionmakers alike are careful to play according to the rules that funding sources establish. State Television in the United States was never formally established as such. Since it is the product of a discreet usurpation, there is neither public protection nor its provision.

A perhaps fatal impropriety of current procedures for the funding and management of public television is their abridgement of the first amendment guarantee of freedom of speech. Through a process long in the making, voices carrying other than approved ideas are disallowed in public TV. There's a "don't ask, don't tell" practice in public television decisionmaking. The rules go like this: Any idea, program or series proposal that might possibly put in question any aspect of the belief system of those holding control of the purse is labeled "controversial", and is *ipso facto* simply disallowed. The single class of exceptions is what are called "issues". These are matters contemplated to arise on the legislative agenda.

By this practice, dissent is not so much forbidden as it is simply not acknowledged.

The possibility of an American Tiananmen Square event (in which dissidents attempt to use the forum of public television to express nonconformist views) is circumvented through the simple instrument of policy — we don't allow the dissidents into the square! Any idea with a life outside Congress' program for themselves is labeled "controversial", or "elitist", and censored by simple non-authorization. The practice of censorship of that which is branded controversial has acted as a prohibition to innovation and creativity, an encouragement to imitation and standardization. Since this abridgement applies primarily to creative people, a disorganized group who do not represent a bloc, it goes unnoticed.

The prohibition of subjects labeled "controversial" allows the application to American public television of procedures that in other countries we label "A Leaden Yoke of Ideology".[4] Those in the media who conform ideologically are rewarded. Not only are they careful not to offend, they are alert to please. The now codified method that is the *modus operandi* of all institutions of public TV has been justified as a survival technique. It has brought public television to its present status as an instrument to produce television programs that are promotions for federally funded or approved activities. Implicit in government funded and promoted promotion/public relations approaches is the assumption that whatever the funder is up to is *ipso facto* a good thing. For a free people, the very idea that the thought control allowed by this method of program production *could* happen constitutes the compromise of some rather basic principles.

The programs you see on public television speak for themselves.[5] The programs are eloquent evidence that the effective management of public television has become effective second-guessing by public TV administrators, an attempt to codify for TV the ideas that are acceptable or interesting to the sources of funding and control.

Control of public television is decentralized. But it can be identified. Locally, control is in the hands of industrialists, businessmen, merchants, bankers and their attorneys and information specialists. These are local public television trustees and board members. They make policy regarding local origination and local broadcast. On the national level, public television policy is controlled by legislators, and by President-designated board members of the Corporation for Public Broadcasting and the Federal Communications Commission. As we all know, the seats, the power, and the influence of some of these appointees are purchased through the simple device of campaign contributions.

Whose interest is served? Government contract-dependent and subsidized military/ industrial donors and their politician benefactors are now and have been for decades the policemen of public television. The financial support they give to a television industry that promotes their own world vision functions as an educational device, beyond the *de facto* censorship that is the funding or not-funding of program subjects that do or don't conform to a legislator's definition of his interest. Federal prohibition of what they choose to call "controversial programming" guarantees no dissent from whatever views they declare to be controversial. The similarity of this device to regulations that Chinese Communism[6] undertook to "ensure stability" is illuminating.

The management of public television in the interest of status quo politics and commerce is inimical to the long-range interests of both the medium and the people it is meant to serve. The bogy of "controversy" that dominates public television production is an inhibition to creativity in a nascent art form. It denies a principle that underlies the democratic theory, that "the public consensus, once formed, tolerates and protects questioning voices, which are the sources for ideas that will make future advances possible."[7] Or as Rosa Luxemburg pointed out regarding Lenin's suppression of democracy, "Without a free struggle of opinion life dies out in every public institution."

The actions of the federal funders of public TV reveal a power structure threatened by creativity . . . a culture in need of props to its own legitimacy. The practice of banning controversy from public television is effectively an abridgement of the free speech guaranteed by the first amendment to the Constitution. In the course of time, in its suppression of any "other", a doctrine disallowing controversy, threatens itself.

In policy decisions regarding public television we see not democracy but tribalism at work. The power of appointment, of hiring and firing the public television leadership, is political power. A coterie defined essentially by political party membership selects the leadership of public TV. These selected leaders hire people they understand.

And what kind do they understand? What kind of person would you expect government functionaries to understand? Experts in management, resource allocation, budgeting, of course; people comfortable in a corporate or bureaucratic context. That's who bureaucrats understand — people like themselves, people they can talk to. These are people with a valuable but limited subset of knowledge, a subset of awareness disciplined by the necessity to achieve defined, limited goals. Fueled by the rewards of marketing, advertising and lobbying, they represent the currently dominant culture, adopting strategies that mimic those of a momentarily ascendant consumerism.

Together, this limited stratum is today's TV gatekeeper. They are the *de facto* censors, withholding funding from the programs they don't want. These are the definers of the federal Communications Acts' terms, "public interest, convenience and necessity". These are the promoters of programs that carry a message congenial to *their own* interest, convenience and necessity. The knowledge of the nature and meaning of reality, the conception of excellence, the imaginativeness, the insight, the vision, the originality of the kind of person content to spend a lifetime totting up numbers implementing regulations, sitting at conference tables reporting on and being reported to, and vying for advancement — *theirs* is the originality, the conception of a significant life *you* get on public TV. American public television viewers see the programs that meticulous functionaries accept and fund, the programs that meticulous functionaries want them to see. As a viewer, as a citizen, how does that make you feel?

As a way to provide people in a democracy with explorations of television's potential richness, the formalized structure of public television as it has developed has become prohibitive. Bureaucratic decisionmaking may work for roads and sewers and bridges and meatpacking. But control of the ideas which form the basis of the content of television by beholden bureaucratic administrators, whether elected, appointed or hired, works as a straitjacket on the creative process.

Our country owes a significant debt to the managers and bureaucrats who keep the complex organizations of commerce and government in trim. As an economy we live by the smooth operation of complex organisms of people and machines. In most of industry, it is immaterial that good managers almost invariably are either uninterested in or are unsettled by genuine creativity. To ask a manager to follow the reasoning of Samuel Taylor Coleridge in distinguishing among imagination and fancy, fancy and caprice[8], is to ask a shrimp to whistle.

The imposition of the corporate/government model on public television was convenient. But it brought managers whose job is simply to keep the ship afloat into a position of making what are fundamentally artistic decisions. When any beneficiary of this (you, that is) presumes that what doesn't get onto public TV is unworthy or stupid, he is placing too much trust in the judgment of functionaries who are not prepared by inclination or training to come to terms with matters of substance. Programs you see on public television reflect not the diverse world as it is, but a particular interpretation as it is perceived by a largely self-selected group of gatekeepers behind the scenes: the industrialists and merchants, their bankers, their lawyers, the people whose electoral campaigns they pay for, their publicists and their public relations people, then by their agents, administrators, project directors, and producers in the field. The hierarchy that pulls the strings in public TV differs from feudalism in that the lords, earls, and princes are self-appointed. And what about the product? In the words of wit and essayist Russell Baker — "Wonders of non-controversial blandness". This is why American public TV is cautious, retrograde, fatuous and unworthy of a dynamic, democratic, open society.

The procedures by which public television is funded and managed today seem oblivious to the lessons of history. History tells us that kings approve of monarchy, and authoritarians of dictatorship; that history is the propaganda of the victors. Democracy was supposed to end that. Freedom of thought was supposed to be allowed.

For the time being, a certain group wields the balance of power in our country. They are the moneyed class. Their guardianship of their prerogatives is jealous; they see it as benign. Because it's true in their world, the controllers of American television extrapolate that human society is dominated by economics. The future that is presented through American broadcast television is an image of the future as they see it, an image of the continuation of a present that will guarantee their interests as they see them. The non-bureaucrat, the person who does not represent a substantial "interest", the seer, the visionary, the artist, the original thinker — that category or person who when examined in retrospect in all previous societies proves to be of the greatest use — these today are represented in the system of American government, education, commercial or public television only in the sciences. They have, in fact, been systematically excluded from other disciplines. Because creative people "make waves" or apply an unconventional perspective to the status quo, they have become *personae non gratae*. In the tree house of public TV, the "weirdos", the "eggheads", the "finks", the "nerds", the "uncool", the deviant, the different have been frozen out. Their places have been taken by the "normal": reliable worker bees whose agendas are dominated by the goals of corporate enrichment. This state of affairs, though real, is not necessarily in the interest of societal development, or even necessarily in the interest of the dominant class, the industrialists, their bankers and their lawyers themselves. It certainly is not democracy. For that matter, if history is a guide, special interest domination is a retrograde influence on the development of any culture. In our interest, in their interest, we *and they* should avoid it. In a democracy, it is a sacred duty.

Why would government, the guarantors of democracy, allow oligarchic power to prevail? One possibility is that its own convenience, its own ambition, its own self-interest as its members define it have persuaded government to co-opt avenues of communication to the public as a tool of self-preservation.

What has this subtle tyranny done and how do we know it? In one of its more public manifestations, it's called News Management. Watch the tube and the front page. Featured you'll see the Big News Every Day from the White House. Press releases and White House Press briefings and conferences have long been a control method of presidents (Nixon and Reagan were particular adepts). Annual funding authorization review of public television is another. Public television is at the mercy of the process of annual congressional surveillance. Congressmen decide, by looking at programs and proposals, whether public TV in their estimation deserves to be funded and at what level. Through the nature of the process, Congress funds public television proposals directed toward a public presumed to be at least a little less knowledgeable, less intelligent, less rational, less sophisticated, less educated, less wise than their elected representatives. To be allowed, a proposal must present no significant risk. A loophole in our system of democratic governance allows a purported alternative communications medium to be enchained.

Every year public television costs the nation's taxpayers about half what we now spend on one warplane, nearly a twenty-fifth of what we spend on prisons. In fact, that's a lot of money for a materialistic technocracy to spend on something as abstract as communication.

If the public is to be served, control of alternative television by the current politico/economic elite must be leavened. Founded as a free country, dedicated to the proposition that free speech is essential to our way of life, we cannot allow our television — the most powerful medium of communication ever invented — to be controlled exclusively by a cabal of two interlocked agencies with majestically demonstrated fallibility: business and government. Those of us in business need criticism. Those of us in government need criticism. Our professional health demands it. Our future, and the futures of those we serve if we are to have futures, demands it.

Chapter 2

PRIVATE AIRWAVES

The TV in your living room is a vending machine. The lineal descendant of radio, it's subject to many of the same regulations — and regulators. Commercial radio was established by government edict in 1934 during an economic crisis, over strong and vocal objections from educators, foundations and others. Some thought commercialization of radio would be akin to allowing street hawkers into the parlor, an intrusion into the opportunity for reflection inherent to a civilized life, and thereby an affront to the fastidious. The fear was that it would undermine a laboriously contrived high bourgeois culture. Those fears, it turns out, were well founded. Fastidiousness has no place in consumer culture. (Apparently, some thought that was okay.) The market role of radio was underlined when the Congress placed it under the jurisdiction of the US Department of Commerce. Commercial broadcasting was put there to move goods to generate revenue for investors, businesses and government. Decades later, "Educational TV" was invented as an alternative to the culturally impoverished "vast wasteland" of commercial broadcasting. Then, after a decade, because educational TV failed to attract the resources needed for its own advancement, public TV was invented.

As it has worked itself out, vending now motivates both commercial and noncommercial TV. The products vended by public TV are sometimes more abstract, more interesting: but the controlling intent that determines the use of the medium limits public television's potential with equal rigor.

Commercial TV calls their TV "free". Public TV says that public TV is made for and supported by "viewers like you". Commercial or public, one or another kind of TV may do what *you* want it to do, but only as a by-product. You may direct your thanks for this pleasant situation to the Communications Act of 1934. This historic federal legislation has been described by Lawrence K. Grossman, former president of NBC News and the Public

Broadcasting Service, as "The greatest giveaway of publicly owned resources in history, the free distribution of the nation's airwaves for commercial use."[9] Distinguished columnist Walter Lippmann called it a "fraud". Nowadays, thanks to the Communications Act of 1934, you can select any TV show you want . . . well, any TV show you want, that is, that *sells a lot of products.* You can select one that sells consumer products to you, on commercial TV, or one that more subtly sells attitudes to you: attitudes like nationalism or "multiculturalism" or "preparedness" or "enterprise", or "political correctness" on public television.

Aren't you lucky? Look at the choices you have! On commercial TV you can get trashy fiction, silly games, fatuous commentary, and a lot of fun ideas about devices you can buy to give you thrills, to make you sexy or to put in your mouth to make you feel good. On public TV you get earnest talking heads to tell you what the government or Wall Street are up to; you get furry animals; murder mysteries; costume drama; people on stages singing, acting or dancing; former celebrities to give you progress reports on government funded activities; auctions, imports and fundraising.

On both commercial and public television you get ideas approved of by essentially the same coterie, just differently wrapped. On both you're protected against any ideas that a large body of people doesn't agree with, or that may disrupt the value scheme or conflict with the perceived self-interest of those who pay the money it costs to put these programs in your liing room. Inevitably, it is rare to find on either commercial or public TV art, poetry, theater, philosophy, or any new or unconventional thing generated to stimulate you to think for yourself. Fortunately, in the television medium, most viewers notice only what is there, not what isn't.

How charming and beguiling and *comfortable* it is. It is, isn't it? Of course it is. And of course we're grateful. Getting this programming to us costs billions and uses up a lot of lives. You may wonder, as you sit back in the eiderdown with the pleasures flowing over you, how it happened that this cornucopia could have come to be there, right in your living room. Well, it happened because your friendly government was there to help you. And do you think that perhaps the Communications Act of 1996 brought any changes? Of course it did. The Communications Act of 1996 is a worthy successor to the Communications Act of 1934 ("to hell with notions of public service", says media historian Robert W. McChesney). Adding to the requirement for broadcasting in the "public interest, convenience and necessity" that for forty years proved more careful to cultivate the idea of an equivalence between commercial and public interest, convenience and necessity, it now specifies a commitment to a free-market "universal service" that promises to maximize opportunities for a veritable Khan el-Khalili Bazaar right in your living room.[10]

How did radio and TV get where they are? Originally, because of the limits of technology. Way back in the 1920s and 1930s radio was a crazy mass of individualists doing their thing. The physics of transmission set limits on the number of signals that could be carried in any given location. To avoid anarchy, by common consent, the government was called in. Petitioners' arguments were entertained by the government. Hawkers competed with universities for access to pieces of a limited broadcast spectrum. Even a labor union got into the act. The Federal Government then established rules and procedures to rationalize the chaos.

Back then, the idea of commercialism was anathema to a vocal segment of the public. It was also taken for granted, then, that if the government were to control radio, democracy would be imperiled. It was a matter of principle, still worthy of note. Eddy Dowling, in *The Form* (February 1934), saw potential danger in government control of information. "Radio is becoming too nearly a branch of journalism to warrant any form of government ownership or operation", he wrote.

The government adopted the role of policeman to a commercial service. It established licensing. A lot of people wanted these licenses. Everybody couldn't have a license, because there weren't enough radio frequencies for everybody. To keep order, the government established a system for allocating the right to use certain broadcasting frequencies. The "no bailout" policy for broadcasting stations was a critical component of the plan: "Make money, or no license renewal." The rationale was that the government didn't want the taxpayer, the "owner" of the frequencies, to be stuck with debt if radio failed. The prospect of radio's economic failure prompted Congress to a great decision to screen out irresponsibles and "do-gooders" and give the airwaves only to those with a proven record of profitable selling. Were visions of increased government revenue dancing in their heads? Who knows? Under the Congress' power to regulate commerce, the whole package was put under the jurisdiction of the Department of Commerce. There could have been no doubt then, as there can be no doubt now: *the structure of American broadcasting is a tactic to push goods. The strategy is to increase governmental, corporate and stockholder revenue. The public is the pawn.*

Back in the 1930s, we were told that our legislators saw the airwaves as a neutral "carrier". The restriction of the airwaves to commercial use under government supervision was justified as a practical constraint for a new useful tool threatening bedlam. The congressional directive — essentially, to "make money, or else" — did limit its use, however. Licensing the airwaves exclusively for commercial use was comparable to the government of Rome, during the Renaissance, telling the crafts guilds of which Donatello and Michelangelo were members that marble, bronze and fresco would be used only by Catholic priests for the making of religious icons. Not exactly democratic, is it?

A decision limiting broadcasting license contenders to the competitive was a decision President Coolidge would have applauded. It was less than ten years since he had announced, "The business of America is business." On top of that, in the early 1930s a gigantic economic collapse was in full swing, and anything that could get us out of it was looked on as a good thing. One of Congress's responses to the currents of the time was to make American radio (and its successor, television) into mechanisms whose primary goal was related to the national economic well-being. The Communications Act of 1934 presaged a national economy dominated by consumerism. In fact, the Act may be seen as a contributor to the domination of political democracy by economics later heralded as "Reaganism".

Licensees thought, correctly, that these licenses conferred the right to make a lot of money just by doing some selling and some bookkeeping. At the beginning, having a broadcasting license was like owning a turnstile: not much responsibility and a lot of collecting.

The development of commercial TV, whatever we might think of it, and the development of educational TV and then public TV, whatever we might think of them, have taken the courses they have as consequences of that act of Congress in 1934. Commercial and public broadcasting today are what they are because they are the descendents of that decision more than half a century ago.

Our Congress handed out access to segments of the airwaves as franchises. Entrepreneurial licensees did with them as could be expected. Their stated mission was to make a living. With a focus traditional among both legislators and merchants, only a tiny minority among the licensees or the Congress conceived of radio as a form of education, as an art form, as an entity with cultural significance, or as a part of human history.

Licenses to use the limited broadcast spectrum were leased to anybody who had the money and who would promise to broadcast in the "public interest, convenience and necessity". In practice, the definition of the public interest, convenience and necessity is supplied by the FCC (a presidentially appointed commission). A good but as yet elusive definition of the public interest is columnist Walter Lippmann's: "What men would choose if they saw clearly, thought rationally, and acted disinterestedly and benevolently."[11] In other words, wisdom.

Radio's licensees, businessmen with federally sanctioned entrepreneurship as their *raison d'être*, stocked their shops with the goods they knew . . . vaudeville, the dime novel, the carnival midway and patent medicine. Licensees used the stations essentially as a shop, to "do well" for themselves.

What came out of the public's radios after 1935? Exhortations to buy. ("Won't you buy Wheaties? They're whole wheat with all of the bran. Won't you buy Wheaties? The best breakfast food in the land!" was a song I heard every day as a child.) Punch and Judy. More selling. Vaudeville. Comics. Escapist drama. The singing commercial (the first: "Pepsi Cola hits the spot! Twelve full ounces, that's a lot! Twice as much for a nickel too! Pepsi Cola is the drink for you! Nickel Nickel Nickel Nickel, trickle trickle trickle trickle"). In the hard-to-sell time slots of Sunday afternoon went "loss leaders": the NBC Symphony under Arturo Toscanini, The New York Philharmonic under Bruno Walter over CBS, Robert R. McCormick's *Chicago Theater of the Air*.

Our country has a tradition of snake oil salesmen. These were quick to realize the possibilities of radio. The historic patent medicine man and his traveling show found he could use the airwaves instead of a horse and cart. Thanks to the curative ministrations of license holders, radio has evolved into what it is today: talk and music, a poultice for the lovelorn, the sex-starved, the angry and those who see about them a world shorn of loveliness. It is a legacy we have inherited. The outcome could have been different.

Licensees encountered problems, of course. An inefficiency of the American system of law (as well as one of its glories) is that everything is allowed that is not prohibited. Limits upon public deception and exploitation are not inherent in the structure of commerce. They had to be legislatively enacted. Laws were passed to prevent narcotic-laden nostrums from making addicts of sick people. A Pure Food and Drug act was passed by Congress. The discovery that gaming could be a cash cow for legislators was yet to come. Duping the gullible with games of chance was a crime in 1934. Section 316 of the Communications Act read, "No person operating any such station shall knowingly permit the broadcasting of any advertisement or information concerning any lottery, gift, enterprise or similar scheme offering prizes dependent in whole or in part upon lot or chance." At the time, all the possible permutations of commerce were not yet sacrosanct. In those days, evidence seemed to support the then commonly-held belief that the consequences of unrestrained entrepreneurship in 1920s had crippled the entire world. In those days, "Marketing" referred to what they did in quaint oriental bazaars. That, we now know, was to change.

When radio's descendant, TV, came into its own, World War II had just been won. To the amazement of anybody who thought about it, our country was suddenly a world power! A world power, though, with some pretty corny popular institutions. To cosmopolitan people who had seen the outside world, our broadcasting, popular though it was, looked silly. England, France, and Canada had intelligent, informative, intellectually and culturally responsible broadcasting services. Here in America we boasted the comics Joe Penner, Fibber McGee and Molly of Wistful Vista, "Banjo-Eyes" Eddie Cantor, Mortimer Snerd of Snerdville; we had stroking neighbors like Aunt Jenny, Mary Marlin, friend of the President in "the little house with the gray shutters halfway down the next block", Ma Perkins, Rush Gook and his never-heard friends Nicely-Nicely and Y.Y. Flirtch, and The Goldbergs with their slamming screen door and distant barking dog. We had consumer products with beguiling names like "Jello", "Lady Esther", "Pepsodent", "New Rinso", "Smoke-no-More Tablets" and "Hadacol", the Eversharp Repeater Pencil — "Guaranteed not for years, not for life, but guaranteed forever!" (Believe me, back then, all of these were known to any five year old as eternal verities, much as Perry Como, Bridey Murphy or Mae Bush were known to every living person in the 1950s or Michael Jordan or Madonna or Ralph Lauren or Magic Johnson are today. In other words, consumer culture's eternally present World of Things That Are Really Important — As It Is and Ever Shall Be.) As the victor of World War II and Ruler of the World, all America could boast of (that was broadcasting's own), that we could objectively regard as stellar, was Edward R. Murrow.

Edward R. Murrow deserves attention here because he represented in himself a promise of mass communications. Murrow was perceptive, intelligent, self-created. He was an anomaly and an accident in broadcasting. Edward R. Murrow, and "Murrow's Boys", were the loss leaders of CBS, servants of the public weal and the jewel of "The Tiffany Network". CBS News, essentially Murrow's creation, was made possible by the amalgam of vision, sense of responsibility, and marketing acumen of CBS Chairman William S. Paley, effectively subsidized by Ma Perkins, Jack Benny, and then Arthur Godfrey. The posthumous deification of Murrow is as much testimony to his particular gifts as it is illuminating to the traditional failure of American broadcasting to encourage, support or promote excellence.

With television succeeding radio as the dominant broadcast form, attempts to "fix up" the less seemly consequences of the Communications Act of 1934 led to increases in FCC regulations, and then to an alternative service, and ultimately to its arduous journey into the present lopsided American television system: a booming advertising-driven system inching toward control of a *de facto* State Television awkwardly engaged in its own co-option. Unfortunately, state television doesn't work any better here than it did in France or in the former Soviet Union. In our own state television, known as "public" television, ten thousand carefully screened *apparatchiks* spend over a billion dollars a year to produce a handful of inspired programs and a wealth of unthreatening, derivative, ideologically compromised, second-class okayed-by-the-government TV. Public TV's government propaganda and imports are promoted in amateurish fundraisers as "the fine quality programs you see on public television". Instead of our dreamed-of alternative, "noncommercial" television system, we have today domestic US Information Service which gives the American public information about government programs, government contractors, government activities, government achievements, and the agencies outside government that support them. We who watch public television with memory mark the process as it works itself step-by-step toward historic irrelevancy . . . with the support of the combined efforts of the hopeful, the docile, the ambitious and the calculating.

Unlike the people who own or regulate them, the people who use the airwaves understand them (correctly) as a "medium" of communication, like paint to a painter, film to a filmmaker. The maneuver of our elected representatives to dedicate a unique medium of communication exclusively to commerce was a characteristic demonstration of congressional breadth of vision. Congressional action to assure stability barred radio and television as tools for unselfish people or agencies for decades.

(In case you think times may have changed, witness the Pilgrim's Progress of High Definition Television. A technology that promises clear television pictures for the first time has been for over a decade kept out of the hands of the public, of creative people, and of imaginative entrepreneurs by a Federal Communications Commission seemingly intent only on the establishment of procedures guaranteeing that the technology offers maximal links in the food chain to corporate sinecures of the media infrastructure. Action to improve television has been halted by lobbyists for owners of the moribund technology of local broadcast television, who have marshaled their not inconsiderable resources to paralyze the introduction of this desirable service so they may usurp the new broadcast spectrum in the interest of higher income through more channels of inferior quality.)

To the legislators, given their mandate as they saw it, the public interest has been served. Money was made, products were sold. Short-term thinking brought quick, quantifiable benefits. But a resource was squandered. Philosopher John Dewey correctly said (around the time network radio was invented), "Societies are remembered not for their politics or their economics, but for their art and their architecture." These factors of importance to the history of broadcasting and the society of which it is a part were given absolutely no consideration by the Congress, being outside their mandate. A telling example: it remained for an Australian, Robert Hughes, to bring a series about American art, "American Visions", to America some thirty years after the formation of public television.

Certainly, members of Congress would be the first to admit that they are not original thinkers, but people who give some publicity or sanction to the ideas of others. Legislators in any society have never been known for innovativeness. That's not their job. Their work at best consists of attempts to patch up the past. Even if one grants that our elected representatives do their best to promote the public weal, they are, as we all are, only interpreters of what that "weal" might be.

Since 1967, the concept of a television that is an alternative to commercial television has been transmogrified into a domestic version of the United States Information Agency, our propaganda arm abroad. That this usurpation has been committed by the Congress of the United States and the beneficiaries of its largesse while the public looked on is a lesson in the subtleties of opportunism. An interesting part of the lesson is that without a critical, innovative public television, those who will suffer may include members of Congress themselves!

Chapter 3

THE MATRIX OF AN ERA:
SHIFTING DEFINITIONS OF CAUSE

I t may be instructive to look back on some congressional focuses of recent decades; emergencies demanding the allocation of tax dollars, these kept Congress in business. At different times, these were the subjects that could command funding for TV shows. They represent the congressional view of priorities that have displaced all or most other priorities in the allocation of those national resources that are not allocated by the market. It may be instructive to look at some of these matters of urgency critically, keeping in mind the question: "Are these what our civilization is about?"

You may remember these all-consuming public concerns: "Left Wingers". "Right Wingers". "The Space Race". "The Communist Conspiracy". "Massive Retaliation". "The Arms Race". "The Missile Gap". "Urban Renewal". "The Great Society". "Equal Opportunity". "The Handicapped". "Supply Side Economics". "The War in {wherever}". "Integration". "Substance Abuse". "The Mentally Ill". "Inflation". "Violence". "Poverty". "The Highway Program" "The WPA". "The Rotting Infrastructure". "Double-Digit Inflation". "The Third Column". "The Fifth Column". "Losing China". "Quemoy and Matsu". "Mutually Assured Destruction". "Star Wars", "Serial Killers". "The Crime Wave". "The Environment". "The Greenhouse Effect". "Child Abuse". "Terrorism". "Stem Cells". These are all (or have been, in my lifetime) on the federal agenda of emergencies: Things That Something Has To Be Done About, Now! These are emergency situations, where our tax dollars (your money, that is), *have* to go. Or so the people whose identity is secured and inflated by spending your taxes would have us believe.

Added to the above, there's high culture to meddle with. Noble enterprises like Art and higher learning are more fundamental and longer lasting matters than those mentioned above. Yet, in the lexicon of legislators, they have to do with the "glories" of democracy. Beyond the ken of political animals, they are nonetheless supported by the Congress — uncomprehendingly. Novelist Gore Vidal characterized the Congress as "Philistines". You can count the number of paintings in congressional offices by a Braque, a Piero della Francesca, a Corot or New York School abstractionist on the fingers of one hand. As with public television, the Congress has difficulty in refraining from making the agencies they fund into the image of themselves.

Through the recent ministrations of government, the dead hand of academism has been successfully brought to public TV. Other agencies have created a benign environment for congressional philistinism. One agency, the congressionally funded National Endowment for the Humanities Media Program, suffers grievously from congressional tunnel vision. The NEH media program is chartered to bring the insights of the humanities to the masses. What it really does is to arrange for television to be a podium from which unexceptionably credentialed academics may address the unwashed. The demonstrated (though not avowed) mission of NEH's Media Program is to use television as a vehicle for Sanctified Truths about Our Nation. How can you tell? By their subjects: Famous American Historical Figures, Famous American Historical Novels, Famous American Historical Wars, presented in reasoned detail by Least Controversial Scholars Bearing the Most Honors.

Although NEH declares its mission to be language-connected, "language" is interpreted narrowly by NEH only in its left-brained, verbal sense. In other words, "Words". NEH reads only the right side of the two-column television script, the "audio" portion. The language of image, of "montage" as applied to film in 1911 by Sergei Eisenstein, has yet to be discovered by NEH. It has not yet occurred to NEH's mandate writers that television is part of the historic continuum of visual communication. The potential of the left column of the television script to further the interest of the humanities is profound. Leonardo da Vinci was convinced of the power of vision as an instrument of knowledge. Visual representation, according to Leonardo, is the primary (sic) method of recording knowledge, and such knowledge enables us to master and control our environment.[12]

But the ideas of pictorial language, of media originality, of television as a vehicle of innovation, creativity or artistic expression, as a potentially significant element of the life of the humanities, is absent from the mandate of NEH. To NEH a television producer is not a creative person to be allowed to form the subject into a vehicle appropriate to the television context, but a kind of groom whose job is to make the needs of the horsemen (the academics) known to the horse (the public). To protect themselves from the criticism in the presentation of materials that innovation might bring, the temple guardians of the NEH mandate must allow only script-dominated, routine, conventional use of the television/film medium. Instead of the content as determinant of the form, as is the case with creative filmmaking inside and outside of Hollywood, NEH's TV, like their scholarship, is "by the book". That's why it looks like student work . . . they require it to. It's their mandate. After all, there's the National Endowment for the Arts to look after TV as an art form, anyway!

The National Endowment for Safe and Politically Correct Humanities promulgates an attempted "scientism" of humanitarian studies. To be considered worthy of government funding, projects must have quantifiable results. Aesthetic, intuitive, instinctive judgments are thereby banished. The approved method is the technique of "documentation and proof" that in social studies brought our legislators, press and public to, among other things, an uncritical reliance on the credentialed authority of the Department of State, the Pentagon and the CIA for a ten trillion dollar misassessment of the real power of the former Soviet Union.

The currently "correct" methodology for our federal agencies is a methodology that denies that truth can be approached through inference, through intuition, through sensibility . . . through art. The procedure for the manufacture of a television program or series by a government agency allows no place for imagination on the part of producers, directors, or writers. The method of the Media branch of the NEH is to line up a troop of unassailable recognized authorities from the world of scholarship and require that the TV producers they fund present whatever the experts say. It is a methodology congenial to security-minded *apparatchik* scholars who think like bureaucrats and trust only their own kind. It also frees NEH staff from risk or blame. What happens, of course, is that the scholars bicker among themselves and cobble together a script that they can all agree on. Whatever its flaws, the methodology of the National Endowment for the Humanities Media Programs is safe for the government agency. Bureaucrats can point to the method and not fear losing their jobs next year. But as a methodology of the unimaginative that denies a hearing to any but its practitioners, a reliance on the infallibility of the application of "scientific method" to the study of ideas has its problems. For example, for nearly a half century, this was the methodology that caused a nation to pour many trillions of dollars into the bottomless pit of war preparation. The reliance on authorities whose primacy may be a result of their own publicity skills in other areas may have cost us our world economic position. Defining the art form of television as only a technique of transmission, and following their mandate to promote intellectual depth and rigor, The National Endowment for the Humanities has succeeded in bringing what in 19th-century France was called the "dead hand of academism" to matters of high importance.

The future of government support of any art form has received a stinging blow from the judiciary. The US Supreme Court in its decision of June 1998 regarding federal support of the arts established a ruling that places conditions of government support of the arts close to the operative position of the *Académie Française* in 1850. Since 1998, to qualify for federal support, an artist must conform to "a general standard of decency and respect". The Supreme Court would have the government apply essentially the same standards to art as it does to pornography. Art should not offend anybody. Art that gets government support must be conventional. It must be "acceptable". On the face of it the 1998 ruling appears to have arisen from a class-bound definition of a work of art. "A general standard of decency and respect" is pretty close to the criteria that a Supreme Court justice's decorator might apply to the selection of a painting to be placed in a Georgetown residence over the fireplace, say, between the Georgian candlesticks and over the Seth Thomas clock . . . something that would be both interesting and respectful of the digestion of educated dinner guests.

The Supreme Court decision exempts any work of art that is a challenge to perception, intellect, sensibility and emotion (that is, any work of art worthy of the name) from federal attention. It looks as if the US Supreme Court members have not thought long or hard about art. It would appear that during the research phase, the clerks of the court were not instructed to consult eminent art historians (at least, none that I ever studied under or read).

The historic mission of art and artists is the exploration of the unknown. A work of art, any work of art, is an experiment. The people we call "artists" are simply those whose experiments have a good success rate. Originality or innovation, prerequisites of a work of art, have never in known human history been notable for meeting "general standards". The standard applied by the US Supreme Court to art requires that what is to be called "art" for government funding purposes must ipso facto be *not* art. What the court is saying is that American "art" should mirror the "official" art of authoritarian states. When they were new movements, the US Supreme Court's 1998 decision would have forbidden US government support of Impressionism, Expressionism, Dadaism, Cubism, Surrealism, the Fauve ("Wild Men") movement, Abstract Expressionism, and the Armory Show. Just as the French Academy did not, the US Supreme Court would not support a new Manet's "Déjeuner Sur l'Herbe" or his "Olympia", or Larry Rivers' nude portrait of his blowsy mother-in-law (exhibited at New York's Museum of Modern Art circa 1960), or Breughel's sexually suggestive peasant dancers. The US Supreme Court's 1998 "figleaf" edict would nicely support the official art of Hitler or Stalin. We can now expect that the National Endowment for the Arts will receive (and fund) proposals for equestrian statues of powerful politicians, muscular patriots, heroes of combat, mothers, babies, landscapes, still-lifes, and quilts. One might hope that in the interest of accuracy, it will change its name to the National Endowment for the Promulgation of Establishment Thought.

The 1998 Supreme Court ruling signals the end for any concept of government support of the arts in the United States. The US Supreme Court has resurrected "the dead hand of academism" that made the *Académie Française* a laughing stock. No less an authority than the US Supreme Court has since 1998 restricted federal arts financing in the United States to *pasticheurs*.

The recourse of an American artist today is curiously similar to that of the early Impressionists. Any future true or innovative American artist will have to rely on the patronage of rich individuals. Thanks to the US Supreme Court, the idea of a renegade artists' movement, a "*Salon des Independents*" or "*Salon des Refusées*", now has fertile ground in which to grow. We need only be patient to see the blooms.

The humanities, too, were once a breeding ground for original thought. In an open, civilized society, a federally funded Humanities Agency would have an independent being. Its purpose would be to provide insights from thoughtful, reflective, educated, original people to benefit the general public and the government, too. Their work would have a valuable role as a basis for thoughtful criticism. Instead, what has happened — at least in NEH's Media Department — is that the humanities have been used by a self-absorbed legislature as another instrument of a narrow nationalism.

The lower echelons in government service have no choice but to follow the dicta of those who pay their salaries. Hot on the trail of next year's funding, and in the interest of job security, NEH's Media Program funds only TV that proceeds from a precondition of patriotism. Almost ostentatiously omitted from the Endowment's congressionally developed mandate is any provision for the Media Program to foster the essential theatricality of television. A television producer is seen by the NEH Media Program not as a creative talent, but as a kind of clerk, an arranger of facilities. In the 1970s, after several years of unremitting struggle and multiple revisions, *The Scarlet Letter* was finally completed. Its producer Rick Hauser was quoted by *New York Magazine* as saying, "I don't know whose show this is, but it certainly isn't mine." Blindness to talent in television production is a significant omission, as well as a hint as to the gulf that separates politicians and their agents from an understanding of the arts.[13] The arts, despite officialdom's lack of concern for them, are a major determinant of the future of our culture. Thanks to the methodology assigned to it, the television that emerges from the National Endowment for the Humanities is a lifeless, ritual obeisance to nationalism and current fads of academic careerbuilders.

The history of National Endowment for the Humanities-funded media signals that something about the process is not as it should be. Unless generously promoted by a General Motors, as was *The Civil War* still-picture show, the television supported by the NEH has a way of just disappearing. Lukewarm public response is the outcome of NEH's media mandate, requiring it to operate under the illusion that television is some kind of illustrated lecture. Looking for another winner like *The Civil War*, NEH allocated over a million dollars for proposals for a comparable series. With Christopher Columbus, the Revolution and the Civil War done to death, what other flag-wavers are there in the field of humane letters that this agency can use to drum up more funding from Congress? You don't have to look far. There's *The West*, Ken Burns' *Statue of Liberty*, *The Brooklyn Bridge*, *Baseball*, *The Presidents*. Feminists. Wait and see what more can be found to tickle your nationalist fervor. Canny proposal writers with visions of Betsy Ross in their heads are surely at work this very moment.

The Congress of the United States has demonstrated little talent as a television producer. They should stop trying. Legislators should stick to what they know — winning the approval of the electorate — and allow others to meddle with wisdom, truth, or their handmaiden, art. If legislators could spare time from career building to read history, they could learn a lesson from the Italian *quattrocento*. This era demonstrated emphatically that the Powers (Popes, on that occasion) understand art only as propaganda. The fact that hundreds of times as many people know the names of da Vinci, Michelangelo, or Della Francesca as know the names of the popes who employed them should give American legislators a sense of their own importance vis-à-vis the packagers they fund. A look at the content of the works of the artists of the Italian Renaissance should give legislators a clue to the existence of a wisdom embodied in works outside the criteria they prize. If traditional American education had provided potential legislators with a better understanding of the meaning of art in human history, they might approach public television in a far different way.

The evidence shows that American legislators, following the tradition of King Louis XIV,[14] understand the media as a tool, as an avenue of propaganda. Examples abound. At the Nationalistic Endowment for the Arts, our public servants in Washington are nowadays trying on the mantle once usurped by the political leadership of a Germany and a Russia we once declared authoritarian, to have the state define the limits of art.[15] With the help of Senator Helms, and the Supreme Court, the National Endowment for the Arts is being "democratized" into the National Endowment for Arts and Crafts. As *The New York Times* once stated on its editorial page, "difficulty is one of the qualities that allow a work of art to keep its voice over time",[16] but easy popular acceptance is inherent in the populist definition of art. Intellectual, esthetic, emotional, or formal sophistication or depth, wit, paradox, ambiguity, irony, innovation — the components of anything that has ever been called "art" — are labeled "elitist" and are declared by politicians (whose sensibilities are most acute in their attunement to the presumptions of their constituents), to be contrary to American political dogma. As a result of their pressure, "the will to think big, to ask uncomfortable questions, and to test unformed and strongly held convictions is now largely absent" (from the NEA), writes Michael Brenson in *The New York Times*.[17] The authentic artist in America today is treated by the politico-economic leadership as, at best, a dissident member of an underclass. Survivors of the maze that is government arts support are often producers of work that is simply bizarre, odd enough to appear to be creative, pointless enough to be unthreatening. This is arts-support-as-steeplechase, and a consequence is that some independent creative artists in America deliberately offend middle class standards. *The New York Times* architecture critic Herbert Muschamp has written that art is "A slice of life that is unruly, irrepressible, not quietly contained."[18] "Great art is subversive to official values", says pianist/critic Charles Rosen.[19] Novelist and social critic Don DeLillo has said that it behooves the artist to stand in permanent opposition to his or her government.[20]

The works of art being produced today that come into my sight are not pretty. As if in response to an arts support that is manipulative and self-seeking, much of the work of American artists today shows the evidence of a corroded sensibility. I remember a class-mate of Andy Warhol's, who lamented to me, "We painters have to paint what we see. We see what the culture gives us."[21] Warhol indicted his culture by copying and framing the banal artifacts that the culture produces. . . . soup cans, photo-offset images, images of se-duction. Warhol's art is comic, embittered, rebellious, insulting, a pie in the face. The so-cial criticism that is demonstrated by the art being produced today and that can be seen by any American in any of our major galleries and museums is devastating. Closer to Goya or Munch than to the portraits of The National Gallery, the works of those creative people not generating income through the production of consumer products today are full of irony, dismay, and clear visions of the myopia and the failures of our times. Viewing a seri-ous contemporary exhibition is not a pleasurable experience. It is undeniable, however, that American artists are doing their duty, are fervently at work at their historic mission.

The currently publicized and commercially promoted styles known as "Deconstructivism" and "Post Modernism" are a minor offshoot of contemporary work. They echo a self-serving, anti-historical, anti-intellectual bias convenient to legislators and consumer industry. Works of living American artists today are sometimes, like Warhol's, aggressive in their capriciousness, and cruel in their wit: a deliberate affront to a public they manipulate. Johnson and Burgee's tongue-in-cheek AT&T building on New York's Madi-son Avenue is a near parody, an application of design devices from early film sets and smug livingrooms to the headquarters of a company long known for buildings whose colonioid *applique*[22] once signaled an unsure industrialist's awkward attempt at respectability. Af-fronted by a market and a government that disavow moral responsibility for their actions, our artists and architects respond with affront. Critic Joseph Giovannini[23] describes the plight of architects: "Deconstructivists are building for a world in which there are few if any certainties left. . . . It is an architecture of doubt that embodies the fragmented and precari-ous times." American legislators would do well to consider that much of the work produced by artists today may be a howl of pain from wounds inflicted by the legislators.

If there is a cultural lag, the *hubris* of our own fallible representatives may incline the electorate to an increasingly more positive evaluation of the National Rifle Association's stance that any citizen has a fundamental right to bear arms against an oppressive govern-ment!

The public would do well to look with skepticism at the makeup of each legislator's *weltanschauung*.[24] It would help them to vote intelligently. They might ask, "What kind of person becomes a legislator?" "Does that kind of person understand the best that humans are capable of?" If the answer is "maybe not", that's important for our futures.

Who are legislators? Legislators are a minority group. Since we try to understand minority groups in America, maybe we can understand legislators, too. I'll make an effort here to define the limits of the particular minority group called "legislator".

A legislator is likely to be a person with legal training (42% of the members of the House of Representatives are lawyers; the average in 18 industrialized countries is 15%.)[25] Gregarious, they mostly have attractive and expansive personalities, plus a gift for self-promotion that is a prerequisite for election to public office. People who become lawyers have minds that work in cognitive verbal fashion. Sensibility and imagination, two of the traditionally most honored attributes of the civilizing forces of history, are generally not attributes of the world's politicians. (Exceptions such as Churchill, Franklin Roosevelt, and Lincoln prove the rule.) The music that is not an accompaniment to courtship, the speculative, reflective or critical thought, the disinterested intellectual inquiry — these are rare occupants of the universe of today's legislators and politicians. That's because the average politician has no use for these attributes to "get ahead". To survive the blood sport of the American electoral process, what a politician needs is the *absence* of sensibility (either real or apparent), originality, or reflective thought. Their ideas come from others, who happily supply them. To get elected, politicians have to be salesmen. Since *they* don't need sensibility or imagination to "get ahead", to gain or to stay in office, legislators conclude that these attributes that historically were considered essential to civilized being are unnecessary or are to be used only manipulatively. (*The New York Times'* R.W. Apple asserted that only two members of Congress, then Senator Daniel Patrick Moynihan of New York and Representative Sidney Yates of Illinois, did not qualify as cultural Philistines.[26])

Plainly, the legislator's background, his orientation, his knowledge of the vast and complex world, is of a kind that belongs to limited group among the diversity that is humankind. He is not everybody. There are other people in the country who see the world differently. Some individuals in America will have a more powerful, beneficent and lasting effect on human culture than members of our legislatures. If only in the interest of their own reputations, legislators should have regard for these other people. The exceptional person may not be a voting bloc, but as Samuel Butler pointed out in *The Way of All Flesh* (in reference to a pale and cowering schoolboy), the exceptional person is worthy of the authoritarian's regard. Butler's warning was, "Headmaster, beware of this miserable cipher you find so useless. It is just he who will memorialize your kind forever!" A legislator cannot, and should not, purport to speak for everybody, even his constituency. Should he presume to speak for people of a different perspective? His is a significant responsibility, some of it to the unborn who are not among his current or future constituency, some of it to his betters. They are the "history" that will finally judge him. They will define the legacy he leaves. The legislator is a facilitator — a better or worse one, depending on the breadth of his knowledge of what it is that he *doesn't* know.

✷✷✷

The Communications Act of 1934 reserved the airwaves exclusively to the control of manufacturers of consumer products through their agents — the advertising agencies — under surveillance by selectees of people elected to public office. Our Congress gave the airwaves to politics and economics and not, as it has turned out, to civilization or to art.

What a boon this law was to American industry in the mid 1930s, cursed as it was with overcapacity and reeling from a worldwide economic crisis of unprecedented severity and duration. Abetted by the fledgling advertising industry whose task was to fan public desire for stockpiles of unsold consumer products, radio and then television became instruments to move products off shelves. And they did it, with unanticipated effectiveness!

Here are a few examples. At the very beginning of radio advertising and in the depths of the Depression, the Bulova Watch Company saw sales jump from $3 million to $14 million in three years. (Multiply that by ten to see roughly how much that would be in today's dollars.) By plugging for just ten days over *Jack Armstrong, All American Boy*, General Mills got orders from children for 1,250,000 Wheaties premium pedometers. (I remember seeing one on a classmate in grade school . . . an ugly, flimsy blue-painted pot-metal thing it was, too!) Cities Service Oil Company credited radio's Jessica Dragonette, Lucille Manners, Ford Bond and Paul Lavalle's orchestra with helping boost their annual gross to more than double during the Depression years between 1930 and 1940. Pepsodent credited *Amos 'n Andy* with keeping their toothpaste on the shelves of economically desperate country drug stores.

Radio's successes in selling then were a small beginning. They opened the door. Radio's financial support — advertising — grew. Ultimately, it became the tail that wags the dog. Advertising, initially a system developed to disseminate information about product availability, in no small measure due to commercial broadcasting has transmuted into a gigantic industry practicing an art form successfully directed toward the generation and manipulation of a culture of desire. Human creativity is now effectively harnessed to the caisson of commerce. The implications of commercial culture present dilemmas for which a law and politics developed for another era are unprepared.

Chapter 4

EDWARD R. MURROW: ANOMALY

Hardly ten years after crystal-set radio was merely a kid's toy, radio served the world. When World War II erupted, radio showed itself to be a valuable tool of information. As Britain's Prime Minister Neville Chamberlain negotiated with Germany's Hitler in Munich, CBS's most distinguished news commentator Raymond Gramm Swing slept in the radio studio at 485 Madison Avenue. A researcher whose career was given an explosive impetus by war, Edward R. Murrow fashioned verbal images that brought Americans close to the experience of the London *blitz.* Those of us who remember Murrow's daily news broadcasts recall that he transcended the limitations of radio. Murrow used language to communicate circumstantial information, and just as importantly, image. You could hear, you could envision, you could almost smell London burning as Murrow described it. Murrow created word pictures. He used his brain as an analytical and synthetical device to compensate for and transcend the limitations of the media he used.

We should not be carried away by the euphoria generated by the likes of Murrow's late loyal subordinate, broadcasting student guru Fred Friendly, when he recalls the "great days" of broadcasting. It was not a perceptive CBS management that "found" Murrow. As Barbara Walters did later, Murrow found himself. Like Walters and many prominent others, he sensed what his medium was, and what his audience wanted and needed — and he gave it to them.

Murrow happened by accident. CBS's Jim Fassett told me that when Hitler invaded the Sudetenland, Murrow was doing a research job for him, setting up concerts of the Warsaw Philharmonic to be recorded for later broadcast over CBS. Murrow phoned in a report from Warsaw — nearer the Sudetenland than any CBS newsperson that day. When Hitler unexpectedly invaded Austria, then declared a break in news silence, Murrow flew to Vienna. His report met with approval. Murrow stayed in Europe through World War II.

Radio, remember, was a shoestring operation . . . a room, a microphone, an engineer, a transmitter. CBS wasn't thought of then as even a serious business. It had been a gift, a "toy" given to young William S. Paley by his father, a Philadelphia cigar manufacturer. The coverage of news added to CBS's losses from cultural programming, the New York Philharmonic and Maestro Alfredo Antonini's CBS orchestra. Nobody knew then if the war would last. Murrow was already there. He was doing Okay. It was cheaper for CBS to leave Murrow in Europe than to bring him back to New York. Why should CBS management incur the cost of sending an experienced hand to Europe? Who could say that the war wouldn't be over tomorrow?

CBS's bean counting offered a career opportunity for Murrow. His astute intelligence was allowed free play by circumstances of the bombing of Britain that obstructed home office supervision. In time, "Edward R. Murrow, from London" became a signal to Americans that they were getting The Word about the war, and getting it straight. Having developed an articulate following, Murrow became a power at CBS. At Paley's request, Murrow then picked highly competent journalists, mainly raided from the Associated Press, to join the "Murrow team" at CBS. Whatever credit goes to CBS management for the development of CBS News goes more for allowing it to happen than for any vision of what it should be. "Murrow's Boys" — Charles Collingwood, Howard K. Smith, Eric Sevareid, Larry LeSeur, Walter Cronkite, the gentlemanly Winston Burdett (who chose exile in Rome over the bruising competitiveness of New York) — a selection that included two Rhodes scholars and a brother of Joan Crawford, together built an image based on sound journalism that caused CBS to be spoken of for years as the "Tiffany" network. Murrow's Boys' provided thoughtful, intelligent news coverage, like Tiffany's Schlumberger, giving CBS "class", a luster that comforted its audiences and that its proletarian entertainment sales traded on.

Murrow was a nontraditional employee. His unpaid expense accounts were a company scandal. When television came, Murrow's status as a popular hero allowed him some leeway. He could originate what later was called "investigative journalism". View-with-alarm programs such as *Harvest of Shame* spotlighted the human degradation that was part of migrant farm laborers' existence. A Michael Parenti of his times, Murrow's specials pointed out the paradoxes of socio-economic injustices that contributed to corporate profit and public comfort. Their effect was more to inform thoughtful people than to alter the inexorable course of the power shift to the economic sector. But Murrow's courage made him vulnerable. His notoriety, and then his salary, exceeded those of the President of CBS. An injudicious choice of adversaries brought this remarkable man to exile at the United States Information Agency.

To members of the craft of journalism, Murrow was a heroic example of creativity that transcended the workaday reality of most practitioners. To the outside world, his CBS News was perhaps broadcasting's crown jewel. To the CBS accounting department, he was a loss leader. To his peers in broadcasting, he was an *idiot savant*.

Chapter 5

COMMERCIAL TELEVISION'S SEMINAL DISCOVERY

When television came around, World War II was just over. Without the War, politicians and journalists thought the economy might just flop back into prewar stagnation. Economists hoped that perhaps consumer products could replace the basic industries of iron, steel and railroads as the economy's engine. The Communications Act's protection of the airwaves as a marketing device seemed as badly needed after the war as before.

Then in 1947, the Supreme Court made a decision of major significance for American business . . . that the government should establish complete religious neutrality. The implications of this decision have played out in ways that may not have been anticipated. On the face of it, the Court's decision appeared to be simply a reaffirmation of the idea of freedom of religion in a separation between any one religion and the state. In practice it signaled the allowability of a separation from one another among the guiding principles of state, commerce and ethics. The Court's decision may have been an unwitting but nonetheless instrumental action in the re-deification of Mammon.

In conventional American thought, traditional religion is the only place where ethical and moral concerns are lodged. "If God is dead, then anything is permitted", wrote philosopher René Descartes. Apparently, many Americans agree. The consequence of the Supreme Court's 1947 decision has been a studious moral and ethical relativism in both business and government and in the principles by which both are regulated. Its implementation was felt so gradually that nobody noticed.

Why should the formal separation of Church and State not have been a benefit? Because the baby went out with the bath water. To those who identified virtue only as the alternative to Satan's trident, the Supreme Court's decision could be seen as releasing lawmakers from one of their former duties of surveillance. This court decision, if accepted unreflectively, could relieve lawmakers from any duty to either the mysteries, or more importantly, to the ethics, of America's once-dominant Judeo-Christian tradition.

For hundreds of years, until 1947, the ethical constructs of England's established Church had informed the English common law of which American legal practice is an inheritor. (Episcopalians know that their Church isn't much interested in the mysteries; establishing it as the State Church in England gives little support for that part of religion.) The Society of Jesus provided philosophers for Roman Catholics. The Supreme Court's 1947 decision effectively cut the legislatures (who were the policemen of the mercantile class) adrift from a source of justification for ethical constraints; and it did so just at the time consumerism took off. The paternalistic corporation no longer had friends in government who could justify costly acts of compassion that might reduce the dividends of stockholders. President Eisenhower pronounced his endorsement of "the rule of law", not foreseeing that in the making of future laws, the historic ethical substructure in the traditional religions had been forsaken without substitution. In the profit-centered technological juggernaut of mid-century America the thought of Plato, Aristotle, Hegel, Kant, Descartes, Hume, James, Russell, Santayana, Hobbes, Leibniz, Sartre, Heidegger, of either rationalism or the enlightenment, carried little weight. (In France, thanks to Voltaire and others, reason was apotheosized, and has served as an effective if unexciting substitute for the ethical constructs of the Church.) It was probably not foreseen that, once liberated from religious constraint, the consequences of value-free legislation would make the economy our theocracy and alter the character of our culture. Nobody foresaw that the television medium would become the prime educator of the masses.

The postwar years were heady. So much had been postponed! There were houses to build, cars to design, babies to make, the modern world to invent! The mood of the country was hopeful, optimistic. Why, I remember that people were even clean and smelled good on the New York subway! The whole south side of Thomas Watson's IBM building on Madison Avenue trumpeted "World Peace Through World Trade" to all the magazine writers and ad agency executives and CEOs who passed below on their way to lunch.

Television qualified as a promised "postwar miracle". Its novelty lured everybody to watch. Audiences grew. Sales were brisk. CBS boasted in 1956 that it had just become the world's largest single advertising medium. Even people who had been to school watched TV . . . there was Bernstein on Bach, Murrow on McCarthy, Charles Collingwood on science, Alistair Cooke on Anglo-Saxon cultural icons. Creativity abounded. CBS allotted an hour a week (but not much money) to *Camera Three*, strictly for TV experimentation. *Studio One* became *Playhouse 90*. Imagine, ninety minutes of a different original "live" drama beamed into your home every week! The future looked good. William S. Paley hired a psychologist as president of CBS. His job — to oversee the production of the best possible programs that would lure the biggest audiences and sell the most products. Frank Stanton presided over a company that tried to do all three. That was the "high road" of commercial broadcasting.

Then CBS Television had its first profitable year. Mr. Paley's and General Sarnoff's prescience was confirmed. After nearly a decade of losses, profit came at last. But, alas! as soon as there was profit, the complexion of the workplace changed. Suddenly, TV was no longer a noble experiment. It was serious business. Suddenly, "real people" became interested. Watching at CBS in the late 1950s, right after its first profitable year, I saw almost

overnight, the laid-back people, the ones with twinkling eyes and tousled hair, who wore odd clothes and molded Space Shoes, just disappeared. It was eerie. Out of the walls came men with smooth faces and hair, wearing meticulously tailored Oxford-gray flannel suits with neatly patterned foulards, and carrying English leather attaché cases. They looked straight ahead. They moved to a quick step, always in a hurry. They didn't joke or smile. The Number People. Their banner of loyalty was a muted necktie of dark orange silk patterned with little black CBS-TV logo "eyes". Like the figures in an architect's drawing, they fit perfectly in the sparsely forested *chic* new tangerine and white and black environment that Florence Knoll had designed for CBS.

As competition for audiences increased, so did pressures from the interests served by television programming. In the late 1950s, preeminent live-drama *Playhouse 90* scriptwriter Reginald Rose complained in *The New York Times* that he was instructed to make his program scripts less demanding so that audiences would be delivered to the commercials in a more accepting state. Some forty years later, *The New York Times'* Max Frankel discreetly noted, "The clamor for a benign 'environment' (for advertisers) haunts even the most trusted media." As we will note later, television's biggest advertiser, Proctor and Gamble, even today pointedly instructs program producers on program content and prohibitions that must be honored if sponsorship is to be renewed. A 1993 BBC report declared with characteristic understatement, "Sponsorship can have a marked effect on the kinds of programmes that are made and broadcast."[27] In 1998, Stephen Metcalf wrote succinctly in the *Washington Monthly*,[28] "TV programs are little more than bait, sleekly crafted delivery systems for commercials."

About the same time as Reginald Rose made his observation, ABC, the then perennial third network, broke a taboo of decades. They resorted to sex and violence to attract more viewers. "S&V" was *Variety*'s anagram for the new trend in broadcasting. Until ABC did it, every network broadcasting licensee's commitment to broadcast "in the public interest" seemed to forbid such a thing. Responsible people believed that violence in the media would breed imitation, that, as Oscar Wilde once observed, "Life imitates art", or, as the decisionmakers of commercial television were learning at the same time, "Monkey see, monkey do". This discovery was to significantly affect American life.

In the 1950s, the media specialists in violence had been tabloid newspapers. Publishers of yellow journalism maintained that the violence in their papers allowed readers to displace their aggressions, rendering them harmless to others. In polite society, newspapers' owners promoted their "defusing" of the disaffected masses as a public service.

The gun as a solution to problems was a tradition of American history and American literature, particularly "the Western"; it was an unquestioned presumption of the cowboy film. The popularity of actor John Wayne rested in some measure on the attractiveness of his identification with problem solving through violence. Comic strips teach that if anybody or anything stands in the way of what you or your crowd wants right now, you just annihilate them with a POW! or a ZAP! "Violence is as American as apple pie", said a 1960s hippie. Thirty years later, Fareed Zakaria, Managing Editor of *Foreign Affairs* magazine, wrote in *The New York Times*, "Problems that might be solved by bombing we readily undertake. Problems that cannot be addressed by this method, we ignore."[29]

In the early days, television felt no need for speciousness. Until ABC did it, for over a century (with the exception of William Randolph Hearst), the low road of sleaze, violence, and sensationalism in the interest of profit had been thought by responsible publishers to be pandering, and ultimately harmful to them. For the more than a hundred years of the industrial revolution, people whose companies engaged in it were *never* elected to the right clubs, *never* listed in the Social Register. The consensus had been that S&V would constitute a violation of the stewardship implicit in ownership of a broadcast license, at least for the networks. But with S&V, ABC's viewership jumped up and the ratings improved. Sponsors read the statistics. "How can you argue with ratings?" shrugged programming executives. ABC got the competitive advantage. What they had discovered is that violence attracts the audiences that buy the products. As ethicist Sissela Bok points out, "Violent programming is designed to put us in a state of semi-arousal for the ads, which act as little oases in between homicides."[30] ABC got the sponsors. The die was cast.

What did CBS do to meet ABC's challenge? Paley repeated what he had done in the 1930s when he hired comedian Jack Benny from NBC. He did what they did in the 1990s when CBS hired David Letterman from NBC. Paley simply co-opted the competition. CBS hired ABC's chief programmer, Jim Aubrey, the man with "a whim of iron", in *Variety*'s words, the one who had masterminded S&V at ABC, as the new CBS television president. It was a watershed in television. Certainly it represented a narrowing of the historic concept of corporate responsibility, which held that any corporation's first responsibility was to the community of which it was a part. A principled gentlemen's agreement on program content was jettisoned in favor of so-called value-free judgments based on viewer count. Human values were on the way to the ash can, soon to be replaced by the absolute tyranny of cash value. Paley, who saw what was happening, observed, "Maybe we should never have gone public." Aubrey soon found his way to Hollywood, where his talents could find more congenial surroundings. As a business decision, CBS's action was unassailable. Its social consequences have been disastrous.

One outcome of ABC's "decriminalizing" of S&V on TV has been that a cottage industry has emerged to count the acts of violence on television. (A record of sorts was achieved by Fox TV's "Adventures in Brisco County", which in one 1993 study depicted 117 acts of violence in a one-hour show.) A study by the American Psychological Association estimates that the typical child, watching 27 hours of TV a week, will view 8,000 murders and 100,000 acts of violence during the formative years between ages 3 and 12. "A television character, by some estimates, is a thousand times more likely to be raped, tortured, maimed, or killed than an average person", writes Stephen Metcalf.[31] James Gilligan, M.D., a psychiatrist who spent ten years with Massachusetts prisons writes, "The use of violence as a means of resolving conflict between persons, groups, and nations is a strategy we learn first *at home*"[32] (italics mine). Dorothy G. Singer, professor of psychology and co-director of the Yale University Family Television Research and Consultation Center,[33] has described psychic circumstances of the viewer-TV interaction in ways that can only cause alarm. Of children, she says, "Kids . . . like to identify with someone who is powerful Kids are small. Their destiny is in the hands of others. So when they identify with someone powerful, they feel strong and powerful." The S&V message children and adults get is the same. We might take Prof. Singer's analysis one step further and apply it to the growing numbers of adults in dead-end jobs, to an emerging army of illiterate or semi-literate, unemployed and unemployable adults with diminished senses of self-worth; they too are "small and not in control of their own destiny"; we can see the attraction of S&V. A possible avenue of academic study is the thesis that the popularity of violence on television may be just a symptom of the need for a safety-valve for the smoldering, inarticulate rage of working people who must publicly pretend to "success" in consumerist democracy while the conditions under which they earn their livings subject them to the shame of castrating robotization, the humiliating dead-end jobs and insecurity of the wage-slavery that is a common lot in the developing mass-market society.

TV violence fills a psychic need. In ways unintended by its purveyors, it also becomes a cause. Singer points out the "ripple effect" of TV violence. She points out that the pattern of thought on violent TV is *imitated* by viewers. "The message is, you fight with your enemies. There's no trying to negotiate. You just get rid of them." "Children who view a lot of action-adventure shows tend to behave more aggressively . . . they *imitate* what they see", Singer writes. In late 1997, a 14-year-old student in Paducah, Kentucky opened fire on his school classmates, killing three. Attorney Timothy Kaltenback said later that the youth acknowledged that he had seen the 1985 film *The Basketball Diaries*, in which the protagonist shoots classmates and a teacher. Dr. Carole Lieberman, chairperson of the National Coalition on Television Violence, writes, "In over one thousand studies, it has been proven that media violence causes real life violence.[34] People who are exposed to media violence become progressively more aggressive, desensitized to violence, anxious and paranoid."[35] "America is more violent than other countries", declares *The Economist*.[36] In *The New York Times*: "Hundreds of studies done at the nation's top universities in the last three decades have come to the same conclusion: that there is at least some demonstrable link between watching violent acts in movies or television shows and acting aggressively in life."[37] If that is true, and if it is true not only of children, does it not make sense to look to violent TV as one element, a signal to be evaluated among others for the light it can shed on an objective assessment of the causes of the epidemic lawlessness and violence that degrades life in our country?

In June of 1993, Cable TV's Ted Turner testified to the House Telecommunications Subcommittee that TV violence can be directly linked to violence in society and that TV executives bear some responsibility for the flood of homicides throughout the US. "[They] are guilty of murder, as far as I can see",[38] Turner declared. In 1994 George Gerbner, Dean Emeritus of the Annenberg School of Communications at the University of Pennsylvania charged the National Association of Television Programming Executives with the promotion of "happyviolence", saying that "guns are a culturally driven habit", the "culture" being TV. Considerable evidence points toward the conclusion that the explosion of gang violence, of prison populations (1.8 million in 1998)[39], of walled communities, of private po-lice forces we endure today, may have its beginnings in the business decisions of television in the 1950s. There was no way to stop it, except by a gentlemen's agreement. Why is nothing done about it? Because "violence sells proddux". Business, after all, is business.

"Monkey see, monkey do", may describe how billions of dollars worth of goods get moved from shelves. It is, however, an unscientific term. Social science, since it is not provable, is not actually a science: a scientifically controlled experiment with a human being is close to an impossibility. In our age of fealty to the methods of science, judges hold back from decisions forbidding acts whose effects are not demonstrable according to science's criteria. So, in a society where everything that is not against the law is permitted, S&V on TV can have no opponents. Its possible consequence, increased violence in our homes and cities, cannot be traced to media stimuli, at least not in accordance with con-ventionally accepted canons of scientific proof. This situation is good for the incomes of many people.

You might ask, "After all, what credentials do broadcasters have that give them the authority to define what's in the public interest?" That's just what the stockholders of CBS asked William S. Paley in 1958. It took a combination of (1) economic uncertainty, (2) the competitive edge acquired by one network through actions that historically had been re-garded as "a decline in standards", and (3) stockholder threats, to bring about a redefinition of the limits in programming. From the actions of sponsors, ad agencies and networks alike it became clear who really owned the airwaves. It became clear that no BODY owns them — they belong to the structure, to the dynamic, to the *process.* The airwaves belong to the dynamic of the movement of the "proddux" off the shelves. *Product sales are the sole determi-nant of whether a program is "good" or not.* It's not a matter of anybody's personal opinion. The movement of the "proddux" makes the decision. They move or don't move. The series stays on or is cancelled. No problem. No arguments. No debatable standards of "ethics". Best of all, it's automatic. The statistics make the decisions. Nobody is responsible! Nobody is guilty! And the money rolls in.

There are an estimated 540 companies that have both the products and distribution systems suitable for a mass public. To woo and to keep the money that rolls in from these 540 companies is a skill. Broadcasting, like any seller, wants to please the buyer. If a spon-sor likes or doesn't like a show, a character, or an idea that surfaces in a show, the broad-caster thinks seriously about making changes. It's only good business. Producers and writ-ers of television series are clearly aware of the sponsors' peeves. Expecting them to neglect the sponsor's desires means expecting them to imperil their livelihoods. As a consequence, a thousand people decide on the approach to human life that should be presented to all Americans.

By law, the license to broadcast is conditional. The license requirements state that broadcasters must broadcast in accordance with "the public interest, convenience and necessity". This, it turned out rather early, wasn't as great an obstacle as it had appeared to be during the first two decades of broadcasting. Two parallel definitions of the "public" became operative. One was the "customer". A separate definition applied for programming in the unsold airtime devoted to what was called "Public Affairs" programming. In this latter area the "public" very early came to be defined in broadcasting practice in a very limited way, as whoever the FCC said the public was. The FCC said "electorate". The deal was done. To broadcasters today you are customer or voter, no more, no less. This goes for *all* broadcasters.

How did your being come to be so limited? In answer to a question from the trainee I was, CBS Public Affairs Assistant Director Jack Jefferson said in 1955 that the definition of "public affairs" was deliberately kept open. His boss Irving Gitlin's program development strategy was apt, a model that would provide a sound basis for programming in public television tomorrow. Irv Gitlin explored the world of higher learning for discoveries and controversies to provide the substance for programs. "Hot" issues among academics in sociology, psychology, technology, and natural science were among Gitlin's favorites. Other disciplines also had some chance. There was an occasional effort at poetry, art, music, or literature. In the late 1950s, twenty or so pioneers at 545 Madison Avenue churned up new stories and new approaches for tele-*vision.*

In our department headquarters, there was a little office in the corner that nobody paid any attention to. A sign outside read "TALKS". Helen Sioussat had been a family friend of the Hoovers (Herbert Hoover had been a staunch proponent of commercial radio in the 1920s); Helen arranged talk shows. Nobody paid any attention to her. Talk? On television? How boring! What a misuse of a visual medium! Poor Helen! We nearly blushed when this relic of radio passed among us. And there was Goodson-Todman productions, the place nobody wanted to go. They did "What's My Line?", "College Quiz Bowl", parlor games in prime-time. They were reputed to have done well at it, but the cadre of visionaries at CBS looked on Goodson-Todman as a place you'd go to work only if you were desperate.

Who would have dreamed that Helen Sioussat's dreary and pedestrian "talking heads" format was to be the wave of the future? From "Oprah" to "Geraldo" to "Washington Week in Review" and the "Lehrer Newshour", over the years the talk show has become a ubiquitous television staple. But it is a non-visual, essentially auditory use of a visual medium. Why would efforts to explore the potential uses of a new dramatic, visual/auditory medium as a powerful vehicle of human communication be abandoned in favor of a reversion to the old model?

Because talk is easy and cheap. For sponsors, the profit margin is high. The Talk Show requires miniscule creativity on the part of administrators, producers, designers. Camerawork is simple and formulaic. Producers act simply as brokers, and the "guests" simply "appear". Set construction represents a one-time cost. There's little rehearsal, saving the cost of the studio, lighting, equipment and manpower. Since the talk show is a formula, untalented or even inexperienced people can do most of the production work. They command small fees, have little leverage with which to bargain for higher wages, and are easily replaced. On commercial television, this has meant that profits from sponsorship don't have to be shared with production staff. On public television this has meant that stations and producers don't have to compete for imaginative, creative, demanding and costly production personnel. Public stations can offer sponsors almost 200 stations to blanket the nation with their message, for the tiniest fraction of the cost of commercial sponsorship.

The demise of innovative, complex, original programming on public television means that public television managers can devote themselves to negotiations with sponsors on price only, and don't have to mess with problems of originality or innovation. This simplifies matters for the controlling, manipulative bean counters whose social responsibility extends as far as their own job. The consequence has been that creative people have given up on public television. Only the brokers remain.

The causes of innovative poverty in public and commercial television lie deep in the history of broadcasting. At the heart is government itself. The root cause is that the people who issued and renewed broadcasters' licenses, and those who policed the stations (i.e., "Washington", as they're known in news shorthand), defined the viewing and hearing public not in terms of any broad definition of humanity but in terms of their own self-interest.[40] Licensees knew which side their bread was buttered on. You can see the limits of congressional vision from the structure of prohibitions and incentives established by the Communications Act of 1934. Unlike the BBC, in American broadcasting there was no incentive to high culture or even "excellence" from the start. There was just "the public interest, convenience and necessity".

How were the public interest, the public convenience and the public necessity defined in broadcasting? Their definitions were conditioned by "the bottom line". Diversionary entertainment is a "convenience", as is information about what toothpastes are available. That takes care of that part of the law. The public "necessity" is pretty well covered by the warning system in case of attack. When you hear, "This is a test", the broadcaster is complying with the law. And the public "interest" was suddenly redefined by ABC's late 1950s *coup.*

With Jim Aubrey aboard CBS, CBS's president Frank Stanton declared that, as a practical matter, "The public interest is what interests the public." The courts declared that the public interest should be defined by the FCC. Cataclysmic! Revolutionary! But who could deny it? More than that, who *would* deny it? (Nearly three decades later Stanton's remark was offered as his own by Reagan's FCC Chairman Mark Fowler.) As a prediction of an economy-driven, "value-free", bottom-line consumer society in which nobody was to blame for any horrors and nobody could prescribe anything defined as "good" (except profits and income), this was a bellwether event in television broadcasting. The stockholders loved it! Gone was the power of a William S. Paley to schedule the New York Philharmonic for reasons of broadcasting's responsibility to the public. Gone was the incentive for General Sarnoff to put the Metropolitan Opera on NBC. Broadcasting decisionmaking was changed forever. ABC's S&V thrust and CBS's counterattack presaged the future of commercial broadcasting. The balance sheet's reign over program decision-making had started on its irreversible march. As *The New York Times* TV critic John J. O'Connor put it, "Accountants and boards of directors beholden to stockholders evolved into the crucial players."[41] The bazaar was open for whatever would bring the crowds. TV had gone Hollywood. That was in the 1950s.

Television did its part to transform America into "the big store". Competition became keener. With keener competition came another big change — part of the audience became superfluous. As a measure of viewership with significance to advertisers, ratings alone turned out to be too imprecise a guide for program support. Advertisers were not content with mere viewers. What good is a viewer who doesn't buy the product? It became apparent to advertisers, then to agencies and to program producers, that the beguilement of viewers who don't buy the product is a waste of the sponsor's money.

I remember reading *The New York Times* on a bus going up Madison Avenue to learn that a Jackie Gleason show with an audience of well over 30 million people had gone off the air. Why? Good viewership, but not enough product movement. The Gleason Show was killed because, the day after the show, the goods didn't move fast enough from the shelves. Another 1950s CBS comedy series failed to sell tires and faced cancellation after its first 13-week cycle. Thanks to persuasive pleas for sponsorship change by a CBS vice-president, the series was given another chance: to see if it would sell soup. *I Love Lucy* lasted more than 13 weeks, only because it did what the sponsor wanted. The sponsor couldn't care less about Lucille Ball[42] or Desi Arnaz or comedy or the hilarious foibles of America's *parvenu* lower class as it fumbled with the unfamiliar trappings of middle-class status. The sponsor couldn't care less about how many watched, who or why. Because the show demonstrated increased sales of the sponsor's product, it became possible for the world to enjoy one of the century's major comic artists. More recently, a critically acclaimed series, *Laurie Hill*, about professional working parents, was cancelled by ABC. Its creators had won an Emmy for an earlier series, *The Wonder Years*. An ABC executive commented, "There is no upside potential in that for us."[43] Simple audience count, "ratings", as these events and others like them demonstrate, are a crude guide to a program's or series' "success". In practice, ratings alone don't count. The ratings issue is a red herring. Commercial TV's purpose is not audience numbers but *product sales*.[44] Product sales alone now determine what is created, what stays on, and what disappears from commercial TV.

The discovery of the suggestible audience explains why the 1950s saw commercial television's abandonment of the middle-class audience. When television was new, generally speaking during the black-and white and early in the color era, programmers and sponsors targeted middle-class audiences. Broadcasters figured that since TV sets were expensive, middle-class owners would constitute the majority audience. They programmed therefore to the largest body of the most well-to-do. That helps to explain the fondly remembered *Adventure, Omnibus, Playhouse 90, Camera Three*, and the Edward R. Murrow analysis programs. But the networks had underestimated the immense appeal of the new medium. Poor people were ready to sacrifice for it. Almost overnight, a TV set became like a car, a badge of membership in the 20th century. By the late 1950s, shacks in America sported a car in front and a TV antenna on the roof. Antenna proliferation was vast and rapid. Astute cartoonist Saul Steinberg's delightful sketches of the antenna-scratched American horizon captured the phenomenon.

At the same time, programmers discovered the truism that one of the reasons some people have money is that they hold onto it. Broadcasters found out that the middle class wasn't the best bet for product sales, ratings, or their own incomes. Tightwads were not the ones sponsors wanted, no indeed! Sponsors want free-spenders! That was the beginning of "niche marketing."[44] Television audience research became more sophisticated, its object to discover the *suggestible* viewer and then to fan *his or her* desire.

Over recent decades, commercial television has provided future researchers with a textbook for a complete character profile of the impulse buyer. The personality portrait of the impulse buyer is not a picture of a cross-section of humankind. The character profile of the impulse buyer is instead an extremely limited but relatively commonly found set of attributes. The character profile of the target audience of commercial broadcasting is essentially this: a person who is (1) unreflective, (2) nonintellectual, (3) short on attention span, (4) self-absorbed, (5) sexually, socially and/or occupationally dissatisfied, and who (6) defines significance in terms of action. Once the impulse buyer was identified and his character profiled by the methods of psychology, it became a relatively simple matter to originate both the commercials and the shows targeted to encourage, flatter, underline, and intensify those elements of the impulse buyer's personality profile that feed into the viewer's gratification through the next day's retail decisionmaking. The underlying philosophy of these commercials may again be summed up by the children's chant, "Monkey see, monkey do". This key piece of nursery wisdom unlocked the sales of billions of dollars of consumer products, determined the future of commercial broadcasting, and modeled the thought patterns of two generations of Americans.

Any application of the enormously sophisticated and vastly documented causality system developed by commercial broadcasting to any noncommercial human activity lies outside the mandate of commercial broadcasting. This particular vast, scientific enterprise into the nature of human response and its conclusions are a secret. They are "proprietary". Fortunately, they may be inferred in their complexity by as simple an expedient as the examination of long-term viewing patterns.

In common discourse, the problems of TV are often said to be the outcome of the cast of mind of the "people in television". One person or another is designated as a demon. Though a traditional and easy application of devil theory, this position mistakes the proximate for the real cause. Critics who condemn the people in TV are both wasting their time and targeting the effect instead of the cause.

Much can be seen by reading between the lines of the government regulations involving broadcasting. The very structure of its being, as established by the laws of commerce and broadcasting, established the mission of commercial broadcasting as the exploration, discovery and intensification of the proclivities, tendencies, likes and dislikes of only that select group of the population that is quick to part with its money. Operatively, the preeminent activity of commercial broadcasting has been the enhancement of commercial and governmental revenues. The social consequences of the mutual reinforcement of the economic interests of government and commercial broadcasting are irrelevant, the public utterances of both notwithstanding. Even though large companies like General Electric pay little or no federal taxes, their suppliers, employees and customers do. Therefore, the better General Electric does, the more tax money your elected representatives will have at their disposal. The assiduous encouragement of corporate growth by your elected representatives may have at least as much to do with their vision of their own potential legacy to be gained by spending tax revenues as with your well-being. (The upsurge in congressional resignations during the 1990s could well be the result of Ronald Reagan's having committed all federal tax revenues, leaving for a time none for his successors to spend on monuments to their own vision.)

From the 1950s onward, the networks simply followed the inexorable course of structural necessity. CBS, once William S. Paley's "Tiffany Network", proceeded apace under Lawrence Tisch in the 1980s and 1990s to become the Wal-Mart network. Tisch, wrote Danny Schechter[45], "strip-mined" CBS. He did so not out of choice, but out of the implacable force of market necessity as sanctioned by federal regulation. Under the unremitting pressure of the favored investors in the consumer products manufacturers who advertise in order to secure a competitive return on their investments, commercial broadcasting took an inevitable course. Commercial design, and as importantly, program design responded to audience demographics and audience psychographics.[46] Today we live with the outcome of these analyses. A key component of both programs and commercials came to be the glorification of the ordinary. Who would have thought in the era of "Playhouse 90" that a series that features people who are fat, ugly, canny and gross[47] would survive, let alone be the most popular series on television? (In 1992 *Roseanne* brought so many of the right kind of viewer that it promised a satisfactory return on its sponsor payout of $2 million per episode![48]) Buyer identification!

Today, not audience numbers but audience profile determines the shows you see. The shows are produced with role models, ego identifications, and stimulus materials designed expressly to have a narrow focus on *only* that portion of the population that is impulsive, suggestible, and prompted by desire. Ages 12 to 24 are a prominent target age group. They're the ones thought by programmers to be most likely to have loose money and plenty of urges they'll act upon. Some agencies are agitating for 43-year-old women as the best target.[49] Any members of either group who have curiosity about life have been written off by now. They're not watching TV anyway.

If you want to watch commercial television, you may watch shows carefully constructed to woo particular groups. If they seem not just right for you, you can go along if you like. But remember, as you watch, if you don't buy the product, you don't count in the calculations of sponsors or the ad agencies, producers or networks they hire. These programs are carefully, skillfully, sometimes brilliantly designed exclusively for people of a specific psychic makeup. Whether or not integrated personalities, skeptics or seekers after some kind of truth "come along" is a matter of indifference to most sponsors. Whatever your interests, whatever your needs, whatever your education, if you aren't an impulse buyer you're irrelevant to commercial broadcasting. If you wonder why TV is vacuous, why the TV screen is full of sirens and chases, crashes and immolations, why it's mendacious, prurient, violent, gossipy, glitzy, vulgar and small-minded, you need only look at the sponsors' annual reports. The viewers who will dash out to buy an advertised product *like* this kind of stuff. TV is only the means; the TV industry is only the mechanism. The end, the real purpose of it all, is a number in the annual report.

A commercial television series, *Murder She Wrote*, was rated among the top ten in viewership for nine of its eleven seasons. It generated the lowest ad revenue in its time slot. Much of its audience was over 50. It was dropped. The producer of the critically praised and then terminated series *Laurie Hill* lamented,

> I don't hear any of these people running the networks talking about "what we need is more diverse, interesting, intelligent programming." No. That's just what they *don't* want! The incentive structure of commercial TV demands that American television take the course it has taken. That's the way it was set up by the Congress in 1934. Commercial television is a machine of surgical precision, manned by people of intelligence and dedication, fueled by the movement of billions of dollars. Its entire being is directed to one end, commerce. The people it has selected to be its audience are a narrowly defined, selected group of impulse buyers. Forget what anybody says about ratings. The shows put on by commercial television . . . *all* the shows . . . aren't made for viewers at all . . . they're made for the *buyers among the viewers*. The shows are mere leverage. The rest is window dressing.

Those agency and production company executives who have winnowed your TV shows down to the ones you see are keen, observant, skilled people. Like soldiers and sportsmen, they play by the rules they're given. They do extremely well what the structure of commercial broadcasting demands. Prominent among them are men like onetime NBC-TV President Fred Silverman, characterized by critic Les Brown as a man with "an extraordinary perception about the television audience that was uncomplicated by taste, idealism or a personal life". In the early 1990s, America's most popular television series featured people with an extremely limited frame of reference, ignorant of history, literature, music, art, philosophy, science, politics. Why? Did these represent the mass of the

American people? Not necessarily. They did, however, reflect the interests of the mass of the impulse buyers who buy advertised products and make TV the big industry it is. And as long as the structure of commercial TV remains, you can expect to see more of the same.

Some think that vulgar commercial television producers deliberately pander to "low tastes", in search of the "lowest common denominator". Not so. These critics give the networks and their producers too little credit. They also misapply their criticism. Demonizing "the networks" is a mistake. It misses the point. It is a matter of fact that a thoughtful, reflective person isn't going to buy *anything* based on a 60-second salesman's pitch. So if your holy mandate is product sales, why bother with that group? If impulse buyers were intellectually constituted like MacArthur Fellows, or the members of The Institute for Advanced Study or I Tatti, you can bet that NBC's, CBS's and ABC's programs would be designed to appeal to them. Paley's appointment of Frank Stanton (a man with a PhD in psychology) as the president of CBS was a corporate application of the concept of "intelligent self-interest". Stanton pioneered use of the research products of scientific inquiry about the nature of human response as an engine of profit. Since Stanton, the history of broadcasting has been a systematic search for the complete psyche of the impulse buyer. The search has been every bit as rigorous as the study of physics at MIT. Studies such as the well-known and much used Myers Briggs personality typologies were only the beginning in weeding out the non-buyers. The revolving door of television production represents a rigorous, informed, controlled, one-day-at-a-time experiment to find more keys to unlocking the impulses of the impulse buyer, and the impulse buyer alone.

Many wooing strategies have been tried. Some producers believe that one only need purvey the deadly sins. Some believe S&V is enough. Some create revenge fantasies to accommodate the resentment and anger brought to "the tube" by audiences demoralized by workaday drudgery. Covert eroticism (once known by the euphemisms of "glamour" and "romance", then yielding to today's percussive salaciousness) has been an effective key to customer types. Today's voyeurism is inheritor of the "T&A" (*Variety*'s anagram for "tits and ass") made manifest in a genre then known as "jiggle shows". Mass entertainments based on the commercialization of athletic conflict are an obvious winner. Games and fictions about ordinary people seem to work. The Fox network ("The Fox in the henhouse" according to *US News & World Report*)[50] has discovered infantilism, unfocused rebellion, and anger; Fox does very well by, in the words of a onetime Hollywood screen magnate, "never underestimating the taste of the American people". What about objective reality? Nonfiction is nowhere to be found. It doesn't draw impulse buyers.

The motto, "NBC News, now, more than ever" straddles the gap between the vapid and the inane. The "In depth" segment of the evening news implies that the rest is "in shallowness". Not to be outdone, CBS intones, "Have you seen your country today?" What do these vacuities mean? Who are they talking to? The question of how stupid, how ordinary, how sensational and how cheap one can go hasn't yet been answered yet, but you can be sure that many extremely talented, industrious people are working on it. An imaginative person can extrapolate a future limit to the trivializing tendency of one or two of Fox/

CBS's current programming geniuses: programs targeted to audiences so dizzy they won't be able to remember the product name all the way to the store. We can comfort ourselves, though, that when that day comes, the inventors of these programs will be "let go". Programs directed to absolute "flakes" won't be renewed, and that won't be because the shows are low, or stupid or awful or that they prompt antisocial conduct. They won't be renewed for the simple reason that they violate the prime tenet of commercial television programming: they don't move the goods from the shelves.

The commercial television industry has attracted people of high intelligence, whose skills are rigorously honed every working day. These vital, ambitious, dedicated, hardworking, clever professionals devote their entire energies to doing what the "system" requires. "You can't fight city hall", they say, meaning "the end justifies the means". It's very interesting that our era is perhaps unique in choosing economic imperatives above all others. Following the demands of logic, in tacit recognition of this choice, working people on all levels have elected a "value-free" governance for their own non-economic actions.

Here's one example. A *New Yorker* "Talk of the Town" featured Scott Sanders, the "voice" of several hundred political commercials aired during the 1994 elections. These commercials were notoriously "negative and nasty". "It's a peculiar position to be in," Sanders was quoted as saying, "I can't sit here and tell you I don't have favorite candidates, or that it doesn't bother me saying things I know are not true. But if I'm being paid for a performance I have to put my personal preferences, and even my personal philosophy, behind me, because they're paying me to do the best job I can, and my job is to get the candidate elected." Multiply Sanders' compromise by a modest 40 million, think about what they as parents advise their children, and you can stop wondering why the behaviors of your countrymen seem uncivil.

Newsweek Magazine devoted an issue to "The Billion-Dollar Battle to Insult Your Intelligence" that *Newsweek* declares is spearheaded by a coterie of veterans of the *Harvard Lampoon*.[51] However smart, though, they have to play the game by the rules if they're to stay and prosper. However undesirable it may seem to an outsider, the constraints of commercial broadcasting limit the creativity of its own people as severely as would the most tyrannical of dictatorships. Inspiration is narrowly channeled by the imperatives of regulation and corporate priorities, and probably more of the latter than the former.

Over the course of years, some preconditions of programming decisions that govern commercial television practice have emerged. They may be summarized thus:

> TV is a device for selling
> Smart people are slow to buy
> Thrill seekers are quick to spend
> Monkey see, monkey do.

These rigid imperatives, unforeseen when the ground was set for them, have funneled intelligent and creative people toward developing a commercial broadcasting entity to appeal exclusively to only one carefully segregated segment of society, the kinds of people who are likely to be easily moved to buy cheap and readily available consumer products. These are the mass "elite", the favored clients of commercial broadcasting ; they are cultivated, bribed, wooed, and flattered. S.P.'s, or "sensory perceptives", Jungian psychologists call them. The target audiences of commercial TV are that 34% of the population who live for the moment, who obey their impulses, who act according to urge, whose behaviors are essentially instinctive, who neither plan nor reflect. The mechanism of mass commercial culture dictates, They Can Do No Wrong — publicly, "the customer is always right", and privately, *"caveat emptor"*.

To commercial sponsors, operatively, no commercial program executives, stockholders, or anybody else in the television audience even exists. As audiences for commercial TV, people who think for themselves are a waste of time and money, as well as being difficult and complex to woo. If you were a manufacturer of a miracle consumer product, which group would you want to sell it to, people you could persuade easily, or people who would question you? The decision is a simple one. The challenge to program developers has narrowed to presentations directed exclusively to this restricted class of impulsive Americans. The programs broadcast over commercial television include *only* the kinds of programs *they* will respond to by increasing their product purchases. Changes in programming reflect changes in attitude or median age on the part of the body of impulse buyers. In American commercial television, the impulse buyer is king. *"Monkey see, monkey do".*[52]

Thanks to the provisions of the Communications Act of 1934 (as amended), a commercial television industry has been spawned that contributes enormously to the US economy. Its method is the distribution of programs designed specifically to meet the preference profile of the gullible. Why doesn't somebody *say* something about this? Nobody needs to *tell* program developers whom they should pitch to. None of them needs even to discuss their structure of imperatives with anybody else. It's the way it is! And it's the precondition of every action taken in the development of programs for television by broadcasters, sponsors and advertising agency personnel. Do it differently? Why? Give up the Mercedes? Take the kid out of Miss Porter's School? Forget February in Palm Desert? Drink cheap booze? What for? The son of the man who didn't tell his children what he did for a living doesn't tell himself how his work relates to any human endeavor outside the company.[53]

Today, gentlemen's agreements in broadcasting aren't about the public interest. A show that's important or desired by the public can't even be considered for broadcast unless it can be virtually assured to bring sponsor satisfaction, *i.e.* increased product sales. Of course! That's what the word *commercial* means! Some Americans may deplore the slide of commercial TV into a succession of simple-minded Punch and Judy shows, but they miss the point. TV has nothing to do with the outside world. It's business. To the industry, it is an irrelevancy that, in the words of George Kennan, Professor Emeritus at the Institute for Advanced Study at Princeton and former US Ambassador to the USSR,

> We export to anyone who can buy it or steal it the cheapest, silliest and most disreputable manifestations of our "culture". No wonder that these effusions become the laughingstock of intelligent and sensitive people the world over . . . so we must expect . . . to appear to many abroad despite our military superiority as the world's intellectual and spiritual dunce.[54]

Despite over 1,000 studies establishing links between TV violence and the way people behave in real life,[55] as yet the defined immediate pecuniary self-interest of those who decide what goes on the air obstructs any acknowledgement by them that "monkey see, monkey do" applies to program content as well as to the commercials, to street violence as well as to product sales. Is street violence their fault? Look to the Communications Act of 1934 for causes.

The narrowness of commercial broadcasting's focus was clear quite early on. Robert J. Blakely, an officer of the Ford Foundation's Fund for Adult Education (1951-1961) wrote, "The goal of most commercial broadcasting is not to entertain or inform but to attract the largest possible audience and to sell . . . not just the programs themselves (which are the bait) but also the commercials (which are the hook)".[56] Makers of commercials invented a device to disarm potential buyers — the glorification of the ordinary. Parents today trying to bring up their children to be responsible adults find roadblocks in the complacency it breeds.

Chapter 6
AN INCHOATE LEADERSHIP

"Ford", as the foundation was known, started Educational Television. "National Educational Television", they called it. Its purpose was "advancing human welfare throughout the world".[57] It would be a television that focused on the evident truth that television was an educational medium. Alvin Eurich, vice president of the Ford Foundation's Fund for the Advancement of Education,[58] wrote, "The key to reforming American education is new ideas. And back of these new ideas is a total *imaginative approach* (italics his) that asks constantly: Why? Why are we doing things this way rather than another, possibly better, way?"[59] From a more shortsighted point of view, former school superintendent Alexander J. Stoddard's influential report (114,000 copies printed) "Schools for Tomorrow, an Educator's Blueprint" (1957) promoted educational television as a way of dealing with a projected teacher shortage. The influence of Stoddard's narrow, short-term position may explain the meager support that atrophied educational television's potential (and may have a similar influence on computerized education).

Educational Television's first headquarters was at the excellent University of Michigan in Ann Arbor, a comfortable and inoffensive distance from the money madness of New York, the power obsession of Washington and Hollywood's intoxicating illusionism, and not too far from Detroit, the home of the Ford Motor Company. Videotape had recently become practicable, so tapes could be distributed by "bicycling" them around the country to be played by local educational stations. The attractions to the educational community included the glorious potential for inspiration from great teachers, easily available to all students. For the budget-minded, they also included the promise that once the hardware was in, the cost of teaching could be reduced. A huge increase in numbers of students was in the offing . . . the "baby boomers", those celebrations of fecundity, that hope for family and love after the privations of war, were coming along. But there weren't enough buildings, classrooms, or teachers to handle this massive influx. Educators explored alternatives. Could modern technology help? Could TV be the teacher? Why not? Why not try it? It would certainly be cheaper than building lots of school buildings that would not be needed after the "boomers" graduated. Making and copying videotapes of teachers would certainly be cheaper than training thousands of new teachers, and then having to lay them off when the boom busted. Good teachers, great teachers, any teachers could be put on TV, and the box could sit in the classroom. Thanks to videotape, the box could teach children. The local "teacher" could become simply a custodian, a keeper of discipline, a giver of tests. Those activities would command less remuneration, less training. It would be cheaper all around. You can see how attractive the prospect of television in the classroom was to "practical" minds! "Educational TV" thus came into being as a marriage between the kind of general-audience informational TV pioneered by NBC and CBS, and instructional TV, the camera in the classroom.

Without a clear mission statement, the development of Educational TV was as a passenger on an *ad hoc* vehicle largely dependent on technological innovation. Instructional TV was the first victim. Dominated by the sales pitch that instructional TV would be cheaper than classroom teaching with a real teacher, instructional TV was able to negotiate only marginal resources. With marginal resources, it negotiated marginal talent.

A measure of the potential for noncommercial television envisioned by some at that time can be seen in a 1959 program category assessment from "Pioneering in Educational Television", by Dr. E. B. Kurtz, Director of Experimental Visual Broadcasting at the State University of Iowa. He wrote,

> A partial list of topics broadcast from stations W9XK is suggestive of the possibilities in combined sound-sight broadcasting with the present state of the television art:

Oral Hygiene	Identifying Trees	Equilibrium
Trail Marking	Shorthand	Charcoal Sketching
Spring Birds	The Constellations	French Pronunciation.

It is understandable that a March 1958 report from the Educational Television and Radio Center to the Ford Foundation stated, "We have preferred not to sacrifice content values for performance, and at times this has resulted in programs which lack the vitality and excitement desired."

In the mid-1960s, Chicago's CAST (Chicago Area School Television) contented itself with placing one camera in the classroom of a teacher who happened not to be assigned at the time it was convenient to make video recordings. The teacher stood at the chalkboard and gave the lesson as usual. The dullness that children were required to watch ranged from painful to excruciating. I saw one of these programs, and even as a professional and

BLACK & WHITE | PORTABLE | COLOR | HIGH DEFINITION

THE ASCENT OF TELEVISION.

Matt Davies
Gannett Suburban Newspapers
Universal Press Syndicate

Dana Summers
The Orlando Sentinel
Tribune Media Services

critical observer, I managed to stay alert for only five minutes. WTTW-TV directors assigned to Chicago Area School Television were at the bottom of the prestige hierarchy in that local station.

Chicago, Massachusetts, Kentucky, South Carolina and Tennessee were serious about Instructional Television. The major stations, in New York, Los Angeles, Pittsburgh and Boston, focused their energies elsewhere: on general audience TV.

The "bicycling" of videotapes from station to station by mail for general audience broadcast was slow. It placed Educational Television in a weak competitive position. "Bicycling" defeated the possibility of topicality, a prime production habit of the network-trained production executives staffing the new entity. With further infusions of Ford Foundation money, Educational Television was moved to New York — in those days, the headquarters of nonfiction television production talent.

There were a number of options this new approach to television could select, all of them expensive. Integrating unsponsored television into the matrix of television as it was would involve exploring unknown territory. The technology was a *prima facie* consideration.[60] Should airplanes fly over the country beaming TV down to the schools? Should there be a national organization? Should there be local centers? What would educational television be, anyway? What kinds of programs should be done? How could they be distributed? Who would do the work? Establishing educational TV was like colonizing an empty continent. We who were working at it were pioneers.

The Ford Foundation's C. Scott Fletcher had the idea that small creative communities could grow up around local stations. At the time, the promising regional theater concept promoted by Tyrone Guthrie looked like a model worthy of emulation. Each local area, each town could become its own *atelier*, its own center of creative expression. The people of each region would have a place to foment works of insight for the rest of the country to see. The creative talents of any town or city would find sustenance through the local educational TV station. There would be grassroots cultural invention, sustained and communicated through the new technology.

By gum! the localities responded. People wanted it! Smalltown universities and big cities jockeyed for licenses to broadcast educational TV. Studios were built. Staffs were hired and production plans were developed. (Of course, they did not know what they were doing, but that didn't matter.)

Sad to say, it was not the Ford Foundation or even the management of Boston's educational television station that discovered TV's first great teacher, it was *lagniappe*.

The first significant triumph in educational television came in the form of a cook, of all things! It's arguable that Julia Child first taught middle class Americans that food could be a "happening", an art form that is fugitive but real. In literate households today Julia Child is an acknowledged national treasure. Julia was the first significant television teacher, and educational TV's poverty made it possible for her to teach us not only her subject matter, but some basic truths about how to use television effectively to teach.

Here's how we got Julia Child: Back in the early 1960s, WGBH TV's Boston studios were housed in a gymnasium at MIT, as the result of Herculean efforts by Hartford Gunn, Dave Davis, the Lowells and other hopefuls, with the support of residents of America's "Athens", Boston and Cambridge. This little, new station really needed programs to fill the air. Funds were extremely short, so they filled the airtime with whatever they could get.

Fortunately for WGBH, at that time the mere idea of "Live Television" had magic for audiences and producers alike. Even if a show had no production value, just by being there it could keep the few outmoded cameras running, the meager lights lit, and the jerrybuilt space in use. Educational TV could provide moving pictures of and by interesting Bostonians for Bostonian living rooms. It could be the start of a global village. The facilities were primitive, but the dreams new and fresh.

WGBH mounted a weekly book review show. It wasn't elaborate, and its volunteer host/producer made a living elsewhere. The show required some lights, a chair, a curtain, a couple of cameras . . . it was as cheap as you could get. The best thing about it was that it *meant* well! It wasn't just *selling* things! It was *clean*! It was *wonderful*!

One day the program manager, Bob Larsen, was phoned by a Cambridge matron. "I have a delightful person for your television station. She should be on TV. She's written a cookbook. It isn't just any old person who's written a cookbook, she's really quite bright and marvelous." "A *cookbook*?" spat the reviewer/host to Larsen. "We don't review cookbooks!" After all, this was *Boston*! The Program Manager apologized to the reviewer, and then to the well-meaning Cambridge matron. But Friday brought bad news. With the book review show scheduled for Saturday, the Program Manager's phone rang. It was the book reviewer. "This week's guest fell through . . . and the standby . . . and my other two standbys! . . . Did you say there was a cookbook writer?"

The cook brought her own hotplate and an omelet pan to the studio. Her stature and demeanor were closer to those of professional golfer Babe Didrickson than to New York television's sleek cooking princess Dione Lucas. Julia's voice rocketed the musical scale. She made an omelet the French way, on camera. "Delicious", the audience said . . . the phones began to ring at WGBH. "Do you have instructions in print?", "When will she be back?"

Nobody knew what had happened. Bob Larsen didn't know, either. But he asked the woman to come back. Magic again. The phones rang. Larsen phoned Mrs. Child: "Can you came back, Julia, and do four more?" Then the studio burned down.

Boston Catholic Television, the first program of the morning on the town's stations, offered the reeling Educational Television station the use of its set, cameras, altar, everything, during the day. WGBH took it. The producer covered the altar with black velour and set up the hot plate, and Julia Child gave Boston's television viewers pointers on how to cook. The phones rang and rang at WGBH. Larsen knew he had something. "Julia, would you do a series on cooking?"

Fortuitously, Boston Edison came forward to offer their demonstration kitchen. On the fourth floor of a loft building in Cambridge, it had no elevator, and it couldn't be moved. Then, another serendipitous gift materialized. The US Department of Health, Education and Welfare gave WGBH a powerful van for remote television broadcast origination. The van went to work at the demonstration kitchen. Julia, her devoted husband Paul, the young producer Russ Morash and production assistant Ruth Lockwood together hauled the magnificent heavy copper cookware up and down the fire escape every week, summer and winter, through rain, sleet and snow, to "do the show". Big Julia, funny, awkward and smart, may have been just the right, unthreatening source to bring the subtleties of Escoffier to meat-and-potatoes America. Distressingly, recordings of those early shows have all been destroyed, "They were too terrible", Ruth Lockwood says. How much they could have told succeeding generations about the development of television as a teaching medium!

The star was paid nothing. At the end of every show, William Pierce's mellifluous voice said simply, "Julia Child is co-author of *Mastering the Art of French Cooking*." Then something happened that is a clue to how to teach by television. The book's sales took off. Here was the first instance of a demonstrable reinforcement between a work of television and print. *The French Chef* pioneered in demonstrating that television can advance learning by providing stimulus through image and affect, folding into the job done by print to provide a complementarity of knowledge and reflection. The combination was immensely satisfying to the learner. Eureka! Here was a key to teaching through television. With the advent of interactive computer education, the lesson discovered with *The French Chef* remains an essential ingredient of media instruction.

Poverty demanded that educational television experiment. Paradoxically, poverty allowed no mistakes, either. Failure was no more an option for educational programs than for commercial programs. The shows had to be cheap, safe, and sure. Since everybody eats, cooking was a natural. With Julia, it worked. The intelligence of Julia, her husband, and Program Manager Bob Larsen and the theatricality of director Russ Morash guided her progress. They made noncommercial TV's first hit.

But the show also exposed some of educational television's weaknesses. To other stations, the subject's commonality and the meager production resources it was allocated commended the studio talk form to managers. Julia demonstrated that you could be both safe and successful, but instead of the real virtues that attracted audiences to her — her finesse, wit and theatricality — managers sought to duplicate only the subject and the miserly production standard. Imitators in other fields made the low-budget "how-to" show a common genre, but never quite reached the transcendence of Julia. Mimicry rather than an exploration of alternatives was the consequence. The lesson administrators took from *The French Chef* was not "innovation", not "international", not "difficult", not "witty", not "elevating to the spirit" or "stimulating to the imagination", not even "left hemisphere-right hemisphere". The message program managers got was "cooking" and "cheap"; this was the way to go. It certainly made sense in terms of cost effectiveness. The "how-to" show became educational TV's equivalent of the game show . . . cheap, easy, and popular. "How-to" is still a staple.

For financially-strapped educational television, prudence led to paralysis. There was no spare money around. In institutional as in personal life, poverty is an inhibition to self-realization. You can't take a risk if there's no contingency option. Here's an example. In its early years, National Educational Television was unprepared to deal with legal challenges to its programming. One staff attorney dealt with all issues involving programs for the whole system, across the whole country. *One* person had to determine whether there might be a legal challenge to any part of any program. The estimable Stuart Sucherman, who was NET's legal advisor to the stations, is intelligent, brave, and compassionate. Every station needed one of him. But no station could pay. How much originality could be tolerable under such constraints? The stations could hardly go to their contributors and say, "We plan an original production. We're going to go out on a limb. We may get into some trouble. We may need money for lawyers." Instead, they maneuvered endlessly to make sure their product was unobjectionable. No legal funds were allocated. In the world's most litigious country, courage is costly. Unable to bear the expense of a lawsuit of any kind, public TV quickly branded courage a No-No.

The paucity of legal recourse to defend originality or dissent in public television programs may well have been a calculated strategy to induce conformism. At any rate, that was its effect.

In the early days, educational television seemed a natural place for young people with vision to go to work. Young visionaries were an incalculable resource. They brought verve, imagination and hope to the stations. And they were cheap. For those with an eye to personal advantage — the upwardly mobile or the ambitious — ETV was a bad bet. It offered no money, no status, no privilege, no power. Willing hands were sure welcome, though. In the early days, everybody, *anybody* was welcome, regardless of race, creed, shape, size, color or national origin. But hardly anybody came.

Nobody came, for reasons that are both a credit to the American past and a discredit to the American present. Just as in commercial broadcasting, in the early days only visionaries, only people with a pioneering spirit were interested. Some good people were able to envisage the promise of an alternative television; people like Nancy Troland at WGBH. They went to work. In the mid-1960s, a career in educational television was a way to act out a dream for young people who had had the privilege of reflection, who thought they could share the joys of discovery and learning with others. They threw themselves into it. Sons and daughters of privilege (often very modest privilege), they elected to give the benefit of what learning they had to these little dream-filled stations that were set up in gymnasia or tucked into the back rooms of a charitable foundation. It was a kind of *noblesse oblige*. The wages were peanuts; they wore their clothes from student days and hoped their family could let them use the old car. They might not have been able to afford a restaurant for lunch, but they could bring in a piece of the quiche they had made the night before (as Janet Weaver did, at WGBH). They wanted to base their careers on doing something useful, something that would "matter". These dreamers went to educational television impelled by the idea of stewardship. It was an ancient idea that those who, through an accident of fate, had access to some knowledge and experience denied to their more circumscribed brethren should share what they had been given with others. This was a translation into action of the traditional belief that the worthwhile life is the life of dedication to something outside oneself, of service of one's fellows (clearly, this was before the 1980s). Here was a Peace Corps, right at home. "From those to whom much has been given, much will be required."

As we all learned, the nastier human qualities are not excluded from operatives in even noble enterprise. But little could we foresee that the time would come when people who had dedicated their lives to noncommercial television, out of a search for excellence, would be pilloried as snobs, as privileged elitists to be targeted and supplanted by skirmishers looking to their own advantage under the flag of populist righteousness.

Chapter 7

POOR BUT HONEST IN
"THE AMERICAN CENTURY"

In the 1960s, the Big Store basis for a philosophy of human organization (which later became known by the euphemism "Reaganism") was merely an obsession of obscure ideologues. People would have scoffed at one of its fundamental tenets, that outside one's own religion and one's own family in their narrowest definitions, the sole criterion of all social value is market value.[61] "Impossible" — anybody who had been to school would say — "Human society is now, thanks to the lessons of human history, dominated by reason, fairness, the goals of social justice and opportunity." Historians in those days laughed about the negative effects of "shopkeeper's attitudes" on Europe's history. Educated people were more than skeptical about Karl Marx's economic determinism as a fundamental engine for a democracy. In those days they still read the lessons of history as affirmation that the most significant human achievements had almost without exception been *outside* the marketplace.

The market had its place; it kept things afloat. But it had no claim to transcendence. The market was seen as servant, not master. In the United States, even in the worst years of the Depression, economically irrelevant and relatively unknown "serious" artists were thought to merit federal subsidy through the Works Progress Administration. It would be quite some time before the White House would honor as "artists" mere entertainers, whose claim to transcendence was that they were at the top of the sales charts. The mass entertainment of commercial baseball had not yet been elevated from the national pastime to a national "sport"; its place as the national pastime was yet to be usurped by shopping.[62] Although the goal of parenthood was for female children to marry into more money and status, and for male children to garner the tools to gain more income and status, the

ideal woman's life had not yet been defined as breakfast, shopping, lunch, shopping, dinner, TV and bed. The ideal man's life had not yet been defined as breakfast, the rat-race,
lunch, the rat-race, dinner & TV on weekdays, and on weekends winding down by fixing
things, playing or watching games and shopping for the "big-ticket items". That was in the
1960s. The revolution was yet to come.

In 1997 *The Economist* magazine declared, "These days, the victory of market over state
is quite taken for granted."[63] It wasn't always so. America's developing market-driven culture was a radical innovation. It was a revolution against ideas that had dominated western thought for centuries. Banished were the preeminence of reason, compassion, reflection, memory, goodwill, philosophical inquiring doubt as ideals. Instead, the revolutionary
thinking of marketing presupposes lives directed by impulse in an eternal present. "A se-
militerate society beguiled by the joys of forgetfulness," Lewis H. Lapham called it, in
Harpers'. With materialism as its guiding principle and consumerism as its agency, opportunism became our operative credo.

A shadowy secret of public television's development may be called the American Sin.
This is a new sin, our own invention. It is the sin of opportunism. The freedom of choice
that is one of the cornerstones of democracy was codified into the structure of our society,
by leaving as many options open as possible. The purpose — to give us all a chance to realize the best in ourselves. Opportunity has begat opportunism. Opportunism gives its practitioners license to pursue any means toward the end of their choice. In American middle-
class culture since World War II, that end has become the feathering of one's own nest.

Evidence daily before us in our workplaces and our public places demonstrates that
opportunism is replacing family values as the defining attribute of the American middle
class. *"Carpe Diem"* could today appropriately replace "In God We Trust" on our coinage.
TV commercials, and of course the programs they used as bait, were proselytizers of this
new way of thinking. They had an effect. The past was junked. "History has ended", one
writer declared. "A torrent of imagery and sound makes every moment but the present
seem quaint, bloodless or dead", said another.[64] A "floating world of timeless fantasy", Lapham calls it.[65] "Market driven culture leaves no place for the nooks and pinnacles of genius
or morality."[66]

As America's new *de facto* philosophy of hedonistic utilitarianism unfolded, there
were some foot-dragging television viewers who knew what they wanted to buy and
weren't going to change their minds because of a 60-second pitch, no matter how jazzy it
was. Unbeknownst to them, they were increasingly irrelevant to commercial television
decisionmaking. Over time, these viewers found that there were no longer programs for
them on TV. A lot of Americans, many of them intelligent, educated and even clever, found
themselves entirely left out. They complained to one another, to no avail. Today, these
people use their television sets only for the screening of prerecorded materials.

More serious forces were at work than the mere convictions of civilized people. *Busi-*

ness was at work. The broadcasting industry had developed into simply "a vehicle for delivering a mass consuming public to national advertisers."[67] What a ride!

One of the remarkable attributes of human history is that in the long run, truth has its say. The workings of democracy and commerce always find out that they can't bypass smart people. Eventually, smart people claimed some of the airwaves back for their own. But only for a while.

In the pioneering days of television, commerce stood on the sidelines. Visionaries, people of imagination (inside and outside the industry) saw television as a revelation. They flocked to work with one of the three networks, the only sources of programs at that time. CBS (thanks to *Omnibus, Studio One, Adventure, Let's Take a Trip, Playhouse 90, Camera Three* and its news department) was esteemed as a locus of innovation and integrity. It was there that I decided to go for my first job, fresh from the army, forcing myself on an unenthusiastic CBS mailroom.

For everybody in the CBS "family", this was a thrilling era. It was pioneer time. Television was an unknown; it was different, new, exciting, a well of possibilities. The air was full of a promise that seemed real and ready to be explored. Here in our hands was a miraculous, unprecedented entity, a temporal/spatial medium that could touch almost all the senses simultaneously, the first of this kind in history that *came right into people's homes.* Television confronted people who had intuition and imagination with a blinding insight: television had potential as a teaching medium of immense and unprecedented power! They were right. Sponsors learned quickly.

A tradition of corporate responsibility that was born in reaction to the abuses of the early days of industrialization in Victorian England protected television's infancy. During the hundred years after the Civil War, the corporate idea was grounded in the notion that the corporation was an "agent of a larger public good".[68] In corporate charters of the late 19th century, the corporation was defined in a general sense, as an entity with a broad purpose: to serve the public weal. These principles were in some measure derived from the idea of service to the Crown and Commonwealth, from English common law, and the Christian ethic. During the early part of the 20th century, in truly conservative fashion, our society had developed a tradition of corporate responsiveness to the principles underlying society at large. As a matter of internal policy corporations saw to it that they promoted to positions of power persons who defined their duty to society as "guardians".[69] Chief executive officers aspired to the status of "gentlemen". A William S. Paley at CBS and a David Sarnoff at NBC acted as fatherly protectors. Back then, benign paternalism was a traditional role for corporate leaders. The body of thought that became known as Liberalism emerged as a strategy to temper the excesses of democracy and market capitalism by applying to them the principles of Judeo-Christian ethical thought and lessons conveyed by the tradition of humane letters.

The end of World War II saw the erosion of this concept. The holy writ of the corporate charter, the principle of democracy, the idea of the separation of church and state and incentives available to legislators conspired to change the American world radically from its roots. In a revolution quite as effective as warfare, with the cooperation of state legislatures hungry for the revenues they could collect from corporations beguiled by hospitable state charters (New Jersey and Delaware were first) the money people took control. The definition of corporate responsibility changed. Corporate purpose became defined as "the bottom line". "Corporate responsibility" became translated into the meaning it holds today: "Whatever sells, we'll produce." Despite protestations to the contrary, in the era now upon us corporate responsibility is above all directed to the gaining of advantage in the competitive intracorporate endurance race that is the Dow Jones Industrial Average. Corporate executives, like basketball players, simply "get a cut of the action" based on their bottom-line performance.

In television's childhood, there were still some people in positions of responsibility in our society who had not dismissed the thought that the Bible was talking experience, not religion, when it declared that "the love of money is the root of all evil". The power television represents, critics thought, was too great to be left entirely in the hands of "low", manipulative people or institutions motivated entirely by pecuniary gain. Intellectual heirs of America's austere Protestant founders, they held to values that now seem curiously archaic. Perhaps they recognized that sponsors are businessmen, and applied Adam Smith's caution that businessmen constitute "an order of men whose interest is never exactly the same with that of the public, who have generally an interest to deceive and even to oppress the public, and who accordingly have upon many occasions both deceived and oppressed it." There were some reflective people then who believed that if television were to become the engine of human betterment it seemed to promise, it would do so only if freed from the inhibition of market domination. The issue seemed to be this: With the power to beguile the populace in their very homes, should television be the exclusive instrument of practitioners motivated by a fault so ineluctably proven to be harmful that it was numbered as one of the seven deadly sins, that is, greed? Should television be allowed to prey on the gullible, trading on base desires as a means to the increase of the dividends of remote, disinterested, essentially irresponsible lenders of working capital? Should television contribute to a two-level society of exploiters and exploited, and become merely a diversion and a distraction for non-integrated people? Would a populace conditioned by television be potentially dangerous to itself? Should this electronic communications medium become a trivializer of human life, an instrument of societal regression, offering escapism, gossip and thrills, or could it be an instrument of cultural uplift? Would our country go down the drain as Gibbon said Rome did, with a leadership feeding the populace on "bread and circuses"? Maybe the GDP wasn't all our country was about! With the trivialization of human life through the "boob tube" a clear and present danger, critical thinkers decided it was time that something should be done.

As commercial TV developed, members of the leadership class developed a sense that it was not fulfilling its potential. Thoughtful people, many of them members of the dominant class, were being shortchanged. Educated people, more than anybody else, recognized television for the art form it is. There were still some people around who loved life in its complexity. There were still some around who felt about art as Jonathan Miller does when he says (about theater), "It galvanizes the spirit and engages the intelligence. If that isn't entertainment, I don't know what is!" Some few even agree with critic Herbert Muschamp: "Art is not a pastime but a necessity of life."[70]

In a democracy, logic tells us, the rich must be afforded the same benefits as the poor. It's only logical that for people who used to read the old *New Yorker*, to whom taste and discernment matter, who love Plato, who go to Tanglewood, who paint a little or can write a sonnet, *people who know who they are*, should have access to television they can watch.

"We'll do it", declared a courageous voice at the Ford Foundation's Fund for Education. The Ford Foundation would fight for tradition, for civilization. The Ford Foundation would be St. George, and it would outmaneuver, if not disable, the dragon of trivialization that threatened to amuse us to death. The motivations of people at the Ford Foundation are unclear. Public scrutiny isn't their thing. Perhaps they saw that the very purposes of democracy were at issue — not democracy the leveler, but democracy that offers to all the option of excellence. It was a dream shared by the founders of the nation. That dream had allowed a country boy with an idea in his head to build the Ford Motor Company. In defense of the Ford Foundation, it has to be said that, at the time, nobody, including the people working in it, knew what television could do. (Unfortunately, from the outset, the Ford Foundation searched too narrowly for its Educational Television template. Instead of the Platonic dialogues, the parables of the Bible, the stories of Sophocles and Shakespeare, it used the didactic model of the pulpit and the classroom. Ford Foundation officials joined educators and lawmakers in failing to penetrate to the essential theatrical nature of the new medium.)

The Ford Foundation faced a sorry television landscape. In 1960, the chairman of the Federal Communications Commission Newton Minow called commercial television a "vast wasteland". Thanks to the combination of corporate imperatives and the networks' grandfathering of the Communications Act of 1934, no commercial broadcaster could any longer bring itself to broadcast in what had for 200 years been defined as the public interest. As had been feared, broadcasting had become an affront to the fastidious. The Ford Foundation therefore took it upon itself to see to it that the instruments of what Western civilization had come to define as education — that is, philosophy, literature, theater, art, science, music, poetry — would break the bounds of exclusivity, and through television be available to all. It was hoped that the immense potential power of this new medium to form better people could be fulfilled — at least, an attempt was worth the effort. Through skillfully applied stimulus, this technological novelty, this trivial diversion, this toy television, could become a tool of the creative impulses of democracy. Educational Television would be invented.

And invented it was, through grants from the Ford Foundation. "Ford" had some help from the "bully pulpit". A critique of commercial broadcasting from their chief regulator, Federal Communications Commission Chairman Newton Minow, came as a blow to commercial broadcasters. Minow's highly publicized "vast wasteland" observation signaled a direction that potential FCC activism could take that might derail the gravy train. In a move that would have delighted novelist Robert Musil,[71] through the Ford Foundation, democracy was to be instrumented by guidance from the top. With a grant of $10 million over a three-year period, Ford established National Educational Television.

After World War II, the Ford and Rockefeller Foundations, and the Carnegie Endowment contributed heavily to the nation's intellectual leadership. Part of that leadership included support of the arts and artists, in the cases of Ford and Rockefeller. Those institutions at the time willingly undertook the risk of supporting creative endeavors of all kinds. Ford Foundation annual reports during this period spell out their beliefs and their needs assessment. As they envisioned it, an alternative television service "can enter controversial areas where government, because of political considerations, or industry, because of economic considerations or education, because of lack of funds, may be reluctant to venture."[72] Their goal was not the consumer. It was not the voter. Instead, "We are interested in the product that only good education can provide: The thinking man." Recognizing that strong forces in the society are willing and ready to mold the population as foot soldiers to serve their perceived self-interest, Ford declared, "Our choices as a nation will be closer to reality if the quality of our thinking is more creative and the number of people capable of constructive thought is larger." That kind of impetus is sorely lacking today; but the goal wasn't given up because it was unachievable. There were other reasons.

Chapter 8

THE INVALIDIZATION
OF EDUCATIONAL TELEVISION

Who should, could or would run Educational Television? Where should its founders look for candidates? In the 1960s, educational television was needy in every way. It needed money. It needed an image. The idea of local ateliers was attractive but problematical. Parochialism was the natural companion of the localism born of the idea of "Group Theater" and the technological necessity of multiple broadcasting antennas (and people to operate them) in the pre-satellite era. Trustees had to decide who would run the new stations that were being built. Where could they turn to minimize risk? Who knew what educational TV could become? Educators who had also been successful fundraisers seemed like a good bet. And that is who was chosen. But they were not winners. Funds were raised — and applied to building programs and technology. Fundraisers and thinkers, it appears, are separate breeds.

Dr. John Taylor, the former University of Louisville president who telegraphed his fitness for television leadership by choosing as call letters for a television station the initials of *Window To The World* (the title of a book about television). WTTW's call letters signaled the quality and originality of Dr. Taylor's insight. To Taylor and Chicago's community leaders, the nascent alternative television was envisioned not as an interpretive theatrical medium needing invention and imagination but as a neutral, non-interpretive medium. This presumption of neutrality was either a convenient oversight or a transparent falsehood. The inadequacy of this circumscribed vision was evident even in the control room, in the selectivity of a director's use of multiple cameras, his camera placement and choice of cutting options.

The convenient assumption that educational TV was inherently objective allowed its commodification. If educational TV was just a conduit, then it would make sense to put good fundraisers and publicity, promotion and public relations people in positions of power. The new medium would not require people of discernment, taste, reflectivity, judgment, sensibility or profound intelligence if it were just a "window" . . . non-interpretive. It would only need people to drum up support, run the machinery, schedule and record what was there, and do the billing. Simple.

Staffing decisions reflected the desire to keep the new medium nonthreatening. But giving the reins to the fundraisers, while it was convenient, was also a shortsighted move. The kind of people who take up the craft of publicity and public relations are drumbeaters by inclination and by choice. People who elect to be publicists and fundraisers are structurally deficient in that part of human intellect that involves the critical faculty. They are good sports: they love *whatever* they promote, and they love *all* their donors. That's their job. It's not part of their job to reflect, to analyze, to measure against standards. They have to be willing to compromise anything, even the institution's avowed goals, in the interest of institutional expansion. A tolerance for mendacity is a structural requirement of the publicity/fundraising craft and its practitioners, and to cloak mendacity in euphemism is all in a day's work. Promoters make dutiful followers and unprincipled leaders: in view of the formidable challenges ahead, in evolving the mission of the nascent alternative art form that was educational/public TV, they were exactly what was *not* needed.

The fundraisers and publicists succeeded. They raised money. They got some power. Then they set the tone. When they moved up from positions requiring tactics to positions requiring strategy, the opportunism, the willingness to compromise principles that had worked well for them as servants compromised the industry they were meant to enhance. Successful fundraisers and publicists established ground rules whose consequences allowed public television to come to its current supine state.

Who hired these Pied Pipers? The boards of trustees. Did they do it as a deliberate strategy to limit the scope of "education" in America? That was the eventual outcome.

If consciously done, it was not a strategy without precedent.

Even at the beginning, everybody didn't share the dream of an alternative television service. And some who did not share that dream pretended they did. Rapid technological innovation made it attractive for commercial broadcasting stations to "dump" obsolete equipment on Educational TV, gaining at once a welcome tax deduction, a guarantee of non-competitiveness, and praise at dinner parties.

KQED San Francisco raised money by inventing a variant on the charitable rummage sale, an auction. The television auction made no enemies. In America this activity was commonplace. It had an honorific place in eleemosynary, well-meaning but powerless institutions like parish churches. But the auction turned out to be educational television's Achilles heel. It raised needed funds, but its ritual significance could not be ignored: it tarnished the image. The public television auction is a ritual homage to the commodification of American middle-class life. It conveys the message, just in case anybody was unclear about it, that within the scheme of our alternative television, to skip down the primrose path of consumerism's glorification of the ordinary is just fine. Shopping is fun.

Since the television auction is essentially another store, another commercial enterprise, the auction's implicit endorsement of tradespeople's values was questionable in an entity designed as a noncommercial alternative. In terms of the options for alternative television, the television auction represents a tacit acceptance of a certain "world view", of an *arriviste* group striving for dominance.[73]

WGBH Boston's president Hartford Gunn, later president of the Public Broadcasting Service, had established WGBH-TV as an *atelier* of creativity. "Here, the producer is king", Gunn declared. The station was renowned among broadcasters. (Its detractors called it "Group Theater", or "the sandbox".) Hartford Gunn embodied the hopes of educated Americans for a disinterested creative forum. Fittingly, Gunn declared the auction to be out of keeping with the character of noncommercial television. He recommended that this haggling and huckstering activity be phased out at the earliest possible moment.

Such was not to be. The fundraising auction became a central enterprise for local stations. Its substantial cost was listed for the public each year as part of a station's programming expenses, conveniently but falsely inflating a station's record for original programming submitted annually to Congress. Local supporters of educational TV sprang at this device for disposing of some of consumer industry's overproduction. The auction fit into suburban habits. Attics were relieved of old books, *objets d'art*, knickknacks, conversation pieces, designer goods, and grandma's watercolors. Retailers came aboard for a little free publicity and at the same time unloaded last season's merchandise as a deductible charity expense. A win/win situation. Bargain hunting benefiting a good cause satisfied competitive materialist acquisitiveness and at the same was honorific. One could publicly dicker to buy something for less than its market value and bring it home to triumphantly show smiling neighbors that you had helped support education! More than that, the auction was an opportunity for people to do good *on camera*. Sleek Junior League matrons in silk dresses and their groomed stockbroker mates flocked to the auction, and gave it social *cachet*. Voluntarism conferred status. "Exposure" satisfied local self-promotion. Educational television could give sanction to vanity. At the auction, the ambitious and the socially prominent could hobnob with rugged sports celebrities, glistening TV anchors and toothsome candidates for public office: career building for charity. "Proof of spiritual refinement", Lewis Lapham calls the trophy of a public TV auction.[74] And it was fun! Auctions boomed. The TV auction became an institution.

"Support your local educational TV station." In the 1960s, with Vietnam, stagflation and the rat race really heating up for the middle class, communities badly needed a modern institution that seemed to do good — whether in fact it did or not. Never mind that auctions consumed a large part of the resources and personnel of the TV station. Never mind that they compromised the service mission of educational TV. They helped a "good cause", and the end justified the means. The communities loved it. Everybody got publicity, some small funds were raised, and the stations remained well-meaning, poor, backward, noncompetitive and manipulable. Nobody in commercial broadcasting or in education needed to fear them. It was an ideal situation.[75]

For all its heroic efforts, the fledgling industry they called educational television found it could allocate only token resources for new programs. The Ford Foundation had limited resources to apply to an enormously expensive television infrastructure. It appointed Fred Friendly, a onetime newspaperman and former CBS News president with a fully expanded ego as TV czar. To Friendly, the promise of television was what he called "actualities". These were live remote programs of news stories whereby television could scoop newspapers. (A wag once said of him, "Fred has a real ear for television"). As educational TV's first priority, Friendly established the primacy not of program innovation but of station interconnection. The 1960s saw an educational television sorely in need of product. Instead, technology, color equipment, national station interconnection, buildings and studios, publicity and promotion, studies and reports (plus, in New York, high rents and union wages) took priority over programs. What programs there were feeble and amateurish — mainly "talking heads" — receding ever farther behind the fare of commercial television in production sophistication.

When I was hired as executive producer at WTTW, Chicago, I was given a prime-time hour a week on Wednesday evening, to be devoted to "cultural programming". An hour of prime-time every week in America's second or third major market — what a plum! It sounded great, to me. Ed Morris, former public relations man and the new Director of Programming for Educational Television then told me that the purpose of WTTW's "cultural programming" was "to make Chicago look good". (Peering over our shoulders was John Ryerson, a Director of Inland Steel and a substantial contributor). Culture as regional promotion . . . how interesting, I thought.

Then I found out what my production resources were. In addition to the hour of prime time, I was given two big black-and-white hand-me-down pedestal cameras. (It was 1965 and commercial TV had converted to color. And for more than a decade, commercial TV shows had been using a minimum of three cameras.) I had some lighting, all the scenery two people could design, construct and paint in five days, and an out-of-pocket budget of $25 a week. With that budget, in those days, I could have a piece of sculpture hauled to the studio — but there wasn't enough money to return it. Withal, we did "Negritude", a live, one hour of performance on Black culture (that was in 1967), and producer Bob Kaiser's inventive show on Archie and Mehitabel won us an Emmy. A grant from the Ford Foundation allowed me to make a film show about poet Gwendolyn Brooks for National Educational Television's *The Creative Person* series. To me, that seemed a good beginning.

We did "still shows" (30 years later they became the source of Ken Burns' renown) using photographs, because we couldn't afford sets in the studio or excursions to a "location". It's difficult to make stills come alive. Because studio cameras weighed 1,000 pounds, camera movement was rudimentary: nothing but cuts, zooms and pullbacks. There wasn't enough money anywhere for the $35 an hour it then cost to animate stills on the Oxberry animation stand used by cartoon-makers in Hollywood. Of course, we knew very well the liveliness an Oxberry could bring to still photographs in informational programming. The Canadian Film Board had shown us a decade earlier. It took a quarter of a century before American noncommercial television could afford the production level of *The Civil War*, a well-done "cheap" show with still-picture animation that's a technological generation behind that of *Star Wars*. The real novelty of *The Civil War* was that somebody was willing to pay for nonfiction! In the general sense, the constraint on all production during the days of educational television was the choice of "doing it badly or not at all". We elected to do it badly, not because that was all we were capable of doing, but because a complex of forces in the society were unready or unwilling to support the cost of noncommercial information attractively presented.

Instructional television proceeded to mount its own assault on education. The "telly teacher" in the classroom on TV was the product of a conjoining of monetary and imaginative poverty that rightly alienated a generation of schoolchildren. But, for educational television administrators, there was a tactical advantage to this situation. As long as the new TV didn't have to deliver, it could continue to make promises people would believe. Nobody minded. In fact, educational TV was like a sick puppy that might die, but was worth nursing to health (if not to vigor). Weak and stupid, it was lovable. It was unthreatening. People could say, "I really love educational TV", and nobody minded that it continually let them down.

The appearance of an unsponsored television entity was a *lagniappe* for commercial TV. With a purportedly public service channel in almost every city, commercial television could now allow "them" (educational TV) to do the cheap talk shows that commercial television licensees once had done as a required "public service" in their unsold time slots — which had long since vanished, anyway. As long as the FCC could read in its reports that the public was getting shows about the things Washington was interested in, it seemed satisfied that public service was being done. FCC members are not trained theater critics. They are, after all, political appointees. As long as Educational Television didn't have to really perform the difficult task of exploring the medium as a creative entity, it could trade on promises while producing low-cost imitations of conventional and outdated network fare. This was convenient for educational TV's management, who might be taxed by problems of creativity. It was convenient for local commercial TV stations, whose professional expertise far exceeded that of their ETV neighbors. It was the road of least resistance, and it's just the one the nation took.

Nobody minded much. As long as the US could claim the 20th to be "The American Century", "frills" like imagination, innovation, artistry, and a voice of a loyal opposition on the alternative to commercial television could be allowed to languish. As long as we were triumphant in armaments and productivity, as long as there was a (cold) "war" on, there was justification for equating creativity with dissent. Since we were "Number One", our businessmen, engineers and politicians could declare that we had no other need than to stay on the course set after World War II: the course of consumer-driven economic expansionism, technological development, military preparedness. President Eisenhower's warning about the dangers of US domination by its military industrial complex had an unintended result; it acted as a signal for the aggressive expansion of just the power he had warned against. In this context, the small voices within the Ford Foundation carried less and less weight.

Other countries like England and Japan, with significantly smaller GDPs, allocated much more significant sums to noncommercial television than we did. The economics of British television, notably the BBC's funding by licensing, was mere frosting on a long-standing theatrical tradition and a serious national commitment to excellence. It was natural for Britain to make a substantial investment in television as an art form. "No strings" funding made it possible for the Brits to provide stylish and intelligently made television. In England, public service TV led and commercial TV followed.

In America, on the other hand, early efforts to produce a few operas and a few plays demonstrated to harried educational television executives that it wasn't going to be easy to be a cultural force. Many executives in educational TV had scant production experience, having recently promoted themselves from roles as fundraisers and publicists. They quickly discovered that it was really quite difficult to keep a station afloat, let alone to make good, original television in Chicago, Boston, or San Francisco. There weren't enough readily accessible actors, for one thing. Talent had to be imported, and was expensive. There was no body of brilliant directors to choose from in Rochester, or Peoria. Working scriptwriters were doing fiction in California or at ad agencies. And which executives who knew anything about the art of theater would accept the pittance offered by educational TV? Certainly there could be no candidates who would be acceptable to a Cleveland banker-TV board member! In time, it became apparent to viewers and educational television professionals that alternative television in America would be more costly and difficult than the Ford Foundation had foreseen. The avenue taken was, again, that of least resistance — that is, simply not to pay anybody a wage comparable to the "outside" and to look for ways to survive with the economic and intellectual resources at hand.

Chapter 9
WHY "EDUCATIONAL" TV DRIED UP

The ignorance we are born with is a personal and social liability. Learning and contributions to self and society are covalent. Schooling of the whole person is a must. The greatest war we must fight for America's future is the war to push back the wall of ignorance. The prize of this war is the great human enterprise: to know. The challenge to education in America is not math skills or science skills or preparing engineers to run tomorrow's technology or consumers to sell and buy stuff. The great challenge facing America in the 21st century should have been the goal of America in the 20th century: to challenge ignorance.

We made a mistake with educational television. A clumsy marriage of narrowly focused prioritization and faulty organizational structure fostered ineptitude. The educators themselves were insensitive, territorial, unimaginative and unwise. An unexamined acceptance of the tradition of Western teaching since Gutenberg closed educators' eyes to the potential of television in the classroom.

Since the founding of the monasteries, since the first university at Gottingen, the written word has been the repository of learning. Learning has been called "the struggle to enlarge yourself to take in a mind greater and more powerful than your own." The written word was for centuries the only efficient way to store and transport records of human thought and achievement. Over the centuries, the worldwide system of libraries, universities, and schools had developed a body of learning and a tradition of teaching that was print-oriented and verbal-sequential in its storage and delivery form. The advent of film a hundred years ago changed the storage/delivery system. The ancient tradition of teaching by story, updated into teaching via the technology of motion picture, came into society by the back door. The first great teacher of the new medium was probably Charlie Chaplin. And Chaplin's secret? *Teaching with delight.* That is also the secret of teaching by television . . . or computer. A *Time Magazine* cover feature on America's best teachers declared, "The most important thing a great teacher communicates is enthusiasm."

Confounded by the new medium of television, teachers missed Julia Child's message. They failed to comprehend the lesson that the first imperative was to enlist television's affective potential as a resource to share the joy of learning. When educational television arrived on the scene, our educational establishment greeted the idea of instructional television warily. They continued to teach as they had taught for hundreds of years. They dug in their heels. They demanded that TV not change anything, despite the revolutionary new storage and retrieval mechanism. Edgar Faure, in UNESCO's *Learning to Be*, corroborates my own experience in the field when he writes, "We find authorities merely inserting television into existing educational procedures, instead of thoroughly reorganizing these so they benefit from this modern technological aid" (p. xxxiv). Instead of seeing television as an opportunity to break down the walls of the classroom and to develop instructional models on the model of Plato's Dialogues or Jesus' parables or Shakespeare's plays or Tolstoy's *War and Peace*, American educators put a camera in front of the chalkboard and called it the "Twenty-one Inch Classroom". Perhaps they felt threatened.

They enlarged their turf. In the 1950s and 1960s a bureaucratized, self-absorbed education establishment made educational television programs that were unthreatening to teachers, that were cheap, didactic, ugly, and unimaginative. Educational TV was thoughtlessly made. It didn't fit. America's educators couldn't shake off the 19th century English pulpit and the English public school. When confronted with the idea of school television, America's educators simply put a camera and a monitor in a classroom, then complained of the difficulty and cost. A captive audience of students caught on rather quickly — students hated the programs and didn't learn from them. This was a misuse of the medium. Students, teachers, parents — everybody hated it. The bad teachers were afraid of it; they, and the good teachers, and the students rejected it.

Perhaps because it would have required curriculum adaptation, the schools never really accepted classroom TV. The error was a combination of bureaucratic inertia, lack of imagination, fear of innovation, pride, job insecurity, and resistance to change on the part of America's educators. Even when an example was presented to them, America's teachers failed to see its universality. In its formative approach, *Sesame Street* was on the right track. It based its forms on story and production value. Its seed fell on infertile ground, however. *Sesame Street* failed to become the developmental model it should have been. A shallow educational and public television establishment conveniently accepted the children's assessment: that *Sesame Street*'s quality stemmed not from its developmental strategy or its adventurousness or its exploration of story and affect, but from "Big Bird".

CBS News' Don Hewitt, veteran of more than thirty years in the television information business, gave a prescription for television as an educational tool when he wrote, "You can strike a more responsive chord by looking them in the eye and telling them a story than you can by dealing with issues. If you want to deal with an issue, tell your audience a story about someone coping with that issue. It's more palatable that way . . . Even the people who wrote the Bible knew that"[76]. The lesson of educational television was there for anybody to see. The models are Plato's Socratic discourses and the Bible stories: "edu-tainment", if you will.

Despite educators, some progress *was* made in the use of television as an instructional tool. I can point to some of my own work during the 1960s — the use of film as stimulus, the bringing together of *cinéma verité* filming techniques and roleplaying in the making of children's films, the bringing together of picture, story, sound and print to prompt positive affect and simultaneously meet various learning styles, to develop stories with concurrent simplicity and complexity of message. Children loved the results. Sensitive administrators awarded my programs with prizes. "What's My Thing?" won an Ohio State Award. "Making Friends" won a Cine Golden Eagle. During those years of trial and error, we learned something about teaching with television. We learned that television provides affect better than information. We learned that a story can stimulate . . . it can open a mind to issues. We learned, too that a guide is needed to help children explore the implications of the stimulus to which they respond. We learned that television can be a part of a rich, interactive classroom experience, in which teacher, video and students are antiphonal elements.

The educational establishment met our discoveries with thundering indifference. Then, in the 1980s, a US president who thought films were a business joined forces with school managements who wanted computers to secure jobs for their students when they grew up. Pragmatic, utilitarian power stopped instructional television dead in its tracks.

The immediacy of television imagery makes it an appropriate educational tool. My own experience in investigating the uses of television/film in conjunction with print has persuaded me that there is still much promise there. Television deals with affect. It uses images in time. It has many of the attributes of theater. The print medium deals with cognitions and their ordering, and allows reflection. The two media, like the two modes in which they excel, are not merely complementary; they seem to reinforce each other.

As we move into the development of educational materials for the new century, we can learn from the failures of educational television and computer instruction. In my decades of producing instructional television and observing its use in the classroom, I discovered something about its capabilities and limitations. These succinct steps are the product of thirty years of failure and success in working with television as an instructional tool.

First, teachers should not be frightened. This "other teacher" is not a competitor. Instead, it is a third hand, available to help them with their task. This "third hand" can do some of the things that a teacher can do, but not everything.

Using this "third hand" needs a little practice on the teacher's part. Only the rare teacher has the instinct to adapt. For the vast majority, teachers' workshops are an important component of familiarization. Workshops can demonstrate to teachers what it is that the medium can accomplish and what is best done by the teacher who is "right there". Essentially, the division between what the audio-visual component can do and what the teacher and texts can do is as follows:

1. *Video:* Through the *particularization* of *story*, an appropriately designed video gives the student *stimulus* and *affect.* It delivers the student to the teacher with a part of the brain enriched in images, in a heightened state of awareness, full of wonder, delight, curiosity and intellectual energy. In the programs I made, I always envisioned that the shot that should follow in a natural sequence, after the last one I made, was the face of the classroom teacher. My shows were a "setup" to "deliver" the student to the teacher in a heightened and receptive state.

2. *Teacher:* Interviews the students to help identify the interrelatedness between characters and ideas.

3. *Then, Teacher:* To deliver the student to the source of learning . . . generalization, information, cognition . . . the WORD (printed and/or spoken).

Television makes possible a symbiotic learning experience among teacher, student, information and stimulus. This, in its simplest form, is the armature for effective use of television as a teaching tool.

However promising the new technology may be, as long as children are diverse, as long as teachers have different knowledge bases and skills, as long as so much is unknown by our species, and however attractive are the economies of media duplication and distribution, there will always be a crucial place for the knowing, dedicated classroom teacher to facilitate the learning process. Still, with expected increases in computer memory, and with increasing capacity of compact videodisc to recreate images in time comparable to those of actual experience, it is worth trying again to profit by the learnings of instructional television. Interactive digital computer/television offers the potential for easily replicated superior instruction that will allow learner choices among multiple learning modalities at minimal cost, as first envisioned in the 1960s with the advent of videotape. If teachers, administrators and legislators are willing to recognize the need to teach each student differently, a video/print/audio technology controllable in time will make it possible to reach large numbers of students more effectively at lower cost. It will be possible in the new century to realize the dream of "teaching with delight" for vast numbers of students around the world.

Economist and financier Felix Rohatyn has written, "The public schools may be one of the last places in America where technology has had practically no impact . . . Beginning in kindergarten, the use of computers, television and VCRs in the teaching process should be part of any program to improve learning and reduce the high dropout rates of our public school systems."[77] I would add that a condition of effective use would be the application of the body of learning about how television teaches that has been accumulated in the last forty years. Television instruction is efficient, labor saving and cost effective. It is interesting that Rohatyn's prescription comes after nearly forty years of school television. He's right. Educational television deserves a try.

What went wrong?

One factor we would prefer not to acknowledge is that the idea of the medium as an educational tool was elbowed out by "urgent" career strategies of people involved in schooling. The "haves", the clever, the aggressive, the calculating, the decisionmakers, having gotten theirs, worked to ossify a stratified social system from which they benefited. New technologies in and of themselves became the vehicle for increasing administrator power. Teachers with ideas not only got no encouragement, they got decreasing discretionary resources.

Legislators saw students as potential sources of their future tax revenues, as potential voters. They got behind programs that might train America's youth as contributors to an enhanced GDP. Businesses saw students as potential customers and employees. Technologists saw public schools as a training ground for "the bottom 50%"[78] as robots, as machine operators for the future's complex technology. None saw their interest as support of the development of television as an innovative educational tool. They dragged their feet and then simply forgot a concept of proven effectiveness.

Many teachers had problems with classroom television because they felt threatened that it might teach better than they could. The makers of the television programs are partly to blame for alienating teachers through their insensitivity. Television as an audio-visual teaching tool should be the teacher's colleague, as books are. Teachers can teach better with TV if they are first led to understand how television *supplements* and *reinforces* the teacher's activities in the classroom.

When television was introduced into the schools, the "box" itself created problems. It was heavy and big, it broke down, it got stolen, it had to be hauled around. A decade of experience with computers may have softened schools toward technology in the classroom.

Television, like a book, is a way of storing and distributing educational materials. The initial cost of software is high, as *Sesame Street*'s Joan Ganz Cooney pointed out in the 1960s. But the life of a good program is long . . . *The French Chef* programs that I helped WGBH-TV produce in 1971 are still being shown in the new century.

In the long term, well-produced television brings instruction to our children cheaply and efficiently, in a form that is akin to the lifelong learning pattern of actual experience. Television can bring image, story, and an engaging approximation of the very act of intellectual discovery to children in school. Television in the classroom can liberate teachers to do other things. When teachers are in short supply, a television-based instructional package can supplement them, and that is an attractive long-term cost saving for school systems. It should be given a try.

THE EDUCATION EMERGENCY

Education vs Consumerism

Any teacher in any public high school today will tell you that most of the students don't want to learn. Our youth are complacent in their self-absorption. Many parents are too busy working and shopping to notice them, so they are, in effect, taught by "the tube" and their peers. The fact is that the effect of a consumerist philosophy is that the engine of our economy is a populace encouraged and confirmed in an ahistoric impulsiveness and gullibility. This is okay for business, it's fun for the kids, and it's lethal to a civilization.

The computer as word processor/book/calculator was opportunistically adopted as part of the revolution of education as America rushed headlong to embrace the dubious political position that the good human life is getting and spending. The computer was sold as a device to bring knowledge. It was bought as a device to prepare students as functionaries in the workforce of an emerging service economy. The push to equip already financially-strapped schools with costly computers at whatever sacrifice was yet another instance of the conception of the school as vocational training institute. The concept of education as job training as it exists in America is a radical idea. It has no precedent in western intellectual history.

An emerging American sovereignty of the entrepreneur relegates to the ash-heap much that has been called education. This new aristocracy accepts the Marx/Engels dictum that the foundation of all society is economic. It damns non-economic activity as "effete and unworldly".[79] The fact that 20% of our population is functionally illiterate may well be an inevitable outcome of consumerism. Novelist Francine Prose writes, "Is it really in the best interests of our consumer economy to create a well-educated, smart, highly literate society of fervent readers? Doesn't our epidemic dumbing-down have undeniable advantages for those institutions (the media, the advertising industry, the government) whose interests are better served by a population not trained to read too closely or ask too many questions?"[80] If our society is to have a future, that has to be changed.

A system of education is effective only if its larger goal is the increase in the sum total of human knowledge. Students must be given the tools to learn to think for themselves. Any other goal is too narrow for education in a democracy that hopes to take a place in the history of civilized societies.

Consumerism leads to the dictatorship of the producer. Some consumer products are of doubtful value (cigarettes being only one visible example). Some consumer product producers' interests are served by uncritical buyers. Therefore, as these producers become significantly large, they find it to their interest to adopt social policies that foster academic anti-intellectualism and political populism. A social system controlled by consumer product producers, and that defines education as teaching people how to get more, own more, and dominate more, is pathological. An educational system that focuses on "professional" training and career "education" euphemizes subordination. Training people to function as *apparatchiks* in a system that dignifies a pattern of life based on the gratification of desires is an abuse of power. Such a system will thwart, inhibit, anger, even derail the innovative minds that represent the generative force of all human society.[81]

Local Control ≈ Loss of Control

I submit that one of the inhibitions to the development of intellectual leadership in America is the principle of localization of control of public education. For over a century, local autonomy has been a sacred tenet of public education in the United States. The concept has been justified on the grounds that it supports local protection from the self-interested tyranny of a centralized government. The position is an understandable one. It derives from the circumstances of monarchy and fascism. Local autonomy in free public education gives the appearance of a system structured to permit equity, to fulfill the promise of equal opportunity for all, and to provide society with the benefits of merit despite accidents of birth, essential to the definition of democracy. Localism is a product of the urban philosopher Jean-Jacques Rousseau's comforting hypothesis that the local, pastoral mind is pure, unspoiled, unsullied, and virtuous. The idea of localism has drifted down to us from conception of the "noble savage", and Poussin's and Lully's romanticization of the innocence of the unaffected, the guileless, the unlearned shepherds and shepherdesses. The error of Rousseauists is well known to shepherds and shepherdesses: the arcadia of shepherds is to be found only in the urban mind. A later commentator has pointed out that the savage life is not noble but is instead "nasty, brutish and short".

The integration of this hope into American practice represents a vision of an American arcadia that has proven to be, unfortunately, wishful thinking.

What's wrong with localism? Localism enlarges the field for the empowerment of ignorance. If you were a manipulative, exploitative, selfish and greedy person (which of course you are not), and you were a member of a board of education, would you encourage the teaching of any literature that declared you a pariah? Or would you encourage a literature that embraced you? In this free society, almost anybody who wants to can become a member of a local board of education — "prominent" people in the community, employers and controlling types ("leaders", they call themselves) included. And which people are motivated to become members of a local board of education? In our democratic society, we must acknowledge that they include those who stand to profit from a certain kind of education of the young and who take jobs that control curriculum to help secure their own advantage as they see it.

In a society legitimately concerned with a local right to educational self-determination, the people who decide how children are to be educated on a local level must be as wise as they can possibly be. Therefore they too must be educated, not just trained. The chicken and egg problem confronts educational improvement in America. Substantial, nay gigantic interests work *against* the education of our people. Localism in public education has a downside. In practice, it limits educational possibility to the scope of knowledge of those who establish the curriculum.

Management theoretician Peter Drucker has declared the power of the local school board ("a law unto itself") to be one of the primary causes of poor education in the United States.[82] Unfortunately, on the parochial level, many decisionmakers in American education are profoundly mistrustful of learning. Learners rock boats. Smart people are troublemakers. Public education has become the instrument of 90,000 local school boards (too often, local controlling types) many of whose *de facto* agenda is simply to train docile employees and neighbors. Stripped of its romance, localism allows provincialism, allowing parochialism and its concomitant, repression of the gifted. Localism was integral to the concept of American public education as a response to the tyranny of royal power. Today, power supports localism: anti-intellectualism fosters the growth of a public that is easier for the clever to hoodwink. Localism has become, diffusely, the instrument of the manipulative. Localism works against the greater good. It works against education. It works against excellence. It is convenient for those who want to have what we have (and more), at the expense of others.

The effect of local school boards on public education is the down side of the hallowed principle of local autonomy in education. No solution to a social problem is ever perfect. The Achilles heel of local empowerment in free public education, however, has allowed critical decisionmaking to fall into the hands of decisionmakers actively hostile to the best and highest purposes of education, the "struggle to enlarge yourself to take in a mind greater and more powerful than your own."[83] Well, we were warned . . . toward the end of the 18th century, William Manning wrote, in *The Key of Liberty*, that in the eternal contest between The Many and The Few, the main weapon of the latter is the ignorance of the former.[84]

This precept is unacknowledged but operative in American public education. What happens in fact in local "free" education is that local school boards are manned by the businessmen, shopkeepers, and factory owners, the "community leaders" who are the local employers. Their educational agenda envisions the training of people with competencies to become *their* clerks, *their* laborers, *their* technicians in *their* enterprises. The agendas of such school board members emphatically do *not* include the education of people who might compete with, displace or challenge them, their interests or those of their children. The less education people have, the easier they are to hoodwink. Why train people who can compete with you? Variants on the feudal customs of "keep them stupid, keep them pregnant" and "bread and circuses" rule are not publicly acknowledged, but are in fact operative threads in American education today. Localism means parochialism means anti-intellectualism means ease of control.

An example: to be sure that free public education doesn't upset the status quo, local school boards almost universally encourage conformist rote learning and team sports. The Eagle Scout who fulfills all the requirements to get all the merit badges, the honor roll student who feeds back all the facts given — they are the "straight arrows". They serve with alacrity. The team captains who rigorously and unquestioningly observe rules of somebody else's making — these are encouraged. "Good kids" *do as they're told*. Students who conform with alacrity are singled out as leaders. The independent student is labeled eccentric. The person who thinks or acts for him or herself is labeled deviant — not only by peers, but by administrations and school boards.

"Smart kids don't need help", say the school boards and administrators, "they can help themselves". This point of view demonstrates hostility to learning and the learned, and a misperception of the fragility of the original intelligence. The tragedy of the brilliant child in the American public school system is that he or she is judged by his or her inferiors . . . and found wanting! Why are they hostile to the smarter ones? Because they won't make good clerks, salesmen, accountants, administrators, middle-level executives . . . employees of the members of the School Board. They rock the boat. Thanks to the limited horizon of local school boards, the principle of local autonomy of public education is a guarantee of the mediocrity, rebellion or self-exile that is so epidemic as to be accepted as a tradition of deviancy in American life. An unwanted outcome of the principle of local autonomy is a public education system that is anti-education, anti-freedom, anti-thought, and anti-excellence . . . anti-American. For all its presumed "democracy", much American free public education is a deliberate tyranny of mediocrity. People wonder why some smart students turn *bad*. It's because they correctly sense their education for the travesty it is.

Who is to protect children of original intelligence from being stifled? The concepts of provincialism and parochialism are not new, nor have they disappeared in America. In the words of Alan Ryan, warden of New College, Oxford, in some cases "Local citizens were 'reactionary, oligarchical, and corrupt'."[85] In some instances, localism's efforts are directed toward the development of a nation of servants. The sensed priorities of localism can promote inhibitions to the development of the broader learning and intellectualism essential to rational dialogue in a democracy. To paraphrase former president Bill Clinton, "No society can afford to lose *one* of its smart kids." Local control of public education as it is practiced in too many American communities is an assault on the gifted, the people any society needs most. For the gifted, the effect of localism all too often is foreclosure of opportunity.

Change or Perish

What can be done? For better or worse, given the way we operate in this country, leadership in this field, too, has to come from a president. Nobody else has a platform. Our presidents set the tone for the country. "He is the artificer of our malleable national soul", says novelist E.L. Doctorow. You may remember that golf players paraded during the Eisenhower administration, and cello lovers bloomed when Casals played for the Kennedys. Educational leadership does not serve the perceived interests of consumerist industry or the media. Their agendas are pro-training, anti-education. Educational leadership, if there is to be any, will have to be up to a president. The tactics of the ministers of Queen Victoria, who turned the renegade country she inherited into one of the earth's most powerful, richest and most upright, might be reviewed as a possible model. Though no president will have Victoria's 50-plus years of watchfulness, there are ways for a president to exercise long-term leadership. Presidents have honored enterprise when we wanted more businesses. They have honored valor when we were at war. They have honored technology, or the GDP. President Clinton's reiteration of the importance of education to America's future was a step in the right direction. The establishment of national standards for educational achievement provides a benchmark. It makes a difference, though, whether education is defined in terms of capacity for analytical, reflective and innovative thought or if it is defined as job training. If we are to have a future, US presidents must continue to honor and help those who provide the tools that will make a viable future.

As we enter the 21st century, the future of the concept of American public education is shaky. It is proposed today (as it has been in the past) that the US institute educational programs for its children to meet the needs of the currently dominant group. Dominant today are our "economic determinists". Their "vision" is modeled on educational policies that failed in Victorian times. "England's wars are won on the playing fields of Eton", they said in the last century. This meant that the educational system of England in the 19th century was designed to train empire functionaries. Today we are being offered the same by policymakers . . . an educational theory that is a rationale for the transformation of our schools into a training ground of the skilled and obedient, factories for the production of worker bees for an empire of high-technology commerce. We must be skeptical of their offerings.

Education to serve the interests of a dominant class as perceived by them at any given moment has been proven always to impoverish societies. Samuel Butler's *The Way of All Flesh* points out that the British educational system trained empire loyalists but thwarted the imaginative, the innovative, the creative . . . the ones who provide a place for the culture to go *after* the Empire. The British Public School, focusing as it did on the administration of empire, made the English less rigorous seekers after truth than they could have been. Time showed the Public School's interpretation of the glory of empire to be myopic. Time showed that their schooling denied intellectual opportunity to children. It left no room for the future, no room for vision. Contrary to its intention, it harmed society. The entertainer Noel Coward mocked this English tragedy, singing, "Why, when the English claim the earth, do they give rise to such hilarity and mirth?" Time has shown that

Butler and Wilde and Coward have the last laugh.

American democracy was founded to deny one class the right to dominate another. Proposed "privatization" of public schools, like proposed privatization of public television, is a mantra used as a device for the private sector to take over that aspect of the formation of children's minds that is now only the province of commercial television. Privatization's duty is to inculcate the values of self-absorption, acquisitiveness, competitiveness, opportunism, and calculation. It will not be able to escape the promotion of public participation in a mechanistic, materialistic way of life with an educational system that simply omits the alternatives offered by history. The private sector envisions a circumscribed educational system that simply trains, without irony, criticism, or doubt. This is a recipe for disaster.

In America we have successful educational models that could be followed more widely. In a tiny segment of America, under the guidance of the church, the headmasters of St. Paul's, St. Marks and Groton, three of America's best schools, try to live between an educational theory directed toward training an elite to rule and educating children to take a place as knowing and hence valuable citizens in the civilized community. One of the century's foremost educators, former chancellor of the University of Chicago Robert Maynard Hutchins, declared, "The best education for the best is the best education for us all." Locally, parochial education has become an attractive option for parents who envision an education containing some "spiritual" or "whole person" components, not mere job training. The church school could be a model for a broader definition of public education in the United States. History has shown, as Samuel Butler pointed out, that people of the greatest value to the society can come from most unpromising roots. No nation has ever been able to afford to "write off" *one* of its children. If in pursuit of empire we propose to turn our public education system into a vocational system with fealty not to learning or thought but to the gross domestic product, we will be denying the meaning of education as it has come to be defined in the last three thousand years, substituting job training in its place.

The signals are out there. A president of Yale resigned his post to join entrepreneur Chris Whittle, who invented "Channel One" as a way to bribe schools into allowing him to show advertising to the malleable captive audience of children in school. Educator Benno Schmidt now works to extend corporate sway over public education through profit-oriented elementary schools. The hegemony of "vulgar commerce" proceeds apace to set the stage for its own overthrow. If we forge academic chains to attach human beings to our economic machine, we will be guilty of the enslavement of a people. We will squander our history, demean our culture, our citizens, and our children. We will lose the race, too.

All of history has honored artists, usually long after their work is done. Democracies have sought to foster them. Post-revolutionary France encouraged artists and saw a blooming of human perception unparalleled in recent centuries. Through the encouragement of artists, democratic France established an eternal credit from humankind. (Sadly, this is reflected in US press reports mainly through the huge prices for works of art sold at Sotheby's, painting a picture of America as centrally committed to barbarism). Our democracy, like France, in its educational system must allow for the option of artists.

Artists are in the forefront in any society. Artists are people who see things differently. A democracy, if it is a fairer, better place, has to provide a place for them. As our seers, they make the Noah's Arks for the future. Original and unique by definition, they are dissenters. We must learn to acknowledge dissent in the interest of art. Honors to wisdom, honors to learning, honors to thought, reason, insight, creativity, to great teachers — these are the tools of the past that we can refashion by changes in our system of public education. Even if only to "win the competition", we must learn once again to educate our children to think, not simply to train them as robots of greater or lesser efficiency.

The reason we don't have decent public education is that the people who make day-to-day decisions for our dominant institutions don't believe we need an educated populace that thinks. Decisionmakers want workers and voters, a docile populace that will function in factories, malls, chain stores, hospitals, banks, offices, courts and jails, and that will buy plenty of advertised goods. Directors, presidents and chairpersons easily succumb to the temptation to look on other people as unlike themselves, that is, to be manipulated. We're setting up for Robespierre.

The invalidation of Educational TV was a symptom. School decline is the product of turning our backs. There's no reason why we can't have good public schools. Educational history tells us how. The schools can become good, and children can redefine success. They need help. Help can come only through a broad spectrum of change.

Chapter 10

THE STATE TO THE RESCUE!

W hat happened to educational TV? Where did it go? Why? With its initial support by the Ford Foundation, educational television established local production centers in major cities. Universities, state legislatures, local foundations and the concerned citizenry were brought in. They gave a lot. But as the years passed, it became apparent that educational TV as it was going hadn't a prayer of becoming the community of creative regional production centers enriching the cultural life of America that some had hoped for. The shows were *terrible*. Commercial television on the channels "next door" was year by year becoming more complex and appealing, more and more like the movies. Budgets, technical quality, performances, scripts on commercial shows were improving by leaps and bounds. Public issues — feminism, poverty, homelessness, disease, abuse, drunkenness, violence, chicanery in high places — all surfaced first in commercial fictional TV. The salaries, fees, and commissions paid to accomplished television production professionals went up. Donations from hopeful viewers of educational television weren't even enough to enable the system to keep up with technology, let alone provide the tools for ingenious people to produce programs that were up to audience expectations. I remember talking one day to WNET president Jack Kiermeir about his hectic fundraising schedule. "I woke up last night and there I was standing at a podium, talking to a hallful of people!" One enterprising Texas General Manager, later to become one of the many presidents of the Corporation for Public Broadcasting, succeeded through euphemism. He prided himself on the programming inventiveness he showed by recording playwright Lilian Hellman in his studio for seven hours and releasing the result as a seven-part series! That was innovative, all right. With mirrors! For educational TV, the money just didn't come in. All the "support from viewers like you" that could be drummed up barely paid the rent and the electricity. Stations could hardly survive, let alone make a place for themselves as contributors to the community. For America at large, this state of affairs would have been okay if we were alone in the world. We could have allowed this alternative to commercialism to sink into oblivion. But there were other countries making us look venal and nasty, not like the Leaders of the Free World. Nevermind reality: educational TV was bad for our *image!*

In 1967, this small insight into the nature of its being was far from the mind of ETV. Educational television program directors and station presidents faced urgent problems. The day of reckoning had come. The way out was to recognize that educational TV was technologically backward. Public support through gifts and donations simply could not bridge the gap. Something had to be done to save face. In the late 1960s, the Japanese, the English, the French, even the Italians . . . *everybody* (except, maybe, the Soviets) was making us look bad. Their noncommercial television had money to spend. Their programs had production values. They had a permanent infrastructure of creative people. Fascinating products emerged, which America could only rent. What did we have? We had talking heads.

Educational television was the outcome of a vision. Educational television dreamed of regional Chautauquas, an image of the regional theaters of Tyrone Guthrie. These centers of creativity were to foster the exchange of new ideas, where designers, writers, poets, picture people, dance people, composers, performers, theater people, image people, and thinkers could gather together to create messages for their countrymen. It died.

The country that can afford to buy two hundred million cans of beer a day, that can pay a million dollars a year to buy softballs for its military, that can give its business leaders fifteen million dollar houses, that can build a two billion dollar bomber[86] and numerous eighty-million dollar fighter planes,[87] couldn't afford it. The dollar cost of regional production centers was more than the country (with only a trillion dollar gross domestic product) thought it could afford. Instead of developing its own creative talent, the Leader of the Free World subsidized the creativity of another, much poorer country — England — where a populace could be found that was willing to allocate the resources necessary to develop and sustain a creative community in the television field.

So, the Public Broadcasting Act of 1967, promoted by President Johnson, came to the rescue. The avowed mission of the new "public TV" was the same as educational TV's mission. The legislation was essentially written from recommendations of the Carnegie Corporation as found in *Public Television, A Program for Action* (Harper & Row, 1967). Federal support for educational television was endorsed by the American Council on Education, the Association for Education by Radio, the Association of American Colleges, the Association of Land Grant Colleges and Universities, the National Association of Educational Broadcasters, the National Association of State Universities, the National Council of Chief State School Officers, and the National Education Association. President Lyndon Johnson declared in his February 28, 1967 message to Congress, "I am convinced that a vital and self-sufficient noncommercial television system will not only instruct, but inspire and uplift our people."

Johnson's endorsement gave renewed hope to public broadcasting. With adequate funding, moribund instructional TV could be rethought. Inspiration seemed to allow for emotion, for theater. "Uplift" implied allowance for an orientation toward goodness. But the lid was in place from the beginning.

Missing from the legislation was any protection for innovation or dissent. A provision in the 1967 legislation that seemed to guarantee fairness served to muzzle originality and creativity. One phrase in the legislation had not been well thought through. It was the command that there would be, in all programming, a "strict adherence to objectivity and balance". This almost required that all programming be restricted to nonfiction reports. It implied that the subjects of television programs would be required to be matters on which there was already general agreement, or at worst two sides. It almost required that all programming deal with public issues — it would be ridiculous to apply the standard of "objectivity and balance" to an examination of the Sistine ceiling, to a chicken leg, to a poem, to an original work of theater or to an essay. More than that, people who have thought for five minutes about objectivity and balance know that these are will-o'-the-wisps.

A demonstration given to almost every beginning law student proves of the variability of eyewitness reports. Objectivity may be desirable, but any thoughtful person knows axiomatically that human ignorance and the omnipresence of subjective factors make objectivity nearly unattainable. The "scales of justice" symbolize that "balance" is a major goal of the courts. Its unattainability is what keeps courts in business. This has been proven thousands of times. Why was such an impossible requirement written into the law? In daily practice, fulfilling this law means "get a conservative and a liberal to talk about this". It also means, "Don't rock the boat."

A further provision in the law snuffed the hopes of cultivated people for an alternative television. Self-sufficiency for public TV was not to be.

A "nongovernmental corporation", the Corporation for Public Broadcasting, was founded — "Not to be an agency or establishment of the United States Government", the wording said. This structure was explicitly an attempt to foreclose the possibility of government encroachment on an independent agency. CPB's separateness was avowedly designed to shield it from government influence or control, in much the fashion of the Federal Reserve System. To most people, it appeared to offer a structural defense against the development of the consequences outlined in this text. Unlike the Fed, however, public broadcasting's structure made it dependent on congressional appropriations. The competitive use of the appropriations and authorization process of the legislative and executive branches demanded, over time, ideological submissiveness from Public Broadcasting. The Carnegie Commission on Public Television had recommended that leadership appointments be in the hands of a blue ribbon committee, presumably apolitical, to include the Librarian of Congress. That was not to be either. Instead, appointment is by the President. . . . and that is a Pandora's box, as you will see. Whether by design or inadvertence, not only is public television not shielded from government influence; government influence determines its very character. The structure of the CPB as a nongovernmental corporation has had the reverse effect from its intention. Exempt from the provisions of the Freedom of Information Act, CPB's status has served as a shield, not from government control, but from public scrutiny and accountability.

As it has devolved, leadership of the Corporation for Public Broadcasting and the Public Broadcasting Service is today in the control of politically-oriented party regulars and trusties. Former CPB President Robert T. Coonrod's 25 years with the US government's propaganda agencies, the United States Information Agency and Voice of America, would seem to be a perfect preparation for leadership in an agency designed to make the case for federal policy to a wider public. His predecessor, Richard Carlson, a onetime reporter, TV anchorman and documentary producer, had also demonstrated ability in the dutiful execution of government policy as Director of the same US propaganda agencies abroad. The Board of Directors of the Corporation for Public Broadcasting is appointed by the President of the United States. President Clinton's appointee was a professor of political science from Fayetteville Arkansas.

It may have been expected when the CPB was born that a president would appoint its leader on the basis of both competence and familiarity in the fields for which the CPB was founded: to "encourage and support research and development leading to an improvement of programming and program production." In practice, however, this appointment is to a greater or lesser degree a token of appreciation for faithful service and/or campaign gifts to the president's political party. The pattern of staffing via selection of people familiar with the byways of government bureaucracy is not new; Eisenhower's first CBP president had previously shown effective leadership of the Post Office. The appointment process assures the dominance of a political orientation on the part of CPB officers and board members. It confirms public broadcasting as a circumscribed governmental agency.

For the most part, public broadcasting functions without incident, but a political tug-of-war results whenever the executive and the legislative branches are controlled by different parties. The CPB board, heavy with political appointees, disagrees over what the Congress should fund. The Board wants broadcasting that will reflect and promote its worldview. The Congress will authorize only that which promotes *its* world view. "We won't authorize THAT!", say the Congress. "We won't appropriate for THAT!" say the president's appointees. By and large, the content of American public broadcasting consists of a middle ground of subjects found agreeable to both sides in this contest. The political/ideological tug-of-war for the propaganda platform that both parties see public broadcasting to be simmers down when president and the congressional majority share party loyalty. When they don't, when President and congressional majority see things differently, war can break out. The result is that control of the content of public television programs according to criteria based on party loyalty can be, in practice, a plum of victory at the polls.

Where is the Arcadia that was promised? A statement of support submitted to the House Committee on Interstate & Foreign Commerce in July 1967 by then Secretary of Agriculture Orville Freeman succinctly stated what has been lost: the hopes of the administration that brought the Public Broadcasting Act of 1967 into being.

"We seek for the artist, the technician, the journalist, the scholar and the public servant freedom to create, freedom to innovate, freedom to be heard."

As agency of last resort, the Federal government had to rescue educational TV. The "danger" of "government control" had to be risked. The alternative was to give up the dream of a television befitting the goals on which our open society was founded. The rescue had to happen, if any part of the dream were to survive. It seemed at the time that somehow, the bogey of "state television" could be circumvented. People who remembered knew the risks. In 1953, eight years after the demise of the disastrous German Propaganda Ministry under Josef Goebbels, the Executive Vice Chancellor of New York University had declared, "Television is dangerous, for it might improperly become the means of a state control of ideas."

Nobody believed then that it could happen here. This was the good, true, honest America we all believed in, and the "American Century" had dawned. The crippled state of educational TV was recognized as an emergency. But it was viewed as an emergency not only because educational TV was doing the wrong thing, but also because its apparent ineptitude made our world image as an advanced technocracy look foolish. "Can plain-Jane educational TV be made to look attractive?" said WNET New York's clever Marya Mannes. "Could we give it a name, not Public Television or PTV, but something familiar, like 'Petey'?" Nobody suggested, then, calling it what it has become — "USTV".

The name wasn't the problem. The problem is control. By control, in America, we mean money. In a society in the process of a revolutionary conversion from a democratic political system served by a market economy into a corporate/market system served by a democratic political apparatus[88] which is itself dominated by an oligarchy of interests[89], how do you marshal resources to encourage creativity in a new *noncommercial* artistic medium in the interest of the general welfare? Or do you? We answered that question by our actions during the decades that followed. The answer was, you dissimulate.

Noncommercial television couldn't escape the silent revolution. While the public education system was being revised into job training for computer clerks, educational television proceeded to consent to compromise the idea of its existence through vassalage to the state.

In the rest of the country there was a "new dawn"[90] of economic globalization. The apotheosis of marketing brought buying and selling to Sundays and holidays. Shopping 365 days a year, day and night brought an end to the 40-hour week. Middle management was replaced by sleepless computers. Part-time employment brought an end to pensions, medical insurance, social security, vacations, time to reflect or create, hope for an old age, or a young age free of drudgery. The sacrifices were willingly, even enthusiastically made. "The bottom line" replaced the judgment of God as the final word on the significance of human life. The injustices, the inequities, the unfairness, the development of a permanent, hopeless underclass, "homeless", unemployed for generations, all once unthinkable in our democracy, became business as usual in the new America. "Freedom", *market* freedom, triumphed. Co-opt ed now, largely through the efforts of radio and commercial television, the American Dream became each individual's choice between "shop 'til you drop" consumerism and some measure of control of one's own life through the marketing of consumer "proddux".

A few perceptive people from educational television saw the straws in the wind. They stated correctly that the problem was the lack of independence of program decision-making. As long ago as 1971, *Time Magazine* pointed out what is still perhaps the basic flaw in public TV: "Since PBS and its producers get much of their financing from the federal government, and since this funding is not insulated from querulous annual scrutiny, the network quakes at the least cavil from the Administration or Congress."[91]

Independent minds in public television made efforts to hypothesize an American television system that could be free of control by any vested interest. They met under the aegis of the Carnegie Corporation, to evaluate the situation. In 1967, The Carnegie Corporation produced recommendations for public television calling for a trust fund that would lessen the possibility of a congressional tyranny over program content through the annual appropriations process. It came too late. The congressional annual appropriation process that determines the nature programs made for and shown on public television has endured for over 30 years.

The process of annual appropriations is the carrot and stick; by money given or withheld, the Congress of the United States decides which programs will get produced and which won't. The Corporation for Public Broadcasting and the Public Broadcasting Service make their annual pilgrimage to court to petition the congressional monarchs. After pleas and arguments, the outcome is the same year after year. Money is appropriated for programs and stations that key committee members "like" and not appropriated for programs and stations that key committee members don't "like". "Successful" public TV stations think up and propose programs that Congressmen may "like". That's how the public television game is played.

There's more. Unfortunately, government censorship of the activities of public broadcasting goes beyond selection of administrators according to political bias, and beyond the funding of television programs that further the priorities of Congressmen. At a February 29, 1996 hearing before the House Commerce Committee, Congressman J. Dennis Hastert of Illinois felt no inhibition to declaring his right of censorship. Quoted in the hearing was his prepared statement, which included this: "NPR allowed Andrei Codrescu to continue working for the agency after making clearly anti-Christian remarks on 'All Things Considered'. He referred to National Public Radio as an "agency" — presumably meaning "government agency" — and proceeded to assume his own right to establish conditions of employment in public broadcasting according to criteria set by vocal members of his constituency. Congressman Hastert's actions imply that he would have a communications entity in which nobody would feel free to disagree with any majority opinion, or any strongly felt opinion held by an organized force, and in this case regardless of the principle of the separation of church and state, let alone the independence of public broadcasting from government control. If Congressman Hastert's presumptions were the standard of any broadcasting entity, it would have little claim on the reflectivity of any person. It would produce what is commonly known as "pap".

The BBC model of licensing fees for set ownership looked attractive. "But how can you ask Americans to pay for TV", opponents asked, "when there's free TV?" There isn't free TV, and they know it. That a commercial television system ruled by the rigorous logic of boardrooms serving balance sheets should be known as "free" is one of the paradoxes of our language. (The word "freedom", declared Herbert Schiller in *Culture Inc.*, "Is a euphemism for private enterprise unfettered by social accountability", or in the words of *Harper's* magazine editor Lewis Lapham, a viewpoint held by "a governing class that defines freedom as the license to exploit.")[92] So in America today the word "freedom" must be carefully examined in terms of its context, regrettably even when used by a president. Somehow, proposers of alternative funding are always defeated by the promoters of commercial television when the commercial TV people declare that the television described by the head of the Annenberg Communications Center as "pay as you wash" TV is "free". Viewers get the shows they want only if they buy enough of the detergent the show pushes. Even the sponsors aren't free to sponsor what they want or like. They sponsor whatever brings in the most loot. Where's the freedom in that?

The idea of educational television as an alternative to commercial television was congenial to the concept of a "fourth estate". The executive, legislative and judicial arms of government, writers once held, must be subjected to the surveillance of another entity, what Morris Ernst once called a "free marketplace of thought" that allows, nay, fosters a critique of all the society's institutions. Or, in Rosa Luxemburg's formulation, "Without a free struggle of opinion, life dies out in every public institution." Intellectual openness presupposes (as democracy does and fascism does not) that there's more to human life than governments know or should know. It presupposes the conventionality of legislators' intellects. It provides a safety valve for dissent, for innovation, for the human and the new. Educational television as once conceived had the option of being the literature of a free people. Educational television was part of an American dream dedicated to efforts fostering steps toward the realization of elements of human potential.

The Carnegie Commission on Educational Television recommended that educational TV be liberated. President Johnson got behind the Carnegie Commission's recommendations. But to suggest that television should be liberated from the siren song of the corporate gestalt was tactically inept. The Carnegie Commission report just alerted the people for whom control is important. As soon as the dreamers had their way with alternative television, when educational television went "public" with the public television Act of 1967, helpers surfaced to make sure the new TV didn't get out of hand. A minor strategy of image building *cum* ideological surveillance through pro-forma support of public television made sense to the leadership of American industry. congressional appropriations became conditional on ideological conformity. Later on, Political Action Committees made the task of control much easier. During the decades following its creation, public television slowly and inexorably mutated from an *atelier* of creative people with ideas about the product to a hierarchy of trustworthy drones earning a living by doing as they're told. How did it happen? How *could* it happen?

Chapter 11

THE CLOVEN HOOF

For a while, with the euphoria surrounding the rhetoric that accompanied passage of the Public Television Act of 1967, the promise of TV democracy seemed more real. Through the workings of our representative legislative system, it seemed logical to assume that at last there would be money for programs. The best would rise to the top, the people would be served. Government would leave television to the professionals. Yes? No. What emerged was a scenario nobody had anticipated, one that is still not acknowledged: state television, politicized.

In our democracy? In our America? How on earth did *that* happen? Well, it took a bit of doing, and more than a little sleight of hand. The remarkable fact is that it was done with such skill that to this day any thought that public TV is the propaganda instrument of a small group of people has not occurred to the vast body of viewers.

The historic memory of ruling elites has something to do with it. Famous in the gossip of elites are the sayings of the rulers of ancient Rome and the kings of Europe about how to assure and keep power. For the Romans, it was to provide "bread and circuses" to the masses, for the kings of Europe, "Keep them poor, keep them ignorant, keep them pregnant."

The "bread and circuses" of ancient Rome is today replaced by "bread", a minimum wage that will clothe and house workers just well enough so they can drudge (with slightly higher wages in big cities to be spent on image, thought to be requisite for a competitive edge). The circuses are provided by a vast industry of entertainment, a poultice for dissatisfaction manufactured by Disney, television, the mass entertainment businesses of commercial baseball, basketball, football and hockey, and now, the expanding field of a government-sanctioned former crime, casino gambling. Through these devices, the suggestible public is, in the words of T.S. Eliot, "distracted from distraction by distraction" . . .

in other words, disarmed. (Another flawed element of the structure of ancient Rome, the Praetorian Guard, has emerged in the United States as the techno-elite of the military-industrial complex, a sacrosanct body that, reason to the contrary, allows no declaration of world peace.)

As for the motto of kings, "keep them poor, keep them ignorant, keep them pregnant" — when it comes to keeping them poor, wage policy in America does that fairly well. Thanks to inflation fears, federal monetary policy is adjusted periodically to prevent full employment. Pressure on Congress from industry and the Federal Reserve to keep the minimum wage down helps too. To "keep them ignorant", educational policy has made vocational schools of our colleges and universities in the interest of providing tunnel-visioned middle-management drones for an age that is now passing. The dumbing of the idea of education has left the public education system in a shambles of neglect, with "higher" education simply a job training ground, having the effect of a deliberate policy of "keeping them ignorant".

Decades of popular fiction in movies and television in which 95% of the plots are about courtship establishes a romantic life goal among the suggestible the result of which is a life devoted to pregnancy and parenthood. The stimulus of commercial music has taken a journey from the suggestiveness of "swing" and "romantic ballads" before World War II to the prurience of "Rock and Roll" and the dionysiac frenzies of MTV. Pregnancy among teenagers, the prime consumers of commercial music, has been added to that among consumers of "romance" fiction in its film, TV and literary manifestations. The poverty, ignorance and pregnancy of masses of Americans that results from a decaying public education system abandoned by young people for a life of mass consumerism recreates the two-layer society of rulers and ruled that in earlier eras has led to the short-term enrichment of some, and later to revolution and revolt.

Power (if I may correct President Nixon's Secretary of State Henry Kissinger) is the aphrodisiac of the impotent. The pursuit of power underlies much of American activity these days. A singularly apt advertisement for Silicon Graphics (1997) said, "Napoleon worshipped it. Genghis Khan killed for it. Now you can buy it. Power."

The executive office of the President of the United States is occasionally the locus of power lust. Efforts to expand presidential power into all areas not expressly prohibited were a defining element of President Nixon's incumbency. Prior to Nixon's election to the presidency, broadcasting as an instrument of thought control had already been amply demonstrated by radio's and commercial television's triumphal promulgation of consumerism. How could President Nixon, given his bias, not attempt a takeover of public television when it was lying there waiting to be plucked? Nixon's actions regarding public television were directly contrary to the warning of his predecessor. Lyndon Johnson, in his February 28, 1967 message to Congress, said that *"non-commercial television and radio in America, even though supported by federal funds, must be absolutely free from any federal government interference over programming."*

Rex Poker was prescient; he wrote in the *Philadelphia Evening Bulletin*, on October 7, 1971, "The fact that more of its [public TV's] funds, and therefore its standard of living comes from a national treasury . . . uninsulated from political considerations . . . is something to worry about." It was.

Under the cloak of "fairness", Nixon hatchet-man Clay Felker instituted an inquisition of noncommercial broadcasting. Nixon's executive branch Office of Telecommunications Policy brought havoc to the Arcadia of public television. The technique was instructive.

Nixon and his ideological brethren defined the issues, defined positions on them, and required broadcasters to function as if these definitions represented a reality. As a power grab on the part of the executive office, an attempt to politicize and thereby gain control of all issues, public and private, Nixon's tactic worked rather well. He set up a straw man and knocked it down. Unlike the failed *coup* to come later with Watergate, the *coup* against broadcasting over control of ideas, staged by the Chief Executive's Office of Telecommunications Policy, was an unqualified success. Beyond an angry and nobly expressed letter from the essentially powerless WGBH-TV Boston's David Ives (who thought the point was intrusive government, not the chief executive), nobody even objected. Public broadcasters, and commercial ones too, capitulated. "Fairness" became not detachment or objectivity but highly partisan cockfights on issues determined by the state.

Clay Felker taught Washington to view media executives as manipulable. He successfully defined the playing field for the "fourth estate" and the rules they would play under were his. He established that, in effect, the Office of the Chief Executive would decide what was and what was not legitimate for public television to deal with. Dissent, the leaven of human progress, was effectively repressed. Reason was defined as subordinate to political partisanship.

Was it right? If it was, this is the first time in history it has been. Brandeis University professor of philosophy Frederic T. Sommers has observed, "When the intellectual is the political, the light of reason goes out." So, as of the time of Nixon's *coup*, between the force of the offices of the Chief Executive and the Congress, any opportunity for openness in the "alternative" television system was hornswoggled. After Nixon, only forbearance determined how much executive office manipulation of both commercial and noncommercial news and information media there would be. (Notable for their forbearance were Presidents Ford and Carter; President Bush I was wrongly chastised for his.) The die has been cast. Never was public television to become free. Thanks to the appointment power of the Chief Executive, today our dutiful public television well knows that the first amendment doesn't apply to cheerleaders. In time, the press has become, in the words of Timothy E. Cook, "a branch of government."[94]

The Congress, meanwhile, was not asleep. They, too, recognized public television as a tool of thought control potentially under their control. They did their best to wrest control of public broadcasting from the executive branch. With yeoman-like application, they worked to mold public television into some semblance of *their* vision of government-sponsored television, an image of the electorate. Forty years of Democratic control of the House and Senate gave Democrats a subtlety that controlling Republicans have yet to emulate.

Through the jealously guarded process of annual authorization and withholding of funds for selected activities of public television, the Congress of the United States embarked on a saga in which the members of congressional committees became in effect TV producers. Every year key committees of the Congress deliberate on the funding level of public television for the upcoming year. Every year, public television must petition the Congress to prove that it has a right to survival. In practice, the process of annual funding authorization by Congress has performed the function of ideological discipline. When onetime House Majority Leader Newt Gingrich publicly declared that public broadcasting should be abolished; when, as they do, congressmen periodically file resolutions like Congressmen Crane & Norwood's 1997 HR 121 "to repeal the statutory authority for the Corporation for Public Broadcasting" or H.AMDT 345 "to eliminate the . . . appropriation in the bill to fund the Corporation for Public Broadcasting", bills calling for the elimination of funding, reduction of funding, or for the sale of broadcast frequencies assigned to public stations, or for privatization of public broadcasting; the message to the public broadcasting tribe is clear. "Watch out!. If you want to be able to continue to make your mortgage payments, don't make any waves. Don't say or do anything that interferes with or calls into question any detail of the value system of any of the people who authorize your funding or those to whom they are indebted! Don't bite the hand that feeds you! We want no unrest in the servants' quarters! One misstep, public TV, and you're fired!"

Needless to say, for the troops within public broadcasting, there is no alternative to ideological conformity. The rent comes due every month. The blame for this tyranny that paralyzes innovation falls on the federal government's annual authorization and appropriation process.

That there might be persons in America better qualified than members of Congress to develop alternative television in the public interest is irrelevant. Dulcet Fourth-of-July rhetoric, mirrors, fanfares and tinted steam notwithstanding, in America the one who pays calls the tune. And Congress has a whole lot of tax revenue to play with. Congress's hidden cultural agenda was the creation of a medium of communications in the image of its own interests, its own mind. Prescient, the *Wall Street Journal* in an editorial of March 8, 1965 on the subject of Federal support for arts predicted, "It is all but axiomatic that Federal subsidization would intensify the tendencies toward mediocrity and phoniness." The *Journal* further predicted that the government would "stand rightly accused of cultural dictatorship". The process of the establishment of the cultural dictatorship predicted by The *Wall Street Journal* in 1965 is the subject of this book.

Chapter 12

NIXON'S *COUP*

The proximate cause of the transformation of Public Broadcasting into Government Broadcasting was a struggle between the executive and legislative branches. For the most part, this took the form of subtle encroachment. This process was considerably advanced by policies initiated by President Richard M. Nixon. The part that became news was his refusal to appropriate moneys to fund public broadcasting that had been authorized by the Congress. President Nixon's massive assault on public television wasn't about public television at all. It was about power, his power.

In practice, the process of annual presidential appropriation politicizes control of public broadcasting through staff appointments and the annual authorization process. In the early 1970s, conflict between the executive and legislative branches over public TV came to a head. The President was a Republican. The Congress had Democratic majorities. The Executive Branch had a goal of extending its power over the Legislative enemy. The method was fear, appropriately packaged in an interesting, an exciting, sometimes even an eloquent mix. A new President, Nixon, rewarded a speechwriter with a place in an executive office, an office of "Telecommunications Policy", headed by T. Clay Whitehead. The speechwriter was Pat Buchanan (in 1996 and 2000, a populist candidate for the Presidency of the United States). He was an articulate street fighter who went for the jugular of the defenseless sacred cow of TV. He declared all public television to have a political bias — most of it not his or that of the President he served. This tactic was probably not about public television at all. It was simply one element of a larger scheme, that of a President bent on opposing the programs of a Congress dominated by the other party. It did, however, acknowledge the ideological bias inherent in the annual public broadcasting funding authorization process.

Well! An attack from the office of the Chief Executive came as a complete surprise to the public broadcasting hierarchy. The players in the public TV sandbox were thrown for a loop! It was like telling Shirley Temple's mother that her child was acting like a seductress. How could it be? At the time, public television still defined itself as an independent, centrist cultural institution. The management of public TV had been carefully selected to be above reproach. There were perfectly credentialed people at all levels. There were industrialists, education fundraisers, attorneys, bankers, even some Blacks on all the local boards, and most of them were big contributors to cultural institutions. Everything had been done according to the rules, for heaven's sake! Public broadcasting was a *bona fide* sacred cow! Suddenly, Goody Two-Shoes found herself a pawn in the political process. How did that happen?

The Communications Act declares that ruling boards should be "eminent in such fields as education, cultural and civic affairs, or the arts, including radio and television." From top to bottom, public television was satisfied that they had conformed. You had only to count the colleges and universities, the industrial benefactors, the prominent citizens on their letterheads. What had they done wrong? Buchanan's declaration came as a terrible shock. In retrospect, the message is clear.

Buchanan's raid served notice to public television that the board of Public Broadcasting's policymaking body, the Corporation for Public Broadcasting (appointed by earlier presidents), would be expected by the Nixon Administration to obey criteria established by the office of the current Chief Executive. Public Television boards had been made up of public-spirited campaign contributors who thought they might have something to contribute to a cultural institution. Appointment was (as it still is) a reward given to substantial donors to the Party. In actuality, boards had never been made up of Sarastros[95] selected for their wisdom, imagination, creativity, or communicative adeptness.

With primary decisionmaking in the hands of presidential appointees, American public television could be counted on never to give decisionmaking power within its hierarchy to an apolitical person. With Nixon, members of the board of the nongovernmental Corporation for Public Broadcasting found that the primary condition of their tenure was the political opinion of the occupant of the White House.

Whatever the outcome, the die was cast. Nixon had politicized public TV. Never in America could there be a public television not subordinated to politics. There could be no one like BBC's even-handed Hew Weldon, no TV Ontario's Bernard Ostry. The structure wouldn't permit it. The way the allowances for its being were structured, no one could move into public broadcasting's future through the apolitical learned and insightful creative community: no Emmy winners, Oscar winners, Nobel laureates or even Pulitzer winners. Furthermore, the Public Television Act declared that appointees to the CPB board should be more or less half Democrat and half Republican. If any is required, this should suffice as a declaration of a common myopia of legislators, who cannot imagine a person of any consequence to be apolitical.

The revolution prompted by Nixon's Office of Telecommunications Policy was a success. From then on, politics, and those who control politics, controlled public television. At the moment of Buchanan's declaration, the issue of control became clear — it was either the Oval Office or Capitol Hill that would use noncommercial TV as its forum. Public TV was to be either the President's or the Congress'. Wisdom, vision, or even open dialogue were now clearly as irrelevant in public TV as they have become in politics or marketing. The "public" of public television was thenceforth to be defined operatively only in terms of its relationship to government power.

President Nixon blocked the appropriation of funds authorized by Congress for public TV. His action had nothing to do with public TV. It was a ploy by a Republican president to show his muscle and wrest control from a Democratic Congress, whose baby was public TV. His aide, Patrick Buchanan, boasted on the *Dick Cavett Show* that Nixon vetoed the CPB authorization bill because he didn't like the public affairs programs on public television. Nixon proceeded to stack the board of the Corporation for Public Broadcasting with ideologues of his own political persuasion. In practice, the virulent political stance of those Corporation for Public Broadcasting members who were of the same party as the administration was their outstanding attribute.[96] For a while, public television was paralyzed.

Eventually, though, Nixon lost. The Congress regained control of public TV through its legislative authority, through annual funding by the authorization process. Public Broadcasting became securely the tool of Capitol Hill. A part of the revolution was duly achieved. One way or another, Washington had politicized ideas, and established an official, party line and a government funded institution to promulgate it.

The politicization of public television didn't go unremarked. During the course of this politicization, protests were made. CPB presidents John Macy, Henry Loomis and Edward Pfister resigned; and the issue was said to be "program independence". "Program independence" means the right of public broadcasting professionals to make decisions about the programs they would make. Warning against politicization of public broadcasting were James Killian, former President of Massachusetts Institute of Technology, Robert Benjamin, Lillie Herndon, and Sharon Rockefeller. Through the process of presidential appointment, everybody who held views like these was moved aside in favor of other figures who could be relied upon to assert the primacy of political thought. One-time PBS President Bruce Christensen observed, with considerable understatement: "It is not unusual for a board whose majority has been appointed by a particular President to believe in the policies of that President."[97] Public television management's reaction was self-protective. It was anti-intellectual, anti-creative, and placed the self-interest of a craven public television bureaucracy above the purported goals of the enterprise. Public television management's survival strategy was to knuckle under to the government.

The immediate result of the intragovernmental *fracas* was a pogrom of creative people from public TV. In all matters of program content, dissent, or even the possibility of dissent was out of the question. Suddenly, with the Nixon administration in power, any program idea that was innovative or original was dubbed "controversial". "Controversial" is the *lettre de cachet*[98] of public television.[99] "Controversial" is a euphemism for "too new", "not familiar", "different", "outside my scheme of belief", "not what we would do", "makes me uncomfortable", "doesn't serve my interest", or "is offensive to my PAC". The very word "controversial" was a tool of censorship, a guillotine to ideas. Through a benign-sounding policy, innovation, originality, creativity, dissent were put on notice . . . there was no place for them in public TV. In practice, any program idea submitted for consideration by station management that was declared "controversial" had, from that moment onward, no hope of production. "Controversial" producers, those who thought for themselves and didn't conform to the party line, found themselves let go. Thus was the result of an officially sanctioned system of *sub rosa* thought control.

The terms "controversial" and "elitist" are now used by public TV inquisitors the way "Antichrist" was once used. It is an unchallengeable weapon to destroy opposition. These terms, used by an executive to a producer, are the death knell of any program. Their application includes the unvoiced statement, "guilty, with no appeal". No producer has ever survived its application to a show idea. "Controversial" means the same as "dead". "Elitist" is a euphemism for "dissenting", and it means death for programs not hewing to whatever happens to be current doctrine.

In practice, a television program that was original, that offered anything outside the scheme of custom or belief of those who had maneuvered themselves into a position whereby they could control the content of this powerful information medium, on a local or national level, was simply not entertained as a possibility for production. Sometimes the program proposal had only to come from a person the gatekeepers didn't like. During the Nixon administration, public television became one of the tools of the politically powerful. And so it remains today.

So much greater a public service would have been rendered had public broadcasting been allowed the freedom allowed to *Foreign Affairs* magazine: the freedom to give voice to opinion.[100] Instead, the politicians made public TV into their own. Independence, the *raison d'être* of educational television, was eroded every year by the arguments of the Congress in committee during funding hearings. Any claim to inventiveness was nibbled away. At the hearings, eloquent spokespersons for an independent television were courteously listened to, thanked, and dismissed. It quickly became clear to the tea-leaf readers who it was who was calling the tune, and what the purpose of public television was to be. The content of public television was to be a projection of the hierarchy of values and principles, the priorities and intellectual grace, the artistic and intellectual sensibility and sophistication held by key members of the Congress of the United States.

Banished from mention today is the body of thought articulated by former FCC Commissioner Nicholas Johnson, in a 1970 statement: "Partisan efforts by government to manipulate and intimidate television to propagandize in behalf of a particular candidate, political party or ideology are simply intolerable in a free society."[101] Legislative and executive efforts to control the content of public television may be illegal. In the operation of public TV, also banished was the thought voiced by Supreme Court Justice William Brennan, that speech may not be suppressed simply because the state disagrees with its message.[102] Public information was straitjacketed and politicized, despite court rulings that government could not ban speech it did not like, despite the fact that "The First Amendment protects all who wish to speak . . . do I really have to say this? from governmental decisionmaking about what and how much they may say."[103] The structural conflict between the congressional power of the purse and the executive branch power of appointment and authorization led inexorably to a convention of the use of public TV as a propaganda forum for the federal administration and the legislature.

Weak and stumbling, public television found few to come to its aid. The agendas of congressional funders routinely determined what public TV would be allowed to do, and what it would not. During the politicization of public television, members of the press (being "doers", not readers or "thinkers"), may not even have known of the ideas represented by Nicholas Johnson's statement. Quick to adapt, though, following the Nixon *coup*, the press quickly took to designating the so-called "nongovernmental" Corporation for Public Broadcasting board members according to political party affiliation.

By 1975, the ideological polarization of the public's alternative to commercial television was complete. *The New York Times*' Anthony Lewis referred to its leadership as the "zealots who now run the Corporation for Public Broadcasting."[104]

Evenhanded?

Educational TV was intended by its founders as an instrument of the kind of democracy the Founding Fathers seem to have had in mind, a diverse system not dominated by special interests. In retrospect it can be seen that public TV was put into execution at a time that proved inopportune, a time when the fastest growing political party was the one that had declared for decades that "government should be run like a business". The dominant socio-political forces of the decades following its founding demonstrated by a combination of neglect and repression that a democratic public television was contrary to the *ethos* of the times. By an accumulation of compromises, an institution brought into being as an open alternative to the constraints of commercial television gave up its independence. A step at a time, it departed from its announced goal. In doing so it mirrored the tendencies of American society at large.

During the 1970s, bias among the judges of television content appeared in what has become a familiar guise, the guise of equity. The underlying goal of equity that prompted the "Fairness Doctrine" and "Equal Time" directives of the FCC was circumvented by government administrators and broadcasters alike. These provisions of broadcasting regulation appeared to be directed toward allowing representation to all, and not allowing the dominant person or culture to overcome its adversaries by dint of simple prolixity. In the day-to-day instrumentation of these directives by broadcasters, as might be expected, it became apparent that the doctrines could be interpreted as requiring attention to be paid to *all* sides, to the "Flat Earth Societies" of every field of thought. Obviously, this level of fairness would tax the intellectual resources of reporters and the monetary resources of broadcasting companies.

A news or public affairs producer who consulted his management was quickly reassured, however. Commercial broadcasters had already learned from the politically-appointed executors of the FCC's "Fairness Doctrine" that they'd be expected to discern and give airtime to only a Democrat and a Republican side to all social issues. Although the Fairness Doctrine declared that broadcasters should allow voices on *all* sides, in practice it came down to *two* voices representing current official positions of two political parties. On a day-to-day basis at the typewriter, in the studio, the office or "on the road", giving voice to all sides of an issue was beyond the capacity or the practical possibility of the working journalists who "did the shows". Thus, the concept of freedom of ideas for broadcast media was politicized.

In time, out of this "fairness" arose a most interesting power grab by the state . . . an ideological *coup d'état* on the part of the President himself. Richard Nixon demanded what was in effect domination of all ideas, all thought, by the President. A furious tug-of-war started between the executive and legislative branches of the federal government for control of the valuable podium that was public television.

How was it done? Much of it through publication in the political journals of various "think tanks". Initially, thought control was introduced through a most devious and subtle process of insinuation. It was introduced by the tacit assumption on the part of the people around the President, and possibly by the President himself, that art, philosophy, literature, religion, every human achievement based on image or word, represented either a "liberal" or "conservative" point of view. Then, by the demonization of people holding differing views, a masked program of thought control could be installed. How Gothic! How Nixonian!

Conservatives of All Stripes

It might be well, here, to define some terms. The definitions of terms in frequent use often change, and they are often implicit. It sometimes takes a keen ear to read behind a "loaded" term to find its real meaning. Nowadays, a person using the term "conservatism" means "an ideology called capitalism". Quite simply, a conservative today is a person who "looks out for number one", and to whom economics is central.

Wolves cloaked in the residual honor of the term "conservative" engineered the ideological coup of the politicization of thought staged by Chief Executive Richard Nixon. These lupine materialists were not at the time regarded as conservatives by people of learning, who considered them to be usurpers of the respectable name of the idea of the historic conservatism that defines itself as an inheritor of the wisdom of all human history. People of learning paid no attention to these intellectual carpetbaggers. They thought that, since they were mere posturers, they'd just blow away.

Broadcast journalists themselves must accept some of the responsibility for the politicization of all issues. An easy opportunism on the part of owners traded programming acquiescence for license renewal (not to mention the sometimes-dubious honor of White House invitations). Tyros themselves, with severely limited resources, public television programmers unreflectively mimicked commercial TV news and information in presenting "two sides to every question". It was cheap. It was easy. It was the way the "big boys" did it.

The effect was curiously reminiscent of the earlier "Red Channels" broadcasting witch-hunt of the McCarthy era. Pat Buchanan, President Nixon's speechwriter, a "street kid" version of the supercilious William F. Buckley, is an articulate spokesperson for a pinched vision. He anointed himself America's TV censor. He instituted a "head count", whereby all issues should be represented by equal numbers of "liberals" and "conservatives". On any public TV program, there had to be equal numbers of minutes of airtime allotted to these purported two sides of all issues. Perish the thought that there should be a "radical" viewpoint demonstrated. (A "radical" viewpoint was any image, idea or concept not a part of the baggage of convention.) The two "sides" were defined not by linguists or scholars, but by political practitioners and their spokesmen themselves. The people who held high the banner of "conservatism" were in power and would not hesitate to use that power to bend public television to reflect their *weltanschauung.*[105]

Whether or not these "conservatives" were as they presented themselves is open to question. Any comparison with the historic conservators of tradition whose name they usurped makes these contemporary "conservatives" look partial. Historic conservatives searched history for lessons leading to the institutionalization of procedures that would encourage justice, equity and fairness. America's self-described "conservatives" define themselves as curators of the common weal through economic self-interest. The writer Marilynne Robernson (*Mother Country*, Farrar Straus & Giroux) points out, "Conservatism has come to mean loyalty to an ideology called capitalism, which is neither named nor implied in once-authoritative documents such as the Constitution."[106] A social theory based on supply side economic determinism is, in historic or even academic terms, not conservative in the least. The more stentorian of American practitioners of "conservatism" endorse by word or action a materialistic, "ends justify the means" philosophy that shares its fundamental precepts with the system promulgated less by Marx than by Lenin, who defined himself not as "conservative" but as "radical." To put an end to this masquerade, a sorting out of political labels is probably in order.

The need for electoral success makes strange bedfellows. To continue with an attempt at a definition: there appear to be several brands of US "conservative". One of them is the prudent conservative; his approach is analytical and cautious. Another is the conservative dominated by historical perspective. One is the traditionalist; his decisions are based on precedent. Another balks at any kind of change from a self-defined norm. Another is the Afraid, who functions as though threatened. We have the Mean-Spirited, with a goal of thwarting others who may differ; and we have the Selfish, who has positioned himself to advantage and rejects change. There is the Vengeful, who uses his "conservatism" as a cloak for misanthropy; and there is the Opportunistic, who sees advantage to be gained from obstruction. Another is the paranoid, who builds life in terms of "enemies". Then, there is the ambitious person who is essentially non-ideological, who simply trades on the views of others . . . any others . . . for advancement. Last, there are "conservatives" who, fearing their own displacement, would repeal for others the conditions whereby their own kind rose from privation to affluence. They use term "family values" as a way to recognize the values held dear by liberals, essentially the Judeo-Christian ethic, but to define its applicability narrowly. This functions as a tactic to restrict the tenets of liberalism to the boundaries of kinship and bloodlines. American "Conservatives" include groupings of these differing worldviews, in varying mixtures. The mixture isn't homogeneous; hence the friction between the anglophile "Eastern Establishment", feudal South and gimmie-grab "Cowboy" conservatives.

All of these "conservatives" demand some degree of control of the "airwaves" from whomever they can get to listen. What they all either reject or downplay is an America of the "Great Experiment", an imaginative projection of the accumulated wisdom of the past extended into the future . . . an effort to create social conditions that will allow all persons to realize their greatest potential for individual and social betterment. To today's "conservatives", the maximum individual and social betterment is already here. The "conservative" businessman's ideology means "get while the getting's good". To the "conservative" *Wall Street Journal*, the "American Dream" means not equity or options for choice, but filling your own pockets. To "conservative" statesmen, the ideology is *Realpolitik*, to win hegemony through imitation of the procedures of imperial powers. For Neo-Darwinists, conservatism means the race goes to the swift and the Devil take the hindmost. Neo-Darwinist theory carries the flattering implication that hundreds of billions of years of cosmic history have led inexorably to a final triumph of the systems and people who produce the highest sustained grosses and dividends, *Genus Entrepreneuris*.

"Liberals" are an embarrassment to conservatives, because liberals espouse the universalization of the Judeo-Christian ethic that conservatives have been unable to bring themselves to reject publicly. Liberals try to apply compassion, humility and forgiveness outside the confines of their own kin. How jejune!

A paradox that should also embarass conservatives is that the qualities some of them prize — aggressiveness, competitiveness, entrepreneurship, self-interest — are character traits found in largest measure in the class they call "criminal". The difference between the essence of the piracy that is called a leveraged buyout or a hostile takeover and a stickup is essentially the complexity of the transaction and the size of the take. Social cost doesn't enter into the picture for either practitioner.

Genus Entrepreneuris saw opportunity for enrichment in the collapse of the Soviet Union. What a potential market! So many people! Such great resources! All those potential profits! American corporate response was swift. The publicity declared the death of the "Evil Empire" (Ronald Reagan's term), and the birth of "freedom"(defined elsewhere in this tract). "Communism failed", was the cry. Actually, what failed was the parasitism of Bolshevik totalitarianism. What won was simply a different approach to the dialectical materialism that had been the avowed credo of Soviet leadership since 1917.

The goal of economics as society's prime mover was paraphrased by Republican President Calvin Coolidge as, "The business of America is business", and by more recent Republicans as "Reaganomics", and by a sign fastened to candidate Bill Clinton's wall, "It's the economy, stupid!" America's official celebration of the end of the Red menace did not exclude the position that a society dedicated to the "greatest good of the greatest number" (Karl Marx's modification of the Christian credo) would flop, that a society dedicated to exploitativeness in the interest of greed (the pre-Judeo Christian matrix) would "win".

What actually caused the experiment in the Soviet Union to fail was not communism but the necessarily fatal combination of greed, ignorance, secretiveness and power lust. These will destroy any society, whether that society goes by the name of Communism, Monarchy, Free Enterprise or Representative Government. Americans would do well to look into the lessons of the late unlamented Soviet Union.

The "conservative" trumpeting of "family values" is code for what were once known as "shopkeepers' attitudes", the embracing of a patriarchal double standard that applies to one's kin a radically different set of values from that applied to all others. "Family values" are an escape hatch for the Neo-Darwinist misanthropy that allows callous exploitation of others (non-family). The code meaning of "family values" is regressive — an outright denial of the fundamental Christian precept of the brotherhood of man.

Practitioners of neo-Darwinist theory have shown that the practice of the theory exposes their own vulnerabilities. An attempt by freshmen at the US House of Representatives to blackmail the executive branch into submission by shutting down the government brought swift public antipathy and censure at the polls. In 1998, House Speaker Newt Gingrich, a prominent practitioner of "the end justifies the means" tactics, was himself toppled by a cadre of colleagues whom he then called "cannibals".

Today's "conservative" solution to "wrongs" (most often against property) replaces selflessness with repression. For many of these radicals who call themselves conservative, there is no thought of a benign future for others but only for themselves and their intimates. My house, *my* car, *my* dining room, *my* lake, *my* portfolio . . . these are life's goals. For many of them, operatively, there is no past beyond their natal day, no future after their own lifetimes. In America, "conservatism", for many, has been a mask. One cannot imagine a conservative member of the House of Lords endorsing the denial of the lessons of history that goes under the name of American conservatism.

Chapter 13

FROM NIXON'S OFFICE OF TELECOMMUNICATIONS POLICY TO THE "REAGAN REVOLUTION"

I n its evaluation of public TV, the agenda of the Congress was aided by the people on whom they could best rely to edit information about public service television, the spokespersons delegated by that congeries of self-selected, underpaid amateurs, the courtiers of the public television industry itself. The Congress may have believed the rhetoric of educational TV's spokespersons, but they failed to notice the cloven hoof.

Public service television was a bureaucracy. In a country where talent follows money, public TV people were paid peanuts. Talented production people were drawn to the idea of what public TV could be, and went away unfulfilled. Canny WGBH, whose somber gray buildings stand just across the practice soccer fields of Harvard's Graduate School of Business Administration, was quick to see that opportunity for them lay as a market middleman. Forget the dream; don't be a tart — that was their key to survival.

By the mid 1970s, public television's one-time programming leader WGBH Boston had radically altered its programming emphasis. During the 1960s under Hartford Gunn, "the producer was king". The working method was collegial. Gunn's method had three conceptual bases: (1) That Television's significance lay in its potential as an art form, (2) That creative people were the source of whatever excellence it could have and (3) That the best results would be attained by a cooperative relationship among the creative people. This was not an unknown or unprecedented working methodology. It was comparable to that of the chamber orchestra, Orpheus, started by Julian Fifer in 1972 and still performing at top level 25 years later. A description of the working methodology of Orpheus echoes that of the early WGBH; hopefully, their working relationship might again be applied to television production one day. Conductorless, "The orchestra is self-governing. The players themselves take responsibility for all aspects of the music-making process, from the creation of programs to the final outcome of the performance." The product of their ensemble is notable for the respect each instrumentalist has for the sounds made by the others in the interest of the composer's goal. The result is music of exquisite sensibility.

The collegial working environment and its results brought WGBH fame, honor, and business, and attracted creative people. Upon Hartford Gunn's departure (for a slow crucifixion as head of the Public Broadcasting Service in Washington), WGBH radically altered its production methods. It dropped all pretense of being an *atelier* of creativity, and started to run itself like a brokerage.[107] It reorganized itself hierarchically, with people at the top who had moneyed "connections", who knew nothing of theater and had never produced a TV show. The publicity department expanded. Consequences were predictable. Christopher Sarson's innovative and popular weekly children's series *Zoom*, a 1960s interactive *cinéma verité* exercise in pre-pubescent self-absorption, was provocative and original. It was cancelled. Henry Morgenthau's much-needed parenting series with Barry Brazelton died aborning. The last opera mounted in WGBH's big studio was Tschaikovsky's *Queen of Spades*[108] in 1968. Julia Child did the color series of *The French Chef* (still being broadcast by WGBH almost three decades later) in 1970, followed by a succession of less ambitious, unremembered ventures seemingly directed toward more "politically correct" minority audiences. The low-cost show-and-tell genre that Julia pioneered, the "how-to" show, mutated, and spawned imitators at WGBH and nationwide. Except for news reading, fundraising, an occasional "talk" show and an obligatory low-budget "minority" series, WGBH's big studio went dark. Why not? Years of poverty and disappointment had assured that creative people in public television were already in short supply anyway. With Washington showing a deaf ear to any but its own priorities, with diminishing opportunities for program innovation, the imaginative people originally attracted to the promise of the new medium simply migrated. The criteria that underlay the tedious and self-serving state television of other countries began to make themselves felt here.

In time, public television stations' accommodation to its deprivations became its tradition. Imitative "talking heads" programs, documentaries modeled on didactic pre-World War II McGraw Hill 16 mm illustrated lectures, copies of network programs of the 1950s (*NOVA* copied CBS's Mike Sklar's 1958 *Odyssey*, *Frontline* aped Aaron & Friendly's 1950s *CBS Reports*) became the staple of American public TV production. Innovation was no more. The structure had seen to that. Any alternative to the dime-novel/parlor game exploitative programming of commercial television (and Hollywood) had been made impossible. Increasingly staffed at local and national levels by adepts at the arts of funder courtship, management infighting and bureaucratic smarm, public TV as it developed became less and less likely to embarrass itself by exhuming its original mandate to even try to be a source of innovative programs. "TV's no art form", WGBH's President and former *WSJ* reporter David Ives tellingly declared in the 1970s, despite evidence to the contrary. With a certain confusion of identification between himself and the medium, he declared, "It's best at *reportage.*" Nobody asked then, "Why bother?" since the commercial networks were already spending many millions every year on *reportage.*

Inertia carried public TV forward. A downward definition of the mission of public television met the agendas of those who intended to use it as a conduit for their own propaganda. If public TV were only journalism, then a person with some money and a message needn't concern himself with complexity. And with the downward definition of public television's mission, production was transformed from custom work (expensive and time-consuming) to a factory system (staffable by cheap hacks) where all subjects were put through the same Columbia School of Journalism format, each program with the same chassis and engine but decorated, like a General Motors car of the 1980s, with a different label and chrome strip. The death of innovation was inevitable since the funders, notably the Congress and people who wanted to influence the Congress, had discovered that they could be the real decisionmakers about which TV programs public television would make and distribute. A hotbed of creativity was the last thing they wanted. What they wanted was a mass outlet for their views; and they got it. There had been a revolution.

Interestingly, it was a revolution unnoticed by most. Voices of protest were cries in the wilderness. "Noncommercial educational broadcasters", said Anne Branscomb, "being largely dependent upon state or local tax sources, are not anxious to bite the hand that feeds them." Anthony Tiano, general manager of KQED-TV San Francisco, observed, "The feeling [in Washington] is that if we're going to take money from the federal government, the federal government ought to have some say in what we're producing."[109] And so they have. Interestingly, some of the fundamental principles impelling the downward spiral of public TV were never explicitly stated. They become clearly evident, however, on examination of patterns of action. Workers in public TV, who wanted to keep their jobs, became noncommercial television's Good Germans.

Congress funded this "TV-that-wasn't-supposed-to-sell-products", but funded it not nearly so opulently as England or Japan did theirs. If congressional intentions were benign, their creation of conditions of privation for public television was a mistake. If their intentions were to assume control, however, their strategy was a good one. Anybody who could tot up a column of figures could calculate that a TV with any hope of reaching a large audience wouldn't be cheap.[110] If congressional intention was to train public television like a puppy dog, tempting and withholding it to obedience, the strategy worked. For the public broadcasters receiving this limited beneficence, initial congressional funding was clearly only an *hors d'oeuvre.* Looking the gift-horse in the mouth made a certain amount of sense, since the funding levels provided were and are clearly inadequate for a service that could hope to be an alternative to commercial broadcasting. Then, every year, as inevitably as night follows day, after the announcement of the current year's funding level, the first priority of the recipients of the money was not to develop strategies to do programs in the public interest, but to develop strategies to get more funding from the Congress next year.[111] As with the whisper from a hooker to her John, the questions "Whachawannado?" and "Howmuchyapayme?" became the primary if unspoken guide for public television success. Inevitably, this goalsetting had to be the natural consequence of the supplicatory position in which public television had been placed by the Congress itself.

Nobody in public television's leadership mentioned it, of course. To mention such a thing would be to violate tribal taboos. As a responsible American executive in any company, you never let on that your priorities are anything but what you say they are. Meanwhile, you are ever mindful to operate to extend the power and influence of your own position, and hopefully yourself, along with it. Isn't that the way it's done in the real world? (see President Reagan's caution on bureaucracies from his final news conference). Danny Schechter, PBS Executive Producer, has pointed out that the center of public television's suicide is structural. "The takeover," he states, "has been internal, prodded by pressure from Congress and a timid leadership concerned about preserving sinecures."[112] Timid? Of course, the leadership is timid! Their organization has neither clear goals nor the authority to pursue them. Instead, it has a mind control strategy by Congress in the form of annual appropriations. It has a barrage of broadsides from every interest group that can command the postage, the fax machines or the lunches with a Congressman to make itself heard. Had clear goals been established for public television as a studio to develop theatrical materials dealing with options for the future of the species, had public television been brought into being in a castellated spirit of free inquiry, free speech and dissent, had public television been insulated from the influence of politicians, pressure groups and their funders, had public television been advised by persons familiar with theater, the arts, literature, what used to be known as "higher learning", would you have a public broadcasting that is a congeries of courtier/bureaucrats just trying to hold onto a job? No. Nor would you have a Congress with the power to determine what goes on public TV. In a way, you can't blame the public TV executives for using their crumbs as bait. They had a realistic claim. Thanks to the fact that funding control was in the hands of Philistines, the specter of second class citizenship for public television was just as inevitable as that for most of public education in the United States.

Was the idea of having public TV operated by puppets and stooges a congressional strategy? Who knows?

Chapter 14

NOT-SO-BENIGN NEGLECT

Public television can be seen as a bellwether for broad tendencies in the operation of American culture. Paramount is the increasing influence and self-confidence of government. By "government", I don't mean government as it is authorized to be in the documents. I mean government as it is, an entity made up of fallible people. Flawed as we all are by ignorance, ambition, and ego, government has increasingly partaken of the style and the methods of business and industry. Why? It was in the air!

Americans who travel outside their country see smiles and nods when our country's name is mentioned. ("Ah, is good, America!", as a Fellah said to me in Cairo.) Why does America make them smile? Because of the gadgets we have? Because of McDonald's? No. I've asked, and it's because to people all over the world "America" means the possibility that a human life could be led in a context of equity, choice, and opportunity for self-fulfillment. A world that embraces what it admires as the American concept of individual self-determination may be surprised when it gets consumer products instead.

That's what it probably will get, too. America's mercantile class is positioning itself to be the next Hudson's Bay or East India Company. Armed with economic theory, sophisticated consumerist and marketing practice, military might unprecedented in human history, and a deep-pocketed industry dedicated to the persuasion and bribery of occupants of elective office, the "materialists" have set themselves up for world hegemony. They call it "globalization."

Within that context, the arrows of the cupid of cupidity are today interpreted as arrows of love. Never mind that for at least fifteen centuries the dominant belief system declared "Love of money is the root of all evil"; the love of money today seems to be the essential engine of American being. "Think Tanks" today provide intricate manifestos to rationalize the makeover of the planet in the image of US corporate imperatives.

The prospect is good for victory in the crusade for American "free enterprise" to take over the world. Over the long haul, the other industrialized countries simply lack the resources to resist. The US continent has a big chunk of the world's natural resources. It has a stunning agricultural base to fall back on. The needy and unorganized of the Third World and the former Soviet Union constitute wide-open territories for shrewd entrepreneurial exploitation and development.

The shopkeepers' infiltration into dominance took a long time. Centuries. Like the compromising of public television, the compromising of the political process by the mercantile class never declared itself. It was like a club secret. A wink, a knowing smile, a touch with the elbow were outward and visible signs. In the years following World War II, communications ownership, lobbies, Political Action Committees, the starving of a historic tradition of liberal education that was born in the reign of Charlemagne, and the simple "nonfunding" of dissent paved the way for the re-deification of Mammon known as the "Reagan Revolution".

The term "Reagan Revolution" made an awfully good slogan. Strangely, speechmakers, policy wonks, and candidates never publicly said what the "Reagan Revolution" was meant to be. If you read the speeches, "The Reagan Revolution" was invoked like a talisman. The term "supply side economics" was about as far as anybody ever got. But initiates could read the code. The mantra "Reagan Revolution" meant a fundamental change . . . it meant a revolutionary conversion in the structure and emphasis of governance in the United States. It meant that democracy would be unseated as the prime motivating force of the society. Fairness and equity lost their primacy in the socio-political spectrum. They were quietly jettisoned.

These events did not contribute to the strength of a television that lay outside the new definition of the good. The Reagan Revolution redefined the good in the United States. As the society had been constructed during its first century and a half, the concept of democracy in the interest of social equity as an *absolute* good had been supported by a market economy that was an *instrumental* good. The supply side economic theory that was the underpinning of "The Reagan Revolution" converted the instrumental into the absolute. From then on, *laissez faire* economics became the absolute good, and democracy an instrumental good. The economy was Number One. The democracy? Maybe we don't care anymore.

The operative credo of the Reaganomics believer could be stated simply this way. "I serve myself. In serving myself, I serve the economy. In serving the economy, I serve the state." Paraphrased, "The more I get for myself, the better patriot I am." Or, in the words of the felonious Wall Street arbitrager Ivan Boesky, "Greed is good."

MIT economist Paul Krugman writes, "There is a problem with markets. They are absolutely and relentlessly amoral."[13] His complaint echoes that of Adam Smith in 1776, that uncontrolled markets cause social harm. With government office now routinely purchased by corporate political action committees, market forces dominate government decisions. The one-time Christian virtues are out. Compassion, humility, wisdom, disinterested intellectual curiosity — they're out. You will look in vain for mention of these virtues in political speeches anymore. The substructure of priority that dominates political and corporate decisionmaking about the world today is *anything* that increases *revenues*. Whether for the family, the school, the government, or for publishing, looking to the past or planning for the future, in practice nothing else matters. Today, if a person is efficient, clean, dresses well, exercises and gets his hair cut regularly, he can be as conniving, selfish, greedy and manipulative as he likes and nobody will mind . . . as long as he increases somebody's revenues!

The philosopher Karl Marx described the dialectic of history as economically based. Christians, bemused by his rejection of the mysteries of Christianity as society's center, often fail to read on to discover that to Karl Marx "dialectical materialism", the economic basis of society, was a negative. Marx mapped in its place a landscape of human fellowship, in which the economic basis was to be overcome by the efforts of good government. Marx proposed that this mundane, calculating economic basis for human endeavor is counterproductive, and should be transcended through societal action. His economically based dialectic of history was descriptive, not prescriptive. His goal for the society that should be constructed was about sharing. It had much in it of the Christian ideal of brotherhood and community. Economic plans, to Marx, were the means not the end. The end was the human community in which each member was dedicated to the well-being of others. This cornerstone of Marxism was conveniently forgotten by Lenin and Stalin. It was forgotten by US policymakers as well.

Over the years, almost without anybody noticing, the dialectical materialism that Marx identified and deplored became America's *de facto* philosophy. Ronald Reagan's "Reaganauts" simply coalesced an operative reality that had been around for years. Remember "Engine Charlie" Wilson, president of General Motors during Eisenhower's time? He scandalized everybody by declaring, "What's good for General Motors is good for America." That sentiment would be endorsed by most Americans today.

Reagan's advisors were crusaders supporting a counterrevolution. They stood to gain a lot, and did so, through both an unprecedented redistribution of wealth in America and the internationalization of corporate American influence and power. "Freedom", code for "free enterprise" in the guise of democratic government, was encouraged throughout the world as an instrumental good in the interest of the absolute good, "freedom" of the US market.

The Reaganauts knew "The Reagan Revolution" was the corporate world's strategic formulation of the tactical campaign phrase, "less government". Translated, "less government" meant less policing, the promise of staff reductions and smaller appropriations for agencies whose purpose was the enforcement of the laws that applied to regulation of commerce. That's why audiences went so wild when Republican orators cried out the mantras "Freedom", "less government", "downsizing"! Substantial investment by those who stood to gain from the "Reagan Revolution" swelled campaign coffers to unprecedented levels. The "payola" was a decade of plundering unseen since the era of Jay Gould and the Robber Barons.

It *was* a revolution. The flag read, "Supply Side Economics." With Reagan as President, the moneychangers now had their priest in the temple. At long last, the shopkeepers who had been waiting for centuries could have it their way. "Vulgar" commerce is now King! At last! As long as there had been Christian- or Confucian-dominated history, the buyers and sellers had been denigrated by the aristocracy, denigrated by the gentry, denigrated by the professions, denigrated by the academies and the learned, and denigrated by the church. The life of trade had been deemed "low", "vulgar". In imperial China, merchants ranked beneath people who worked the fields,[114] "among the despised minor categories".[115]

Now, at last with Reagan in the White House and their people to divert appropriations, they had their chance. They were in charge. Now, having assumed the reins of federal power, they could define the aim of existence for others, as they had always defined it for themselves, as "getting and spending". The "Reagan Revolution" placed democratic society foursquare at the service of commerce. The creed of dialectical materialism described by Karl Marx as a system to be overcome had won in the United States. As it had been among merchants since the time of the "good burghers" whose psychic poverty Rembrandt so mercilessly revealed, implicit in the scenario of "The Reagan Revolution" of the 1980s was that King Commerce was what real life was about. The fact that uncontrolled markets have always created instability and that market instability affects lives outside marketing was conveniently brushed aside.

Public TV, a government-dependent information medium, could not escape the message. The messages of the American Revolution of the 1980s were spread widely by the journalist acolytes of media empire-builders. Like a continual dew from heaven, their comforting messages fell on us all for a decade. The non-economic message of the 1980s declared that the focus of our goal of being was, through individual initiative, to maintain and strengthen a patriarchy in which simple domesticity and uxoriousness constituted the core of personal life. "Life" is getting and spending. The rest is decoration.

In case you have doubts that the new materialism is our religion, think about this. Today's pantheon are enrobed in the radiance of net worth: computer programs (Bill Gates and Ross Perot), petroleum (J. Paul Getty), public entertainment (Michael Eisner), and finance (T. Boone Pickens). Daily our media present to us others the radiance whose sageliness is a direct function of net worth. The pronouncements of these saints, you may have noticed, are infallible. Their presence is holy. Spillover of their economic cornucopia is expected by their peers to create concert halls, universities, and scholarship funds that will, in their turn, spawn more of their kind. The Delphi of the religion is the Federal Reserve; its oracle, Chairman Greenspan. Greenspan's opaque and ambiguous public utterances are examined by the priesthood of the media with reverence of the kind that two millennia ago was reserved for a sheep's liver.

Sinners in the new religion are the people outside the job market. Their purgatory is called welfare. If they don't or can't obey the rules of purgatory, they are summarily consigned to the hell of revenue/balance sheet irrelevance . . . banished to the streets, the gates of America closed behind them. They cease to exist. Nonpersons, their fate is no longer a matter of concern to the drudging faithful. A member of the California legislature has made a proposal, albeit in jest, that poverty be declared a crime! The renegade mother who chooses to barter, to grow her food in a vacant lot in order to devote eight hours a day to the upbringing of her children rather than flipping hamburgers, is left to go under — with the sinful rest, with visionaries, with the poet, the writer, the composer, the sculptor, the philosopher, the painter whose works don't sell today. These are some of messages that we receive daily from the acolytes on the evening news.

Our new market religion revises history. Some of the uncodified messages of the new religion that surfaced in the 1980s were these: Art is a commodity to be bought and sold for status — the measure of greatness of a work of art is the most recent sale price at Sotheby's. Music is either a bath or an erotic stimulus. Architecture is a movie set "Babylon" whose purpose is to make an impression of institutional importance and dominance. Books are written to be sold at high cost to be made into movies. Ironies are allowed late Saturday night, when the children are asleep. Banished to oblivion are philosophy and poetry, meditation and reflective thought (like the poor and homeless, their existence is simply denied). Thinking is out, planning is in. Education is redefined as job training. New neighborhoods, both urban and suburban, are atomized units of worker incubator/dormitories — cookie-cutter real estate housing developments for all classes are designed as places to eat, sleep, procreate, watch TV, park the car, show off economic status . . . and get ready for work! Criticism is out, promotion is in. Like a Ferrari automobile, a totem of the decade, the economic engine has been brought to higher and higher tune, with its own being an end in itself. Commerce is Serious Business. The "bottom line" is, as they say, the bottom line.

For decades, fiery attacks on the corporate-owned press for "liberalism" and "secular humanism" (two radiant achievements of the Renaissance, the Enlightenment and democracy) justified the pruning out of independent minds. An effective tactic, broadsides at the red herring of "liberalism" provided a diversion that allowed rapacity to proceed unchecked. Signs of metastasizing acquisitiveness sprang up over the landscape. California's chock-a-block instant suburbs of trendy villas, in effect designed by lenders, stampeded over the helpless hills of nature. Residences of size and vulgarity not seen in a century materialized in resorts and suburbs . . . one million dollar dwellings were followed by $2, $5, $7, $15 million "homes". Arches, towers, strips of gold, recollections of Sam Goldwyn's Babylon proliferated. In California, some of these jukeboxes were even built by speculators. The styles of the most advanced residential architects mimicked the glitzy and stentorian ahistoricism of commercial building, a symbolic obeisance. With a courtier's sensitivity to the tradition of *parvenu* clients, architectural theory discovered virtue in the jejune fantasies of boardwalk and midway. In the 1980s, those who may have raised voices in opposition to "the big store" were treated the same as the poor, the ignorant and the mentally ill: they were shut out, and effectively robbed of power, money, authority, access.

In public television, the term "controversial" continued to be used against the concept of a free marketplace of thought. "Controversy" was forbidden to public television. The term was used as a simple censorship device. How far this practice deviated from historic American thought can be assessed by reference to a statement of the esteemed Supreme Court Justice Oliver Wendell Holmes, in a dissenting opinion (US v. Schwimmer, 1929): "If there is any principle of the Constitution that more imperatively calls for attachment than any other it is the principle of free thought . . . not free thought for those who agree with us but freedom for the thought that we hate." Not on public TV, you can bet your life! American dissidents are muzzled by official censorship; in public TV, they call them "controversial".

Dissenters from subjects on which the political parties have taken positions, or from subjects on which the political parties had taken no position, are branded "controversial" and therefore *ipso facto* forbidden to public television. Any idea that lies outside the belief system of the network of control is inadmissible. Since art almost by definition "challenges society's rules and norms at every level",[116] and "one ambition of art is to get people to think what they did not already think",[117] and since any new, original concept or approach in any form is "controversial" and therefore formally declared to be impermissible in public television, art is quite explicitly forbidden to American public television.

Elsewhere, the structure of government funding inhibits innovation. Key words in the "requests for proposal" issued to those applying for government grants give a clue as to who and what is to be excluded. Results of government-funded projects must be "quantifiable". They must "demonstrate" something. They must be provable. They must be "objective". In other words, any recipient of a government grant must be able to document (preferably with an adding machine, but sometimes survey questionnaires are acceptable as supporting data) that the taxpayer's money was "well" spent. This is understandable as a method for elimination of risk-taking by government, a way to defuse criticism. It is, however, a methodology that puts bureaucratic convenience ahead of achievement. One consequence is what Michael Ignatieff has called "a queasy moral relativism".[118] It's also a way to promote the safe, the conventional, the accepted, the status quo, and establishment cant. In an art form like television, it is a retrograde practice that does long-term harm.

An illuminating example: Filmmaker Richard Attenborough made a costly movie about a dissident intellectual. The Academy of Motion Picture Arts and Sciences gave the film academy awards for Best Picture, Best Director, Best Actor, Best Screenplay, Best Cinematography, Best Film Editing, Best Art Direction, Best Costume Design and Best Sound. The Queen of England conferred a Lordship on Richard Attenborough. Attenborough has since written, "Unless it is daring and risks failure, any art form will wither and die." Can anybody imagine any US government agency conferring honors on a person who countenances not only a dissident, but also an intellectual? A person who dares to take controversial risks? The film was *Gandhi*.[119] Better "Baseball" or "The West".

Human knowledge is contingent, partial, tentative. Every discovery of science and art demonstrates how little we know, how vast is the landscape of the unknown. The music of Debussy in the late 19th century stated unequivocally that the real world is full of accident, randomness, partialness, what poet Robert Frost called "hint'n". Einstein called it "the intuitive leap". Governments will have none of such nonsense. What is stopped is innovation. History forgets governments, probably for the reason that they have small tolerance for innovation. . . . ideas and innovation come from others. The best thing a government can do is to permit a climate to exist that will allow ideas, thought and innovation to flourish.

You may say, "Oh, yes, but look at the Metropolitan Opera on television! That's art." Or is it celebrities? As written, the subversive opera *Tosca* is about class warfare, and *La Bohème* is, too — and societal neglect of its creative people. *Madama Butterfly* can be seen as a metaphor for the American establishment's (the Navy was the "gentlemen's' service") callous disregard of the sensibilities and honor of others. But you'll never hear *that* from the ladies in gowns or the men in tuxedos who introduce them on public TV. Read what critic Edward W. Said writes: "The contentiousness of debate about opera's social and philosophical meaning (is) now almost totally lacking in US productions, dependent on corporate sponsors who will have none of it."[120]

A contemporary comment on grant-getting may be seen in the film *Twister*. Jonas Miller, its villain, is ambitious, organized, well-groomed, articulate, imitative and well-funded, but without intuition, imagination, wit or an operative knowledge of fundamental principles. "High-tech gadgets and no instincts", says Bill Paxton. The Miller character depicts the conventional grant-getter. Opposed by a raggle-taggle group of people attuned to their craft above all, the competitive Miller and his well-funded entourage of sleek black sport-utility trucks are last seen being wafted skyward by a huge black tornado. George Lucas' message to business and government? Open up the criteria of the proposals you fund beyond the provable, the quantifiable and the demonstrable, or be resigned to failure. A good message.

It's a curious paradox that a country that effectively forbids the airing of dissent on its commercial or public media sends flocks of reporters to canonize "dissidents" in countries other than our own! It's a curious paradox that a country that pretends to honor the arts forbids to its public media four elements essential to the definition of art: creativity, originality, innovation and provocativeness.

How could this have happened? The same way it always does . . . power in the hands of manipulators. There was a "Cold War" on. There was a "Threat to The American Way". Compliance with Washington was the route to advancement. It was the route to influence. It was the route to big contracts, faculty appointments, a job on the newspaper, advancement in the public television hierarchy. Intellectual freedom in America was a casualty of the Cold War (except for engineers and technocrats); the academy, the press, the bourgeois intelligentsia, faced with rigorous opposition, laid down their arms. Or they went underground. Or they bided their time. Whatever route a free mind selected, the avenues of power or influence were not among them. In television, censorship laws could not have been more rigorous or effective than the simple prohibition of "controversial" programming by the Federal Communications Commission.

The "Reagan Revolution"

In my craft, the development of ways to use film and television to reach people more effectively, Ronald Reagan brought the curtain down summarily. Upon Reagan's election, support ended abruptly from government agencies that once defined their mission to (as Senator Edward Kennedy once put it in a letter to me) "minister to the needs of elements of society not otherwise served." During a period spanning the Johnson, Nixon, Ford and Carter regimes, I had made some relatively successful, low-budget government funded films whose purpose was to let people know about how space science applied to our daily lives, to bring young children to an understanding of their organic relationship to a larger society of the city, to help children to come to terms with disabilities, and to communicate current knowledge of mental illness. Some small freedom for experimentation was allowed in this context. I was allowed to innovate a little. It wasn't easy even then.

As a civilized person, I tried to make a contribution through film. I undertook to produce a series funded by the Ford Foundation and the US Department of Housing and Urban Development. The purpose of the series was to instruct children about their responsibilities as citizens. The series was called, *If You Live in a City, Where Do You Live?* The Ford Foundation well knew what it wanted children to do. It wanted them to stop vandalizing. From my own childhood, I remembered that as a technique to influence action, indoctrination is not lasting. Children, particularly the smart ones, rebel against those attempting to control their actions or their thoughts. So, in the interest of children, I produced films that reached children on two levels. One was the script, the other was the story. "Ford" got everything it wanted in the script. What I wanted was for the children to be piqued with curiosity and a sense of empowerment, to get some tools to look at the world for themselves. Thought is never what controlling types want. It most certainly is not what the Ford Foundation wanted. They wanted children to respect urban "furniture".

There was some learning for me, too. On a hunch, I asked four children from Winthrop Street, off Flatbush Avenue in Brooklyn, to show us their "secret place". To my surprise, every child had one, and was happy to show it to us. One was a huge tree in Prospect Park. One was a cellar of an abandoned building. Here were parts of the city that the children themselves declared to be valuable. I started the story there, not with the findings of researchers or the projection the sensed needs of grownups.

Because they explored to some degree the potential of an infant medium to communicate "difficult" ideas, some of the films I produced were awarded significant television honors. Then, suddenly a chasm opened in front of me. I was informed that the new President, Reagan, had declared that "the government isn't in the film business." This was a telling signal of the times. Presidential leadership signaled the tenor of a decade dedicated less to enlightenment than any other in the century.

What was the President saying? His Hollywood origins spoke. The phrase he used, "The film business", means the use of film as a device to generate profit. In Hollywood, the more profit the better the film. That is what "Hollywood" means. Hollywood today is a society and a culture made influential and strong by riches gained from fulfilling the legacy of Pandarus.[121] Except for one night a year, nobody pretends that Hollywood has any other mission than maximizing returns on investment. On that one night a year, people who spend the other 364 days thinking about money, think about art. The results are predictable. A film that involves the largest number of people (voting academy members) or the film made by the company with the most employees (voting academy members) or the film that makes the most money (that's what it's about) is declared "best". After all, votes count. The voting members of the Academy are people who work for a living. They use their votes to guarantee insofar as possible that they'll work again next year. An academy Award for their company is good for members' resumes.

A natural consequence of the nearly total dedication of Hollywood to profit is that, thanks to the videocassette, an underground information network regarding films of consequence exists completely outside the blatherings of "the business". This extra-commercial network will probably be the determinant of history's assessment of films as literature.

The "Reagan Revolution" signaled that public broadcasting would get no help from the chief executive. It became clear that noncommercial *anything* was *ipso facto* bad. Reagan threatened to banish public television. Sonia Landau, former head of Women for Reagan/Bush was deemed to have the best credentials for guiding the Corporation for Public Broadcasting. Under her leadership, board meetings became near-riots. Her Vice Chairman, R. Kenneth Towery, supported programming that emphasized patriotism and national achievements.[122] So much for the memory of public TV's insulation from government and the political process. Reagan packed the board of directors of the corporation with obstructionists, who did all the harm they could.

Public TV turned to Congress for help. Congress obliged . . . it was an opportunity unprecedented since Hitler turned to Goebbels. Unlike Nixon, President Reagan didn't want to use public television as a forum for his ideas. The legislature, however, was still left with the power to allocate resources to public television . . . to a public television not interesting to the incumbent president. Congress had its own, different agenda. Reagan let them pursue it.

The congressional agenda for public television was and is essentially a reelection strategy that has become known as "political correctness". The paradox of Political Correctness is that it springs from a concept that has been dead since the French Revolution: that persons should be granted special privileges solely on the basis of an accident of birth. The current theory of political correctness springs from the idea of fairness. In a democratic society, as it does and must play out, inequity is iniquity. Political correctness simply complicates the scenario. As it plays out in practice, "political correctness" is inequity, a mask of fairness worn by self-interest. It rightly asserts "minority rights" and proceeds to define "minority" narrowly, in a way that serves the political/economic self-interest of the people up for election. To Washington, a "minority", we learned in the 1970s, is not simply a coherent group that is less than a majority. It's not the 400,000 Armenian-Americans or the Irish-Americans or the Italian-Americans or the Episcopalians. It is instead a group or a member of a group that the Congress *defines* as a minority. Not Germans or Catholics or Americans of Hungarian descent, not intellectuals or gays or artists or writers or people with Down's Syndrome. These are not congressionally-defined minorities, and therefore they don't exist functionally as minorities at all. In other words, these others have no claim on aid. A certified "minority" person today is a Hispanic, a Black, a Native American, an Aleut, an Asian. And that's it. No others. Why? Because these groups have been selected by Congress for special help, to be, in George Orwell's phrase "more equal" than other Americans.

Why were these groups selected? On the basis of need? Partly, but not entirely. There are many fragile and needy people who are not considered deserving of particular attention by the Congress. Why? If you read the numbers, they say that official "minorities" must have been selected because *their populations are large enough to represent potentially powerful voting blocs.* When you hear the term "minority", you may want to think of the term "swing voter", which will help you to understand the congressional code. The cultivation of these "minorities" in any agency that might be a candidate for a federal grant is known as "political correctness". Here's how it works. You hire members of the approved "minority". Then you get the government grant. The minority person then presumably votes for the grant giver to whom he or she owes the job. There! the taxpayers' money has bought a vote. The rule applies for atomic physics as well as independent television. Any agency or company or foundation or university that receives federal funding, for anything, must staff with a quota of sanctioned minorities or it doesn't get a dime from the Feds.

We may find a precursor in our literature . . . Carlisle Floyd's opera *The Passion of Jonathan Wade* features a character, Enoch Pratt, who is sent by the War Department to set up the Freedman's Bureau in Columbia, South Carolina at the beginning of Reconstruction. "Our party will raise up the Blacks", he sings, . . . "and gain their loyalty for a hundred years." It might be instructive for members of Congress to attend this opera, and to note that the character Enoch Pratt is one of the opera's two self-serving villains.

Political correctness functions as a diversionary strategy, a pretense that diversity is allowable. "Political correctness" is not color blind, but color coded. It does not hypothe-sizer one class, one culture, one people, who are all equal. It does not see its people, as does the new South Africa, as "one people". Operatively, political correctness establishes that only a particularized genetic diversity is allowable. Its precepts implicitly declare that intellectual diversity is forbidden. Political correctness has dominated the allocation of resources in public television for 35 years. It has done some good. It has exposed many funders, administrators and recipients as cynically manipulative, too.

Chapter 15

KNUCKLING UNDER, GETTING THE GRANTS

In 1926, threats of a government takeover of the British Broadcasting Corporation were fended off on the grounds that government involvement would inflict fatal damage on the BBC's credibility. The belief that such pressures should be resisted is central to British broadcasting philosophy.[123] So is that *belief* in the United States! But action sometimes can be contrary to belief.

The legislating into being of public television as successor to educational television was a signal for opportunists to regroup. With Congress footing the bills for this supposed alternative to commercial television, with Congress seeing itself as in part "responsible" to the voters who elected them to office and might (or might not) elect them again, a new and interesting game began. This game is a strategy whereby public television functionaries structure their own well-being by second-guessing their funder, the Congress of the United States. Lest we credit public TV management with too much imagination, may I point out that this procedure is an exhumation of the old *CBS Reports* "butter up Washington" technique. In 1971, *Time Magazine* wrote, "Since PBS and its producers get much of their financing from the Federal Government, and since this funding is not insulated from querulous annual scrutiny, the network quakes at the least cavil from the Administration or Congress."[124] Well, what of it? Obviously, the likes and dislikes of the federal legislators are the key to program funding.

Here's how it's played in public TV. Each station is on its own . . . "Independent" is the euphemism. Some managers are savvy; some are not. The savvy ones, the ones who get the grants and do the most business, do this: Program proposal development executives determine which congressional committees oversee or are likely to have influence on the funding of their turf. That's easy. The executives have access to the literature, just like you and me. They find out that six committees have direct or indirect influence over funding of public broadcasting. These are the House Energy & Commerce Committee, the Senate Commerce, the Transportation and Science Committee, the Senate Communications Subcommittee, the Telecommunications Subcommittee of the House Commerce Committee, the Committees on Education Arts and Humanities, and Children, Family Drugs and Alcoholism. Around eighty people run these committees and make the decisions about authorization of funding for public television. Most of these people, of course, are lawyers. Many are businessmen.

How can a public TV station compete with other public TV stations for grant money? By finding out the names and biographies of members of the decisionmaking committees, and tailoring appeals accordingly. You can start with *Who's Who*, where you can find out what was their college major, which is probably the best indicator of who you're dealing with. Then you will have to assess organizations in which membership may or may not be merely politically expedient (like the Rotary, and Masonic Orders). What have they written? Before talking to them, find out what their hobbies are, what their sartorial preferences are. Can you connect with their places of origin? Their children and their children's interests? Who are their primary contributors or clients? Phone their office. Talk to staff members. Read their speeches. Make an appointment to go and see them. Take them to lunch.

For the smart PTV executive who wants a bigger piece of the pie, the smart thing to do is to assess what the powerful Congressmen who are members of these committees want. Or, perhaps more realistically, "What do these powerful Congressmen want, that they can persuade others and themselves to think their constituencies want?" It's not too hard to do.

Here's a helping formula: Attorneys and businessmen are likely to be verbal types. Not terribly imaginative. Conventional. "Suits", clerks call them. Congressional committee agendas are published and available to the public. "Issues" that could be program subjects are right there in the Congress Business Daily, The Congressional Record. Congressional staff members can be helpful with agendas. You as a smart public television program executive can then find out what issues are interesting to Congress, or at least to the key members of the committees that make decisions about public TV. Get a sense of which way the winds are blowing. Then go back home and write proposals for TV shows that deal with just these subjects! The approach to the programs you propose is easy, too. You know that Congressmen will define their constituencies not in their larger dimension, but as electorate. So you do, too.

You sit before your word processor to devise a proposal. You combine the talents of television producer and surrogate Congressman. Start with "American", of course. George Bernard Shaw wrote, "Patriotism is not the last resort of scoundrels but the *first*." So that's your first word, "American". Then what? Then it just flows out. American Power? American Pride? American Wealth? American Business? American Patriotism? American Victories? American Government? American Presidents? American Heroes? American Monuments? Try warming it up a bit. American Sentiment? American Nostalgia? American Pastimes? American Children? American Marriages? American Old People? American Babies? American Movies? American Novels? American Music? American Issues? American Games? American Families? Gee, the proposals almost write themselves!

Never fear that Congress will want to fund a public TV series on American Jingoism, American Arrogance, American Pruriency, American Selfishness, American Opportunism, American Greed, American Manipulativeness, American Violence, American Self-Deception. Naughty! Unpatriotic! That'll make bad TV! In other words, Congressmen who funded shows like those could neither win elections on the basis of their support nor be secure from retribution from all their campaign contributors!

In writing proposals for public television, it's profitable, too, for a public television executive who wants funding to ascertain *unstated* congressional goals. That's not hard to do either. These will be the goals of the PACs and the big lobbies contributing to the members of the above committees. You can be assured at least modest success if you remember that the underclass needs defusing, or that the technocrats needed as troops in the next generation of our industrial development will have to be given the "right" attitudes and the right skills, or that Spanish-speaking and Asian-American citizens will soon represent a substantial voting bloc. Given a little insight into congressional workings, the public television TV shows arise with majestic inevitability!

So, just as CBS guaranteed its license renewals and Washington influence in the '50s by reading congressional agendas and then producing *CBS Reports*, so did the public television leadership make itself courtiers to Congress after 1967.[125] Searching for guarantees for their own futures, public television executives, instead of asking themselves, "How can we, representing the entire community, best move toward a goal of an alternative television service?", took the safe and sure route for their own job security, asking "What's the funders' agenda?"

There! Now you know. That's how you get the programs you get! And that's how you don't get some you may want: programs of insight, of originality, of philosophic inquiring doubt.

Given the congressional power to select programs as a result of their annual review of public television's funding, viewers would do well to cast a critical eye on what, in fact, public television is *doing*, what good is being served through this fealty to congressional intent. *The New York Times'* Leslie H. Gelb has observed, "Washington is largely indifferent to truth. . . . Handlers create appearances and they churn out scripts to combat truths and untruths alike. Television trains citizens to judge all this by who gave the better 'performance'."[126] "All men have their price," Sir Robert Walpole said of a now infamous era when principles were compromised to favor one's advantage.

An elected official, a congressman who wants to be reelected, can't object to public television's doing programs that a Congressman's constituency might approve of paying tax money for. So there are a lot of these shows, second-guessing the Congress. As observed above, many of them have the word *American* in their titles. (How could a Congressman resist funding renewals for a show with the word *American* in its title?) The shows came rolling out. No doubt you've seen some of them. Talk shows about American writers. Cheap-to-produce concerts of American musicians. Talk shows about what Washington thinks are social issues. Talk shows about money (as if a country obsessed with money needed public TV to talk about it too). Of course, a talk show or two about Washington. Naturally, talk shows about the issues before Congress. And political correctness, in spades.

Some of the shows are pretty dull. Public TV executives don't want to ruffle any feathers, or there won't be any money next year. It's best to make the shows as unexceptionable as you can. Remember the power of the political action committees, remember voter self-interest. Remember that most influential people won't see the show, they'll just see its name on a list. Forget any subject that could even be interpreted as questioning the prerogatives of either the moneyed class or vocal elements of the electorate. Eschew "controversy". Fly from even an appearance of dissent. Forget why the Ford Foundation brought an alternative television into being. Run your scripts and raw materials through committees at all stages of production. Don't produce any programs on subjects that will arouse vocal opposition from *anybody*. Make "Wonders of uncontroversial blandness", as Russell Baker called them.

Some random examples seen on public TV: How about White Water Rafting . . . who could object to that? Remember the one about Presidential airplanes, with a five-minute shot of just President Bush's plane passing some mountains? How about a *NOVA* show about llamas? And the former Surgeon General (Koop) telling a sweet old person how to get up out of bed. . . . now who could object to that! How about a series on *babies*. Only a monster could object to that. A public TV series has been brought into being that focuses on the most common denominator of all (unless we can find another for a series next year), childhood. This one presents the latest in "what is known" by social science, or at least those portions of social science that have merited grants from the funding agency, the National Academy of Science (funded by the Congress of course), etc., with a painfully carefully orchestrated, pictorialized narrative, showing the evidences of meticulous attention to correctness in its preparation.

The committee that authorized the funding will want the recipient of the funding to develop the work through, of course, a committee. That's how we can guarantee its impregnability!

Chapter 16
CREATIVITY BY COMMITTEE

.

T he product, factually correct and designed to please all contributing agencies, alternates between the unctuous, the condescending and the fatuous. Energy, thrust, movement, direction, drama, brilliance in any aspect, an overarching creative design may be searched for in vain. This is the "style" of committee-generated public TV. It is not a style envisioned perceived by a producer or a writer or by anybody, for that matter, but issimply the outcome of the organizational process of the committee that controls the funding. Although there is a nominal "producer", essentially these programs are produced *by* the committee *for* the committee to watch. The medium of "TV" has been selected as the recipient of largesse, not because of the subject's particular appropriateness to an audio/visual/sequential presentation, but because "everybody watches TV". When the committee has finished putting into the show everything they think should be there, all America is expected to rejoice in their new knowledge. The advisory committee fails to realize that everybody in America doesn't think like a member of a committee. In fact, lots of perfectly good people don't *want* to think like a member of a committee. They hate the methodology and hate the shows. Few ever watch these government TV shows. They see them as patronizing and wrongheaded, Thanksgiving turkeys that "Lady Bountiful" committees make to guide the poor benighted public. These are our own domestic examples of our new American state TV, a version of France's detested state TV or the state TV of any other country. TV produced by government bureaucrats is deservedly hated for what Wolper's Warren Bush used to correctly call "Onanism", bringing delight only to their perpetrators. Monotonously, these shows come and go, with nodding acceptance from those who have to accept. Then they vanish onto the shelf.

The Congressional Broadcasting System seems unresponsive to criticism. The power of authorization is its shelter. It has carte blanche. Shouldn't public television have an investigative journalism team, say, on *Frontline* that will investigate public TV? "If you're publicly funded, how can you expect to go around investigating public institutions?" asks Barbara Gordon in *Newsweek* (October 18, 1971, p. 127). Of course you can't, you'll get your funding cut! Dummy! Censorship, alive and well, wears various disguises.

A sideshow of dubious merit and purported threat distracts people from the issue of who really controls the content of public television. "Political correctness", the new "Red Channels" as it has affected public television, has performed some measure of wing clipping. Any shrill voice demanding "rights", if strident enough, now commands attention. (By that is meant a show here, a show there, an appointment to a minor decisionmaking body . . . never enough to make any real difference.)

A long tradition of anti-intellectualism in America has found a place in public TV. "A mediocracy that distrusted excellence and suspected creativity as un-American or subversive"[127] has always defined a broad spectrum of opinion in America. Some of it is reflected in the people's representatives. Quickly, people in public TV with a nose for their own advancement discovered that this was an acceptable bigotry, since it was shared both by many taxpayers in our democracy and their elected representatives. Intellectuals, people of imagination and/or experience, people who pursued an abstract idea of excellence within public television, found themselves branded as "controversial", as "elitist". Like the term "aristocrat" during the French Revolution, these labels meant the guillotine. People who cited precedent or gave evidence of academic or experiential support for their proposals or ideas were effectively driven out of the system. The opinions of dissenters within the public broadcasting hierarchy were simply ignored. People in public television who prize excellence or are creative in the sense that they bring originality to known context are as welcome as a child molester in a suburb.

There can be only one reason for this bridling of dissent: a conviction that it is justified. A confident person, a confident institution — particularly a confident democracy — rejoices in dissent. The airing of alternatives tests the soundness of positions. It's what free speech means. Public TV's abrogation of the responsibility for the presentation of "controversy" has given its viewers the equivalent of bread and circuses. Viewers are given reportage that runs the gamut from excruciating blandness to vigilante charges against high-visibility, highly vulnerable targets, and entertainment based on nostalgia, patriotism or equivalent irrelevancy.

There are abundant examples of patronizing ignorance among the creators of programs. A fictionalized public TV series about tribalism in an American high school presumes an acceptance of the urban high school as a warehouse for libidinous working class boys and girls, a prenuptial sandbox in which the pitfalls of rudimentary courtship form the plot. The series was probably formulated and sold as a condescending device "to reach our youth in terms they understand"; in other words, patronizing populism. The production value, casting, direction and acting, and, I'm sure, its production budget make this effort no threat to real broadcasters. To you who may not have seen it, I have to tell you, this stuff is unworthy.

What purpose does this treacle fulfill? It keeps the populace, in the words of T.S. Eliot, "distracted from distraction by distraction". Public TV has become another diversion added to each person's drudgery of the workplace today: to seven-day-a week shopping, re-choosing telephone services, keeping up with food fads, replacing batteries, throwing away the trash, reprogramming the clocks after every power outage, servicing the car, keeping up with the styles in clothing, cosmetics, hair, furniture, houses and cars, paying the bills, poulticing family squabbles, and the daily "crisis" in news. Public television presents its antidote . . . toothless American history, de-fanged art forms, soft, furry things, special interest pleading, and Lawrence Welk. Rented English reruns take the "high road" to stroke the wives of the bankers and stockbrokers, a minor funding source.

Remember the "documentary film"? The respect given by critics always outweighed the popularity of the nonfiction film genre. *Nanook of the North, Louisiana Story,* Wasserman's *Out of Darkness,* these remarkable *stories* are taught only in the classroom today, where they sometimes inspire those students who are sensitive to the enormous potential the genre offers as a locus for their own statements. Once a staple of US public service television, the nonfiction essay is still a traditional form in Europe. The documentary tradition, which eschews the party-dress metaphor of fiction and lays its truth bare, enjoys a rank in US arts today somewhere in the vicinity of dough sculpture. A documentary producer does not qualify as a credentialed person in Washington. Perhaps a reason for this was pointed out by T. S. Eliot, when he wrote, "Humankind cannot endure very much reality."

The "entertainment industry" is one of America's biggest. One can speculate on how dreadful must be the lives of most of the public, to reduce them to need so much stroking. "Music and movies are America's contribution to today's world", says conventional Japanese wisdom. The wild success of film fantasy, of cartoons not to mention popular immersion in gambling casinos and empty issues like flag-burning to the neglect of real problems like those of manifold debt crises, robbery of the poor by the rich, the revolution of falling expectations, the perils of globalization, family dissolution, criminality, ignorance, mass infantalization for profit, or the pileup of junk, gives some credence to the position that Americans cannot endure any reality at all. Being not popular, the nonfiction film as a potential resource for an alternative to commercial television has been a casualty of the twin forces of mass-audience presumptions and controversy-paranoia among public television purveyors.

There is some laughter to be gotten from public television's second-guessers' attempts to accommodate to their understanding of the congressional imperative. Maybe the funniest example of a public TV station's tries at populism happened at Boston's WGBH. They came up with "Disco Dazzler", a Sylvia Davis "dance-athon", designed to pry contributions from suggestible teenagers, a target of vulnerability already proven by commercial TV. The fundraiser's call-in viewers were to vote for their favorites and make a pledge. They did. But WGHB neglected to provide for the duplicity that may have signaled the audience's identification of WGBH's guile. The voters never sent in their promised pledge money! A potential pop genre was nipped in the bud.

The fundraising power of treacle is not to be underestimated. The assumption that the elderly are "dotty" and not in control of their pocketbooks has spawned a genre of public television fundraising through nostalgia for the pleasurable stimuli of their youth. Public domain dance music of a half-century ago is favored bait. The vulnerability of the elderly was discovered early. A story told at WGBH auctions was that one of the telephone volunteers informed a person on Cape Cod that she was the high bidder on an item, to be answered by the cry, "Oh! Nursie! We won!"

Public television's patronizing in the interest of fundraising is forgiven by forgiving and hopeful apologists who shrug their shoulders and say, "Well, they've got to get money somehow." *Swing Alive* was a 1996 fundraising "Benefit for public television" performance at the Hollywood Palladium presented by WEDU Tampa. This evening of nostalgia was purported in its flyer to support "programming that puts content and quality ahead of any other criteria." This is precisely what the fundraiser did not do. The priority of bottom-line calculations of how best to raise money traded not on Granny and Gramps' love of quality but on their nostalgia for the chortles and treacle of their courtship days. Francis Kidd & Associates exhumed Bob Hope, Les Brown, Doris Day, Patty Andrews, King Creole and the Coconuts and other one-time profit centers, for what other purpose than to bring toothless smiles of memory to the rocking chair set on the way to unlocking their pocketbooks? It sold tables to anyone dotty enough to pay $25,000, and individual tickets for as much as $10,000.00 per person, to witness the making of a TV special built on public domain songs and old jokes. PBS's Florida West Coast Public Broadcasting Company was behind this effort to capitalize on the stroking of the uncritical elderly, purportedly in the interest of "quality programming".

A condescending turn of logic allows public television executives to pander to ignorance. The reasoning goes that since the masses are trivial and vulgar and since the elderly are senile and childlike, it must follow that infantile, trivial and vulgar programs "represent" the taxpayer and are therefore inherently democratic. A result of this patronizing logic has been a metastasizing of what *Time Magazine's* Kurt Andersen (July 26, 1993) has called public TV "Pop crud". (Has anybody seen Lawrence Welk's oldies on public TV? There's "fine programming" for you!) Says Georgie Anne Gayer, 23-year veteran of public television's *Washington Week in Review*, "Local public television stations all over the country were now leaning toward the popular and the cheapened."[128]

Radio has not been immune. The May 31, 1998 issue of *The New York Times* devoted one-and-a-half pages to the "dumbing down" of radio, with the headlines, "Classical Radio Plays Only to Sweet Tooths"; "In Boston, a Last Broadcast Bastion Falls"; "In a city with a renowned intellectual culture, WGBH is dumbing down. Why?" Why? Dummies are easier to get money from, and there's the rent to pay!

There's a related logical pitfall that catches broadcasters who try to program to target the "average" American. They try to gain business support for public TV by campaigns based on research gathered from statistical projections of sales charts. This is lazy thinking. When public TV tries to get "hip" (meaning "hep"), with specials on Elton John, Paul Simon, Billy Joel, Joe Cocker and The Beatles, they misapprehend their own mission. They learn from Hollywood films that celebrity represents prepaid sales promotion. So they try to attract "names". The "stars" public television courts into its fold are commercial. But with budgets calculated to prohibit public TV from ever becoming a threat, public TV can hire only fading and former stars. These, public TV discovers, lack drawing power and confirm the audience impression that public TV is "uncool".

The formula that prompts the search for "star" power contains a fundamental error. The pop icons called "stars" do not necessarily spring from the hearts of the people, as their promoters would have you believe, and perhaps they themselves believe. Public TV opportunists, taken in by the ad agencies' *weltanschauung*, beam their "popular" message to that slice of the public that is already well served, the shopping mall crowd.

The only documented statistics readily at hand on ordinary Americans' taste are sales statistics from movies, commercial music, and the product sales from commercial TV. These represent a limited spectrum of the people. What is known as "pop" culture is merely the sum of commercial products bought by an impulsive, unreflective, egocentric, self-indulgent segment of society. To identify this limited group as "the people" is inaccurate. Functionally, the use of the term "popular" in the commercial context is both euphemism and a form of censorship. This common, limited definition of "popular culture" excludes any artistic production outside conventional "high culture" and the mass consumer marketplace. For public broadcasting to pitch to this restricted group of impulse buyers as if they represented "the people" is not only an abrogation of the mission of public television but it is even false populism.

Why do public television executives take this route? Because it's easy. Besides, who cares? A survey of the taste of people who don't buy records would be costly, and time consuming. It would require effort and discernment. That a public service, "alternative" broadcasting entity bypasses this unserved population is myopic. As an informational avenue for alternative television, it's self co-opting. It leaves out the non-consumers, exactly the same people left out by commercial television.

"Popular culture" is not popular culture at all. It is instead a limited manifestation of mass marketing. More properly termed "Consumerist Culture", it is defined not by the nature of the consumer but by the commercial returns of the producer, and is therefore not popular culture at all. It is sales charts. Noncommercial popular culture is an unknown: the noncommercial popular culture is America's lost generation. Who will find them?

America's "popular" music business is not our folk culture. Commercial music today is among its practitioners simply a device for prying pennies out of the capricious to provide incomes for songwriters and record companies whose role edges ever closer to that of panderer. The people who make the songs, of course, never publicly acknowledge that they do not represent the spontaneous upwelling of inspiration among the uncultivated that they pretend. Why? It's a living! Singer Andreas Marcovicci has declared, "Since the advertisers only want to reach people between 18 and 35, sophisticated music is dying."[129]

Public TV's selection of Big Sellers as indicators of popular culture indicates the level of insight to be found among public television decisionmakers. Their crude attempts to gain public acceptability by grafting commercially profitable clichés onto their works demonstrate to a commercial television delighted to hear their message that there is no American folk culture in the historic sense. It reassures commercial people that there are no songs people sing, poems they write, artifacts they make, performances they give, beliefs they hold, or books they read just because they want to.

Analysts' use of the blanket term "popular culture" as a euphemism for mass-market performance creates a logic that validates the impossibility of an alternative television. The uncritical method of mimicry that public television functionaries elect when they choose "pop" or mass-market commercial as representative of the tastes of the taxpayer merely "proves" that the penny arcade that is broadcasting today is okay the way it is. The false populism of the taxpayer representation school of public television programming is convenient. It is also shallow. The harm it does to the integrity of the idea of an alternative television, as to the concept of America as a civilization, is erosive.

Lord Reith, founder of the British Broadcasting Corporation, pointed out the underbelly of populism. He said, "He who prides himself on giving what he thinks the people want is creating a fictitious demand for lower standards which he will then satisfy." WNET New York's one-time president John Jay Iselin echoed Lord Reith, and raised the level of American populist discourse for a moment by asserting that WNET had no intention of denying to the poor of New York the cultural life traditionally reserved for the rich.

Where are public TV's new show ideas? Why are there so many talking heads on public TV? Why so much verbalization? Hasn't commercial television at least taught us that TV is a medium that uses picture and story and sound in a temporal matrix? Isn't it axiomatic in scholarship that "primates are primarily visual animals" (the words are those of Harvard anthropologist Stephen Jay Gould)?[130] Are the people who originate public TV programs blind? Yes, and no. The reason is that in the calculations of our public TV world, economics outweighs sensibility, insight, experience, even wisdom. Talking heads in a studio are simply the cheapest way to fill airtime. In any contest with excellence in public television, cheapest wins. Talking heads on TV are the most convenient way to fill the most time at lowest cost. They're the cheapest way to create show titles to fill in the blanks on federally mandated documents tallying a broadcasters' public service commitment, to be read by legislators, commissioners, trustees, donors, potential donors and others too busy with interesting matters to take their valuable time to watch dull, boring talk shows on public TV. Talk shows complement the agendas of station business managers, those balance-sheet servants whom it is falsely hoped will be teammates of the gatekeepers to creativity.

The cheapness of talking heads is reinforced by another important plus: satisfaction in the places where satisfaction *really* counts. The money/power people who have to be pleased by what the public TV bureaucracy does are verbal people. Talk is what they understand. Television that is radio is no aberration to them! Legislators, industrialists, lawyers, bankers, the ones who make the fundamental decisions, who allocate the funds, are all word people — "left-hemisphere dominant", some call it. It's not their fault. This is simply the way people who are attracted to these professions happen to process information, by an accident of birth. And it happens that nowadays these people are economically dominant. For their convenience, and probably unwittingly, they staff the TV production entities with people who speak their language. They read reviews written by critics who make words for a living. The verbal people listen to the television that verbal people make, and together they secure funding for more like it. And what is lost? The people who sense the enormous potential of the pictorial dimensions of the medium tire of talking to stone walls, and quit. Stations save money. The drones keep on working. The talk goes on.

The bureaucratic model for the managerial structure of public television is based on past practice in American industry. It's a paradox that the corporate organizational model of mid-20th century American business should have been based on a model of social organization abandoned by European culture as unworkable — that of hierarchical, authoritarian feudalism. A "bureaucrat", by the way, is a government functionary who, if he were in business, would be called an "executive". That is, a line officer functionary in a feudal, hierarchical organizational structure. Like athletes, they are tacticians.

When educational television became publicly funded, for reasons of efficiency and corporate/government convenience, the corporate/government model was selected for a structure of public television management. Abandoned was the strategic, collegial, *atelier* structure appropriate to an organization whose essence was and is innovative, exploratory, generative. A corporate-model decisionmaking process/power structure of public TV presumes intelligence only on the part of management and treats creative people like robots. Hierarchical organizational structure has acted as a deterrent to originality, exploration of the potential of the medium or even its use, in ways demonstrated daily by the example of commercial TV. The cause isn't deliberate decisions by malevolent or even misguided people in public TV, it's just the way the system that has been selected works.

This condition prevails not only in public television. *New York Times* art critic John Russell observes, "Worldwide, it is now the manager and the moneyman who rule, while the creative people — the editor-in-chief, the museum director and the curatorial staff — are discarded."

Masterpiece Theater isn't the only theater on public television. The system itself has become a marionette show. Powerless marionettes do make-work in the public television stations. Fundraisers pretend that a system of creative production on the local level is a reality. Congress annually authorizes tax money to maintain the charade of localism.

The decisionmaking process of public TV was closed to creative people by the structure public TV developed. A winnowing process that has purged independent thought has left the field to ten thousand trusties willing to knuckle under, grateful for the sinecures of Affirmative Action and feminism. The programs you see on public TV show that their continued employment implies production of programs limited to the recycling of hoary icons as Significant Cultural Events, avoidance of criticism in exchange for crumbs that allow them to inoffensively bleat their pride in accidents of birth or to whimper about the injustices those accidents have caused. These subjects along with civics lessons that inflate the egos of the primary funders constitute the major part of public TV programming made in America

Understandably, those public TV executives who have survived the winnowing process don't want change. They don't want to see those troublesome creative people calling the shots . . . people who laugh at the wrong times, who don't take serious things seriously . . . they could imperil the next funding cycle! Martin Mayer complained in 1972, "What has been lacking [in public TV] is any significant sense of experiment or any idea of what might constitute either art on television or television as an art form."[131] The cause, Mr. Mayer, is the organizational structure; the remedy is structural change.

Chapter 17

THE TEAM AS ORGANIZATIONAL MODEL

W hat about sports as a model for structural change? "England's wars are won on the playing fields of Eton"; a cliché of the 19th century points out the importance of sport in the making of Obedient Servants to The Crown (whoever "The Crown" happens to be.) The attitudes engendered by sport: uncritical obedience to authority, high energy, competitiveness — were found in 19th century England to be functional as an adjunct of empire. In 20th century America, school sport was used as a form of boot camp for corporate employment. Skills gained in sport are attractive to power people looking for foot soldiers in the hierarchical feudal systems that are corporate/industrial enterprises. But as Samuel Butler pointed out in *The Way of All Flesh*, what is good in a feudal fiefdom is not necessarily good for civilization. Olympic champion diver Greg Louganis argues that sport retards rather than educates the soul.

What is called "sports" in today's broadcasting parlance is a far cry from the noncommercial athletic games engaged in for "the fun of it" that once defined the term. If we go back to the origins of the idea of "sport", we return to Plato's Socratic Discourses and the Olympic games. In Plato's dialogues, Socrates tries to establish that a meaningful life for a thoughtful person includes the disciplining of the body to maximize its capacity, as a kind of ordeal of self-discovery in the interest of one's experiential potential. Romanized in Juvenal's "Satires" to *Mens sana in corpore sanem*, "A sound mind in a sound body", Greek thought held that the well-being of the body was an enhancement to reflective thought — that the mind works better if the body is in transcendently good tune. What is today known as "fitness" was to the Greeks simply a device, a means toward a more important end: the enhancement of the intellectual faculties. Privately, the English aristocracy and their cultural inheritors in America have held Plato's analysis to be a good guide.

Over the centuries, the purposes of sport as derived from the Greek ideal have eroded. Sports in Queen Victoria's public school system were modified. The goal of self-discovery was removed; it was a matter of small interest to the Queen's ministers. The purpose of sport in Victorian England was a particular kind of socialization. "Bullies" were tolerated; they could be useful to the Crown later on in the subjugation of Lesser Peoples. The games and sport of the English public school functioned as a training ground for co-operative participation in the management of the Empire. During the course of the life of the British Empire, however, sport was always voluntary; voluntarism was an essential part of the phenomenon.

Sport in the interest of commerce was an innovation of Americans. That professional sport is an oxymoron may have made it more attractive to television sponsors. Commercial athletics, euphemized into "sports", were (for reasons detailed elsewhere) attractive to commercial media. Athletic contests that set high value on competitiveness, that provide "winners" and "losers", are convenient for broadcasters and even more for sponsors. They multiply profits at the same time as they inculcate whatever School of Business Administration belief system is at any given time thought convenient to corporate expansionism.

The belief system fostered by "sports" adds to their attractiveness to consumerist industry. "Show me the money", says the sports agent played by Tom Cruise in the film *Jerry McGuire*. Sports and its derivative, mass-audience team competition, are a useful tool for the promulgation of attitudes convenient to controlling types. Though competitive athletics may take a variety of forms, "We compete and cooperate . . . in the sporadic, bucolic manner of professional baseball or in the corporate, bureaucratic manner of professional football or in the fluid, improvisatory manner of professional basketball", writes Dave Hickey.[132]

One of the desired social outcomes is that competitive athletic games inculcate attitudes that "help the economy". Uncritical obedience to "rules" is as essential a component of competitive athletics as it is to slavery. Efficient collective action among toilers is considered necessary to military, corporate, industrial effectiveness. The discipline of vigorous and uncritical obedience to rules among workers contributes to effective group function. Competitive athletic games are good training for troops. These games, be they voluntary or commercial, are authoritarian. Their cornerstone is "rules". "The rules" allow no questioning. They allow only the most miniscule of deviations among its members, generally restricted to the fields of skill and quickness.

"Sport" gives structure and goals to people who may lack the imagination to establish for themselves the goals of achievement, innovation or excellence. Instead, sport substitutes a reachable and socially admired goal, victory. Sportsmen make good employees. They value group effort, work hard, can stand up under stress, and their more durable bodies are less likely to eat up the accumulated capital of health insurance premiums before retirement time.

Football has long been a handmaiden of the industrial economy. College football players used not to have a problem getting a job anywhere. This sport's history, however, should give some pause to those who would use it as a universal model. Invented in Rowley, Massachusetts in the late 18th century, "football" was greeted by a Boston newspaper of the time as "an activity suited only to ruffians, and not worthy of the attention of a gentleman". As recently as 1993, football was declared by an editorial in *The New York Times* to be "the athletic expression of the worst aspects of corporate life — a celebration of coordinated group movement and the ability to suppress independent thought".[133] The explicit rage, destructiveness and heedless violence embodied in the wife-abuse problems of celebrity football hero O.J. Simpson, whose misapplication of lessons learned as an American football hero were the preeminent news story of 1994-95, might well cause some rethinking among America's more reflective corporate leaders about the "sport" of football as a behavior model.

Basketball's lessons are timelier. Within a relatively simple framework of allowances and prohibitions, a behavioral lesson is established and confirmed. The lesson of basketball is that the deft use of cunning, guile, speed, physical strength and opportunistic alliances makes "winners". In this game one can bring one's group to dominate others, and can bring oneself to dominate the group. Basketball is a ritual performance of "street smarts", a survival strategy for today's industrial/urban/corporate life. Because he embodies desired attributes of the corporate gestalt, and because he sells so many sneakers, basketball "superstar" Magic Johnson, like other sports celebrities, is rewarded with a cut of the profits.

The princely rewards that commercial competitors gain today are the best clue to what matters in our society, and to who is in control.

In our newly apotheosized market economy, sport's focus on competition confirms behavior attributes necessary to keep markets growing, dignifying the economic rat race as an article of tribal oneness. For business, next year's dividends must be bigger if one is to stay in business, next year's profits must be higher to maintain the ability to borrow. One way to achieve these goals is to make all the oarsmen row harder.

Stalin's Stakhanovite program, a cheerleader's device that established rewards of notoriety for increased industrial output, was designed to encourage everybody to work harder. It didn't. Soviet citizens saw it as manipulative and controlling, benefiting greedy authorities rather than themselves. In America, though, the Yuppies took the Stakhanovite bait. That little red car that shot in front of you this morning was a willing acolyte, a lemming goaded into serving his company's stockholders better in the best way he knows, by being quicker, jumping ahead of the other guy. Aggression, opportunism, ambition: these three added to cleverness in employees help to make businesses prosper.

Outside business, it's another story. The streets of America's best resorts have become the locus of scrimmaging among 7 Series BMWs and sport-utility vehicles owned (or leased) by people who simply cannot stop competing. On today's freeway racecourses, speed limits are universally violated. The emergence of aggression and competitive driving has led to a calculated version of "road rage", a custom that I call "driving to intimidate" (at least on the highways of California, where I live). Police along the Washington Beltway have campaigned against these "road sharks" by driving rental cars that signal a road shark's actions to cruisers. What they don't understand is that these aggressive, self-absorbed people are simply using the highway as an extension of the principles behind their conduct at the office. The attitudes they demonstrate on the highway are those they've been told are crucial for success in today's world.

A Canadian singing group known as "The Android Sisters" was interviewed on public radio. Asked, "What is an android?" a member replied, "A robot that looks and acts just like a human being . . . they're everywhere!" Their program reads, "GET AHEAD!" Television's role in this corporate future is to keep the sports-loving audience keyed up for competition, in a permanent trembling state of anticipation of the next Super-Star Grand Slam World Championship Bowl Whiz-bang.[134]

"Sport" since the Roman Empire has been an extremely attractive device of public manipulation. Since the days of "Die for dear old Rutgers", worker bees among the populace have been trained through competitive athletic games. "The rules" are to be obeyed. That's the drill. Implicit, unquestioning obedience to "the rules" makes Eagle Scouts, star athletes, Stakhanovites, parish priests, office drones, foot soldiers, fast-track hot-shots. It makes "good Germans", too. An acceptance since World War II by the American middle class of the utility of this set of motivations and goals is probably a major factor in staff complicity in the betrayal of the founding principles of public television.

"Games" are immensely convenient for "leaders", as people who want control are wont to call themselves. Down from Valhalla onto the playing field come rules that aren't open to question, from rule makers who choose to be anonymous. The peons get out there on the field and break a leg for a score. They forget today's score tomorrow, and are ready to go out and fight again. It's remarkable how close the culture of "sports" is to what the tyrants of human history have always wanted of their troops. . . . Unquestioning obedience; nay, willingness; nay, enthusiasm; nay, effort; nay obsession for preset goals, without thought that any sacrifice is made. What more could you ask of your foot-soldier employees to help your company beat out the competition? *Not*, however, good training for independent citizen responsibility in a democracy!

What does this have to do with television? American sport today is the parade ground for the foot soldiers of industry and commerce. Television is their *Champs de Mars*. For TV producers, accommodation to these assumptions among sponsors, licensees, and agencies constitutes the line of least resistance and highest reward. The business of commercial athletics now known as "Sports" is a congenial medium for television to advertise to the "ignorance is strength" crowd. The "fans" represent a self-selected group who without reflection identify themselves as malleable, suggestible, uncritical, willing and energetic. A self-identified market in the millions, "the fans" are a gift to sellers, a gift already tied up in ribbons. An "easy mark", what more could a sales department ask for? Commercials directed to this group need only imply that a customer should take pride in the instinctual, that if he drinks beer, drives heedlessly, smokes cigarettes, lusts after women, enjoys comradeship, that just by purchasing a product he will be magically transmuted into somebody more manly, more sociable, a "winner". This is good news for Joe Sixpak conjuring up a hazy consumer haven for himself at the end of a week of frustration and impotent anger in the mines.

A thoughtful person sees no point in wasting his time watching another person chase a ball. Thoughtful people have better things to do than sitting around drinking beer. Those truths of human differentiation set the limits on TV commercial athletic sponsorship that networks are glad to accommodate. The documented results of "sports" on television are astounding. The two hundred million can/bottle-a-day beer drinking habit in the USA owes enough to television advertising so that beer and the TV football, baseball and hockey industries are almost synonymous. (These sports may be displaced by *Fortune* magazine's 1998 discovery, cited above, that "[auto] racing fans, a third of whom are women, are more likely to buy sponsors' products than fans of any other sport.")[135]

Public TV fundraisers once tried to mimic commercial TV's sports-goldmine. Despite ample evidence that, as Esteroff Maran, editor of *Psychology Today* has written, "Sports are a primitive ritual of aggression and release"[136] and their place on an educational service is questionable, other factors dictated the kind of compromise that has become endemic to public television.

Perennially in need of funds, one public TV station, WGBH Boston, uncovered a hidden truth about a segment of their audience. Boston's public TV station discovered "fans" among *their* public, the (then prosperous) middle class! Back in the 1960s, competitive athletics were an established fixture on the commercial networks. Their history went back to newspapers and radio. An astute public television person in Boston, with an eye to income enhancement, had an intuition that almost paid off. What if public TV could get into the "sports" act! Sports people are free with their money. If public TV could find a "classy" competitive athletic game not on commercial TV, maybe it could be used as an income producer. Well, they tried it, and it worked . . . for a while.

In the 1960s, there was no tennis on commercial TV. The reason was prejudice. Tennis is a metaphor for survival through a combination of dogged competitiveness and adherence to rules long associated with the leisured among the dominant Anglo-Saxon culture. The sport of the then dominant culture, tennis had a *cachet* of snobbism and exclusivity. Too "toney" for the masses, representing too small an audience, tennis was "not interesting" to commercial TV.

But if it didn't work for commercial, how about tennis as the "sport" for public TV? Back in the late 1960s, WGBH Boston tried broadcasting the Longwood Cricket Club's tennis matches from Chestnut Hill. Classy. Toney. Elitist. Obsessively competitive. Evocative of school and club. Suitable for the image of the leadership mass medium, public TV.

And what happened? A surprise. Fundraising pitches for the first tennis game on public TV brought in *a lot* of pledges of financial support for the station. A Sports Department sprang up at WGBH quicker than Athena out of the head of Jupiter. It didn't last long, though. Success killed tennis on public TV. The commercial TV people weren't asleep. They saw that public TV's discovery produced *income.* It didn't take long for market forces to prevail. "If they're that quick to pledge to public TV", Commercial TV reasoned, "tennis people will be quick to buy our advertised products." Quickly co-opted by commercial TV; WGBH's discovery that the tennis audience are free-spenders continues to work on commercial TV to the benefit of brokerage houses, IBM and BMW.

WGBH in effect did the tennis research for the networks. Commercial TV saw that even though tennis was "elitist", its fans weren't the self-reliant, self-assured non-consumers their image projected. Tennis fans, too, were "doers", conformist, competitive, "wanting"; q.e.d.: there was potential sponsor coin in tennis, too. Tennis magically disappeared from public television. Now it belongs to commercial TV. Tennis sells proddux, lotsa proddux!

The esteemed position of commercial competitive athletics as mass role-model in the agendas of corporate sponsors may now be in jeopardy. The vehicle of instant obedience, impeccable adherence to imposed rules, the tireless energy that once was taught to the soldiers of empire and of commerce has undergone a mutation. Now these virtues are available as a computer program. The computer program does all that the middle level executive once did. The computer does it tirelessly. It's fast. It never makes a mistake. It asks for no raise, nor does it use its knowledge to join the competition. The casting-off of hundreds of thousands of middle level executives by American industry in the 1980s and 1990s signals their replacement by the computer program. These people's virtues are no longer marketable skills, so why does industry need to inculcate them with the attitudes promoted by sports? We can expect to see sponsorship of "sports" on television fall off. Sports, however, will leave their residue.

I'd like to suggest here that the growth of "sports" on television is related to the growth of violence on television. "Sports" is only a part of it, but part of it nonetheless. The relationship is presented by sales departments as a by-product of purely "neutral", "value-free" commercial decisions. Over the years, through trial and error, it has emerged as demonstrable that depictions of conflict on TV seem to prompt product sales. More violence shows, more competitive athletics, q.v. more sales. Terrific for business.

Why and how does this happen? One theory is that fictional violence enables a viewer through a process of transference to passively cope with the resentment and frustration of his own workplace. Having "come to terms", so to speak, with his bottled up feelings through the vehicle of violent fiction, the viewer buys the advertised product to some degree out of relief and gratitude. In addition, sponsors, ready to advance the life strategy of competitiveness and conflict that has led to their preeminence in their own fiefdoms, incline favorably toward the shows that sell their products through strife. The economic consequences are the desired ones. The psychosocial consequences . . . who cares?

Sponsors, agencies and networks conveniently forget *as commercials affect the viewers, so do the shows.* Yes, sponsors grant that "Monkey see, monkey do" applies to the public as viewer of the commercials. All the way to the bank. But, it is more difficult for sponsors or broadcasters to accept, or at least to acknowledge, the fact this also applies to the public as viewer of the *programs.* As the *Washington Times* said (12/27/93) "Television . . . probably incubates a sump of social pathologies." Viewers leave the "video nasties" and go out into the world primed with the juices of competitiveness, strife and violence. (Just watch the drivers at the foot of Boston's Mystic Bridge after a "Brunes" hockey game at Boston Garden. They're continuing the game on Storrow Drive. It's not a good idea to be in their way.) A 1996 San Diego Police Domestic Violence Unit study revealed that domestic violence in San Diego households increases by 12% whenever the San Diego Chargers play on TV, increasing by 18% if the Chargers lose. For Joe Sixpak, if you add the infection of violence from TV to the reality of limited income frustrating an inflamed desire for gratification through consumption that commercials promulgate, what do you have? You have television acting on some viewers to define their desires, reality frustrating them, and then TV again offering anti-social action as a model method for getting what you want. . . . this is TV encouraging crime.

Remember that these stimuli are presented to people many thousands of times in a lifetime. One consequence? The epidemic anti-social activity that dictates living conditions in America today. "Those who watched the most violent television as youngsters grew up to engage in the most aggressive behavior as adults, from spouse abuse to drunk driving" declares a report of a 30-year study by psychologist Leonard Eron of the University of Michigan's Institute for Social Research.[137] What are we to do with the tempted unfortunates who swallow the "go for it" teachings of commercial TV but circumvent the money part? We have to examine the context of motivation. That their behaviors may be a consequence of the economic imperatives of those engines of wealth, consumer industry, broadcasting, and advertising, is something that's not comfortable to confront. So we turn our heads, we sweep the idea under the rug. When we must, we put people who act according to principles that we promulgate into prison. It's called "blaming the victim". It's called "scapegoating". It's done all the time. Politicians make a career of it, diverting public concern from the real issues.

And what of the public relations professionals, the advertising executives, the marketing vice-presidents, the attorneys, the accountants, the laborers who earn a living from them? "We're tarts, not whores." "We support charities." "We go to church." "We vote." "Don't be *naive.*" Besides, it helps The Economy!

Chapter 18

TV JOURNALISM
AS LITERATURE, AS THEATER, AS SPORT

hanks to the organizational structure that public television has developed, most of the homegrown product we now get on American public TV is a product of the tradition of newspaper journalism. Some of it is of high quality — for a newspaper. Television journalists and journalism professors cite the examples of thoughtful, insightful reporting that are our heritage. Walter Lippmann, the Alsops, Scotty Reston are ornaments to the tradition of newspaper journalism. Broadcast journalism has a history of a thoughtful and evocative description of the significant events of the day recalled by the names of Eric Sevareid, Chet Huntley, David Brinkley, Howard K. Smith, John Chancellor, Roger Mudd, Bob Trout, Raymond Gramm Swing, and, of course, Edward R. Murrow. The tradition of "serious" journalism on television, however, has slowly, almost imperceptibly eroded.

It should be borne in mind that journalism is not and never has been considered to have the stature of literature. Leo Tolstoy called the practice of journalism "an intellectual brothel" — despite *The New York Times* Editor-in Chief Hodding Carter's unequivocal *ex cathedra* 1950s pronouncement, "*The New York Times* prints the truth." (Not "The truth as nearly as we can fathom it", or "as much of it as our readers can read in the time they're willing to give", or "Those parts of it that our readers may find interesting, informative or useful." No, "The truth." That was it.) Carter stood alone among journalists of my acquaintance. His pronouncement was of little use to a struggling TV person trying to find methods to inform the public in the new medium.

The Pulitzer Prize, journalism's highest award, is held by most literary professionals in less esteem than the Nobel, or the National Book Award. Journalism is a *poseur* of literature, not without reason. Examined in the perspective of history, journalism has to be seen as a mere subset. It has to be . . . its *raison d'être*, unlike that of literature or art, is not itself, but the selling of its matrix. Critic Larry Sabato has written, "The press depends on controversy to generate the headlines that sell papers and attract viewers . . . so they're in the business of creating conflict, not just reporting it." Following in the footsteps of William Randolph Hearst, who declared "The public is even more fond of entertainment than it is of information", publisher Rupert Murdoch once tellingly revealed, "After all, news *is* entertainment." Or, as *Entertainment Weekly* magazine's senior editor, Mark Harris, put it, "Television . . . all television, even television news . . . is show business."[138]

If the memory of William Randolph Hearst's *American Weekly* is too remote, try the supermarket checkout counter tabloids or the leering tabloid journalism of a Geraldo, or of NBC's Steve Friedman/Paul Greenberg's *Exposé*. WSVN Miami's "Disaster *du jour*", "If it bleeds, it leads" journalism[139] — in the long discredited traditions of *Grand Guignol* and public execution — are inescapably among the credentials of the journalism fraternity. Says political analyst Richard Parker,[140] "By taking a highly personalized approach, by seeing issues in terms of good guys and bad guys, journalists trivialize debate."

Tabloid journalism's only justification is marketing. Like the "search" function of a computer, commercial broadcasters are forever scanning ways to increase audiences of "suggestible" product buyers. Tabloid journalism attracts gullible people, as headlines like "World War II Bomber Found on Moon" attest. This audience is rationally, methodically, astutely selected *because of its credulity*.

Tabloid journalism's attraction to broadcasters is that the credulity of the viewer that opens itself to the show's outrageous content extends to the commercials. That the substance of tabloid journalism becomes part of the knowledge/action system of the viewer is accidental and irrelevant to the decisions of both producers and sponsors. That these buyers of the vended proddux in their role as citizens vote "a law-and-order ideology that promises that public safety and well-being can be achieved without addressing such underlying issues as racial conflict, education and poverty"[141] is irrelevant to sponsors' decisions, and simply not considered by their "journalists" just "doing their job", who present today's "stories" and tomorrow go on to others.

Journalists fit easily into commercial broadcasting. The term "journalism" itself is apt. From *jour*, "day", the term correctly implies that the concerns of the craftsmen are limited to the immediate present. With a few notable exceptions, journalists look neither forward nor backward. The greengrocers of literature ("snow sculptors", Lewis Lapham calls them), they deal in perishables. It should be said, the more perishable the better, since they want to work on a "new" story tomorrow.

During 1966 and 1967, I produced *Newsfront*, a weeknightly hour-long news show for public television Station WNET, New York. My approach to news was that any story should be justifiable as connectable with the viewer's decisionmaking in his own life. One evening, two "news items" competed for primacy on the show. One was a just-reported rowboat afire in the East River; the other was a morning announcement of the publication of the autobiography of one of the century's important philosophers. My team fought for the rowboat, but I led with Bertrand Russell.

Hubris intact, I tried to redefine news, to do something less trivial, less casual, less titillating, something with proportion. I thought that the news they see and hear could be functional in people's lives. My underlying assumption was that the audience had practical needs but was also curious about any sea changes there might be in the fundamentals. My staff resisted me.

Another evening, we were pondering our lead story. "I know the President's plane just landed thirty minutes ago", I told them; "Did he say anything? No. Why should we declare that to be a Matter of Concern to our viewers?" "Because it wasn't on CBS at 6:00", they pleaded. "Empty", I declared. "Let's do something else." We looked for and found a story that was more "important". I thought then (as I do today) that a news program should include what I call "today's significant achievement, accomplishment, or discovery." "Not news", my staff snorted. I knew they thought I was some sort of weirdo. Now, thirty years later, a domesticated version of my approach is suddenly "in", promoted as "News You Can Use".

My "news judgment" was seen as faulty. "News" is not "that which is important". "News", at least in television, is "that aberration that happened nearest to right now". That the Impulse Writers of news departments should serve the Impulse Buyers among viewers in an eternal present is symmetry between both commercial television news and entertainment.

Of course, factors having nothing to do with objective reality influence the development of news coverage. An unacknowledged mission of many journalists of my generation was the career pursuit of "the big time". Taken in as children by fictions largely fostered by the press itself, from "Front Page" to the self-promotion of Walter Winchell to Rosalind Russell movies and Superman, boys grew up motivated to enter the fictional world of their own childhood admiration. Their lives attempted to be a self-fulfilling prophecy, to imitate their tough heroes. Many newspaper and television journalists are just little guys who love snuggling up to power and riches: "If Mom could see me now! Here I am in a limo going across Paris for an interview with the Foreign Minister! Whee!"

"A pack of mongrel dogs" is the way writer Tom Wolfe describes the press. Journalism in its "news" garb fits neatly into the practice of commercial broadcasting. Its concern for the moment has no conflict with a sponsor's appeal to your current impulse to purchase a product no later than tomorrow. Photojournalist jackals hounded Jacqueline Onassis and Princess Diana to the end of their days, mercilessly pursuing the vulnerable for the delectation of the mean-spirited and the profit of the unprincipled. The ideas of reflection, memory, planning, a sense of past or long-term future are not congenial to the sale of nostrums, ornaments and snacks, or to the sale of newspapers, magazines and The Nightly News.

Journalism in its magazine garb fits neatly into American State TV. Here, journalists doing their job can be used as publicists for issues facing legislators at any given moment. The co-opting of journalism by the US government, however, has implications of seriousness beyond that of selling proprietary medicines. At their worst, journalists are simply literature's barking dogs, remarking anything deviant, be it a 200-pound baby or a high-priced Cézanne. At their best, journalists are a "fourth estate", interposing themselves as articulate members of the community between transient but powerful special interests and historic ideas of the general good. Like all barking dogs, however, even good journalists are expected to wag their tails at their masters. We do well to identify those masters. "Power corrupts" everyone: legislators, industrialists, reporters, you and me.

Efforts to co-opt the American journalism fraternity by retail merchandisers through newspapers and magazines, by government through commercial and public television, have succeeded. In America today, *every thing* uncongenial to the perceived self-interest of the media is simply omitted, simply not authorized. Simply "not there". Writing skill has nothing to do with this form of censorship. A reason can always be found ("budgetary cuts" are a favorite) for any journalist who tries to offer an uncongenial message to be simply "let go". As Danny Schechter has observed, "A growing partnership between public relations specialists, political leaders and corporate interests routinely screens out unwanted perspectives."[142] Any freelance writer who "heeds his own drummer" is simply not published, not put on. Censorship by omission in America is a daily reality.

The public should read their journalists selectively, always bearing the carrier's interest in mind. Their craft is not literature; it is sales. As Lewis Lapham noted, "If the writing of history resembles architecture, journalism bears comparison to a tent show." Or, as *The Economist* states, journalism is "a literary form where truth and accuracy come low on the list of priorities".

In the interest of objective decisionmaking, the public should be aware that presidents and congressmen use their journalists as propagandists. Clever presidents like Nixon and Reagan make sure the propaganda goes their way. Nixon and Reagan were instinctively adept. They "made" the news. Every morning they arranged a headline of their own choosing. Manipulative presidents do the journalists' work for them. The journalists eat it up. It's flattering. They grow fat and happy, and learn to neglect the rest of the world.

There are exceptions. President Bush I's dutiful press secretary Marlin Fitzwater lacked the guile and showmanship of some of his more manipulative predecessors. He forgot their lessons. He forgot how the Washington press corps had been co-opted by the tinted steam of Nixon and Reagan. Fitzwater left the press hungry. Some days there wasn't even a bone for the press corps to gnaw on. Fitzwater forgot that journalists have a deadline to make, a check to earn. Some mornings nothing important had happened . . . there was no big story revealed at the briefing. "Presidential inaction!" the press howled. What they were really saying was, "Where was my pre-made story today?"

The early training given to members of the press forms the ideological assumptions of working journalists. As "cubs", American newspaper journalists for the most part apprentice on sports pages, chronicling the ritual of conflict and conflict resolution on the playing field that is a cultural metaphor for the corporate struggle that is the real activity of advertisers, broadcasters and publishers alike.

Not surprisingly, journalists as a breed have a tendency they've been conditioned to, that is, to apply the sports page armature to all of human life. You may notice that as news is presented on television, the political process in the United States is a "race". When heads of state meet, the outcome is described in terms of an athletic contest: "Gorbachev came out the clear winner on this one, Reagan the loser", is typical. Some have a talent, called a "nose for news". Reporters who have it can see a "story" (an apt metaphor) where others may not. These Good Reporters have the key to journalistic success. They recognize its difference from other literary endeavors.

Playwright Vaclav Havel noted, "Journalists . . . are simply more interested in the game of power, and they consider ideas about the nature of 'being' irrelevant to their journalistic task."[143] Subtleties and complexities are irrelevancies to reporters. "To explore the mind of a journalist is to trespass on virgin territory", George Will once wrote.

Simple-mindedness sells papers. ABC's Av Westin sees the audience's world as enormously self-centered. Westin listed three more or less universal audience predilections as guidelines to the scripting of daily news programs:

1. Is my world safe?
2. Are my city and home safe?
3. What happened in the last 24 hours to shock me, amuse me, or make me better off?

The bias of a reporter is more than brainwashing, though. The reporting career attracts a subset of the left-brain dominant who actually see these journalistic formulae as an image of reality. A consequence is that journalism presents to the public a whole world inhabited by "street kids" bent on dominance within their group. Academic historians searching for both the nature and meaning of events quite properly never use newspapers as primary sources. A *Newsweek* executive editor, fawningly interviewed on public TV, was stroked by his interviewers. "I guess you'd say that *Newsweek* is the chronicle of the history of our times." "That's not the way we see it at *Newsweek*", was the reply. The editor's terse confession illuminated the fact that his job, like that of any editor, is to select stories that sell the magazine to its readership. *New York Times* executive editor emeritus Max Frankel wrote devastatingly, "News is not a rendering of reality, only a quest for novelty."[144] It would be unsound, incorrect, *wrong* for an historian to write the history of the world according to a vision of a person whose essential purpose is to sell today's advertising space!

Television journalism had its roots in newspaper journalism. Thanks to the timely demise of the New York *Sun* at the moment NBC and CBS were developing their television networks, the *Sun* staff moved right over to TV, and did what they used to do at the *Sun*. These were all word people. It took a decade for people in commercial television news to realize that TV had pictures. Only years of incessant daily experience persuaded TV news that the medium offered opportunities like vastly enriched pictorialization and limitations like constraints on verbal thoroughness.

The careers of some of the members of the TV press, as members of what has been called "publiciety", persuaded some ego-driven journalists that there could be a place for them in TV. The television matrix, a world of "star"-driven fiction/fantasy, provided a substratum in which a journalist might himself or herself become a "personality". The journalist as "personality" became his own commercial; the news he gave today was either more or less effective as bait to bring the viewers back tomorrow. "That's how it is", Walter Cronkite intoned at the finale of his daily newscast . . . it wasn't, but viewers wanted to think it was. "See you tomorrow", lies Tom Brokaw. People who lament the bias of TV news fail to recognize that the newsman is not showing bias at all, only merchandising his product to maximize returns. What he does isn't ideological; it's commercial. The blow-dried hair, trendy attire and coloration of the day's events are simply appropriate to the sales context.

News is our Babel. It is also our theater. "Hey! Extree! Extree! Read all about it!" Hucksterism is itself an evolved, unburied tradition of news. News cries for attention. The need to sell demands customer reorders. It is to the interest of news organizations to keep you on the edge of your seat, to get you to come back tomorrow. Dan Rather's worried face says, "Pay attention to me. Come back for another delicious worry, tomorrow." Tom Brokaw's puppy face says, "It was okay, wasn't it, and when I 'see you tomorrow', I'll make that okay, too."

The process of trivialization of the news appears to be recognized by NBC News. One segment of the NBC Evening News is called "In depth", implying that the rest is in shallowness. *Exposé* and gossip journalism of the "American Journal" genre, a prime-time syndication fad toward which NBC management is pushing an ill-equipped Brokaw, gives viewers titillation unencumbered by reason or reflection.

Public television journalists labor under harsher constraints than either newspaper or commercial television journalists. They are vulnerable to nearly everybody who wants to take a shot at them. Fragile public TV is acutely susceptible to retribution from voter blocs, the military/industrial junta, hysterical fringe groups, local donors, legislators, the entertainment industry, nearly any loud person or group who happens to take exception to anything they do. Having no clear mandate, no clear agenda, they have no armor. Public TV could be ruined by pickets, bomb threats, letter campaigns. They couldn't pay for their own legal defense. Theirs is not an enviable position. Vulnerable, they choose the safe course. Like consumer products developed in response to consumer surveys, safe television is what gets produced. Public television that is bland and unexceptionable is produced the same way as Kraft Cheese, with comparable results.

Perhaps, one might hope that the information specialists in public television would use their ingenuity to discover ways around the tyranny of the army of self-appointed censors who beset them. No. Instead they have chosen the inoffensive route of the tried-and-true. They stand as referees between the "this" and the "that". The outcome: pap. As with politicians, originality is not the journalist's forte. Look at public TV's shows . . . the ones made in the USA could have been invented by a committee, produced by a committee. Who needs talent for that? *NOVA* is a repeat of CBS's *Odyssey* series of the 1950s. Paid for by the National Science Foundation (funded by Congress), *NOVA* is part of the NSF propaganda mission, justified initially by a need to motivate schoolchildren who are science adepts as future cold war technologists. The public issue inspired *Frontline* is a copy of the old *CBS Reports* and *NBC White Paper* "view with alarm" journalism modeled on *The New York Times Magazine* with a dash of Hearstean tabloid adrenalin to draw a bigger audience (viz. December 1996's Lee Harvey Oswald pseudo *exposé* . . . created for what reasonable audience?). As a measure of the system's conservatism, there's even been a remake of Ed Murrow's 40-year old *Harvest of Shame.* From all of these you get, as Barbara Grizzuti Harrison wrote, "comfy-cozy beatitudes . . . for an inspirational buzz that exacts no intellectual toll and obliges one to do nothing but be the passive recipient of factoids."[145] Public television is clearly not an alternative to commercial television, where, as *Variety* says, "tried and true is alive and well".[146] Public television is just as timid, just as frightened, just as self-serving as commercial television. Significantly, too, it is much poorer.

Having been desperately poor is a curse you never get over. Public TV is like a person who has been hungry. It can't get beyond step one. . . the talk show. As an art form, the talk show can claim a level of distinction comparable the productions of a front stoop *yenta*. With the talk show, technology has added a spurious *cachet* to gossip.

I confess to have been present for the ratification of the talk show. Long ago, in the 1950s, CBS Public Affairs filled CBS's unsold time with experimentation. Then the recession of 1958 hit.

From a production standpoint, all of us at CBS Public Affairs thought that "Eric Sevareid Speaks to The Shankaracharya of Puri" was a *reductio ad absurdum* of television as an audiovisual, theatrical phenomenon. The show was a quickie-cheapie talking-heads filler, the result of a declaration of financial emergency. We pulled it together in minutes. I was Assistant to the Producer. The sage-like Shankaracharya came into an empty studio, we sat him down, and Sevareid questioned him. Three cameras, two chairs, some curtains, some lights. CBS didn't even pay the Shankaracharya's cab fare to the studio. It was as cheap as you could get at CBS.

In Monday's *New York Times*, the angel choirs sang. TV critic Jack Gould gave our no-budget quickie a rave review. A praiseful review from *The New York Times* was all it took to establish this form as a genre acceptable outside a local TV station. Suddenly, I realized the business I was in. A good review in the *Times* was all a congressman needed or a licensee could ask for! This show turned the tide. It showed the way to the networks and later to educational and public broadcasting. It proved that the people who make the important decisions either don't watch the shows or can't judge them. It proved that people in power will let journalists make their esthetic decisions for them. It showed, too, how little money and effort a broadcasting company needed to expend to gain critical praise . . . a lesson television's financial opportunists were quick to learn.

How could a mere newspaper critic contribute to a limitation on television? Because a lot of journalists simply don't read visual images. Left-hemisphere dominant, they probably can't. Their talent lies in another direction. Some journalists whose brains don't read images even get to be TV critics. It's a job on a paper or magazine, sometimes it's a promotion . . . and a reporter doesn't turn down a promotion. Being TV critic isn't a job people seek or stay with. It's a dreary life, because you spend your life watching garbage. All your colleagues know it. Your *mother* knows it. It's a job sensible people don't want. For an editor, the Russell Bakers and Scott Restons are too rare, too valuable to waste on TV, so the standards of selection for reviewers of TV aren't very high. Look at it from the publisher's standpoint. Where is there for an image-oriented critic to go on a newspaper? We at CBS discovered that *The New York Times'* critic only *listened* to its public service cheapie show. He loved what he *heard*. The Shankaracharya was a wise, well-spoken man, so the review in the *Times* was laudatory. Nobody important to CBS watched, of course. Busy people "don't watch that stuff". They learn what CBS does from the program titles on the reports they read, and from the papers. CBS learned from Gould's review in *The New York Times* that radio on TV is okay with *The New York Times*, and *ipso facto* with Washington. CBS profited from their learning.

A recession was on. Quickly, CBS fired the theater people on the Public Affairs production staff, the innovators, the people with the funny hair who wore Space Shoes. CBS replaced them with people in suits, broker/schedulers they dignified with the title "producers". (I was so lowly and cheap they let me stay. I also had some suits, left over from college.) Since Jack Gould liked talk shows, and since the only knowledge most people in Washington (they renew the licenses, remember?) had of television was what they read in *The New York Times*, CBS could fulfill its public service obligation by radio with cameras. Cheap, cheap. I'm sure CBS's treasurer loved it. As long as Gould was at the *Times*, CBS could do talk on TV and call it "Public Affairs".

"New" TV formats followed apace on Jack Gould's rave review of a money-saving talk show. A young NBC attorney was appointed Vice President of Public Affairs for CBS. For some years he invented attorney-like television programs for America to listen to. New formats proliferated: (1) A Famous (staff, on salary) Correspondent and an Important Person (who would accept a mere honorarium). "At the Source", this was called. Then, something New and Different! (2) *Two* staff correspondents, not so famous, and a *famous* person who would accept a mere honorarium. How about "Joint Appearance" for a title? Then (3) Two staff correspondents and *two* guests (two honoraria), and presto! Another series with another title. There were more . . . all the permutations of numbers of staff correspondents and guests, all picture-radio, all with different titles, all purporting to be something different than what they really were . . . cheap. This talk genre reached its zenith at CBS with Howard K. Smith, then the Gibraltar of staff correspondents, and (a sign that the economy was picking up) . . . on camera at the same time, *five* persons known for writing well. It was called "The Great Challenge", with the finale of Beethoven's *Eroica* as theme music (chosen and edited by me). "The Great Challenge" final show from Paris' *Union Interalliée*

sported a black-tie audience, a marble stairway and the Garde Republicain. Like a chambermaid in mink (although it did fool some), from a television production standpoint "The Great Challenge" was radio with pictures. Good for the balance sheet. Satisfying, even gratifying to Washington and the stockholders. An unimaginative use of the television medium.

In 1959, I made a daily trek to my desk sandwiched in at the CBS Public Affairs offices at 545 Madison Avenue. There, I researched the subjects of the weekly "live remote" talk shows that were the latest wave of cost-cutting public affairs television. Every week we had a new subject, a new crisis to present. Every week I had a new subject to learn. Every week we brought in a new "expert" or "guest".

After a time, I found that my Bibles were the New York and Washington telephone directories. Armed with the crisis-of-the-week, I looked under "American", or "National". There was bound to be an organization in New York or Washington dedicated to the furtherance of the goals of practitioners of any subject our mission might call upon us to deal with. During the week I'd phone these associations to find America's most renowned experts on whatever-it-was. We'd bring them to New York and "put them on". Then as now, thinking people had little access to viewers. Nobody I invited ever said "no" to me, except the then master of jurisprudence, nonagenarian Judge Learned Hand, who said, "I'm just too old."

Washington was a sleepy southern town, at the time, with only one good French restaurant. The pace was slow, agrarian, and friendly. The American Association for X was just building its immaculate, pleasant, neat, reserved but substantial new headquarters somewhere near Dupont Circle. Over the years I found myself going to those buildings more and more, talking to the polished people with doctorates. They always had material to share with such as me. They had all learned that if they were to have influence in their country, they had to conduct studies, publish reports, draft legislation, take people to lunch, have a presence in Washington, talk to people like me. . . that is, to lobby. They found they had to compete with others doing the same. Their work became Washington's industry.

When the Ford Foundation came up with some money for an alternative television service, then News Vice President Fred Friendly had just closed down the modestly inno-vative CBS Public Affairs in favor of "live" news "actualities", multi-camera remote produc-tions that allowed viewers to have immediate television experiences *as they happened*. "Actualities" programming promised the holy intensity of the immediate present, defining significant television experience as viewers' simultaneous witnessing of real events through the magic of TV. I remember witnessing one of these: the actual Pope as his actual car passed an actual Chevron station in an actual raunchy district on the way from an air-port to Somewhere Important. (Defining history as the immediate present, of course, was congenial to journalists at a network supported by impulse buyers.)

Shortly after commercial television networks discovered cost-saving talking heads, the Ford Foundation founded National Educational Television, and moved its headquar-ters from Ann Arbor to New York. Back at the networks, an economic upturn in the early 1960s enabled the networks to sell the "sustaining" time they had devoted to public affairs talk shows. There was no more unsold time to put experimental shows in.

Educational TV hired the displaced producers of the commercial network talk shows as decisionmakers. Why? They were "network". They were out of work. They were cheap. The residue of the talent genocide that was CBS's response to the recession of 1958, these network second stringers brought with them virtues to excite ETV's accountants. Their talk show skills freed educational television from being troubled by advocates for costly innovation. The predictable happened. Educational TV emerged as talk shows. As time passed, when any money did come to educational television, it came to the people who only knew how to talk, to verbal people, people with no "eye", non-visual people without knowledge of or training in theater, the art form of which television is an arm. The new producers of educational TV were able to spend more money on the only thing they knew how to do: radio on TV.

Their legacy is with us today. The intellectual star of public television for two dec-ades was Bill Moyers. His cheap talk show got budget increases, more shows, and better time slots, and expanded by going to locations where Moyers delivered lectures. Why? He had ideas. He cared. He was a preacher. He pushed away the veil of common duplicity just a little bit. Some of his ideas even defied positions held by some members of Congress, the funder of public TV. Although Moyers' shows were low on production values, they were intelligent talk shows. In the desert of public TV, Moyers cultivated an oasis.

There's only so much you can do with even intelligent televised radio by pouring money into it. Other talk series are initially attractive to business managers simply because of their minimal production cost, as *Wall Street Week* or *The Lehrer News Hour* once were. With continued audience acceptance and prosperity, they get slicker, glitzier, more pompous, even lavish. A gardening show initially justified for production on the grounds of economy celebrated its prosperity by travels all over the world. The genre remains radio programs.

Thousands of public television professionals were hired to do these cheap shows, shows like the studio music performance show *Austin City Limits*, shows requiring minimal production facilities, skills or knowledge. The people who made these cheap shows have now moved into positions of prominence. Wearing expensive suits, the same people go about securing ever increased funding for the kinds of program ideas they know, the ones that were only done in the first place because there wasn't enough money to fill the time with anything better. This winnowing process took years to accomplish. In that time, of course, all the people who could have done better work disappeared into Hollywood or Madison Avenue or some other stressful place where (however perverted) the goal is money and a challenge to imagination.

The legacy of public TV's poverty has been two generations of formulaic managers. They are now preened, polished, ossified and decently paid — "a bloated and engorged bureaucracy", in the words of Frederick Wiseman.[147] That inbred tribe, after over twenty years, has given birth to a notable cultural achievement, "politically correct" programming. (As described by *Newsweek*, "PC is, strictly speaking, a totalitarian philosophy[148]). Alas and alack!

And what about the purpose of it all, the programs? Could commercial television have prayed for public television to become the fatuous thing it has? When commercial TV first unloaded those outdated cameras, maybe this was what they had in mind!

Some of public television's parochialism can be traced to its fealty to the Congress as funding source.[149] Aside from the source of funds being the entity perhaps best known for the filibuster, you may have noticed that there's almost never a program and certainly never a series originated by our state TV about a subject outside the continental limits . . . where there are no voters. There are three allowable exceptions to jingoism: (1) One of "our" wars, (2) The congressionally subsidized American economic interests who fund the PACs and pay the lobbyists, or (3) The homeland of a substantial American voting bloc. With the exception of some soothing imported culture-as-ornament, shows designed to enhance a funder's image (Mobil, Exxon, Martin-Marietta, Archer Daniels Midland) programs on subjects on which our political system takes no position have no place in the production schedule of American public television.

The consequences of this setup are an inhibition of the very purpose of an alternative to commercial television. Originality, subtlety, or intellectual depth have never been the strong suit of politicians in any culture, or of the journalists who make a living by cranking out exciting descriptions of their doings. Since politicians and journalists are key controlling groups in public television, those aspects of its potential that do not reflect the priorities of these two groups go unattended. These are some of the reasons we in the United States have made no serious efforts to reach, let alone transcend, the program quality of Kenneth Clark's *Civilisation*, or James Burke's essays, two of the most elegant and inventive uses of nonfiction television ever.

That's not to say that there haven't been some worthy efforts. In late 1991, a onetime WNET/BBC Weinstock/Jackson/Krulwich try at the essay form was sometimes wry, sometimes amused, always semi-detached. It served no special interest. It provided a gentle and ironic comment on pop culture for the pleasure of the intelligent viewer. Its piece on Cowboy Poetry was superlative . . . witty, kind, insightful, it added a dimension to a hackneyed subject. The series, called *EDGE*, died within months, never even given a chance to build an audience. It had wit, intelligence, and charm. Why did it die? *EDGE* served no funder interest. Public television, and all of us, then lost Krulwich to CBS (who didn't know what to do with him either), then to ABC's *Evening News* where Peter Jennings regarded him with amused interest, as one would a performing billy goat. Krulwich, now doing essays for Ted Koppel, may have found a place that gives some allowance to his wit and insight. ABC uses him as a court jester . . . a source of damaging truths cloaked in wit. Krulwich is a stellar talent.

In 1994, we had an occasion for public television's funders to show their muscle. San Francisco's public station, with major funding from England, produced a TV version of an acclaimed, 20 year old novel, Armistad Maupin's *Tales of the City*. The novel was a composite of people in what would once have been called a "Bohemian" environment in San Francisco. The story depicted a very traditional American reality of young people who have gravitated to a metropolis in a fumbling search for a society that relates to their own sensed inner truths. Production values approached those of commercial TV. The people were fairly conventional characters, mostly young people with jobs. One of the characters insulted her employer and was fired. The identity search of more than one character involved some unconventional sexual experimentation. Some of the words used were the argot any soldier hears hundreds of times a day. A brilliant performance by Olivia Dukakis capped very able work by the rest of the cast. Here was a story of people who were searching for themselves . . . they weren't doing what they were told.

The day after broadcast, a giant sucking sound came from Washington. It was the sound of funding drying up. Certain members of Congress didn't like the show. Shame! Didn't public TV know that they should make sure the messages they were promulgating were Congress' messages? Public TV had gotten uppity. They're supposed to know that it's their job to put on shows congressmen like. That's the name of the game.

The word came down . . . The series wouldn't be finished. The man who pays the piper called the tune. Public TV presumably got the message. Cable produced and aired the sequel.

We can all figure out from what we see on our home screens that public television stations produce precious little local programming. Because we must search, we see that the small quantity of high quality original American work that they do produce is a tiny fraction of the quality and diversity of commercial television. Why can't public television produce large quantities of diverse and inventive programs? Where is that desperately needed inspiration to the public, that opportunity for the development of artists of the television genre for America? As a basis for television in the interest of the public (in any of their aspects save that of electorate), the overall performance of US TV has been, in a word, poor. Our *system* of public television *guarantees* pap. The *system* of petition by the dreamer servant for largesse from the pragmatic master has deprived the medium and the public of the leaven to human discourse that are dissent, innovation and imagination. The *system* has deprived public TV of First Amendment rights. That, you may agree, is a serious flaw.

Chapter 19
WHO MAKES THE RULES, ANYWAY?

The public television viewer's "interest" is guarded by boards of trustees or overseers, who set public TV policy on the national and on the local level. Their decisions establish the policies according to which the programs we see are made. Their function is causative. The names of trustees of national and local public television are seldom mentioned, except in the final pages of an annual report. Who are these trustees, anyway? "Distinguished persons", we all assume that. But who? If they make the policy whose results we see every time we turn on the public channel, shouldn't their names be household words?

Are they the ones you see on the auctions? No. On the auctions and fundraisers you see station personnel, line officers, not staff officers. The guy who signs the station on, the one mugging before the cameras at the auction, and the Directors and Managers who do crossovers and sell tables, their duty is to execute the policy of their boards, not their own. The ones you see are the "front men", the marionettes. Somebody else pulls the strings. Ever wonder who?

Policymaking in public television is of critical importance. We as a country have a history of government agencies' use of public entertainment to shape culture. The story of how two decades of Hollywood films about courtship has affected the baby boom generation is yet to be measured.

The extent of intervention by the Office of War Information in the content of Hollywood films during World War II is only now being revealed. After World War II, Douglas MacArthur's occupation government of Japan was sensitive to the power of mass culture to shape attitudes convenient to the occupying power. In the field of mass entertainment, a conscious decision was made to promote "The Three S's: Screen, Sex and Sports" as devices to defuse Japanese public resentment. Just as the Shoguns had encouraged the aristocracy they replaced to attend Kabuki drama, so the US occupiers of Japan encouraged the public diversions of movies and sport[150] as a control device. Can we assume that our own government is less knowledgeable about public manipulation than one of their occupying forces? If not, we should look at the policymakers of public TV.

The boards interface between the organization and the community, so their role is important. Board policymaking is by definition manipulative and controlling. The public should know about that. The Corporation for Public Broadcasting has a board, appointed by the President of the United States. The Public Broadcasting Service has a board, every station has a board, etc.

Who are they? Substantial citizens, of course. Support in case of economic catastrophe is guaranteed by the presence of community "leaders" on the board. These are mainly well-to-do people dedicated to the public interest, as they define it, plus, these days, a minority person or two (hopefully also prosperous; if not, then at least a "winner", that is, a person on the way up, who merits media coverage). Very occasionally, you'll see a journalist or a lawyer, that is, a clever person who can be counted on to guarantee the interests of other board members.

Axiomatically, any Establishment person has a vested interest in maintaining the conditions that led to his or her preeminence. It only follows that part of the public interest for these people is to see that people unlike themselves don't get too far out of line. Public order is, after all an important consideration of leadership. Frequently trustees are open-minded and intelligent people, but they can be counted on to scuttle any suggestion of change that might in their estimation adversely affect their interest as they define it. That's only natural, isn't it? It's a hard world. Has a man who made his own money ever willingly foregone a seat on the Concorde? We should look to see what trustees' interests are, because its their interests as they see them that dictate the policies they set for the broadcasting we will all turn on in our living rooms.

It's the trustees who decide how deep, how broad, how complex, how wide-ranging the programs you see will be. So, let's look at who public television's policymakers, its trustees, its cultural mandarins are. Of the forty members of the boards of the two parent organizations, the Corporation for Public Broadcasting and the Public Broadcasting Service, in 1992 you could find the following: eight members representing some aspect of broadcast management, seven from business and finance, six journalists, four lawyers, five from advertising and public relations, four who are politically connected, two educators, an engineer, a theologian, a surgeon and a social service worker. These appointments give credence to the view stated in the *Economist*, that "politicians are more likely to regard intellectuals as a liability than an asset."[151]

On the local level, most trustees are members of the corporate priesthood, businessmen and lawyers. As you might expect, these people have some attributes in common that color their interpretation of human life. They are people whose lives are built atop a working circumstance structured as a feudal power relationship in which the primary goal is profit, the secondary goal a relationship to a market. Their cultural habit restricts creativity to the advertising and design departments. Tribal mores define creativity outside the locus of sales as deviant. Okay? Maybe. Do the interests of these policymakers seem a lot like those of the policymakers of commercial TV? Well, yes. Maybe an education administrator will be thrown in to this power elite majority as a public TV trustee, for image. The "image" of the education administrator as having some vague familiarity with wisdom is as likely as not to belie the reality, since "educators" who have institutional control today are more than likely to be fundraisers for their institutions, hustlers, not educators in the classical sense of scholars whose primary interest is learning. If you want to see an institution with a decisionmaking entity stacked in favor of the group at present holding the most power in our society, that is, the people whose interests are to see the society as an economy where people's proper primary dedication is to getting and spending, you may want to look at the life-roles of the last decade of policymakers of public television.

The effect of trusteeships on public television has been a brake on innovation, progress and the development of a nascent art form. As expressed in day-to-day decisionmaking from top to bottom, throughout the staffing and decisionmaking of public television, the *Weltanschauung* of the tradesman is a precondition of the policymaking process of the boards that control local public television in the United States.

What kind of person do these boards select to implement policy, to manage public television? What kind of people do they hire? People they can count on. A favorite candidate is one who has experience in public relations. The reasoning behind this preference is illuminating. A good flak is like a good infantry second lieutenant. He does what he's told and only what he's told. Charming and companionable, he throws himself into what he does with a wholeheartedness bordering on obsession. A board of trustees who prefer not to endure the discomfiture of an executive officer with critical imagination does well to give the reins of power to a public relations person. If they want an unquestioning servant, the public relations person's job profile provides the necessary guarantees. But if the trustees expect originality, imagination, innovation, probity or a devotion to truth, they would do as well to expect these attributes of a marionette. And the outcomes are predictable.

Public television's "Cultural" programs seem to be afflicted by patterns of thought peculiar to public relations and publicity. Advertising and book jacket copy have established the literary standard. Euphemism married to sales promotion has produced a minor literary form known as "blurb". This is the language of public TV scriptwriters. The narratives of cultural programs that public TV shows are scripted not as expositions but as press releases. Poor Martin Buchspan and Peter Allen flutter about the performing arts on public television breathlessly spouting press-agent hyperbole about the performers, in a language that is less literature or communication than advertising copy. In this approach, Buchspan and Allen yield the prize to "Bubbles" Beverly Sills. Is blurb what the public needs if it is to recognize art?

What the public gets on public TV is the spa approach . . . to be salved, comforted, massaged, and soothed. Heaven forbid that viewers should be aided toward a confrontation with the transcendental rigor of that sublime conjunction of sensibility, reason, perception, memory and emotion essential to the perception of a work of art. The people who make the decisions that encourage this form of manipulation aren't stupid, but they are conveniently silent. They will continue unless the public asks why they do this. Are works of art so offensive that they must be bathed in treacle? Whose interest is served by this condescension? That is the question; and public television managements nationwide should be held accountable for the answer.

A reason may be simply that executive incomprehension leads to ritualized obeisance. Art has always been difficult for businessmen to understand. Its perception requires intuition, compassion, breadth of understanding, humility, a willingness to learn, an exploratory linking of thought and emotion, the ability to perceive image as language. Not many are able or willing to take this route to understanding the world. Some components of science are easier for accountants and businessmen to understand, like the technology that is called science, in common discourse . . . you just tot up the numbers and let them say what they say. Science is descriptive and predictive. It deals with commonalities. Art is trouble. It deals with uniquenesses. Art has only one number, the number one. It's much harder to deal with — like God. It is much easier for practical men to deal with art as craft, as process, as a skill divorced from any subject. So defined, art becomes shared, a commonality. It becomes understandable, subject to rationalization, regulation, codification, legislation, bureaucratization, and extinction.

Both art and science are congenial, even important, to the theory and practice of democracy. The will of the people is the commonality of democracy. Commonality is tabulated by survey and averages. The uniqueness of the individual is closer to art. It defies bureaucratic record keeping. Keeping track of the unique is difficult, inconvenient, and perhaps impossible. Science is "easier" than art. A consequence is that government by NBC/Wall St. Journal survey renders the very concept of uniqueness, of art, of individuality, as aberrant. Art is the friend of uniqueness, of individualism, of democracy as opportunity. "Every work of art . . . is a challenge to the consensus", says playwright and historian Charles L. Mee, Jr.[52] Part of the American heritage, our art is part of our greatness as well. Legislators may not understand it, but they need it. Many trustees of public television, like the members of Congress whose decisions they implement, are successful members of a dominant culture ignorant of the essential nature or long-range importance of the art form whose policies they set.

An examination of the membership of the boards of trustees in national and local public television shows that public television policy is controlled by interests whose procedures and daily assumptions may be related more closely to commerce than to democracy. Some may say that the corporate priesthood, bankers, lawyers, industrialists, businessmen and their apologists *have a right* to dominate noncommercial television in the United States. Some would also say that not only is it a redundancy, since they already dominate commercial television, but it is still to some degree a questionable assumption that commercial interests converge at all points with the interest of the public. It is of the essence of reason as well as a hallmark of democracy that questioning of questionable assumptions must be allowed.

Our economic system is new to human history, and its brief tenure alone should give pause to those who would give it universal and eternal validity. Britain's Member of Parliament Anthony Wedgewood Benn, neither a stupid nor an unreflective man, declared doubts never heard on this side of the water, when interviewed for the *MacNeil/Lehrer Newshour* in 1991, after the collapse of the USSR.

> I think . . . democracy . . . will turn its mind to the defeat of capitalism, and
> I think capitalism is a very undemocratic system, because capitalism gives
> you power according to your wealth, whereas democracy gives you power
> according to your existence, so that I've always seen the real conflict in
> the world as between capitalism and democracy.[153]

If there is to be an examination of the appropriateness of decisionmaking in public television residing in the hands of persons whose primary interest is economic expansionism, we could not look to Presidents Reagan or the Bushes or Clinton for leadership. The code word "freedom", used by these people in conjunction with "democracy", indicates by the separation of the two that "freedom" is not to be interpreted as political, but economic.

Understandably, any government regulation represents a cost. Every cost to a corporation means a reduction in profitability. Any reduction in profitability means a reduction in dividends or an increase in debt. These reductions reduce corporate competitiveness. Since economic expansion is a prerequisite of corporate survival today, it can be understood that the "party of business" calls for less government, less regulation.

But beyond the freedom from regulation that the "free enterprise" party meeting "huzzahs" indicate, when the word "freedom" is orated, the energy of its reception might lead one to believe that to many followers, "freedom" has something to do also with their dreams for "less government" as a spur to the augmentation of their own power through American corporate world hegemony (now known as "globalization"). A president's use of it gives away a bias that conjoins "freedom" and economics as in the emotionally charged euphemism of campaign oratory, "free enterprise". A prejudice favoring the centrality of economics to America's cultural destiny was not out of keeping in President Bush I, who chose to be an "Econ" major at Yale, President Bush II, who earned a Master's from Harvard's Graduate School of Business Administration, or in President Clinton, whose law degree places him professionally as a committed corporate servant.

If you look at the makeup of the decisionmaking bodies in public television, you find a distinct bias in favor of a definition of man and society in economic terms, an economic determinist — a Hegelian/Marxist causative bias, if you will. In a lonely recognition of the historic primacy of values other than economic, the Carnegie Commission in 1979 recommended that public broadcasting "include as decisionmakers the outstanding members of the creative community itself." The current board membership of the two leadership agencies of public television show that the Carnegie Commission's recommendation has been disregarded. "We are the first people in history who condescend to art", said Agnes De Mille. The congressional directive to appoint people from "the arts including radio and television" appears to have been interpreted as meaning that the inclusion of administrators from prominent public television stations sufficed as representation from the arts. To the best of my knowledge, it remains for the future to declare budgeting or fundraising an art!

Why this state of affairs? Legislation. The Federal Communications Commission "has authority to prescribe the qualifications of station operators." The people prescribed to control the stations are people in whom the members of the FCC, who are Washington lawyers, can have confidence. People like themselves. People they can understand at hearings.

The television we watch today is the descendent of a literature that has been immensely important in the formation of what we call civilization . . . a literature that includes theater, dance, poetry, the novel, opera, easel painting, philosophy, and nonfiction genres. For those who dare to go back to sources whose validity is proven by experience other than America's since our last president, Aristotle's *Poetics* gives insight into television's being. Television has the earmarks of an art form as defined there by that long-dead Greek. It would seem only logical, "conservative", that the direction taken by this form of artistic communication would be substantially influenced by people experienced in creative fields who had at least read Aristotle.[154] Instead, public television programs give the appearance of being created by technocrats, business and finance people, their journalists, fundraisers and the beauticians whose jobs are to make them look good. As a culture we have long been accused of having an anti-intellectual, and anti-artistic, bias. The composition of the governing boards from top to bottom of public TV, confirms this assertion. If an outsider needed to confirm the penetration of corporate attitudes into the fabric of American life, they need only look at the structure of our state TV. The nearest to a culture czar public TV has been able or interested enough to allow is Jac Venza, an articulate and charming one-time window dresser, now major-market station director of Cultural and Arts Programs, whose "culture" programs are nowadays not original creations but almost exclusively simple "coverage" of events produced *outside* of television.

An optimistic assessment is that the public television genre's present pedestrian state is the consequence of shortsighted decisions in the selection of people to run it. A pessimistic one is that it is intentional. Somewhere in between, it may just be that worthier people don't think the game is worth the candle. The presumptions of board members who do the selecting, the structure-dominated industrialists, businessmen, and their bankers and lawyers, theirs are the unstated preconditions of rules to be followed by the managers and marketers they select to oversee the development of this alternative art form. These selectees of these boards, these obedient managers, marketers, promoters and journalists, are the real culture czars. On a day-to-day basis, they have the decisionmaking power over the kinds of television materials that will be presented to people's minds and sensibilities. It is *their* grasp of human history, *their* vision of the future that informs their daily decisions. In practice, it is *their* knowledge of history, *their* vision of the future that is communicated to the television audience. *They* execute the cultural pap, *they* eschew programs and ideas feared to be "controversial", *they* give the public the diet of fatuous establishment cant that is the material of the public television schedule. They do as they're told.

It may or may not be true that in the final decades of the twentieth century Americans with imagination found their most significant outlets in the fields of marketing, franchising, leveraged buyouts, corporate raiding, insider trading, savings and loan profiteering, real estate speculation, celebrity fashion design and pop entertainment. If so, the decades just past represent an historic first. In our national preoccupation with the diversions of the moment, both we and the people who spend our money may simply have misasessed both the need and the remedy for public television.

It is our thesis here that it is not in the field of corporate enterprise that the kind of imagination public television needs is to be found. To learn where it should be found, we need only look, conservatively, to historic precedent. Before the industrial revolution America looked to its creative people in the arts for leadership, even in government. Men of learning, Jefferson, the Emersons and the Lowells guided our leaders. Pursuit of learning toward wisdom once ruled in our culture: onetime Harvard President Lowell, when away from his office, was described by his secretary thus: "The President is in Washington, seeing Mr. Taft." Today the very Congress of the United States is awed by the insight of little Czechoslovakia in imitating American history and choosing an intellectual for its president. Perhaps we should note, similarly, that the former USSR, in their liberalizing efforts toward *perestroika*, appointed Nikolai Gubenko (a film and stage director/actor), as Minister of Culture. The first President Petrossian of Armenia was a noted scholar. France never hesitated to give high government office to novelist and critic André Malraux. Our national goal, if I read the last few presidents' public statements correctly, appears to be the generation of more money for us and more detritus for the planet through more complex technology. The nearest we get to a minister of culture in the United States is presidents' wives and appointments secretaries! Have populism and consumerism committed us to denial of excellence? Must another force prevail if the United States isn't to become a Stone Age society with microchips?

After thirty years, no significant body of creative public television production expertise has been developed. Where are the playwrights working in every region, with every station? Where are the directors bringing us interesting work from Cleveland or Montgomery? Where are the actors? Where are the resident companies in our major cities?

Where are the creative animators using computers? Where are the producers generating formats any different from those the commercial networks developed decades ago? WHY HAS THERE BEEN NO SIGNIFICANT BODY OF INNOVATIVE WORK PRODUCED BY AMERICAN PUBLIC TELEVISION IN THE LAST THIRTY YEARS? SHAME!

If our public TV spends a billion dollars a year and comes up with only a raft of English recuts, imitations of pre-World War II McGraw Hill-style illustrated lectures, civics courses and a few talk shows, we're doing something stupid — even by accounting standards. Maybe it's time to wonder why creative people in America do not have a significant voice in the development of what is essentially an art form, an auditory and visual language of communication?

A common complaint is that "creative people can't manage". People characterized primarily by insight and imagination could hardly do worse than the technocrats have done. Of course, by looking at public TV you couldn't be blamed for believing that, aside from Bill Moyers, there weren't any clever people in America. From what you see on TV, one can only wonder if America has any distinguished playwrights, critics, novelists, filmmakers, philosophers, real educators who might have that rare thing called vision, so essential to the effectiveness of any person who presumes to be a "trustee" of the public weal. These are the people who should be informing policy decisions about alternative television!

Chapter 20

THE ROOT OF ALL TELEVISION, TOO

ost of the money spent on public TV comes from you. In the whole nationwide system during a year there's a grand total of about a billion dollars spent. Seems like it would make a lot of shows, doesn't it?

Where does the money come from? Around $400 million a year comes from federal, state and local governments (that's you). The lion's share earmarked specifically for programs, about $186 million a year, comes from you via the Feds. A little less than $250 million comes from subscribers (that's you, too). That's a total of $650 million from us through taxes and donations. Colleges, universities and foundations provide about another $130 million. Auctions gross $22 million for stations.

Businesses kick in $173 million. (Compare these amounts with the $790 million that one company, General Motors, spends on spot and network TV ads alone in a year, or with the average single TV network's $2.75 billion in commercial billings in 1987, and you'll get a clue as to how the amount spent for public TV compares with amounts spent for commercial TV.)

Where does the money go? The money allocated for public television doesn't all go for TV shows. How much does is a matter for speculation. The Corporation for Public Broadcasting confesses that they themselves keep no tally of the production budgets of the programs the stations produce, or the areas of program subject into which they fall. They themselves lack data as to how many programs are original and how many have been bought, how much is spent on news, how many of the programs implied to be original are mere "coverage" — piggy-backs of events utilizing the creative and organizational skills of people outside television. The Corporation for Public Broadcasting has been declared by the Congress to be not an agency or establishment of the United States Government, and so doesn't have to respond to questions based on the Freedom of Information Act if it doesn't want to. They do, however release selectively categorized totals of their expenditures. Some of it goes for TV shows. The rest goes for Other Important Activities, like raising money, studies and administration.

The federal money is mostly distributed by the Corporation for Public Broadcasting. All the federal money is supposed to go for programs. Part of it goes to pay for the production of auctions and fundraising, by a convenient stretching of the definition of what is a program. A big chunk of it goes for the programs you see on the air, through a mechanism called the National Program Service (successor to the Station Program Cooperative). The nationally distributed programs you have seen in recent years were selected for production by the structure of the Station Program Cooperative. This was a clever system whereby the 202 local stations pooled their ideas for programs and the bucks available to get programs to broadcast. At first, it seemed a reasonable, democratic and very safe way for stations to get programs. Each station got a chunk of money from the Corporation for Public Broadcasting, bigger or smaller depending by and large on the size of the community the station served. Each voted on what programs it was willing to contribute to. Station managers and program directors (trained extensively in esthetics, theater, criticism, and the performing arts, or in management, public relations, fund-raising, marketing or self-promotion — you can guess the proportions) proposed new programs and voted.

They started out with every station wanting all the big-name, blockbuster shows they couldn't afford. Station managers want big-name, blockbuster shows because they believe it means sure-fire audience draws, higher ratings and recognition, q.e.d. "showcase" programs to draw audience for fundraising, a better job at more pay for them, and more money from the government, the funders, subscribers, etc. later on. But reality intrudes. Simple calculation demonstrated that there's a lot of airtime to fill, and not enough money for all "biggies". When Round Two came, the buyers decided that if they couldn't get the "biggies", they might as well lower their sights to about maybe one or two "biggies" and the rest cheapies to fill the time with stuff they could at least declare to be "NEW!"

Since there's a lot of time to fill in a year and not nearly enough money, the economics of the situation dictate that from among the "biggies", first they chose the cheapest "biggie" with the biggest drawing name, say, the Boston Pops, anything with Pavarotti, or the sure-winner musical variety show "gala". The Gala, you may have noticed, is a glitzy parade of warhorses and "personalities". That the Gala blithely compromises the very idea of music as a language expressing the deepest and most subtle emotions of mankind, transforming it instead into a parade of complacent celebrity, makes no difference. Once the few affordable "biggies" have been chosen, with one eye fixed on the next year's congressional budget authorization and their own fundraisers, those agents of the common weal look next to cornball nostalgia, publicity and political correctness for your "fine" public television schedule.

Our government television has lubricated avenues of influence to you from Washington. People with high Washington connections are more likely to have an opportunity to host programs than you or I. Former State Department spokesperson Hodding Carter, Jr. and former Surgeon General C. Everett Koop joined former presidential press secretary Bill Moyers in access to prime time. Former Reagan and Bush speechwriter Peggy Noonan pitched *Peggy Noonan on Values* to an interested WNET New York (*Variety*, May 3, 1993).

Former Education Secretary Bill Bennett's series *Adventures from the Book of Virtues,* on ethics for children, (the realization of a goal that I proposed unsuccessfully to NEH and that a relatively unknown Bennett endorsed in 1977) decorated the cover of a 1997 PBS Home Video flyer within weeks after a Republican majority was elected to Congress. Later came a PBS Home Video cover featuring an ecclesiastic known less for his theological probity than for his multiple White House guest appearances during the occupancies of a succession of Republican presidents. An early 1998 issue, prominently displayed on the first page the cover of a four-hour cassette featuring the beaming countenance of "Reagan". Could these choices possibly be read as public broadcasting's genuflection to a Republican dominated Congress?

In 1992, three series with the word "American" in their titles were funded from Washington. Seven "cheapies", *Austin City Limits, Evening at Pops, Frugal Gourmet, Great Performances, Mark Russell Comedy Specials, Mister Rogers' Neighborhood,* and *The Victory Garden,* were all funded. Washington continued to examine its navel with *Washington Week in Review* and the *Lehrer News Hour.* Stockbrokers and investors, apparently in need of financial support, continued to be encouraged by *Wall Street Week* at taxpayer's expense. The future of neo-Darwinism was assured by two nature series, and encouragement of the science and technology so necessary to US economic expansionism were sanctioned by *NOVA* and Smithsonian continuations. Lovers of kitsch could be happy that encouragement was given to those neglected arts, commercial music and commercial culture, not excluding "Baseball". Bidding rounds, in which program managers try to make their money, go farther continued. New program ideas were entertained, providing they were "timely" (news?), "compelling" (to whom? to the funders, of course), "accessible" (to whom? to the review panel) and reflect "the actual diversity (of bloodlines only, in practice) of the *American* (italics mine) population" (that's Political Correctness, there!). Drama, humor, comedy and satire dealing with "important issues" (as defined by the Congress, if the precedent of the last fifty years is any indicator) were said to be under study. Any option allowing for an educated, or insightful, or creative or accomplished filmmaker's essay of choice was nowhere to be found. You can see that nothing here questions the status quo. Opportunities for dissent or intellectual challenge either inside Congress or public television are not specifically blocked by the process. They are simply not acknowledged.

The ultimate destination of the penny-ante process of program selection by station and program manager "voting rounds" has been a disincentive for the stations that present original program ideas for production. Original stuff is more expensive and less likely to be picked up. It's both cheaper and safer to let somebody else hire the actors and the hall, do the rehearsals, and sell tickets, and then for public TV to come and "cover" it (or better yet, get a cut-rate used rental tape, preferably from England, that requires only a fanfare and a "presented by" tag) than it is to do all those things yourself. Since coverage of somebody else's play, somebody else's opera, somebody else's ballet, somebody else's symphony orchestra is a heck of a lot cheaper, it's more attractive to program managers with an eye only on their budgets. They just give it to their publicity people to promote as "A Presentation of. . . Us! . . .", as if it were something they had a hand in creating. ("Those fine programs", etc.)

What's *wrong* with public television's just going into a theater or opera house with cameras and shooting? Well, that's a lesson the film industry learned in about 1920. What's wrong is that it fails to explore the potential of the very medium that it uses. The limitations, opportunities and conventions of staging for an audience from a proscenium are a far different thing from the limitations, opportunities and conventions of staging for one take at a time by multiple, moveable viewer-surrogates on booms and cranes and then editing. To be effective, body movement, costuming, makeup, positioning, and delivery differ substantially for theater or television audiences. Even Kirk Browning's estimable real-time coverage of the Metropolitan Opera as presented "live" to 3500 people in the opera house has less impact as a television presentation than Zefferelli's films. Peter Gelb, Executive Producer of the TV version of Wagner's *Der Ring des Niebelungen*, declared that the challenge of the $5 million TV version of the $4 million stage production was "to shoot it for television without killing it".

Of course, doing it on the cheap is an acceptable option to people without imagination, taste, or sensibility. Letting somebody else do all the creating and then sending in a public TV crew to record the result is easier, quicker, cheaper and worse . . . worse because it encourages procedures that deprive the television audience of both present and future *television* artistry as appropriate to the special character of the *television* medium. Years of the winnowing process have led to the current state of affairs, where the Brits do the creating, or the Metropolitan Opera does the creating or Hollywood does the creating and public TV gets "spinoff", at best recording as well as they can get under the circumstances from whatever somebody else sees fit to do or, at worst, merely brokering it.

A dilemma arises when a choice must be made between an institution's avowed mission and institutional survival. Retrenchment was once considered a viable option. But times have changed. Institutions like public television, presumably dedicated to developing alternative materials for wide-scale broadcasting, decided to elect opportunism over principle. That choice has been exploited by their funders. The stations that knuckle-under get the money. Over time, the public TV stations have learned that they can continue getting both funding and public support while staffing themselves with brokers, salesmen, schedulers and technicians, and cloaking themselves in the mantle of "impresario". They've let the creative people go, and now nobody left at the station knows how to make an original anymore.

What I've just described is part of the process whereby innovation, inventiveness and creativity have come to achieve their present invisibility in public TV programming. To others, in other countries, our crude use of the remarkable technology of television demonstrates a fundamental American insensitivity. **Where is the evidence to prove them wrong?**

Chapter 21

HOW PROGRAMS REALLY
GET PRODUCED

T he number and range of potential television programs is as broad as human imagination. In practice, however, the forms that today's programs take are rigidly disciplined. Situation comedy, action/adventure, cartoons, professional athletics, parlor and other games, fictional drama and "talking heads" have settled in as the staples of television program format. When one considers the potential variability of dramatic performance, this seems a small variety indeed. Why are there only these?

Which programs do get produced? The programs viewers want? The programs producers want? Of course *not*. Don't be ridiculous. Of the millions of possible TV shows, only a selected few make it through the process. This holds for both commercial and public television. The nature of the process determines the character of the programs produced. As we noted earlier, in commercial TV, it's the shows that sell the products that stay on the air.

But what about noncommercial TV? The programs public TV produces are what can get through the constraints, prohibitions, and allowances of all those hard working people spending that billion dollars a year who have dedicated their lives to bringing you the finest kind of programs *they* know. The *they* includes a bunch of agencies, all of which are dedicated, (once their own expansion has been taken care of), to the goal of getting what they consider to be the "best" programs to you. There's the Corporation for Public Broadcasting with their oversight role and the studies they do, and The Public Broadcasting Service that keeps all the 202 (down from 385) independent stations all over the country together somehow. Then there's The Development Exchange, Inc. ("Development", in case you don't know, is a euphemism for raising money). There's The National Association of

Public Television Stations, The National Federation of Community Broadcasters, PBS Enterprises (trying to make a buck out of "spinoff"). Then there's National Public Radio (for a time, it was the best part of the system, allowed to pursue excellence because radio was not seen as an avenue to the Big Time[155] and it costs almost nothing. Even now, Pacifica Radio, funded in part by CPB, stands as perhaps the only media institution that regularly criticizes American economic interests). And there's the Public Radio Program Directors Association, the Radio Research Consortium, and the Station Resource Group. (Public radio addresses with intelligence a broader definition of government than has been allowed to public television programs. Although manifestly an agency of the state, it deals with governments and issues affecting governments abroad, and with US state and local government issues, not just Washington. Sadly, with the infrequent use of Stamberg and the loss of Krulwich, irony has vanished. The diversity of public radio mirrors the diversity of congressional thinking).

There are the local TV stations with their staffs and managements. A total of over 10,800 people nationwide are working for you in public TV. Television programs that get through this great big system to finally make it to air are essentially those that succeed in reaching the people that the people in all these organizations are second-guessing. And who are the people being second-guessed? Generally speaking, they're the ones with money and any appearance of a mandate to give it to public TV. Jobs are involved, too. Astute programmers in public television direct their efforts toward next years' funding level. Proposals for next years' public television "offerings" act as bait for next year's funding. You can watch the programs you watch with more interest when you view them as allurements deliberately contrived to be dangled before congressional committees as inducements for greater amplitude in next year's public broadcasting appropriations.

It's only fair to note that there have been acts of heroism in public TV. WGBH's president Ives once opted for principle over gain, drawing the line between himself and an agent of the very President of the United States (the same one Buchanan mentioned earlier), declaring that his station would not allow overt presidential control of his funding. With the press bawling, David Ives was against the wall, publicly. He adopted a potentially costly position. The president of a feeble public TV station was, of course, no match for a US President bent on self-aggrandizement. The result of the St. George and the Dragon playlet was that the dragon puffed off on other missions. Aside from a life-or-death instance such as this one, and aside from the handful of stations that prefer to be poor-but-honest, it is tacit policy for public TV never to actively discourage a major potential funding source.

Whose programs do you see on public TV? You see the proposed programs that make it through the selection and review process. "Juries", "boards", carefully selected judges identify programs. The expressed criteria of selection are limited by the unexpressed . . . that is, the assumptions of the real target audience . . . the funders. The programs you see on public TV are those programs that public TV managements sense will appeal to their major sources of financial support. These are people known as "the state" and those they are beholden to, today known as the corporate plutocracy. And what are their special attributes? These are most likely to be people whose communicative style is verbal, who have been trained in the law, who see the world the way politicians do, who have the attitudes, the goals, the principles that bring success at this moment in time to people who run for public office, and their designees, generally people who have similar backgrounds, attitudes and thought patterns.

Once production funds are awarded, funder review points generally include outline review, script review, rough and fine cut edit review. A committee meets to screen and to make sure that the message as they understood it to be at proposal stage is in fact coming through. At "milestones", the "creative" production team is reminded who is boss. It makes sense, doesn't it? Funds are allocated and programs get produced that politicians trained in the law *guess* their PACs, lobbyist friends and constituents will view as not a waste of their money. So it's the programs that the *system* wants, not the programs that any of the individuals in the system want, that get produced. As in commercial TV, *nobody's to blame!* Everybody does what the structure dictates. Just as in commercial TV. The poor audience, the people for whom state television is supposed to be produced have to be glad for what they get. It is, weak as it is, in some ways better, more diverse, more intelligent than TV available through the more overtly commercial sources.

Who calls the shots? The people who made the rules, who established the structure and left the loopholes, call the shots. The structure of incentives built into the system is the map followed by its staffers. Nor can people in institutions presumably dedicated to public service be expected to hold themselves aloof from opportunism when it is the standard for their peers in other fields. Nowadays, if the law doesn't prohibit, and if it helps you get the better of the other guy, even in public TV, you do it. The rules don't prohibit it . . . it's the way all the rest of them are playing the game. Big promotion, big publicity, big fundraising, "development" and design budgets are the way to get ahead of the other guy. Does it matter that the gullible are being hoodwinked into supporting the propaganda platform of the state? Not really. Who thinks of that? Instead, devote your attentions to more current trends . . . why not a mail order boutique to sell promotional merchandise that includes "Compost Happens" and "*Carpe Diem*" (today's motto for the opportunist who went to school) T-shirts, like the Yankee tradesmen's in Boston?[156] Or a glitzy Newport Beach mall shop near Brooks Brothers, like KQED's? Or KPBS' beguiling grotto at San Diego's Horton Plaza. Or tapes of "The Doo Wop Box", Sinatra, or Barbara Bush reading her memoirs, available from Minnesota Public Radio.[157] Forget about creating unsponsored public service television programs! This is the post-modern era!

"Programs of high quality, diversity, creativity, excellence, and innovation", says paragraph 396 of the public law authorizing public television. Who defines these terms? This part of the law is set dressing, tinted steam, dreams, keynote addresses, nothing you can pin down as science. Nothing to stand in the way of an alert opportunist. Except that there are some simply civilized people with a vision of a desirable future who work within the public television structure. They function as subversives. They swim upstream. Their agenda is supposed to be amalgamated into the structure of public broadcasting, but in practice it is not. People dedicated to service — and our society does produce some — effectively function as "window dressing". These times are not their times.

The rest, the executive directors, the managers, the presidents, have their eyes on more practical ends. They do their best to "get ahead" while not breaking too many of the rules. They call it "the name of the game". In today's environment, TV stations (like individuals) see themselves as in a competition not unlike that of any joint-stock corporation. New business comes to the Big Names. For a public TV station, too, winning has become more important than achieving, image more important than reality. People in any organization find themselves in a job in a structure with certain parameters, with certain "do's" and "don'ts". If there's a job to get done, few in public television are up to the standards of commercial broadcasting's William S. Paley's insistence in the 1930s that CBS carry the New York Philharmonic, foregoing an opportunity for gain because of a sense of obligation to the audience (for which the writer, who was a child of parents struck into near penury by the economic collapse of 1929, has known a lifetime of gratitude). You may or may not be pleased to know that Sammy Glick is alive and well working, for you in public TV.

The categories into which the productions of American public television fall demonstrate some confusion in the minds of members of congressional appropriations committees. Our representatives seem to fail to recognize a possible distinction between the "public interest, convenience and necessity" that dominated the language of legislation from 1935 to 1996 and the promulgation of ideas that enhance the prestige, power and influence of people engaged in governance! There is no agency to police a Congress that sees itself as cynosure. Therefore, as things stand now, this job must fall to the Fourth Estate.

Chapter 22

THE SELF-INTEREST/PUBLIC INTEREST EQUATION

A contradiction of capitalism as society's tool is that the interest of the consumer is its *secondary* goal. Primarily, it serves its own monetary gain. The current "success" of capitalism in America has promulgated imitation. The governmental system has co-opted the structure of duality that is a structural essential of the corporate system. It has developed a "public" television service that secondarily serves the public interest but, in the major part of its being, serves the perceived interest of the two major branches of the federal government. The current runaway success of the double standard inherent in the operations of business and industry appears to have ratified it as a model for other institutions.

Public Television spends a billion dollars a year. It employs 10,816 people. The money and the people produce programs most of which (if critics could bring themselves to watch) would be called fatuous. A mountain has given birth to a mouse. Who could have allowed it to happen? It was the America Establishment, the old industrial leadership with lack of insight into the foibles of others. Their sins were of omission. The old Establishment thought it enough to establish high-minded, imprecise goals for the new art form. They anticipated continued cultural dominance by educated Episcopalians. They assumed that universal literacy and democracy would automatically produce an Arcadia. They reckoned without those enterprising folk now known euphemistically as "buccaneers", a whole new US power elite,[158] a new class, enriched by the nation's fear and hatred of the bogy Soviet Union, who would not hesitate to use their power to co-opt the mission of a public television that patently did not share *their* mission.

The rules for educational TV had been made by men of the old school who had learned some of what history as they knew it had taught and who tried to profit by it. They assumed, incorrectly, that others would know the same history, and profit by it. Remember that hoary leadership, the American Old Guard? Clear eyed, upright, disciplined, implacably principled, they are now fading into history. The pioneers of industrial society failed to recognize that although they may have learned the lessons of the past, consumerism would bring newer, richer, more powerful others for whom all that is past is irrelevant. For these new holders of the reins of power, "consumption is a useful social as well as personal occupation . . . righteous, in other words."[159]America's old leadership failed to pass on the remembered knowledge of millennia: that only wise men know what it is they don't know. The leadership failed themselves to remember that educators often fail to act in a learned way. They mistakenly assumed that a modest public service entity such as public television would neither attract nor be vulnerable to clever and ambitious men, men who pursue gain before principle. A public service mandate offering small opportunity or remuneration discouraged imaginative achievers and instead provided a domain for a cadre of pettifoggers, infighters and nest-featherers.

"Poor but honest" is no more honorable a status in public TV today than at any retail shop. Our education system and our corporate life now train people to use any system to their advantage. This "cowboy" ethic, this taking what there is for oneself, may not contribute to the greatest public benefit or even be to the takers' own advantage, but momentary advantage *as they see it* overcomes the attractions of other options. The former president of WGBH, Boston, a station that presents itself daily as under the guidance of the viziers of the Lowell Institute Cooperative Broadcasting Council (representing Harvard University, Tufts University, Brandeis University, The Massachusetts Institute of technology, The Boston Symphony, Wellesley College, etc. — and presumably some of the wisdom attendant thereupon), advised his producers to pay no attention to the Broadcasting Council. The real function of the Lowell Institute Cooperative Broadcasting Council is to add *cachet* to an astute WGBH's ideological courtesanship to the US Congress and beguilement of the local community. This is the same station that rents outsiders their subsidized, tax free, taxpayer funded facilities and equipment at prices equivalent to those that commercial stations have to charge because of layers of middleman profit-taking.

People will always be willing to snuggle up to others for their own gain. There will be people to "get around" any regulation or warp it to their own interest as they see it. Examples include the Fairness Doctrine, the Communications Act of 1934, and the Public Broadcasting Act of 1967. People who meant well promulgated these ideas. In fairness to them, how could they as people of good will see that public service television could become a field of contest among those possessed of what Shakespeare called "vulgar ambition"? Inadequate funding guaranteed that only small people could be hired. That was a fairly good guarantee to the networks and Hollywood that they could rest secure. Still, the formers of public TV underestimated the power these little people would get through the incentives offered by the administrative model of the Harvard School of Business Administration, with its structural hallowing of competitiveness, exploitativeness, adversarial relationships, an emphasis on winning rather than achievement. These even a not-so-bright person can understand.[160] Added to this, public television adopted for its "literature" the skills that would serve it as State Information Agency. It abandoned any pretense of genuine literature, which in its descriptions of reality derives its form from its content. As it developed, public TV opted instead for journalism as its literature. Journalism imposes it own formulaic template on a reality from which all that does not conform is excluded. Public TV adopted the Columbia School of Journalism model, which teaches our journalists to see the world as a competition in the image of the "B" School.[161] Fed into the Cold-War enriched technology power structure, which sees human society in mechanistic, technical terms, and equating education with training, American state-supported television's lopsided, partial worldview emerged.

A "fairness" doctrine was sensibly intended, initially, by the Federal Communications Commission to discourage broadcasters from using program time to overtly promote the public agendas of sponsors. The Fairness Doctrine showed itself over time to have an Achilles' heel. It was vulnerable to political jawboning. In practice, annual broadcast license authorization review became a tool of a politics that required all human concerns to be interpreted as political issues, with Democrat/Republican or liberal/conservative options and no more. Broadcasters interested in protecting their jobs took the avenue of least resistance, and followed obediently. A 1981 study showed that national political figures had become far and above the most frequent subjects of network news.[162] A law designed for "fairness" indulged the politician's bias (promulgated most vigorously by Richard Nixon) that every issue has only two sides. It muzzled dissent by blockading as "controversial" any and all new and original ideas on which positions of agreement or disagreement between the two major political parties had not been formulated. Creativity became, in effect, dissent, a subversive activity. The Fairness Doctrine frightened timid broadcasters away from anything not a known quantity. Their fright translated into aversion to all things ambiguous, tentative, unknown, new or creative. The people who formulated the Fairness Doctrine may have formulated it in the interest of equity. Unfortunately, they reckoned without the accumulated force represented by the opportunism of self-interested politicians exercising power over small broadcasters. What emerged from application of "The Fairness Doctrine" to radio and television programs was an image of a false reality of the status quo, itself described not as it was seen by power but as it was seen by the courtiers to power. Talented broadcasters were expunged for not observing its tenets.

After doing its harm for decades, the Fairness Doctrine is no longer with us. Its abolition was an enlightened act. Its effects remain in what amounts to a policy of the stifling of artistic freedom.

Before Reaganism, the Charitable Foundation was encouraged by US tax laws. Before the re-deification of Mammon, the charitable foundation, like government, served society as a device to attend to human needs not met by the marketplace. Then, in the 1980s, the insatiability of beneficiaries of a burgeoning GDP and the delight of the populace in its playpen of acquisitiveness provided a justification for the redefinition of the role of the foundation. The foundation role, in recent years, has been modified to extend the influence of the system of beliefs that brings market dominance. Thanks to the much lower costs of "nonprofit" public television, the relatively modestly funded charitable foundation now has an affordable megaphone for the ideas of its founder. For a rich person who loves control, the "charitable" foundation adds yet another weapon to the opinion-forming arsenal of newspaper ownership, broadcasting station ownership, magazine ownership, advertiser control of television programs and editorial policy, book publishing, education funding, and political action committee campaign funding. The financial backing of the Heritage Foundation by beer baron Joe Coors, money magnate Richard Mellon Scaife and former Treasury Secretary William Simon, Scaife's backing of the Bradley Foundation, the backing of the Cato Institute by the Koch family (owners of the second largest privately owned company in America — oil, natural gas, land-management) constitute a hefty subsidy for their own views in the free market place of ideas, a guarantee of legislative protectionism for those ideas that serve their interests as they define them. Foundation support of public TV adds yet another control mechanism, bringing the beliefs of owners to the public through still *another* medium. Hamstrung public television programmers, desperate for time-fillers of any kind, have become willing partners of foundations' proselytizing missions. Stations that know where the money is, with no more moralizing than any commercial entity, seek out the foundations, write proposals based on the foundation's declared spending priorities, and mount television shows and series funded by these foundations with tax-deductible dollars laundered through public television in the interest of the promotion of the *Weltanschauung* of a person the source of whose greater right to be heard is that he has control of a lot of money.[163]

The new private-sector "support" of public television, (what *Variety* aptly calls "sponsorship") is used as an instrument of control. Again, because of the way institutions are structured, what is thought by the unreflective public to be a neutral entity, public television, through private sector "support" becomes fiscally dependent on an agency with a mandated agenda for the promulgation of ideas and attitudes that selectively advance its own institutional self-interest.[164] A corporate "gift" to an entity in which a Congressman has a stake, like public TV, when the Congressman also can exercise a benign influence on the passage or enforcement of legislation affecting that corporation, is to that corporation a legitimate exercise of business investment. For the publicly held corporation, there's no argument about the appropriateness of this "charity" . . . the corporate agenda is mandated to the television sponsor in his corporate charter. It's his sacred duty. Corporate structure allows no deviation. If there is to be cooperation with the state (i.e. public TV), it must be to the corporation's advantage . . . that is, to the stockholders' advantage, and that means the cooperation must bring profits. Any corporate spokesperson will tell you, when you ask for a donation to a worthy cause, "I must be able to justify this to my stockholders." Any PR person will also tell you, "Doing good" as a justification for support carries no weight with a stockholder.

Implicit in the acceptance of corporate support of public television, as with sponsorship of commercial television, is the endorsement or acknowledgement of the inviolability of exceptional qualities common to corporations and corporate life. Some of the assumptions that differentiate corporate thought from, let's say, academic or religious or philosophical thought are an unquestioned adherence to:

- Materialism
- Ahistoricism
- Economic Determinism
- Competition
- Precedence of ends over means
- Quantitative over qualitative measure.

The above may have significance as corporate contributions to human progress. But a practice whereby these concepts should be sacrosanct, kept outside the realm of question, is itself open to question. Why? If only because the above attributes are abjured by many of history's great thinkers. They may even in fact be not quite unassailable to a Drucker, a Deming or a Galbraith today.

In any case, the education and communications institutions of a democratic society should be guaranteed the opportunity at any time and in any way to call these values into question — and they are not.

An early 1970s WNET New York-based series entitled *The Great American Dream Machine* was called "imaginative, "droll", a "Sesame Street for post-pubescents", "one of the liveliest and brightest of television's magazine formats" by *The New York Times*. "Explosive", said the *Atlanta Constitution*. "Making waves" said the *Cleveland Press*. It had essays, cartoons, film profiles, theatrical skits, and stand-up comics. More than that, it had verve, style and originality. Executive Producer Al Perlmutter said comfortingly that *Dream Machine* was about "people's goals, their ideas of themselves, their country, their hopes and their dreams." It was also about imagination and risk. One skit, "The selling of the American Flag", came afoul of the FBI's J. Edgar Hoover. The segment was dropped. Then the *Dream Machine* series itself disappeared.

Under the headline, "Public TV Censorship and Government Funds", Rex Polier, in *The Philadelphia Evening Bulletin*, wrote: "Although a public TV spokesman denied that the segment was dropped in fear of unfavorable reaction by the FBI and Congress, the possibility that public TV was so influenced cannot be dismissed." He went on to write, "The fact that more of its funds, and therefore its standard of living comes from a national treasury — uninsulated from political considerations — is something to worry about."

Not too many years earlier, in 1967, WNET New York produced a live, late evening drama series. In one episode, a couple could be seen going to bed together in the same bed. The camera faded to black, and came up on the couple smiling. The next day a WNET trustee, also a vice-president of Philip Morris, had WNET's most valuable employee, program manager Louis Freedman, fired.

We all know of instances when sponsors of commercial television have "dropped out" when they have disagreed with a program that takes a courageous stand about a sensitive public issue. The loss of sponsorship causes economic hardship to networks and inevitable warnings against repetition to producers from those in positions of fiscal responsibility.

In the field of public television, "Corporate support", like "sponsorship" in commercial television, entails a respectful regard for the operative principles and the advertising goals of the funder. It is *de facto* censorship.

Sponsorship does not violate the principles of accommodation on which public TV operates today. But it violates the principles on which public TV was founded, the principles to which it must return if it is to survive.

Public TV can no longer pose as Caesar's wife. To expect the public to see the "support" of *Wall Street Week* by two investment houses as evidence of a disinterested concern stretches credulity. Corporate "support" of public television is an act of generosity in the minds of those who wish to see it that way, but hardly to the participants. Since public TV is the vehicle for the promulgation of the interests of those who authorize its budget, "support" of public television is justifiable to corporate stockholders as a legitimate activity of the enterprise of lobbying the Congress. In the *quid pro quo* of corporate government relations, corporate support for public television is a "quid", and the ear of the Congress is its "quo" . . . with the implication that corporate support may be reconsidered next year. Now, just guess whose interests are best served by "corporate support" of public television. The public's?

The discovery that US public television could tap the reservoir of British television drama was a watershed event in public television. A short-range cost-benefit justified action on the part of US public TV that effectively ended any potential for public television in the United States to become a creative, innovative, professionally competent force. A budding Pandarus at Boston's WGBH discovered that it could broker an imported drama series from England to an oil company. This is a company engaged in a business that *Barron's* editor Alan Abelson has declared shows no limits to its deviousness and guile. Mobil Oil, at the time it undertook sponsorship of *Masterpiece Theater*, had one of the worst records for charitable donations of any Fortune 500 corporation. Consumer lobbies were denouncing Mobil at the time for price gouging during the oil crisis of 1973. (A bill introduced by Senator Jim Abourezk of South Dakota to break up the oil companies was defeated by only three votes.) Mobil's president William Tavoulareas looked to the model of Texaco's sponsorship of the Metropolitan Opera, a proven device for securing corporate goodwill from influential middle- and upper-middle-income viewers. Taking advantage of the desperate straits of public TV, Mobil's public affairs vice-president Herb Schmertz lassoed *Mahstepiece Theahtah*, and juiced up the image of its sponsor at Filene's Basement prices. "Herb Schmertz decided to capture just the sort of middle and upper income support sought by Texaco thirty years earlier with its sponsorship of Saturday afternoon broadcasts of the Metropolitan Opera . . . Schmertz engineered this by placing Mobil commercials on public television."[165] Mobil was abetted by WGBH's then President Stan Calderwood, who had recently retired with a substantial fortune earned by saving the stockholders of the Polaroid Corporation from risks attendant on the inventive genius of its founder Edwin Land. As a public service, Calderwood transferred his corporate acumen to Boston's public TV station, setting opportunism in place as a basic model for the operation of a public television station.

For WGBH, Calderwood engaged in the prime American art form, "the deal". As a deal, the marriage of Mobil to BBC had the luster of purity. Here was some second-hand foreign merchandise available for a tiny fraction of the cost of its manufacture. Used tapes of TV dramas made for British consumption were available for peanuts. Boston licensed them, and sold sponsorship. And wonder of wonders, a public TV station actually made some money! But not much, by commercial standards. Sponsorship of *Masterpiece Theater* was one of the great bargains in broadcasting history. *One* one-minute commercial on network prime time would have cost Mobil about what it paid for the *whole* first thirteen-week series. What a deal!

WGBH Boston's deal really knocked out its competition, the other public TV stations. Actually, it administered a death blow to any remaining hopes of a viable creative noncommercial television service in America. In 1970, the British product was simply too good and too cheap for nascent regional production centers in the United States to compete. The station-as-broker concept ended the era of the station-as-innovative-producer. With the help of Chris Pullman's brilliantly photographed and lighted table-top opening sequence, plus Christopher Sarson's not-quite Kensington intonation and Alistair Cooke's sheen of polite good manners enrobing even works of dubious merit, *Masterpiece Theater* offered middle class Americans who had suffered through college survey courses in the humanities what was perhaps their only opportunity to see meticulously produced original television made for an audience defined as something other than customer.

Calderwood went on to reorganize the public station on the model of his earlier triumphs. His changes would today be perceived as regressive. Abandoned was the collegial, cooperative institutional structure. Hartford Gunn's "playpen", the relaxed, informal family (you could bring your dog to work) was replaced by hierarchy. Somewhat like the practice in the 19th century mills of Lowell, Massachusetts, creative people were redefined as "labor", hired on a piecework basis. Decisions about new programs were thenceforth made by "management", many of whom had little to no experience in assessing and putting together the infinity of variables that make the components of a television program.

WGBH's program producers rebelled. The people who knew most about program production, they were shut out of decisionmaking about programs by the hierarchical reorganization. In an effort to have some say in the subject area where they were most knowledgeable, WGBH's producers tried to unionize. In this way they thought they could require administrators to consult program makers about program formation. But The Department of Labor of the Commonwealth of Massachusetts declared that, since producers had some say in the hiring of directors and writers, they were "management" and couldn't unionize.

With a *de facto* adversarial and/or "worker" status vis-à-vis WGBH management, and with no say in what would be produced, the cadre of creative people formed under Hartford Gunn simply drifted away. WGBH adopted the newspaper model for its own productions. Commercial networks had already found the *reportage* model for programs both creatively anemic and a poor income source, and only did them as a sop to Washington. They happily yielded up this type of endeavor to WGBH.

WGBH Boston's *Masterpiece Theater* deal with the BBC made superlatively-produced drama available in America. It also brought the curtain down with a thud on the promise of innovative television from American sources.   An easy and profitable strategy was borrowed from Hollywood. WGBH discovered the "pickup". A "pickup" film "bore the company logo and, to the uninitiated at least, appeared to represent the company's product."[166] The public thought that "presented by" meant the same as "made by". England became a Kimberly lode of "pickups" for public television. In the public perception, public TV institutions got credit for shows that US public television didn't produce. Meanwhile, the stations saved wages, rent, equipment costs, "headaches", and mostly, they saved risk. The federal Government, the prime funder of public television, looked the other way. They saved risk, too . . . the risk that inevitably goes with innovation, and is perceived as politically disruptive. Other stations emulated WGBH. Their thought was "Can we do something that Mobil will pay for?" writes former NET president John Day. Public television stations like WTTW Chicago sent scouts abroad to look for second-hand product to peddle, and fired their creative people. Innovation and innovators in public TV became history.

At the time of the passage of the Public Television Act, CBS gave a gift of $2 million. On that occasion, CBS President Frank Stanton stated, "With federal help, you'll have the resources to develop creative people . . . and you can bet the commercial networks will do our best to steal them from you!" Innovation takes time. Innovation takes reflective thought. Innovation takes painstaking care. None of these are allowable in a competitively driven television (or much else, for that matter). Dr. Stanton recognized that the prerequisites of commerce established an impenetrable limitation on the potential of commercial broadcasting to innovate. It was his hope, as it was the hope of others in broadcasting, that public television would have the structure and the resources to establish a stable of innovative talent in production, that it would evolve television forms of excellence and potential that could serve both as achievements in themselves and as models for commercial television to follow.

The hope that public television could be a school for production talent went unfulfilled. What innovation there has been could be found in commercial TV. It has been a long wait, too. Thirty years later, in 1995, when NBC wanted to produce a "reward" for Ted Danson for eleven years of profitable servitude as star of the series, *Cheers,* NBC spent $28 million to produce a four-hour special, *Gulliver's Travels,* as a Danson vehicle. "Jubilantly imaginative", wrote TV Guide's Jeff Jarvis. Imaginative, witty, and in excellent taste, this production fulfilled the half-century old promise of American television to bring intelligent theater to millions. To produce it, NBC went to Englishman Duncan Kenworthy and to Englishman Charles Sturridge to direct. After thirty years of public television's ostensible encouragement of "independent" talent in the United States, there was evidently no creative talent in the United States accomplished enough to produce a program characterized by subtlety, wit, invention, grace, intelligence and style. So, in 1995, NBC's 28 million US dollars were spent by the Brits overseas. The decision to so allocate resources was a perfectly rational consequence of decisions made over the years by the US Congress and public TV.

English television itself is not a model of innovation. The subjects of the productions rebroadcast as *Masterpiece Theater* were, in their country of origin, generally famous, novels . . . proven successes, tried-and-true. Their innovativeness was well buffered by history. Most were dramatizations of novels that had "stood the test of time." English programs broadcast by public television under the title *Masterpiece Theater* had already fulfilled their mission at home when offered to the US market. Meticulously, sometimes brilliantly, produced and acted, they are a joy to watch. Their production budgets were for the most part far in excess of any that could be garnered from the junta of US Congress, US corporations, from "viewers like you" or any combination thereof for dramatic presentations by American public television producers.

An argument can be made that the products of British broadcasting that became a staple of US public broadcasting represent foreign goods "dumped" at prices the local competition is unable to match. WGBH's field of leadership was akin to the outsourcing to foreign suppliers by American industry that produces joblessness in many American industries today. In no particular was the new leadership style directed toward the development of a viable alternative television in the United States. Its consequence was indeed joblessness . . . for creative people in America. Cheap imports made it possible for American public television to fire its own creative people.

WGBH's marketing inventiveness proceeded from a cynicism and opportunism that compromised its own avowed mission. Its motivation was short-term, "value-free" and bottom-line. WGBH's marketing *coup* secured it a competitive advantage over other public stations that remains to this day.

From the success of this recycling of foreign product, other public stations learned that, just as in *Filene's Basement*, used designer goods are available to a canny entrepreneur at cut-rate prices. After Boston's fire sale of *Masterpiece Theater* to Mobil, the public TV stations of the other regional markets sent their minions over the world to search out cheap product that *they* could offer to PBS. But WGBH "got there first", as Armand Hammer did with Lenin. Like Armand Hammer, they exploited and publicized their advantage as virtue.

There are lessons to be learned from this episode, lessons that should be useful in case there is ever a rebirth of that idea of a civilized alternative to commercial television that first prompted educational/public TV in America: lessons in the definition of quality television. Because they represent markers for effective public service television that were long unknown and because the lessons of quality public service television were derived from long and painstaking experience, and because whatever its state today, there may a future for an alternative to commercial television, I will highlight two of them.

One is that *a common thread of all successful television, fictional or nonfictional, is theatricality.* Television communicates best as an extension of that long tradition of fictional stage performance, the essential nature of which was described centuries ago in Aristotle's *Poetics*. *Masterpiece Theater* programs are, by-and-large, thoughtfully and meticulously written, acted, lighted, designed, and directed. They are part of the ancient tradition of theater.

The novel, *an intimate, personal story,* can be translated effectively in television terms. The development of a genre for theatrical presentation emphasizing vast panoramic landscapes is testimony to the success of television as an intimate medium.

The merchandising of "pickups", second-hand imports for public television, was a lethal move for American public television stations as creative entities. With the success of brokering, the role of the public station as producer of original programs using local creative talent ended. The station abandoned its role as creator/innovator, and became retransmitter, or euphemistically, "impresario". WGBH Boston, with its handsome "WGBH Presents" tacked onto the head and tail of others' products, led the change.

Under the Lowell Institute's guidance, WGBH-FM became legendary as the best FM station in America. When the elder Lowell passed away, he left Lowell Institute oversight of the TV station to his son. It may be that Mr. Lowell sensed that the Congress as funding decisionmaker for public television would not long support Hartford Gunn's idea of noncommercial broadcasting as an *atelier* directed toward the exploration of creative opportunities. Perhaps he foresaw that the structure of CPB and PBS and the annual congressional funding review process inevitably dictated that public television would be authorized and budgeted as an instrument of the agendas and the presumptions of members of the US Congress.[167] Perhaps he reasoned that "political correctness" bore some relationship to his family's Institute's historic educative role. In any event, from the decisions made in Boston, it appears that a fight for the preservation or extension of the creative tradition of Western civilization through the new medium of television was not to be pursued by Boston's public TV station. Under its new leaders, Michael Rice, a brilliant Rhodes Scholar and Mozart of memos (he could write a long, complex memo and never need to correct a word), his successor and fan of animal shows Henry Becton, and David Ives, former *Wall Street Journal* journalist, publicist and impresario of auctions, the flagship production house developed by Hartford Gunn ("where the producer is king") was transformed into the "pick-up" brokerage house, talent scheduler, recut center and Congressional Agenda Newsmagazine center it has become.

It could be said that the exporters and importers of second-hand European TV effectively waged and won a price war against public television's national production centers. An important attraction of the imports was their reasonable cost. Another part of the reason for the triumph of the second-hand was that many British programs were superbly produced, written and directed. They were the outcome of a serious commitment by their funders to the proselytizing of English culture, "one of our country's few remaining resources", lamented one English broadcaster. Through British television, American audiences were given an opportunity to experience drama of subtlety, grace, wit, intelligence, and sensibility . . . very unlike American commercial fare. Some *Masterpiece Theater* programs, *The Jewel in the Crown*, for example, gave Americans an opportunity to witness human interactions determined by civility, courtesy and respect — a world apart from the crude interactions depicted in *All in the Family*, *Married With Children*, or *Beavis and Butthead*. England's best television demonstrated a commitment on the part of its production agencies and funders to the potential of the medium as a civilizing force. British television's accomplishments could have provided a lesson for American public TV. Instead, its success orphaned any impulse to creativity in American public television. WGBH achieved cost-effectiveness while it abandoned its own place as a center of innovative television.

Thanks to the success of British drama in America, the estimable and now defunct *American Playhouse* was delayed in its dramatization of American novels by perhaps twenty years. David Davis and Ward Chamberlin deserve a medal for tenacity for "sticking it out" while public television's courtiers nationwide shored up their meager power and influence with accommodating programming. Davis and Chamberlin's right-thinking effort to establish noncommercial television as an outlet for its own kind of innovative American theater, however, could not compete with other imperatives. A series that understood that the medium is essentially a theatrical form, and that reached toward the development of a creative American voice in that medium, could not survive. *American Playhouse*, perhaps the best hope for public television as theater in the last twenty years, is no more. Its place has been taken by an American Wing of Masterpiece Theatre, funded to the tune of $15 million by (who else?) Mobil. The new *Masterpiece Theatre* includes a nice feminist drama from a novel by Willa Cather, a portrait of a safely long-dead American past by Henry James, a nice minority work by Langston Hughes and a peek through the keyhole at the domestic tribulations of Mr. and Mrs. Mark Twain. No ruffled feathers here!

The paralysis of creativity in American public television has a long history. Bear in mind that WGBH's, 1968 *Queen of Spades* was the last opera ever to be produced, rather than merely "covered", by public television.

A casualty of *Masterpiece Theater* was the Ford Foundation's hope that the creativity of regional production centers would enrich noncommercial broadcasting. There was a short-term corporate benefit, though. Through these TV shows presupposing stratified British culture, public television acted to promulgate the Mobil Corporation hierarchy's feudal/corporate ideal of group relationships. With these routine presentations, upwardly mobile American audiences captured by the attractiveness of rank and privilege were indulged by costume soap operas masquerading as "culture". While a heroine of an American soap opera might say, on any given day, "Oh, Madge, I don't know what to do! George phoned. He's coming back from overseas duty next week, and Dottie's pregnant!," a character in a British historical drama might instead intone "Ah, Lady Margaret, I am perforce distraught. The King's heralds have ridden their palfreys into the Great Hall to announce his return from the Wars of the Roses, (pause), and the Queen (pause) . . . Oh, shame! (pause) is with child!" Culture? Of course not . . . pretend culture, soap operas for parvenus comforted by mundane tales decked out in the trappings of rank and privilege. An admirable feature was the doughty sportsmanship of host Alistair Cooke as he labored to ascribe literary merit to some of these penny dreadfuls.

The audiences of *Masterpiece Theater* are legion, and committed. Why? Partly because British drama is generally masterfully performed and brilliantly directed. The downside is that, with this series, public television's contribution to American culture is the importation of fictions that salve the common literary taste. Safe adaptations of once daring but now time-honored English classics feed comfortable American middle class snobbery while at the same time inculcating the values of feudal tribalism. At bargain basement prices, too!

Masterpiece Theater fell on its face only once. The reason could have been an unfortunate presumption on the part of the BBC about American attitudes. A 1991 WGBH/BBC "co-production", *Portrait of a Marriage*, reflected what could only the bowing of producers before the opinion of a bigoted funder. The producers stooped to a keyhole-peeping, prurient interpretation the lives of two of the century's more accomplished sensibilities (fortunately for them and for their detractors, deceased). Harold Nicholson and Vita Sackville-West were among the most eloquent products of their era's civilization, education, intelligence and sensibility. These two were poetry and prose writers of sufficient accomplishment to be included in university curriculums. Vita was thought worthy of the affections of the brilliant sensibility, Virginia Woolf. Together Sir Harold and Lady Nicholson brought their flower garden at Sissinghurst Castle to the level of art form. Their lives together were an original creation, possible because of a confluence of currents at a particular historic time. But nowhere in the television program was the personal distinction of these two people evident. Instead, the co-production treats the audience to a backstairs maid's-eye view. It gives the "couch potato" viewer sets to envy, and costumes derived from photographs but intensified in every aspect of peculiarity. The lead characters are caricatures, presented as a weak fag and a willful dyke, whose lives revolve around stupid, gross and loveless sexual deviancy. This barnyard version of the lives of the aristocracy may have fed into the preconceptions of dustmen, readers of checkout-counter news, and Senator Helms. This interpretation of the lives of two original beings was an insult to the idea of the self-created human life.

Why was it done this way? How much of the coloration in scripting and editing of this lopsided interpretation we owe to the co-producers' second-guessing about American bigotry or congressional/funder reaction is a matter of speculation. *Portrait of a Marriage*, whatever the cause, is porcine.

Exhumed and therefore unchallengeable "classics", England's sumptuous, retrograde costume soap operas in tooled leather binding are unctuously re-titled *Masterpiece Theater* and promoted by public television to credulous viewers as cultural leadership. They aren't.

Mobil's Raymond D'Argenis once pointed out the instrumental value to his company of public television sponsorship. "These programs build enough acceptance to allow us to get tough on substantive issues."[168] For a corporation, public television sponsorship has multiple advantages not the least being the image of corporate probity generated by support of noncommercial television as an enhancement to investor confidence. Decades later, agribusiness giant and government agricultural subsidy beneficiary Archer Daniels Midland, ("supermarket to the world") sponsored public TV before, during and after being fined $100,000,000 by the federal government for price fixing. They also represent the marriage of public television to the corporate abandonment of cultural responsibility.

The shift from *atelier* to brokerage house carries serious implications; it means moving from creator to merchant. It means moving from analyst to accountant, from teacher to banker, from intellectual adventurer to hermit, from pioneer to miser, from outward to inward, from active to passive, from risk to security. The brokering style is the reverse of that of the *atelier*. Its style, "repressing one's own convictions and withholding judgment in the interest of bringing profitable relationships"[169] is value-free and essentially amoral. In adopting the role of brokerage house, public television "flagship station" WGBH mimicked the dominant agencies of its culture, established its redundancy, and set the stage for its own comfortable irrelevance.

This is not to say that some of the imports repackaged and re-labeled as *Masterpiece Theater* are not serious, intelligent, even inspired uses of the television medium. A few are convincing demonstrations of the power of television as a civilizing force, as undoubtedly were the BBC's *War and Peace*, or *A Passage to India* and Granada's *Brideshead Revisited*, and the brilliant nonfiction television odysseys of James Burke. These could be models for American public television production, if America had the will.

That the highest use of the television medium should originate in England is both a tribute to the sense of priorities of the British television production establishment and an indictment of American willingness and ability. Like the American shoe companies that let Italian laborers make our shoes, like the TV set manufacturers that let Japanese and Koreans make our TV sets, like the automobile makers who let the Japanese make their parts, public TV discovered that it could let the English make our good TV shows. English wages were lower. The producers in England had talent and the experience gained from a solid theatrical tradition. This approach saved money. What else mattered? So what if it killed the possibility of noncommercial television in the United States as a contributor to the artistic or cultural life of the planet? Who would sue because their jobs were being taken by foreigners? Nobody — perhaps because nobody in public television production made enough money to hire an attorney.

Private sector participation in public television like Mobil's has been advanced as a method for balancing ideological control against "too much government." The argument is based on the assumption that the interests of government, business, and "viewers like you" diverge, that each will to a degree temper the other. The unspoken assumption is that business and government will do just what they have in fact been doing, using public television as a platform from which to give voice to views that they want others to hold in order to serve their interest as they currently define it. Businesses have been solicited for two decades to support public television. Some do, but selectively and conditionally. Initially, to avoid "corruption of the unbiased nature of public television", businesses were solicited for contributions not targeted to specific programs. Except for Mobil, there were no takers. "Underwriters" since then have been able to select the programs they will contribute to. They select programs that serve their commercial interest. They select public TV if it serves their lobbying interests. They trumpet their support of public television as if it were disinterested. Public television calls them "supporters" or "funders". *Variety* calls them "sponsors". Former CPB Corporate Communications Director S.L. Harrison points out, "Corporate sponsors[170] declare candidly that they do not throw money away on programs that don't promote a 'feel-good' image for the company."[171]

Chapter 23

"UNDERWRITING" FOR WHOM?

W hy should a corporation be interested in noncommercial television, anyway? Because of a generalized desire to further the public interest? The truth is much more interesting.

Corporate support of public television follows a path with illuminating sidelights. It has to do with the essence of what and why a corporation is. The structure of any American corporation demands that it meet the demands of its creditors first. Corporate creditors are the people whose money corporations operate on. That's the stockholders from whom the corporation has borrowed. The stockholders took a risk. Any corporation must be able to justify *any* move it makes in terms of the interest of the stockholders whose money it rents. As we know from reading reports of stockholder meetings, corporate management is closely bird-dogged by stockholders. Washington's National Association of Whatever or the American Association of Whatever, these lobbies and Political Action Committees support the interests of corporate stockholders. That's why the stockholders allow them to spend money that could be theirs. The expansionism of American industry, the consumerism, the efforts to influence world hegemony by the state, are utterly innocent. There is absolutely no evil intent. All derive rationally from primary corporate responsibility to owners, the stockholders. The positions American corporations take on these matters are easily divined; they are merely consequences of the ineluctable logic that follows from their charters. Their first obligation is to provide as large a return as possible to all the people who elected to let them have their money instead of putting it in a bank. It has nothing to do with personal motivations, with good and evil, or any other of the motives often ascribed as causes of the dislocations the society at large suffers as payment for industry actions. Like the products they manufacture, the television programs they sponsor are to them value-free. They are part of the mechanics of doing business, simply a device to get the most return they can for their stockholders. For all of us who think about corporate sponsorship of public television, it makes sense to remember why business is in business. They give to get. They are obligated to take in more than they give. A good enough clue to understanding may be found in the corporate bible, *Fortune Magazine*. An example from "Reality Check" (August 21, 1995, p. 35) declares, "Assuming that everyone is utterly selfish, it turns out, allows you to predict pretty well how people in general will act in a given situation."

There is a fundamental flaw in the wish that commercial sponsorship can provide a completely diverse range of fare for a democratic society. The flaw is the hypothesis of identity between commercial and public interest. Implicit in corporate support for the making of television programs (the broadcasting itself costs so little as to be essentially free) is endorsement or acknowledgement of the exceptional qualities common to corporations and corporate life. Some of the assumptions that differentiate corporate thought from the thought of significant elements in the rest of humanity are these: (1) Materialism, (2) Economic determinism, (3) Ahistoricism, (4) Competitiveness, (5) The priority of ends over means, (6) A greater tolerance for greed, self-seeking, egomania, and manipulativeness among its practitioners. The above, it should be noted, are attributes if not abjured at least cautioned against by one or more of history's esteemed thinkers ("It is shameful to make gain your sole object", said Confucius, for example) but these six are, at least for the time being, either implicit in or sacrosanct to corporate thought.

The condition of these attributes as essential to corporate thought may be temporary, or it may represent the corporation's permanent contribution to human progress. In one case, criticism would be ineffectual, in the other, appropriate. In no case should a corporation participating in the free marketplace of thought that is a democracy have the option to withhold support from entities that call the above values into question. Corporations should be prevented from encouragement of the assumptions mentioned in the above paragraph in programs or commercials. They should certainly be prohibited from censoring materials that suggest alternative methodologies for human well-being.

If a free communications industry is to survive, it must be able to operate in recognition of at least the contingency of the above-defining corporate attributes.

As it is practiced, corporate underwriting of public television is not an attempt to proselytize. It is instead an extension of lobbying activities. The congressmen who fund public broadcasting are beholden to corporations who pay the enormous cost of getting elected today. The "political correctness" that underlies programming decisions is part of an incumbent's election strategy that must be paid for. Program sponsors Archer-Daniels Midland,[172] Boeing, and others who stand to benefit from congressional favors, can "stroke" a legislator who has an agenda for public TV by funding a show or series whose subject is close to his heart. In return, the legislators give their benefactors legislation favorable to their economic interests. "One hand washes the other."

In reality, the position of sponsors relative to the First Amendment right of public broadcasters is roughly comparable to their position relative to commercial broadcasters.

Underwriters or sponsors want said what will serve the interest of their stockholders. IBM has declared that it will support public television programs that support IBM's interest — programs on science and technology. The *Lehrer News Hour*, paid for by you, dear taxpayer, to the tune of $12.8 million in 1993,[173] is "must-viewing" for congressmen. Described by *The New York Times* as "The television arbiter of mainstream Washington thought",[174] the *Lehrer News Hour's* participating sponsorship, subsidized by your tax money, waves the flags of AT&T and Pepsico. Their assumptions about you lead them to present themselves as caring companies trying to ingratiate themselves with *you*. Why should their stockholders allow them to do that? As we have pointed out, people who think for themselves are far down in the list of target audiences. The money they spend on public television is good money that adds to the company's PAC money as a nice contribution to Congress' domestic USIA. When legislation comes before Congress that affects PepsiCo or AT&T, how hostile can a congressman be who's flown on their corporate planes and been nicely treated on the *Lehrer News Hour* that they sponsor?

In practice, industry support of public television is tentative. The criteria are often crude and shortsighted. Sponsorship of the *Bill Moyers Journal* was withdrawn because of sponsor objections to program content. "I should have been able to air controversial views"; he declared. "I wasn't." *"The system leaves no room for an independent journalist or a serious inquiry into our society"* (italics mine), says Moyers. Moyers' independence of mind is a valuable public asset. He describes a circumstance that should disgust Americans. Conditional support from sponsors of public television implies the option of editorial control, the suppression of dissent, otherwise known as censorship. If Moyers is right, there hardly seems need for public television at all, does there?

Biased messages promulgated on public TV by special interests may be, quite literally, in sheep's clothing. An example is public television's recent staple, the "harmless" animal show. If you look beneath the fur, in these shows animal life is used as a metaphor for the old-time corporate struggle, in the guise of neo-Darwinist opinion. The way they're edited, these animal shows show all life as a contest in which the strong and guileful overcome the weak and trusting. Called by Stephen Jay Gould a "progressionist credo", it declares that "the motive force of progress is entirely martial; animals prevail by dint of force and muscle, humans by the ever more potent instruments of war." Their message feeds into the current views of the "B" school segment of the political spectrum inside and outside the Congress.

This convenient corporate fantasy has not always enjoyed a following in the scientific disciplines. (See Gould's book *Wonderful Life* for a detailed explosion of this myth). To expose a self-promoting teleology of the development of species to a generation of young people in the guise of science, as these animal shows do, is duplicitous. In the free marketplace of thought, there's nothing wrong with promulgating a point of view, but there *is* something wrong with not being upfront about it. Fence and greenhouse makers' sponsorship of a gardening show, a brokerage's sponsorship of *Wall Street Week*, etc. are not-so subtle co-optings. We know what those sponsors want — an audience of customers for their products. But, how can we know what are the interests that the Scaife Foundation promulgates? How can we know what is Martin-Marietta's influence on the programs we see? Public television, obviously, has its price. What is it? They'll never tell, but the regulations governing actions of joint stock corporations are a guide to understanding.

"Every man has his price", said a character in Edward Bulwer-Lytton's *Walpole*[175] over a hundred years ago. "I will bribe left and right." Bulwer-Lytton's lines were meant as a warning. A culture that is influenced, primed, prompted, moved, cajoled, bribed, rewarded or denied, halted, redirected, and punished by the deft use of money keeps its integrity only by the watchfulness of its citizenry. Public television, as if unaware of the lessons of Aesop or Baron Lytton, has not only consented to but has sought out its own co-optation.

It can be expected that retail advertiser dependent organizations like *The New York Times* would wait until the trendy and expensive Barneys declared bankruptcy before outing their owners as "garment district Borgias."[176] Owners and advertisers in America have built-in protection from the media. In commercial television, the inevitable influence of owners on information content is seen by some observers as a measure of societal corruption. John Horn once wrote, "Affluent whites who have control of television employ it to their own economic ends, not for human communication. It is a deprivation of grave consequence."[177] Former *New York Times* editor Max Frankel points out that "Some corporate behemoths have bought favor and protection simply by buying the media . . . . Not incidentally, that also gives them control over all the television news concerning their own conduct."[178] Russell Baker pointed out that it follows from the source of his income and status that Tom Brokaw knows better than to say anything that might seem damaging to the corporate self-interest of NBC's owner, General Electric (described by CNN founder Ted Turner as "the most corrupt corporation in America").[179] Danny Schechter[180] quotes as a rather special interpretation of the legislative mandate to broadcast in the public interest a General Electric Communications manager who declared, "We insist on a broadcast environment that reinforces our corporate message." While balancing his loyalties between the idea of public information and his own well-being, one could expect Brokaw to be aware that his talents could command an income of over a million dollars a year in few other activities, though I'm sure his boyish charm could bring success as a door-to-door magazine salesman.

Barbara Ehrnreich has written, "Show me a mainstream journalist today and I will show you a broken creature living in mortal fear of being downsized or dismissed for offending some advertiser, some executive or some company that happens to belong to this poor journalist's ruling media conglomerate."[181] That Tom Brokaw and other NBC people occasionally wear the unflattering two-tone tribal-signal shirts favored by GE board members[182] may be a symbolic reassurance to them about Brokaw's ideological conformity. Somehow, NBC News failed to mention the 16 instances of fraudulent activity against the government by GE since 1990.[183] We might ask if Brokaw would be able take it upon himself, in his selection of news topics, to risk influencing actions that might ruffle the feelings of GE's owner, France's Thomson CSF, or to mention raise negatives in management regarding the pollution control, mortgage insurance, financial services, chemicals in which they have a huge financial stake? As a further guarantee of corporate interest, we can surmise that the credentials of Brokaw's onetime boss, Michael G. Gartner, both president of NBC News and a columnist for *The Wall Street Journal*, gave GE assurance that he could be trusted to arrange terms of daily operation of *NBC Nightly News with Tom Brokaw* that presumed an identity between corporate and public weal. (If Gartner had not permitted a news segment that faked evidence against a product of big TV sponsor General Motors, he might still be NBC News President.)

Former FCC member Nicholas Johnson has stated, "No newsman would be able to erase from his mind the idea that his chances . . . might be affected by his treatment of issues on which (the corporate owner) is sensitive."[184] Further, Johnson declares it unwise to "harness the enormous social and propaganda power of a national television network to the service of a politically sensitive corporate conglomerate", . . . "a company whose daily activities require it to manipulate governments at the highest levels."[185] That's General Electric, the owner of NBC, he's talking about.

General Electric has paid fines for defrauding the government on military contracts: $2 million in criminal and civil penalties to the Air Force in 1985, $3.5 million in 1989 for issuing faulty time cards, $30 million in 1990 for overcharging the Army for a battlefield computer system, and $69 million in 1992 for bribery in defrauding the Pentagon. As an NBC executive was quoted in *Variety*, on the firing of "Scud Stud" reporter Arthur Kent, "You can't forget that General Electric owns us and those guys play hardball like nobody else."[186]

On the basis of standards it applies to its own conduct, General Electric's probity and therefore its fitness to control an educational instrument as potent as a television network is questionable. But the issue of the lawlessness of their corporate owner cannot be addressed by the investigative journalists of NBC. On reflection, a reasonable viewer must therefore be driven to a degree of skepticism on the positions that NBC News promulgates on *any* issue. To fail to do so would be to marry gullibility to vulnerability.

Commercial news broadcasts signal their fealty by other devices. Their matrix, commercial broadcasting, is one in which you may have noticed that all characters represented on screen, in fiction or nonfiction programs, appear as just a little more "consumers" than you or I. Even persons whose avowed purpose is to communicate information to a disinterested public are themselves packaged like consumer products. News anchors, male and female alike, stay abreast of trends in hairstyles . . . the total amount of hair spray used on newscasters annually can only be a matter of conjecture. Fashions in shirt wear and neckties for the men, the "dress for success" look for the women, are *de rigueur*. (Remember how NBC's Andrea Mitchell wore just the kind of loose-necktie blouse that Nancy Reagan did, as long as Nancy was in Washington — and you may have noticed that Ms. Mitchell abandoned them when Nancy left Washington.) Makeup, a consumer product, is used liberally. Those hardheaded female reporters made up like Barbie dolls with lascivious hair, pout-painted lips and encrusted eyes that sparkle with calculation are a necessary paradox of TV news. Yes, on-camera talent in commercial TV have to be very models of how to improve one's image by enthusiastic use of consumer products. (Can you imagine what Barbara Walters would look like without having been "done"? Only she knows what's under there.) Images to be imitated, they'd be traitors to commercial television if they didn't dress and look expensive, like a salesperson in a shop . . . or "Miss Piggy", take your choice.

Gresham's law of economics — that bad money drives good out of existence — is a good enough metaphor for network news/information programming. As part of the continuing saga of debasement, network news has tacitly admitted that the TV audience that is delivered to their news programs by the fare on the rest of the schedule may be in search of something other than intellectual gratification. A trend to *exposé* journalism, so successful nowadays at supermarket checkout counters, serves two ends. It draws some customers (the less skeptical ones) and keeps them perennially distracted, perennially in search of the next tidbit showing others to be just as flawed as they are, or even more. Customers in such a state are no threat to their manipulators.

One criterion of a news story used to be the viewer's presumed questions, "What does that have to do with my life? How can knowing this help me?" It seems today that an editor's selection of a story for broadcast is based on how *little* it has to do with the viewer. An alert viewer can read the signals. News programs are taking tentative steps toward "the low road". One signal is the music you hear. There's a perceptible increase in "ominosos". (All the options among John Williams' inspirational theme music for NBC *Evening News* have been jettisoned in favor of one unsettling fugue). An increase in alarmist subjects. An increase in subjects that can in no way alter the sum total of a viewer's wisdom. You may have noticed more police-blotter stories of cave-ins, floods, fires, murders, police chases, and unavoidable wrongs or accidents to individuals, dubbed "tragedies". "You have these famed anchor people who need a drama for the evening news", says Hugh Sidey, veteran *Time* commentator.[187] Titillation by horror sets 'em up for a soothing commercial. You'll also see less analysis, more "heart-warming" features like miracle medical advances, elementary school teaching improvements, soft furry things in peril. These are evanescent subjects that in no way could prompt a viewer to threaten institutions that the sponsors hold dear. They also keep the public occupied.

It isn't that news honesty hasn't been tried. It just doesn't work. One-time ABC News President and Eisenhower's White House Press Secretary Jim Hagerty tried to bring honesty to TV news. He put real, working print journalists on camera. Viewers disappeared. Why? It happens that the hard lives led by working newspersons scars them (just check the press room at the White House or anywhere else). Hagerty's results were strictly noncommercial. Viewers didn't rejoice to see terrible-looking good journalists with bad delivery.

Money is power. That's why controlling type personalities become CEOs in the first place. What small attractiveness public television has to corporate sponsors can be explained on the basis of power. A sponsor can elect to fund or not to fund, choosing shows with a congenial message (often, as noted before, served up to him by the knowing and compliant, ever-courteous PTV "development executive", tellingly differentiated from a rumpled production person by his Wall Street suit).

Periodically the press reports that, on commercial television, Oprah Winfrey, Geraldo, etc. have sponsors who influence program content by withholding of sponsorship when the show features too taboo a subject.[188] Whatever opinion you may have about these programs and their hosts, the principle of sponsor dictation of program subject matter in commercial or public TV is coercion. What works inside a corporation may not work outside. In a democracy, it's plain wrong. Is a candy bar manufacturer by his very nature favored with so exalted an understanding of the nature and meaning of reality that he can tell us what we can and can't know? *Variety* aptly states the relationship between American industry and the art world: "Shows that receive a sponsor's nod are those that correspond to corporate tastes and marketing needs. Rarely will businesses support experimental or controversial art forms, opting instead for safer or more conventional works."[189] No innovation, only icons, no art. The same goes for the TV shows.

Now that we have commercial sponsorship of public TV, can we trust public TV objectivity any more than we can commercial? Hypocrisy, it has been said, is the tribute of vice to virtue. These hungry, clever public TV people discovered "infomercials" years ago, starting with "auctions". Public TV shows, as I hope I demonstrate here, already advance the interests of politics and industry. Commercial sponsorship of public television denies the reversibility of what is now merely duplicitous.

If our alternative TV is going to be controlled by people with the circumscribed set of attitudes appropriate to commercial and political survival, what's the reason for PTV's existence as an alternative? To give work to an army of trusties who have flexible principles? In the field of public service in a democracy, Caesar's wife must be beyond reproach. With sponsorship, public TV has installed a turnstile!

From the standpoint of a viewer's access to unbiased material, sponsorship of public television is a doubtful proposition. The institution of lobbying in Washington being what it is, we can speculate that public television, like all the arts in America today, is a locus of mutual handwashing between industry and government. The public benefit is at best a means, not an end, for a sponsor. Philip Morris once distributed a tasteful and dignified public service television campaign in "favor" of the Bill of Rights. This polished and beautiful exercise can qualify as the very definition of manipulative propaganda. Philip Morris' "Public Service Announcement" was a benign veil for some very serious corporate lobbying in favor of the application of First Amendment guarantees to the advertising of their lethal product.

From a strict cost perspective, to a prospective sponsor the advantage of public TV sponsorship is demonstrable. The shows are cheap. Often they are made abroad by talent whose wages are lower than Americans would command. Import production costs have been written off in their country of origin. The programs can be offered to America at low prices, as used goods, providing a little extra gravy for their producers through international distribution channels. Next, their distribution here is subsidized by the taxpayers. Advantages to a sponsor are that, whereas national broadcast of his commercial message over a commercial station will require a fee payment to every local station that carries it, public broadcasting requires payment to no station at all! And price is only one advantage.

Public TV audiences are less likely to be consumer product impulse buyers, so sponsorship by toothpaste companies makes little sense. Companies like Proctor and Gamble avoid it, of course. But if your company has an image problem, "Public" may be a good idea. The audiences, though small, are generally more intelligent than the audiences for commercial TV, for reasons we've noted above. The flip side of this is that now, with more and more sponsorship in public TV, the advantage of a presumably uncompromised public broadcasting system to give acceptability and prestige to your organization is offset by the fact that public television is now becoming more transparently an image-polishing tool of commercial interests. The objective of commercial sponsorship of public TV may not be the sale of consumer products but instead may be such a useful corporate enterprise as the pacification of disgruntled stockholders. The "participation" of industry in the "support" of public TV brings public television to a position where its essential difference from commercial television lies in the corporate goals it's buying. The advertiser's choice in commercial television is product sales, in public television it's image. Unfortunately, public TV's willingness to sell itself has compromised the image that once distinguished it. Public TV's cry for private sector "participation" is a discreet version of the third world urchin calling, "You f___ my sister? she virgin." Everybody who's doing it knows the true state of affairs. The word gets around . . . as *Variety* says, "The sponsors call the shots on public TV." Where anymore is the *cachet* for a sponsor in PTV? People aren't stupid. Soon they'll catch on . . . and then where will there be an alternative television for American viewers?

Public television executives, in securing their own advantage, pay court to funding sources. Legislators, whether they wish to or not, influence the content of public television programs. The result of the process whereby this happens is a narrowing of the definition of democracy. It's in the nature of mankind that there will always be those who find ways to toady to the moneybags. The wrong is that the practice of shaping program content to sponsor's agendas is encouraged by the funding structure of public television.

One can only ask if the funding structure of public television may not have been created with the intent of producing the result it did. There is no shortage of examples in chronically impoverished public television. It is chronic poverty in public television that has defoliated its creative landscape. Chronic poverty has caused hope to be abandoned, and principle to be compromised, and has handed over operation to opportunists. The example of "the oldest profession" is not inappropriate here. The lessons of history tell us that this will ultimately be destructive to the institution that harbors it.

Chapter 24

ELITISM VERSUS MULTICULTURALISM

Americans gather together to stone the people they don't like. Bigotry helps American Calabans in their war against history, against wisdom, against criticism. The academics who advise government agencies trumpet ahistoricism, philosophical/moral/esthetic relativism.[190] Bureaucracies demand "measurability of outcomes".[191] Government agencies follow. The application of these criteria predict an inevitable outcome: non-adherents "don't get the grant". An underground, a "fifth column", this cast of mind has not yet published its "Red Channels", its blacklist of "elitists". But there is one . . . the list is kept in the back of the mind.

With the tacit support of the rich or powerful, the bludgeon of anti-intellectualism functions effectively in the United States.[192] Tolerated and encouraged in some settings, "anti-elitism" has some positive consequences. It helps redistribute some of the wealth. Within organizations, it gives cover with which to fire nonconformist, or senior, expensive employees. It helps ambitious people clear away those in their career path who may know more. It diminishes or discourages excellence. Anti-elitism helps give minorities a "leg up", but even more it helps keep the rich rich, the powerful powerful.

Composer Matthias Kriesberg writes this about music composition:

> To suggest today that writing music is about more than pleasing an audience is to commit the most horrific cultural crime of the late, late 20th century, "elitism". There is broad agreement across the political spectrum: wisdom resides in the will of the people. Granted, our embrace of the collective philosophy we used to mock has a new twist: yesterday's masses are today's marketplace. And since the power of the market is the flip side of democracy, you can't challenge one without ostensibly opposing the other.[193]

Anti-elitism is a strong instrument in the maintenance of the status quo. It eliminates threats to sitting bureaucrats. Anti-intellectual assassination through accusations of what is called "elitism" has become so conventional as to be sanctified behavior in America. Any subject characterized by complexity or subtlety, any product of accumulated learning, of imaginative originality, of intellect or sensibility, can be a target. A person whose works proceed from or are characterized by these attributes may be singled out and exiled without a hearing. American Robespierres stand ready to call, "off with their heads". And the heads come off. Arts administrators, university administrators, culture administrators, lie supine before any accuser.

"Ignorance is Strength", Orwell's tyrant declared in *1984*. "Elitist" has today joined "abuser" or "sexist" as a judgment without appeal. "Elitist" has replaced "pinko", "Sheenie", "Mick", "Coon", "Pansy", "Com-symp", "Egghead", "Fellow-traveler", among signals of irrevocable censure. The victim of this currently enshrined bigotry has no recourse.

The strategy of anti-elitists is transparent. Under the cloak of democracy, the purpose is to unseat those equipped to make judgments informed by experience and/or education, with the object of replacing them with oneself. How duplicitous, how guileful, to adopt a righteous mask of conventional prejudice as an opportunistic device to damage those who stand in the way of one's personal advancement! The effect is a cultural "sacking of Rome". Does it represent a loss? Read Gibbon's *Decline and Fall of The Roman Empire* for a report on today's events.

Elites were once seen as groups sharing common definitions of excellence or worthiness. That was a productive and useful way to define the term. A convenient misconstruction of C. Wright Mills' unmasking of America's "power elite" (usurpers of positions of leadership formerly awarded to persons of merit, concerned with public well-being) fifty years ago has bowdlerized common use of the term. Since Mills, the term "elite" in any context has been negativized. The word in any of its contexts, as used by those for whom words are arsenal, has, quite without reason, taken on the overtone of "usurper". It is used in much the way as Robespierre's rabble used the word "aristocrat". Far from describing holders of a body of knowledge or experience, it now implies Machiavellian intent to any who stand outside the crowd.

Thanks to the witch-hunt against them, elites have gone into hiding. They present themselves attired in what sociologist David Reisman has described as "proletarian drag". Their language is monosyllabic, their cadence diffident. Elites are, however, very much with us — which is good, since they are part of the promise of America.

The cudgel of accusation of "elitism" does damage to the venerable idea of America as a meritocracy. A meritocracy is perfectly compatible with democracy. In fact, reward and promotion for merit is one of the most attractive features of democracy, its allowance for advancement of the good regardless of previous station. Anti-elitist demagoguery attacks and subverts the very idea of advancement through merit.

An elite is a minority, deserving of the protection of law accorded any minority in the United States. An elite can suffer from bigotry as well as any minority. A person dominated by a search for excellence is both a minority and an elite. A stance that casts doubt on the motives of persons of principle, always few in number, compares with aggression against minorities as we know it in other theaters of our society. As in other manifestations, the weapon of accusations of "elitism" is the outward and visible sign of a hostile takeover bid by persons unsure of their own qualifications. There is precedent among the bigotries of our national past. It's done all the time. The victim of the demonizing of "elitism", however, is excellence.

Whose interest is served by this particular corruption? Of course, the interests of some of us are served by public ignorance: the purveyors of shoddy products, the purveyors of shoddy ideas, demagogues. They profit, sometimes immensely. They bray loudly, sometimes on the floor of the US Congress. There have been so many in our recent past in fact that their exposure nowadays causes only yawns.

Among populist public television apparatchiks, the tactic of demonization of whatever is unique and special has been a remarkably effective part of the arsenal used against innovativeness. Never mind such well-taken cautions as the declaration by the Carnegie Commission that "a call for excellence is not a retreat to elitism". Richard O. Moore, a former manager of KQED San Francisco, has seen cause to lament, "Public television has devised a system wherein the power rests with a collection of institutions and boards as a protection against the exceptional. It is a system that guarantees the second-rate in the name of localism and system survival." Mr. Moore wrote this in 1975, before the invention of the latest manifestation of "Caliban's revenge",[194] now called "political correctness" and "multiculturalism".

What *is* multiculturalism? What *is* political correctness? "Multiculturalism" is a diversionary tactic. It makes a shibboleth of cultural diversity, defining it in a mechanistic, noncultural way. True cultural diversity is the richness not only of America but of any society. "From each according to his abilities", is the way Marx put it. In cultural terms, that means each shall contribute in accordance with the resources at his command, including cultural heritage. The tradition of multiculturalism is a long one. Latin, Gaelic, and Welsh language and thought are part of the English language and culture today. Shakespeare cribbed from the Romans. Leonard Bernstein cribbed from Voltaire. The French today declare themselves the intellectual descendents of the Periclean Athenians. Margaret Mead and Ruth Benedict identified the universal validity of multiculturalism in the 1940s. Arnold Toynbee observed (correctly) that as long as there has been human history, wherever peoples have met they have mixed. Multiculturalism lies outside biological differentiation. It exists within genetically similar groups. Multiculturalism is intellectual diversity. Multiculturalism is the way history is and the way it has always worked. Radio, television, newspapers and jet plane travel have just made it happen faster.

In the hands of public television, multiculturalism has become a device for the suppression of art. A clue can be found in a report of public television's 1991 Forum for Producers of Culturally Diverse Programming.[195] Tellingly, the report defines a cultural diversity that may be "cultural" in some aspect but is essentially a highly limited, racially/ethnically-defined ghettoization that ends at the Atlantic and Pacific Oceans. It defies the principles of integration. Participants in the 1991 Forum were predominantly Spanish speaking, Asian American, Native American and Black. They were brought together to assert their differences, not to share. The report gives away the secret of "cultural diversity". It declares that America's "new pluralism" means that "the demographic scales will tip in favor of minorities by the beginning of the next century."[196] You can see from this that multiculturalism as defined by public TV has little to do with human diversity, little to do with the complex knowledges of differences that Margaret Mead and Ruth Benedict revealed half a century ago, little to do with the development of a cosmopolitan society. Instead, it has a lot to do with a statistical projection that in America there will soon be significant voting blocs for the Congress to beguile. Suddenly, thanks to a demographic statistical projection, the concept of "multiculturalism" is defined as a concomitant of congressional self-interest. Suddenly any shared belief of a voting bloc is deemed worthy of priority assignment by congressional funders of public television. The motive of Congress is transparently political. Art, and those minorities being thrown a bone, are ill-used.

Why the push? Why the sudden discovery of what has been there all along? Beyond a signal by four groups that they can soon represent a substantial voting bloc, there is that old motivation, opportunistic personal ambition. Multiculturalism is being used today as a "revolution" in the sense we have seen it many times in South America — a traditional power grab by "have-nots", the more talented of whom want to make their own valid place in the scheme of things, the less talented of whom want to displace somebody else, with an eye toward usurping their power, influence and emoluments, and see this as the easiest and quickest course.

Affirmative Action in employment, the principle whereby an accident of birth (for congressionally defined "minority" persons) may qualify a person for preference that overrides merit, is a flawed maneuver. Judging people on the basis of an accident of birth is a denial of one of the underlying principles of democracy. Among the reasons democracy came into being was to end inequities resulting from the concept of the aristocracies of birth that were derived from "the divine right of kings". A casualty of rationalism and the science of genetics that brought into the question the inheritability of character traits and intellectual capability, this scientifically discredited concept was replaced by the concept of meritocracy. The end of primogeniture, the discrediting of nepotism, the rise of feminism as a redress of the wrongs of patriarchal privilege, all are a part of the democratization of the relations among people, the social purpose of which is the general welfare.

In *Animal Farm*, George Orwell described a flagrantly irrational concept justifying preference as "some people are more equal than others." The restitution of the practice of conferring unearned privilege due to an accident of birth is the flaw in the policy of instrumentation of the potential cultural enrichment that "multiculturalism" offers into an employment quota system called Affirmative Action.

The multicultural intent of Affirmative Action has been perverted. Affirmative Action has been used in practice as an instrument of vendetta by a particular spectrum of second and third generation Americans against descendents of the oppressors of their ancestors. And (like an English hereditary lordship) it has become a tactic for opportunistic career advancement of the less qualified. Its opponents rightly see the events around them as proof that the reality of Affirmative Action is ignoble, patronizing, flawed. A flawed remedy put to an ignoble, opportunistic end is a situation in need of reevaluation.

There are certainly some among all races and classes who have the potential to make a contribution to human wisdom in excess of those who "affirmatively act". Today, however, if these happen to be not of a designated group, if they are Armenian, or gay, or intellectual, they may find themselves pushed aside. Not only must these minorities look out for themselves, they must defend themselves against people who are of less social utility but have a sanctioned preference due to an accident of birth.

Affirmative Action is exclusive. It is patronizing. It proceeds from an arrogance and condescension on the part of its instigators. It proceeds from a hypothesis that the decisionmakers of the currently ruling group are "better" than others, and have a duty to bring others who are less fortunate "up" to their empyrean perch. The presumption that a person who can create a specification, create an organization chart, organize categories, formulate a strategy or tactic, operate a network or count up to a trillion is somehow "better" than his fellows is not necessarily supported by historic precedent. Its opponents rightly see Affirmative Action as a denial of the primacy of human imagination, intelligence, inventiveness, merit. It implies that America is some kind of futureless, finished factory, and that the jobs in it can be filled by interchangeable drones. The clever among its beneficiaries rightly see it as shallow and manipulative, and so they manipulate it to their advantage. As the tool of backlash, it has demonstrated that an opportunism that sets its highest premium on self-advancement regardless of the consequences to others is not restricted to Anglo-Saxons. Aggressive "multiculturalism" has become a cloak for self-seeking. The term "multicultural" is now code for "I want a job in a university." Certainly that must be evident to any observer. Governmental sponsorship that redefines multiculturalism as restricted to only six selected US genetic and biological "minority groups" reveals itself as shallow opportunism: behind the smoke screen lurks a simple electoral threat and its self-serving response, a bid for votes.[197]

Functionally, for a legislator, this false "multiculturalism" is a neat synthetic issue, a red herring that diverts public attention from real issues facing our society. Harvard's Prof. James Russell has declared multiculturalism to be "a cover for a political agenda", "an ideological bit of chicanery, a mask for bigotry." Legislators should be wary. The harm it could do was pointed out by critic Frank Kermode: "the self-ghettoizing of Black history or women's history presages a more general social fragmentation, and endangers the precious ideal of political unity in ethnic diversity."[198] The world has always tended toward multiculturalism. This goes for their cultures, too. "Multiculturalism" and "Political Correctness" as simple job-and-role-usurpation, as a cultural "coup", is unworthy of the support of reflective people whatever their origins.

A 1953 comment of David D. Henry, Executive Vice Chancellor of New York University, bears repeating: *"Television is dangerous, for it might improperly become the means of a state control of ideas"* (italics mine). Public television, by its fealty to government funding sources, has through the natural course of pursuit of its own self-interest been rendered incapable of taking an objective position. "Public television is so immersed in its problems about congressional funding that it's impossible to measure the degree to which they're caving in to pressure . . . but it's enormous", wrote Malcolm Carter in 1971. With survival perennially in doubt, it "knuckles under" uncritically to the congressional agenda, be it Affirmative Action or "noncontroversial programming". Its potential as an organ of the "fourth estate" defused, public TV is a victim of government censorship . . . beholden, deprived, held on the short leash of annual appropriation. Our public television can't bring itself to be either critic or contributor. Its self-interest forbids it to be the "other voice" any culture's establishment needs. Public television may prefer not to let on, but like a courtesan in a modest apartment, on the "good" side of town, its well-being is contingent on the favors it gives. Public television is the powerless victim of the abuse of power of the executive and legislative branches of the US government in their use of the authorization and appropriation process as a tool of censorship.

A long and involved process has led public television to its position as publicity agent for the federal legislature. The loss to the public dialogue has been massive. Because of its fealty to funding through the political process, public television cannot be a critic of that process. Instead, it remains for other organs than public television to inform the electorate regarding political nonperformance. It remained for a magazine, the respected *The Economist* to state, "It was Ronald Reagan who ran up the ($4 trillion national) debt as if it were Old Glory on the Fourth of July."[199] Why not somebody on our alternative television? Three guesses.

The British Broadcasting Company, perhaps seeing the American example, has declared explicitly, "The BBC's acknowledged strength as an independent information provider . . . should not be compromised by close association with or dependence on the government of the day."[200] American public television has served the people ill because the people who have elected to make public television their careers have yielded to pressure to compromise with the fundamental principles that constitute public television's *raison d'être*. They have allowed their decisions to be made by people whose unspoken but overriding priorities are government contracts, retail sales, worker docility or their own job, power or status. They have consented to live with abuse of power and censorship by major agencies of the federal government.

Chapter 25

PROGRAMS AS PRODUCT:
FORTY YEARS OF CAPITAL FORMATION

O f the library of programs that have been broadcast over American public television, some should be owned, or at least seen, by any intelligent person. A minimal collection of four (Jacob Bronowski's *The Ascent of Man*, Kenneth Clark's *Civilisation*, James Burke's *Connections* and Robert Hughes' *American Visions: The Epic History of Art in America*) would be welcome in the library of any person blessed with the capacity for reflection and inquiry. These essays are landmarks in the history of television. They explore its uniqueness and power. They qualify as a basis for study by any would-be makers of television, and by anybody seriously interested in television as a civilizing force.

How did they happen? What is the root cause of these triumphs? How can the causes be duplicated?

The universally acknowledged "great" television series were *all* made outside the United States. Why weren't they, or others like them, made in the USA? I offer here the beginnings of a solution and a remedy.

"Programs are our only purpose", says *The History of Public Broadcasting* (page 74). Okay. A traditional measure of the success of any enterprise is the durability of its product. If we want to establish at least a general outline about the success of public television, it is logical to ask the question, "What programs made for educational and public television have stood the test of time?" A basis for assessment can be found in documents circulated by public television itself.

Guides to programs were circulated to the general public by PBS. PBS made three "levels" of catalog available. "PBS Home Video" was the most widely distributed catalog.

It listed the programs that public television offered for sale in VHS cassette form. To anyone who asked, public television would forward the booklet of over 60 pages listing and describing almost 300 VHS videocassettes offered. (Inside its cover was a photograph of Ervin S. Duggan, President and CEO of the Public Broadcasting Service, whose broad experience in the emerging art form that is noncommercial broadcasting includes a life-experience more than heavily weighted in the field of government service, as a presidential assistant at the White House, and in various functions at the Departments of State and Health, Education and Welfare, and the Federal Communications Commission. Mr. Duggan is pictured with *Sesame Street's* "Big Bird".)

A second source of available public TV cassette offerings is the "PBS Video" catalogue, which includes listings for the school market. For the most part, it is redundant to "PBS Home Video". Included with general interest and civics are instructional videos about math and science. The instructional videos differ in that many are perked-up with beguilements, amusements and "celebrities" in imitation of commercial television.

The third catalog is called "PBS Video Catalog of Educational Resources" and is clearly intended for more serious users. 240 pages long, measuring eight by ten inches, it includes most of the entries in the other two catalogs and many more of a didactic nature.

The catalogues, and the beguiling public television shops opening in selected shopping malls, are commercial. Therefore, we may expect that some titles that PBS might have thought were desirable or appropriate are, for reasons of ownership, copyright, etc., unavailable. Nonetheless, a listing of cassettes distributed by PBS and their origins is instructive.

A compilation follows, made by the author from listings of available videocassettes during the years 1993-1996. The category headings I've used to organize the following listings are not those used by PBS. The reason may be that the categories I've established, though probably fairly accurate, wouldn't "look good". You'll notice that a high proportion of the offerings were produced by independent production entities, sometimes in cooperation with a public TV station. A majority, mainly imports and public issues programs, are brokered or produced through one public station, Boston's WGBH, with WNET New York and WETA Washington as a distant second and third. Other public stations, like Wisconsin, Chicago, Maryland, Los Angeles, Phoenix, Chicago, and St. Louis are represented by a few entries focused on regional subjects. This list seems to indicate that the lion's share of programs, and by inference the lion's share of the money from Congress, has been going to WGBH-TV, Boston.

Over the long term the two American heroes of the list, obvious recipients of really major funding, are WGBH's *Frontline* and, in recent years, Ken Burns' ride-the-tide Florentine Productions. Frontline's "in-depth", "hard" news program effectively continues the 45-year-old butter-up-the-FCC tradition of *CBS Reports*. Like *CBS Reports*, its subjects are closely attuned to the agendas of official Washington. An ideological tie-in may be found with Columbia University's School of Journalism, where former CBS Reports/Ford Foundation powerhouse, the late Fred Friendly, had a professorship, and which produces its own talking-heads series featuring Washington Bigdomes.

Then there's the meteoric Ken Burns, who burst on the scene with *The Civil War*, liberally supported by no less than General Motors. You may detect a halo of national pride in the subject matter of nearly all Burns' meticulously produced paeans to competitiveness and techno-nationalism. Burns' dioramas mine the tradition of 19th century history painting, historic tourist sites, calendar art and *Saturday Evening Post* covers. The astute Burns, sensitive to the image concerns of major governmental and corporate funding sources, has discovered that stroking the funders in government and industry and the public all at the same time is a wondrously effective strategy. His tactical device has made him into a one-man industry behind a resurgence of self-congratulatory down-home populism of "The Things that Make America Great".

An apparent presumption underlying the productions listed is that television (contrary to my contention here) is neither art form nor theater. An underlying thread of nationalism permeates the American product. You'll notice that in these listings there are no programs about France, Germany, Italy or Eastern Europe; there are only 23 titles about non-American people of achievement, nothing about small countries of any continent. You'll find no operas and only four plays listed. There is little, particularly in the American product, that could be called "original" or "creative". What historically has been known as "high culture" is fig-leafed under the guise of subjects for the idle curious, like "travel". There are dramatizations of time-honored English novels, but little literature from any other country, almost no theater, a formal minimum about the stellar achievements of most cultures, painting or sculpture, architecture, art or poetry. As I mentioned earlier, "Civilizations are not remembered for their politics or their economics", declared philosopher John Dewey, "They are remembered for their art and architecture." America public TV evidently marches to a different drummer, with politics and economics setting the pace.

In the list that follows, the brilliant essays of Britishers Kenneth Clark and James Burke (both recycled to US Public television) stand out in high relief. These two represent an astute and sensitive nonfiction use of the medium, and are treasures of television achievement. Alone among American essayists is the voice of Bill Moyers, like a ballad from an earlier age, singing of creativity, speculative thought, the arts, or higher learning. (Moyers' former role as Press Secretary to a dead president, his history as a man of the cloth and the modest outlay required by his mostly interview and talk shows, gives his opinions a certain immunity from attack by congressional cultural watchdogs).

If you examine the list carefully, you'll find programs about "political correctness" in many guises . . . anthropological, economic, artistic, sociological, and legal. There are 28 such programs and series under the category I've headed "Our Great Country's Heritage: Gender/Race/Ethnicity" — offerings that appear to have arisen from the idea of differentiation of one class of people from another, not on the basis of achievement but on the basis of attributes over which they have no control, like accidents of birth. Historically, in the days of cultural dominance of the idea of an American Meritocracy, this particular form of differentiation was known as "bigotry". By a curious reversal, these arbitrary isolations of classes of people into categories based on an accident of birth are presented as a source of pride. With propaganda of inverse bigotry, the powerful, attempting to defuse them, patronize the powerless. Are they fooled? Probably not.

"Issues" facing the electorate (taken from the headlines) abound. You'll notice substantial efforts designed to generate a climate of acceptance and support for the underpinnings of the late unlamented Cold War: appreciations of warfare, of science and technology, of the learnings that workers were thought to need in order to support commerce or the armaments industry. You'll find folklore, that of Washington establishment professionals, in the Columbia University Seminars.

The following lists present the product of forty years of noncommercial television—the programs Public Broadcasting has selected for preservation. By far the largest number, 70 programs and series, fall under the heading, "Government Issues Shared With America's Electorate". In this category you will find subjects that the federal legislature apparently thinks should occupy your mind. You will see there that the viewer is defined not in terms of human breadth but in terms of his or her relationship to the political process. This selective definition of the viewer is indicative, of course, of the presumptions underlying a TV system defined in practice as the propaganda arm of the federal legislature.

Next in number to you-as-electorate programs come you-as-someone-in-need-of-self-improvement, 43 "how-to" programs and series ranging from weight control, nutrition and exercise to sports, self-defense, computers, math, writing and even one on how to get old. These useful programs explore one of the most effective attributes of television as a teaching device: its application to a tell-show-do teaching method. These can be seen as fitting into the funders' agenda as exemplars of the validity of techno-fix methodologies.

Back to nationalism — there are 31 non-fiction programs and series celebrating Our Great Country's successes in combat, and 7 fictional celebrations of America's martial supremacy. Other people's wars, mostly ancient, merit four programs and series. Next come 35 celebrations of our achievements in technology. There are eight programs and series about other nations' technology. The national goals of developing a Fortress America and a market technology spawned 26 programs and series celebrating our achievements in science, the underpinning of weapons and consumer product technology. 30 programs and series can be described as simple civics lessons, to help you vote knowledgeably for the program's funders. 28 programs and series look to be "personality" portraits of the nation's politicians.

The 22 varied programs and series about mysticism and religiosity are beyond my power to explain.

The same number, 22, feature biographies of exceptional *nonpolitical* Americans. Who are these exceptional Americans whose efforts merit canonization by public television? A diverse group — included among the twenty-two are six writers, four musicians, two

Senator Byrd realizes that, during the impeachment trial, not one new Federal installation, highway, bridge, sewage treatment plant or hospital, bearing his name, has been built in the State of West Virginia.

WELL, ENOUGH OF THIS...

Jeff Danziger

"But how do you know for sure you've got power unless you abuse it?"

aviators, two murderers, one mathematician, one inventor and one anthropologist.

Eighteen programs from our noncommercial TV feature the achievements of American commerce. There are 20 programs on what for fifty years has been touted as the potential glory of television: the arts and architecture.

Approximately 20% of the offerings culled from forty years of American public broadcasting are British in origin. There are 19 British costume dramas, and 17 programs and series on British humor. Perhaps to indulge the American TV viewer's taste for violence, so well cultivated by commercial network television, there are 17 British murder mysteries, a total of 54 British programs and series. The British product is instructive. It is characterized by intelligence, inventiveness, production skill, imagination, theatricality, taste, and an investment of time and resources in production far in excess of the standard of the American product. In themselves the British products constitute as good a critique of American public television as you might ask for.

Sixteen programs and series celebrate Our Great Country's heritage. Thirteen are about status architecture, of all things. For Neo-Darwinists, there are 12 programs and series about animals. There are 10 about how things work, from the human mind to the baseball industry. Non-American subjects of all kinds get short shrift. There are 3 about non-American political figures, one each about American theater and British theater. On the subject that has been the crowning intellectual achievement of human civilization, philosophy, there is *one* series, about ethics, from the perspective of children.

If you were a member of Congress, you'd want tax dollars spent so that Americans could see these TV shows, wouldn't you? On the other hand, if you were someone other than a post-World War II American politician . . . God, for example, or Plato or William James or John Dewey or the Librarian of Congress or Bertrand Russell or the President of Brown University or John Updike, the list would be rather different, wouldn't it? The studious will observe that most works proceeding from major funding from federal sources reflect a mind-set long ago identified by Stendhal in a description of the French Directory in the Paris of 1796 . . . "a mortal hatred of anything not mediocre".[201]

You may see before you an American noncommercial television that is a Potemkin Village. The categories and numbers in this incomplete listing indicate the ideological bent of the makers of programs for American public television. Their eloquence is unmistakable. Pay particular attention to the programs and series produced in the United States. The imports, despite their high quality and the diversity of subject matter, can be seen from the perspective of the funding of US public television simply as discount merchandise, programs the system that funds American public broadcasting doesn't feel seriously enough about to commit "real" resources to.

The degree to which these titles demonstrate the goals of public television, the single alternative to commercial television extant in this 200 million member, two trillion dollar GDP democracy, is telling. The number of programs under each subject heading is a key to the priority structure and the uses to which public television is put.

The list below summarizes the subject categories into which the programs may be said to fall, with the number of titles in each, in descending numerical order. (Category titles are my own.) This is followed by a closer look at each category and the titles represented therein; the categories are grouped according to related topics.

SUBJECT/PRIORITY	NUMBER OF TITLES
Issues Facing Your Elected Representatives	71
America's Technological Successes	42
Learn Skills	42
America's Combat Success: Nonfiction	41
Science	36
The Historic"Melting Pot", Cultures Behind Ours	34
Mysticism/Religiosity	34
Our Great Country's Heritage: Gender/Race/Ethnicity	31
Civics Lessons for the American Electorate	30
American Political "Stars"	30
British Thought: Costume Drama	28
American Nonpolitical "Stars"	23
Art	22
British Thought: Humor	22
British Thought: The Thrill of the Hunt	21
Celebrating Our Great Country's Commerce	20
Architecture	19
America's Technological Heritage	11
Behavior Lessons for a Competitive Culture:	13
Behavior Lessons for a Competitive Culture: Sport	12
How Things Work	12
America's Combat Successes: Fiction	7
Beyond Our Borders	6
Non-American Nonpolitical "Stars"	6
British Thought: Theater	5
Non-American Political "Stars"	5
American Thought: The Thrill of Murder & the Chase	4
American Thought: Humor	3
American Thought: Theater	2
Ethics	1

ISSUES FACING YOUR
ELECTED REPRESENTATIVES . . . 71 TITLES

CASSETTE NAME	ORIGINATOR
A Couple of Beers	Soapbox
A Decade of Hard Choices	Columbia University Seminars
A Public Voice . . . '95 Contested Values	Milton B. Hoffman Productions
A Public Voice . . . '95 Violence, Immigration	Milton B. Hoffman Productions
Addictions	Mind
After Goodbye: An AIDS Story	KERA
AIDS Fighters	Club Connect
AIDS	Life Matters
AIDS In Search of A Miracle	Managing Our Miracles
AIDS, Blood and Politics	Carole Langer/Health Quarterly/WGBH
America's Managed Care Revolution	Columbia University, WNET
America's War on Poverty (5 hours)	Blackside
American Schools: Who gives a Damn?	Columbia University Seminars
An Appointment with Death (Euthanasia)	Virginia Storing/WGBH
Andy Rooney Collection	CBS
Arab and Jew	PBS
Ashes of the Cold War	June Cross/WGBH
Behind Bars	Sue Castle
Breast Implants on Trial	Jon Palfreman
Business vs. the Media	Columbia U. Seminars
Caring for Tomorrow's Children	WETA
Censorship or Selection: Books for Public Schools	Columbia University Seminars
Choosing Death	WGBH
Currents of Fear (sexual abuse)	Jon Palfreman/WGBH
Dilemma in the Newsroom	Columbia U. Seminars
Divided Memories (Sexual abuse)	Ofra Bikel/WGBH
Does TV Kill?	Michal McLeod
Drug-Free Youth	Club Connect
Drugs and AIDS: Getting the Message Out	State of the Art, Inc
Go Back to Mexico!	Hector Galan/WGBH
Godfather of Cocaine	William Cran & Stephanie Tepper/WGBH
Great Crimes & Trials of the 20th Century (5 cassettes)	————
Hard Drugs, Hard Choices (4 cassettes)	Columbia University Seminars
In the Face of Terrorism (4 cassettes)	Columbia U. Seminars
Liberating America's Schools	Corp. for Educational TV & Radio

Listening to Children	PBS
Living on the Edge	Tom Casciato & Kathleen Hughes
Mafia (4 cassettes)	Arts & Entertainment
Managing Our Miracles:	Columbia University Seminars
Health Care (10 cassettes)	
Medicine at the Crossroads (8 cassettes)	WNET/BBC /WETA/Australian BC,
Mixed Messages and the Media	Club Connect
Murder on Abortion Row	Virginia Storring & John Zaritsky
Picture This-AIDS and TEENS	Spellbound Video Pdctns/WFYI-TV
Public Lands, Private Profits	Stephen Talbot
Rachel Carson's Silent Spring	Neil Goodwin
Return to Alcatraz	————
Safe Speech, Free Speech	Columbia University Seminars
& the University	
Sarajevo: The Living and the Dead	Radovan Tadic/WGBH
Secrets of a Bomb Factory	Mike McLeod/WGBH
So You Want to Buy a President?	Michael Kirk
Substance Abuse Prevention I, II, III	Club Connect
Tabloid Truth:	Tom Lennon/WGBH
The Michael Jackson Scandal	
Teaching Students with Special Needs	Maryland Instructional TV
(15 parts)	
Teens Talk AIDS	In The Mix
The Death of Nancy Cuzan	Elizabeth Arledge/WGBH
The Health Care Gamble	Noel Buckner & Rob Whittlesey/WGBH
The Kevorkian File	Michael Kirk,/WGBH
The Media and the Military	Columbia U. Seminars
The Military and the News Media	Columbia U. Seminars
The Mob(4 cassettes)	Arts & Entertainment
The Nicotine War	Jon Palfreman
The Orphan Trains	PBS
The Other Side of the News	Columbia U. Seminars, TV Espanola SA
Waco-The Inside Story	Michael Kirk, Michael McLeod/WGBH
Welcome to Happy Valley	Paul Sapin and Marc Etkind/WGBH
What Happened to the Drug War?	Jim Gilmore & Joe Rosenbloom
When Doctors Get Cancer	Ruth Yorkin Drazen
Who Shal l Be Healed?	WNET
Who Will Teach for America?	Drew/Fairchild/Conn. Public TV
Who's Afraid of Rupert Murdoch?	Jim Gilmore/WGBH

CIVICS LESSONS FOR
THE AMERICAN ELECTORATE ... 30 TITLES

Alaska: Man & Nature (4 cassettes) Frontier Collection
Amerika (5 cassettes) ———
America's State Capitals (4 cassettes) City Productions
Baraka   Mark Magidson
Campaigning for the Presidency UCSD/ KPBS
Chicago 1968 Chana Gazit
China in Transition MacNeil Lehrer
Clarence Thomas & Anita Hill Ofra Bikel/WGBH
Dark Passages Tanya Hart & Valerie Whitmore
Divided Nation: Americans Speak Out WHYY
Economics USA (7 cassettes) PBS
History's Turning Points (6 cassettes) Ambrose
Inside the FBI (4 cassettes) WETA, Channel 4 (England)
Inside the Republican Revolution Manifold
Is This Any Way to Run A Government? Martin & Frank Koughan/WGBH
Mississippi, America Judith McCray, WSIR Carbondale
Presidents and Politics with Richard Strout Moyers/WNET
Reinventing Government in America Wisconsin public TV
Search & Seizure: Film Odyssey, Inc.
    The Supreme Court & the Police
That Delicate Balance II: Our Bill of Rights Columbia University
The Best Campaign Money Can Buy Steven Talbot/WGBH
The Challengers '96 (5 cassettes) WETA
The Constitution (7 cassettes) PBS
The Modern Presidency (5 cassettes) Enterprise Media, Inc.
The Politics of Power Jan Legnitto/WGBH
The Power Game (4 cassettes) Philip Burton Productions/U. of Md.
The Presidency and the Constitution Columbia University Seminars
    (7 cassettes)
The Presidency: Light Side Up UCSD/KPBS
The Rage for Democracy University of Chicago
The Unelected The Power Game

AMERICAN POLITICAL "STARS" ... 30 TITLES
Civil War Legends (4 cassettes) ———
Eisenhower Austin Hoyt, Adriana Boxh/WGBH
FDR David Grubin/WGBH
Frederick Douglass WETA/ROJA
George Washington David Sutherland/WGBH

Hilary's Class	Rachel Dretzin & Jane West/WGBH
Huey Long	Ken Burns & Richard Kilberg
Inside the Republican Revolution	Manifold Productions
Jackie, A Tribute to the First Lady	Discovery
LBJ	David Grubin/WGBH
Lincoln(4 cassettes)	Peter W. Kunhardt
Malcolm X	Blackside/ROJA
Monuments to Freedom	History Channel
Nixon (3 cassettes)	Elizabeth Deane/WGBH
One Woman, One vote	Educational Film Center
Real Richard Nixon (3 cassettes)	———
Roundtable '95	David Paradine/WETA
Summer of Judgment (2 cassettes)	WETA
The Challengers (5 cassettes)	WETA
The Congress	Ken Burns & Stephen Ives
The Kennedys (4 hours)	Mellowes, Whitehead, Espar, DeVinney/ WGBH
The Kennedys of Massachusetts	Orion
The Lincoln Assassination (2 cassettes)	History Channel.
The Long March of Newt Gingrich	Stephen Talbot
The Men Who Killed Kennedy	Starmaster
The Power Game (4 cassettes)	Philip Burton/Maryland public TV
Thomas Jefferson	Central Virginia Educational Telecommunications WCVE/WHTJ, WNVC
Thurgood Marshall: Portrait of an American	Hero Columbia Video Productions
TR and His Times	Bill Moyers
United States Presidents (5 cassettes)	City Productions

NON-AMERICAN POLITICAL "STARS"
. . . 5 TITLES

Churchill & the Cabinet War Rooms	History Channel
Churchill The Speeches Collection	MPI Home Video
Mandela	BBC/Panorama
The Churchills (3 cassettes)	WGBH/Brook Associates
The Struggle for Russia	Sherry Jones/WGBH

AMERICAN NONPOLITICAL "STARS"
. . . 23 TITLES

A Portrait of Elie Wiesel	WHYY, Philadelphia
Amelia Earhart	Nancy Porter
American Heroes: The Educated	Press & The Public Project
Edgar Allen Poe, Terror of The Soul	Film Odyssey

Einstein	VPI Vidifilm/Lumen Pdctns/WNET
Fires in the Mirror (Anna Deavere Smith)	Public Television Playhouse
Ford: The Man and the Machine	Cabin Fever
Hemingway in Cuba	——
In Remembrance of Martin (Luther King)	Idanha Films
Rabi: Man of the Century	Moyers
Leonard Bernstein's Concerts (3 cassettes)	——
Lindbergh	Stephen Ives/WGBH
Margaret Mead: Taking Note	Odyssey
Marian Anderson	WETA
The Odyssey of John Dos Passos	Stephen Talbot
Oscar Peterson (2 cassettes)	View Video
Pauline Kael	Writer's Workshop
Barnum: America's Greatest Showman	Discovery
Susan Sontag	Writer's Workshop
The Battle over Citizen Kane	Tomas Lennon, Michael Epstein
The Grateful Dead	——
The Man Who Shot John Lennon	Kevin Sim
Who Was Lee Harvey Oswald?	William Cran/WGBH

NON-AMERICAN, NONPOLITICAL "STARS"
. . . 6 TITLES

Franz Boas, Anthropologist	Odyssey
Mozart	Arts & Entertainment
Piaf	FFI
The Homecoming (Solzhenitsyn)	Archie Baron/BBC/WGBH
The Life of Leonardo da Vinci (3 cassettes)	Questar
Three Tenors Encore (2 cassettes)	——

AMERICA'S COMBAT SUCCESS: NONFICTION
. . . 41 TITLES

The Alamo	History Channel
America Goes to War:	
The Home Front-WWII	Anthony Potter Productions
America's Battleground	JoAnn Garrett
America, Love it or Leave It	ALIOLI Associates
Between the Wars (8 cassettes)	Anthony Potter Productions
Churchill and the Secret War Rooms	History Channel
D-Day	Charles Guggenheim
Campaigns in the Pacific (7 cassettes)	——
D-Day to Berlin	George Stevens

Emerging Power	Wall Street Journal
Enola Gay and the Atomic Bombing of Japan	History Channel
Espinosa	WGBH
Home Away From Home, Yanks in Ireland	
Honor & Glory	Arts & Entertainment
Last Stand at Little Big Horn	Paul Stekler/WGBH
Medal of Honor World War II	Cabin Fever
Postwar Hopes, Cold war Fears	Moyers
Raising the Bamboo Curtain	Questar
Sea Wings (3 cassettes)	Discovery
Sunken Secrets of World War II	————
The American Revolution(6 cassettes)	Arts & Entertainment
The Century of Warfare	Time-Life
The Battle of the Bulge	Thomas Lennon/WGBH
The Civil War (9 cassettes)	Burns/Florentine
The Great War-1918	Tom Weidlinger
The Gulf War (2 cassettes)	Eammon Matthews
The Hunt for Pancho Villa	Hector Galan & Paul
The March of Time:War Breaks Out (6 cassettes)	New Line
The Prize	Public Media Video
The Revolutionary War (3 cassettes)	Discovery Channel
The War Years	FFI
The Way West (12 hours)	Lisa Ades and Ric Burns
USS Intrepid	History Channel
Victory at Sea (6 cassettes)	New Line
Vietnam Memorial	Steve York and Foster Wiley
Wings of Glory: The Air Force Story	
(7 cassettes)	————
War in the Gulf (6 cassettes)	CNN
World War I (5 cassettes)	CBS
World War II (7 cassettes)	Arts & Entertainment
World War II with Walter Cronkite	CBS
(8 cassettes)	
World War II Collection:	
General Schwarzkopf (5 cassettes)	

AMERICA'S COMBAT SUCCESS:
FICTION . . . 7 TITLES

A Rumor of War (3 cassettes)	————
Guns of August	MCA
Holocaust	Republic Pictures
Piece of Cake (6 cassettes)	————
Schindler's List	MCA

The Winds of War	Paramount
War & Remembrance (12 cassettes)	————

COMBAT . . . 5 TITLES

Ancient Warriors (3 cassettes)	Learning Channel
Crusades(4 cassettes)	Arts & Entertainment
Great Commanders	Ambrose Video
Knights & Armor	Arts & Entertainment
War and Peace (3 cassettes)	Kultur

SCIENCE . . . 35 TITLES

A Glorious Accident	JFI
Bill Nye, Science Guy	Disney
A Brief History of Time (Stephen Hawking)	Errol Morris
The Blue Planet	Smithsonian
Children's Encyclopedia of Science (3 cassettes)	Oxford
Cirque du Soleil	Telemax
Cosmos (7 cassettes)	Turner
The Creation of the Universe	Northstar Productions
Discovering Great Minds of Science (6 cassettes)	————
Earth: The Changing Environment	Global Links
Edison's Miracle of Light	————
Gemstones of America	Smithsonian
Icewalk (4 cassettes)	Icewalk, Inc.
Insects	————
Life on Earth (2 cassettes)	Warner
Mechanical Universe	PBS
Nature's Symphony	Reader's Digest
The Nature Connection (6 cassettes)	————
Other People's Garbage	Odyssey
Planet Earth (7 cassettes)	PBS
Planet of Life(4 cassettes)	Discovery Channel
Stargazers	Discovery
Symphony to the Planets (2 cassettes)	Questar
The Brain (3 cassettes)	Discovery
The Creation of the Universe	Northstar
The Earth Explored (14 cassettes)	KRMA-TV/BBC
The Great Comet Crash	WHYY
The Living Smithsonian	Smithsonian
The Nobel Legacy	IMG/TWI

The Private Lives of Plants (6 cassettes)	———
The Ring of Truth (6 cassettes)	PBA
Tornado Video Classics	———
Tornado Chasers	Arts & Entertainment
Under the Microscope I & II (13 cassettes)	Prince George County Public Schools
Voyage to the Outer Planets & Beyond (Asimov)	Allied Artists Entertainment

AMERICA'S TECHNOLOGICAL HERITAGE ... 11 TITLES

Amazing World of Trains	Arts & Entertainment
British Rail Journeys	RV Television
Connections (10 cassettes)	Ambrose Video
Connections II (10 cassettes)	Ambrose Video
Floating Palaces (4 cassettes)	Arts & Entertainment
Great Eastern Train Rides	Questar
Irish Railway Journey	BBC
The Hindenburg	History Channel
Train Journeys in Australia	Banksia Productions
The Great Indian Railway	National Geographic
The New Glacier Express	Switzerland

AMERICA'S TECHNOLOGICAL SUCCESSES ... 42 TITLES

America by Air	Windows of the World
America's Railroads (7 cassettes)	———
America on the Road	Moyers
Apollo 11:Missions to the Moon	———
Apollo 13 (2 cassettes)	MCA
Ben's Mill	Odyssey
Bush Pilots of Alaska	Migratory Films
Change, Change	Moyers
Colt Firearms Legends	Sony
Cyberfuture	MacNeil/Lehrer Productions
Driving Passion	———
Edison's Miracle of light	Matthew Collins
Empire of the Air: Radio	Ken Burns, Morgan Wesson, Tom Lewis
Eyes in the Sky	Discovery
Fire Fighters	Arts & Entertainment
Flight Over the Equator	Discovery
Formula 1 Saga (4 cassettes)	White Star

Guardians of the Night: Lighthouses	————
Great Drives (5 cassettes)	PBS
Great Eastern American Train ides	Questar
Harley Davidson	American Motor Classics
High Stakes in Cyberspace	Martin Koughan & Frank Koughan
Implant II, Knee Replacement Surgery	KAET
Life on the Internet (13 half-hours)	Georgia public TV/Cochran
Moon Shot (2 cassettes)	Varied Directions International
Triumph of the Nerds	Oregon Public B'casting, Johan Gau Pdctns
Out of the Fiery Furnace	Opus Films
Panama Canal	Arts & Entertainment
Skyscraper,	KCTS/Ch4 London
Spaceflight (4 cassettes)	PBS
Spy in the Sky	Linda Garmon
Subway	Arts & Entertainment
The Brooklyn Bridge	Burns, Stechler, Squires, Sherman
The Building of the Boeing 777 (5 cassettes)	Karl Sabbach
The Implant	KAET
The Information Society	Aspen
The Internet Show	Brandenburg/Production Co./Rice U.
The Iron Road	Neil Goodwin/WGBH
The Wright Stuff	Nancy Porter & Kate Hudec
Trucks: Masters of the Open Road	Arts & Entertainment
Tunnels	Arts & Entertainment
World's Greatest Roller Coaster Thrills	————

LEARN SKILLS . . . 42 TITLES

Minute Acupressure Facelift	————
The Art of Coffee	————
Against All Odds: Inside Statistics	
(7 cassettes)	Brandeis
Algebra (7 cassettes)	PBS
Art Linkletter on Positive Aging (2 cassettes)	Kip Walton Pdctns
Autism: Reaching the Child Within	WHA-TV
Books from Cover to Cover (15 cassettes)	WETA
College Composition	————
Conquer the New S.A.T.	USC
Cooking for Good Health	California Culinary Academy
Covert Bailey's Fit or Fat (13 cassettes)	KVIE
Covert Bailey's Smart Exercise	KVIE
De Medici Kitchen	Direct Cinema Limited
Discovering Psychology (7 cassettes)	PBS
Eat Smart	MacNeil/Lehrer Georgetown U.
Fighting Cancer	MacNeil/Lehrer

Fit or Fat for the 90s	KVIE
French in Action (7 cassettes)	PBS
Futures (24 parts)	FASE
Here's To Your Health	KERA
Internet Starter Kit	————
Introduction to Spanish (7 cassettes)	PBS
Is Your Number Up? (Cholesterol)	New Jersey Network
Leo Bascaglia Specials (7 cassettes)	KVIE
Life Matters (7 cassettes)	KERA
Living & Working in Space	FASE
Math Talk (20 cassettes)	Children's TV Workshop
Math . . . Who Needs it?!	FASE
More Books from Cover to Cover (16 cassettes)	WETA
Nutrition: Eating to Live or Living to Eat	Here's to Your Health
On the Issues	Perlmutter
Powers of Ten	Eames
Quarterbacking the Spurrier Way	White Hawk Pictures
Read On: Cover to Cover (16 cassettes)	WETA
Tai Chi	————
The Coming of Age (5 cassettes)	Wisconsin public TV
The Eddie Files (4 parts)	FASE
The Kay Toliver Files (4 cassettes)	FASE
The Ring of Truth (6 cassettes)	PBS
Working Solutions	Rutgers/WNET
Writer's Workshop (15 cassettes)	U. of South Carolina
Writers Reading	Trinity Church

HOW THINGS WORK . . . 12 TITLES

A Place for Madness	DeWitt Sage/WGBH
Computer Animation Festival	SONY Music Entertainment
Discovering Psychology	CPB
Last One Picked	PBS
Madness (5 cassettes)	BBC/KCET
Prisoners of Silence (Autism)	Jon Palfreman/WGBH
The Body Atlas (6 cassettes)	Ambrose Video
The Glorious Accident (8 cassettes)	JH
The Implant	KAET
The Mechanical Universe (7 cassettes)	CPB
The Mind (9 cassettes)	WNET
The Transformation of Man (2 cassettes)	Mystic Fire Video

THE HISTORIC "MELTING POT": CULTURES BEHIND OURS . . . 34 TITLES

Ancient Greece (2 cassettes)	Kultur
American Traditions (6 cassettes)	TEG Video
Crusades (4 cassettes)	Arts & Entertainment
Charlemagne (5 cassettes)	Acorn
Days of Majesty	Yorkshire Television Ltd.
Epic Voyages of History	FFH
Florence	PBS
Forbidden City	Discovery
Gargoyles	————
Great Cities of the Ancient World	
(2 cassettes)	Questar
Great Splendors of the World	Reader's Digest
History's Turning Points	Ambrose Video
Jerusalem: From a dream to Destruction	History Channel
Legacy	Ambrose Video
Life on Earth	Warner
Lost Civilizations	Time-Life
Macedonia (2 cassettes)	Kultur
Mummies & The Wonders of	
Ancient Egypt	Arts & Entertainment
Majesty, the History of	
the British Monarchy	————
Maya: Lords of the Jungle	Odyssey
Myths and Moundbuilders	Odyssey
Odyssey of Troy	Arts & Entertainment
Petra	Arts & Entertainment
Pharaohs and Kings (2 cassettes)	Discovery
Pompeii	Arts & Entertainment
Roman City	Unicorn Projects
The Incas	Odyssey
The Light That Failed (the USSR)	MacNeil/Lehrer
The Power of the Past With Bill Moyers:	
Florence David	Grubin/WETA
The Silk Road I & II (12 cassettes)	Central Park Media
The Twenties	Corp for Learning & Technology
Inside The Vatican	Multimedia Entertainment
The Way West (4 cassettes)	PBS, American Experience
The Western Tradition (7 cassettes)	UCLA, PBS

OUR GREAT COUNTRY'S HERITAGE: GENDER/RACE/ETHNICITY

. . . 31 TITLES

A Class Divided	Janet Elliott,/Yale University Films
A Lynching in Marion	Wisconsin Public Television
America and the Holocaust	————
Black American Conservatism:	
An Explication of Ideas	Corp. for Educational TV & Radio
Can We Get Along?	MacNeil/Lehrer
Clarence Thomas and Anita Hill	Ofra Bikel/WGBH
Dark Passages	Tanya Hart & Valerie Whitmore/BET
Eyes on the Prize, I & II (14 cassettes)	Blackside, Inc
Far Away from the Shamrock Shore	————
Flyers in Search of a Dream	Philip Hart/UCLA/WGBH
Held In Trust: The Story of	
Lt. Henry O. Flipper	KCOS, El Paso
Journey to America	Charles Guggenheim
Mafia	Arts & entertainment
Memory of the Camps	Sergei Noblandov & Stephanie Tepper
Midnight Ramble	Northern Light Productions
Mississippi, America	Judith McCray/WSIU
Native Land: Nomads of the Dawn	
New York: The Way It Was (3 cassettes)	Acorn
One Woman, One Vote	Educational Film Center
Out of Ireland	Shanashie Entertainment
Pocahontas	————
Primal Mind	————
Roots of Resistance	Orlando Bagwell
Save the Males: An Endangered Species	KUHT
Survivors of the Holocaust	Spielberg
Seeking the First Americans	Odyssey
The Spirit of Crazy Horse	PBS
The Mob	Arts &Entertainment
The Native Americans (6 cassettes)	————
The Orphan Trains	Janet Graham & Ed Gray
Women First and Foremost (3 cassettes)	————

CELEBRATING
OUR GREAT COUNTRY'S COMMERCE
. . . 20 TITLES

An Ice Cream Show	————
Bill Gates	David Paradine & WETA
Global Links (6 cassettes)	WETA/World Bank
Heartbeat of America	Steve Talbot/WGBH
Hot Money	Peter Malloy/WGBH
How to Steal $500 Million	Jim Gilmore/WGBH
Japan Reaches for the 21st Century	PSG
Off Limits: Your Health, Job, Privacy	Educational Film Center
On the Issues I & II (48 cassettes)	Alvin H. Perlmutter
Popular Culture: Rage, Rights and Responsibility	Columbia University Seminars
Power in the Pacific (4 cassettes)	KCET
Profits and Promises:	Friendly/Columbia U/WNET
Public Lands, Private Profits	Stephen Talbot/WGBH
Team Spirit	MacNeil/Lehrer
The Begging Game	Joe Berlinger & Bruce Sinofsky/WGBH
The Diamond Empire	WGBH/BBC/Australia/Impact/Inca
The Entrepreneurs (6 cassettes)	Martin Sandler/Concepts Unlimited
The Story of Federal Express	Moyers
Working Solutions (4 cassettes)	Rutgers/WNET
Your Money and Your Life: Managed Care	Columbia University/WNET

BEHAVIOR LESSONS FOR
A CULTURE OF COMPETITIVENESS: SPORT
. . . 12 TITLES

Bad Golf Made Easier	Rocket Pictures/ABC
Bad Golf My Way	Rocket Pictures/ABC
Baseball (9 cassettes)	Ken Burns
Dorf Goes Fishing	Fish n Hole Partners
The First Olympics Athens 1896	————
Idols of the Game	————
Lindbergh's Great Race	————
Liquid Stage	Michael Bouce
The Marathon: A History of the Great Race	————
Greg Norman's Golf	CBS Fox
Years of Olympic Glory	Panasonic
Warren Miller's Ski Package	Warren Miller Entertainment

BEHAVIOR LESSONS
FOR THE CULTURE OF COMPETITIVENESS:
WILD ANIMALS . . . 13 TITLES

Audubon Society Specials (8 cassettes)	Christopher N.Palmer/Turner/WETA
Dive the World	Kuredu Rangalli & Angaga Fish Head
Dolphins	PBS
Encounters with Whales	One World Films
In the Wild (3 cassettes)	Tigris/Meridian/WNET New York
Nature of Australia (3 cassettes)	PBS
Sharks(3 cassettes)	National Geographic
Southern Africa Safari	Video Expeditions
Tales of the Serengeti (4 cassettes)	————
The Chimps of Gombre	Discovery
The Dinosaurs! (4 cassettes)	WHYY, Philadelphia
The Vertical Environment	Echo/Idaho public TV
Untamed Africa (2 cassettes)	Questar

MYSTICISM/RELIGIOSITY . . . 34 TITLES

Abraham, Jacob, & Joseph (4 cassettes)	————
Amazing Grace with Bill Moyers	PBS
Ancient Secrets of the Bible	CBS
Angel Stories (2 cassettes)	Cascom
Angels	Time-Life
Bermuda Triangle Secrets Revealed	Questar
Body, Mind & Soul(2 cassettes)	Mojo Productions
Castle Ghosts of England	Discovery
Conversations with God	————
Crusade: the Life of Billy Graham	Turner
Discovering Everyday Spirituality	Laura/ Hanuck/Scott
Dead Sea Scrolls	Arts & Entertainment
Inside the Vatican (4 cassettes)	Multimedia Entertainment
Joseph Campbell & the Power of Myth (6 cassettes)	Mystic Fire
Life After Life	————
Mary Magdelen	View Video
Maya Angelou: Rainbow in the Clouds	WTVS
Nostradamus	Arts & Entertainment
Pharaohs and Kings	Discovery
Reincarnation: Coming Home	Vladimir Kabelik
Reaching Beyond the Magical Child	
Seeking God	————
Seven Spiritual Laws of Success	Mystic Fire

Sights & Sounds of Nature (7 cassettes)	———
Sunday Morning	Soapbox
Teenagers and Religion	Soapbox
Telegrams From the Dead	Matthew Collins/WGBH
The Bible(8 cassettes)	———
The Old Testament Collection (6 cassettes)	Arts & Entertainment
The Glory and the Power: Fundamentalisms	WETA/U. Of Chi/BBC
The Search for Satan	Ofra Bikel & Rachel Dretzin/WGBH
The Shakers: Hands to Work, Hearts to God	American Documentaries, Inc.
The Vatican	Glenn Warren Entertainment
Zen: The Best of Alan Watts	

ETHICS . . . 1 TITLE

Listening to Children, A Moral Journey	Social Media Productions, Duke U.

BRITISH THOUGHT:
COSTUME DRAMA . . . 28 TITLES

A Town Like Alice (3 cassettes)	———
Bah!Humbug!	WNET
The Black Candle	Tyne Tees
Bramwell (4 cassettes)	Carlton UK
Catherine Cookson Collection (4 cassettes)	BFS Video
Charlemagne (5 cassettes)	Acorn
Elizabeth R (6 cassettes)	BBC
Emma	BBC
Eye on the Prize (7 cassettes)	PBS
Hard Times	BBC /WGBH
Claudius (7 cassettes)	———
Jane Eyre	BBC
Jewel in the Crown (8 Cassettes)	Granada, England
Martin Chuzzlewit (5 cassettes)	BBC /WGBH
Martin Scorsese Presents 4 Films (4 cassettes)	Republic Pictures
Middlemarch (6 cassettes)	BBC/WGBH
Moby Dick	Comic Classics/WPBT
Northanger Abbey	BBC
Nicholas & Alexandra	Sam Spiegel & Franklin Schaffner/Columbia
Persuasion	BBC
Pride and Prejudice (6 cassettes)	Arts & Entertainment
Pride & Prejudice (2 cassettes)	BBC
Sense & Sensibility	BBC
Six Wives of Henry VIII (6 cassettes)	BBC, England

The Buccaneers (3 cassettes)	BBC
The Far Pavilions (4 cassettes)	———
Three Sovereigns for Sarah (3 cassettes)	NightOwl Productions
Upstairs Downstairs (7 cassettes)	Thames TV

BRITISH THOUGHT: THEATER ... 5 TITLES

Discovering Hamlet	Unicorn
Shakespeare (6 cassettes)	Films for the Humanities & Science
Three by Shakespeare (6 cassettes)	———
Riverdance: The Show	———
Torvill & Dean:	
Face the Music Tour (skating)	———

AMERICAN THOUGHT: THEATER ... 2 TITLES

Fires in the Mirror	Public Television Playhouse, Inc.
Tales of The City	Propaganda/Working Title

BRITISH THOUGHT:
THE THRILL OF THE HUNT ... 21 TITLES

A touch of Frost (3 cassettes)	———
Brother Cadfael (7 cassettes)	Central Independent TV
A Dark Adapted Eye	BBC
Dr. Who (4 cassettes)	BBC
A Fatal Inversion	BBC
Gallowglass	BBC
Hands of a Murderer	England
Ian Richards, House of Cards, Play the King	
(6 cassettes)	BBC England
Inspector Morse (6 cassettes)	BFS
Inspector Morse V (6 cassettes)	England
Memoirs of Sherlock Holmes	———
Miss Marple (5 cassettes)	Arts & Entertainment
More Sherlock Holmes (5 cassettes)	England
Murder of the Century	Carl Charlson
James: Devices and Desires (6 cassettes)	Arts & Entertainment
Prime Suspect (3 cassettes)	Granada
Sharpe's Collection (4 cassettes)	England
Sherlock Holmes (5 cassettes)	———
To Play the King	BBC England
Treasure! (3 cassettes)	Treasure Seekers
Two by Catherine Cookson	England

AMERICAN THOUGHT:
THE THRILL OF MURDER,
THE THRILL OF THE CHASE . . . 4 TITLES

Mafia	Arts & Entertainment
The Mob	Arts & Entertainment
The Secret Service	Arts & Entertainment
COA the Secret Files	Arts & Emtertainment

BRITISH THOUGHT:
HUMOR . . . 22 TITLES

Absolutely Fabulous (4 cassettes)	BBC England
Alec Guinness Collection (4 cassettes)	British Sterling
Are You Being Served? (2 cassettes)	BBC
Benny Hill's New York	British Sterling
Black Adder Collection (8 Cassettes)	BBC
The Darling Buds of May	Yorkshire
Fawlty Towers	BBC
Class Act (4 cassettes)	Carlton
How to Irritate People	David Paradine
Jeeves & Wooster (6 cassettes)	Arts & Entertainment
Keeping Up Appearances	BBC
Mr. Bean: Ron Atkinson (6 cassettes)	BBC
Monty Python Collection(3 cassettes)	England
Red Dwarf VI (2 cassettes)	BBC
Root into Europe	Aspect/Central TV
Take a Letter Mr. Jones	Questar
The Amazing Mr. Bean	————
The Best of Benny Hill	British Sterling
The Best of Red Green	————
The Little Rascals (9 cassettes)	Cabin Fever
Wallace & Gromit (2 cassettes)	Republic Pictures
Waiting for God	BBC

AMERICAN THOUGHT: HUMOR . . . 3 TITLES

Burns and Allen Show (9 cassettes)	Screen Gems
Honeymooners, Lost Episodes	MPI
The Three Stooges (10 cassettes)	Columbia Picture

ART . . . 22 TITLES

America By Design (5 cassettes)	Werner Schumann, Guggenheim Productions
American Indian Artists	KAET
Art of the Western World(4 cassettes)	Kultur
Artists of the Harlem Renaissance	NJN
Cezanne: The Riddle of the Bathers	———————
Civilisation (7 cassettes)	Public Media
Creativity (17 cassettes)	CEL Communications
Degenerate Art	David Grubin Productions
The Fantastic World of M.C. Escher	Michele Emmer/Film7
Golden Age of Silent Films (7 cassettes)	—————
Great Tales of Asian Art	—————
The Hermitage	—————
Louvre 2000 (3 cassettes)	Stan Neumann
Teen Artists	Club Connect
The Art of Illusion	Smithsonian
The Battle over Citizen Kane	Thomas Lennon & Michael Epstein/WGBH
The Bernier Art Lectures (9 cassettes)	Metropolitan Museum of Art
The Dancing Man-Peg Leg Bates	Hudson West/South Carolina ETV
The Unquiet Library	WETA
Thomas Hart Benton	Ken Burns & Julie Dunphey
Visions of the Future	Club Connect
Women and Creativity	Moyers

ARCHITECTURE . . . 6 TITLES

The Architecture of Frank Lloyd Wright	ABC Multimedia
Pyramid	Unicorn Projects
Castle Unicorn Projects	
Cathedral	Unicorn Projects
Frank Lloyd Wright: Prophet Without Honor WHA-TV	
Uncommon Places: Frank Lloyd Wright	WHA-TV

STATUS ARCHITECTURE . . . 13 TITLES

America's Castles (6 cassettes)	Arts & Entertainment
America's Castles II	Arts & Entertainment
Britain: The Garden Kingdom	—————
Camelot	Arts & Entertainment
Castle	Unicorn Projects
Chatsworth Manor House (3 cassettes)	————
Gardens of the World with Audrey Hepburn	————
Historic Homes	Arts & Entertainment

Palaces of the World	Discovery
Statue of Liberty	Buddy Squires & Ken Burns
The Irish Country House	———
The Places We Live (2 cassettes)	Films for Humanities & Sciences
Washington National Cathedral	WETA

BEYOND OUR BORDERS . . . 6 TITLES

An Irish Country Calendar (4 cassettes)	———
China in Transition	MacNeil Lehrer
Red Flag Over Tibet	David Breashears/WGBH
Scotland the Brave	———
Three Faces of Scotland (3 cassettes)	———
Nature Perfected: the Story of the Garden (6 cassettes)	———

This list reveals a hierarchy of priorities for American public television. Of 562 programs and series, the largest number, 344, can be interpreted as furthering either the mission or self-interest of one group — the federal legislature. For the most part, these reveal a bipartisan agreement that citizens should have knowledges and skills regarding the workings of government, the underpinnings of Cold War preparedness (science, technology, skills), and the contributions of persons involved in political life. The forty-year control of Congress by Democrats is evidenced by some 65 titles dedicated to "politically correct" issues regarding selected minorities. A favorite subject of Republicans, competitive commerce, its sporting training ground and its theoretical adjunct neo-Darwinism, are represented by 45 titles.

If *Masterpiece Theater*, *Mystery* and single British series are excepted, we are left with approximately 145 of the 562 programs and series, only around one fourth of the public television programs of more than momentary interest, that can be said *not* to involve issues or subjects of concern to the US Congress. That only *one* of the 562 titles is concerned directly with ethics should come as no surprise to those familiar with procedures of campaign funding and lobbyist originated legislation within the democratic process.

Issues of direct interest to the federal government — programs and series about government and governmental concerns — number 136 titles. Warfare numbers 53 programs and series, "political correctness", 53; "enterprise", 45. So, there are 299 programs and series distributed by public television as its "oeuvre" that could be described as government propaganda.

The 34 programs and/or series about mysticism are themselves somewhat of a mystery; that there should be only one about ethics is probably not. The 73 programs and series devoted to the dramatizations of English novels, to British humor and to mystery fiction should bring satisfaction to the guardians of British culture. Forty-one programs and series about art and architecture are a tribute to those who are willing to tolerate jittery images caused by 525 visible lines of visual information and bad color in order to experience something of the domestic savoring of visual esthetic that was the historic promise of the promoters of television. That there should be as many as 41 programs and series about art in this list may be a clue that visual representation of a high order represents a promise of more arts programs for the coming days of High Definition Television.

These programs demonstrate the structure of our priorities. How many of these could be seen as self-serving and self-promoting to some members of the US Senate and House of Representatives? About three-quarters of them.

The programs made in America are revealing. Are these programs a picture of the "public", of a broad spectrum of alternative television? Do they represent the needs of that public, the civilization of which we are a part? Is this a list of programs whose content would be determined by donors, by public TV executives, by the creative community? Do they demonstrate American creativity, verve, ingenuity, humor, sensibility, and depth of thought? Or do they demonstrate short-term objectives of a cadre of politicians who happen to be politically dominant? Decide for yourself. Is this a picture of America we would want others to see, or to emulate in their own countries?

What this list does is to reveal the priorities of those who have authorized and appropriated funding for public television during its lifetime. Behind the TV announcer's agreeable promise of "The fine programs brought to you over public television", a specific kind of animal is bedded down. The evident substructure of these "best" programs, as you can see from this list, represents something other than the set of priorities one might expect from an organization devoted to the exploration of our cultural diversity and accomplishment.

The above statistics reveal a substructure of program development for public television whose engines are nationalism, propaganda, publicity, self-seeking, self-promotion, manipulativeness and thought control. What this list reveals is the degree to which opportunism has found loopholes in the Public Television Act of 1967, the law that established the structure of noncommercial television production, loopholes that the US Congress has used to make public television into its own instrument. If a democratic society is an issue, this list is an argument for systemic change.

Chapter 26
THE CULTURE OF CONSUMERISM

ommercial television teaches, as I have said. What it teaches feeds into the broader education of the populace, with effects far broader than the immediate sales goals of sponsors. Inevitably, not only the commercials but also the content of the programs reflect the worldview of the policymakers . . . boardroom members who, at the same time as they make decisions regarding commercial sponsorship, also make decisions as to how their own lives may be led most conveniently and satisfyingly.

Public service should be a factor in the decisionmaking of a person who seeks membership on a board. However, public service for these folks is likely to be defined in terms of their own self-interest. Universal understanding, even broad understanding, is not a necessary attribute of the corporate mentality. It is neither claimed nor sought. A customer is a means, not an end. The corporate mentality is honed to razor sharpness, like a spear, highly directional, entirely directed to the goals set by the organization's charter. It's a sacred duty. Any assumption that the goals of a fast food or entertainment company and the traditional goals of human civilization may be congruent has validity that can only be temporary and local.

534 corporations are big enough and distribute widely enough to qualify as sponsors of network television.[202] The cognitive habituations of a fast food or entertainment company today do not necessarily prepare its leadership to assume the role of educator. It's nonetheless true that in commercial television, as in politics, the people who run the rich companies *are* our educators. This is what we have to live with, wherever there is "commercial sponsorship" — simply an instrumentation of the corporation's "sacred duty" to its stockholders. The laws governing corporate activity require corporate leadership to look out for corporate advantage first. Corporate leaders who identify with their company can be expected to approve and encourage (as part of their corporate responsibility) be-

haviors they see as being to their own advantage.

There's a necessary parochialism. You can almost predict how a sponsor will receive an idea. The sponsor's first and most significant question is, does this idea or does any idea stand to improve his company's balance sheet?

Can you imagine any commercial sponsor who could see his interest furthered by your knowledge of history, your reflectiveness, your philosophic inquiring doubt, your originality, and your sensibility? It simply follows from the logic of the circumstances that there are no TV shows today, commercial or public, that encourage attributes that were once deemed essential to any civilized person. "America is a place of lies and bitter disappointment . . . It promises everything but eats you alive." This sentiment, articulated by a character in E. Annie Proulx's novel, *Accordion Crimes*,[203] calls forward the downside of consumerism. "Internalized self-censorship is now the primary threat to free-speech journalism in America today,[204] writes media historian Robert W. Machesney. "The penalty for veering way from the corporate world view is the guillotine." That is a reality that we'll have to face up to. Our society is materialistic. Its philosophy is utilitarianist. Its method is economic determinism. Its acolytes are advertisers. As long as each of us realizes that, to the vast majority of our countrymen, the life of each of us as an individual is a means to *their* end, we'll be able to cope. Since World War II, our relationships to our fellow Americans have changed. Nowadays, far from being those of community held together by multiple acts of selflessness, our noncommercial relationships are more nearly simply a truce.

Even Christmas has been commercialized. Compassion and love have been trivialized into a retail circus. Commerce laughs Christianity out of existence by creating cartoon characters like pneumatic sex-kitten Santa Clauses and Rudolph the Reindeer to romp over a religion's most holy day, selling presents.

As long as each of us keeps up his guard, as long as we remain skeptical, as long as we recognize that today the meaning of the term "the public", far from meaning a body of unique individuals, means "consumers" or "electorate", as long as we factor into our decisions that we are only the instrument of the actions of others, not the goal, we'll be able to approach workable decisionmaking. We know what we're dealing with. We know that there are galaxies of human wisdom and understanding that don't serve corporate charters, and so are outside the mission of sponsors and CEOs. There is another world out there . . . the world that the idea of the joint-stock corporation was brought into being to *serve*.

Some among us seem to have forgotten that the society out there is not a tool, a means to corporate ends, an instrumental good leading to the absolute good of corporate well-being. No, the reverse is true. The economy has some other purpose than to enable the people who inhabit it to meet their material needs. The corporation is the tool, the instrumental good leading to the absolute good defined as the well-being of society. Tails must not wag dogs.

The lesson that the unreflective may be controlled through beguilement is a new formulation of the primrose path. The "Disneyfication" of consumerist America appears to be the market economy's extrapolation from our constitutionally guaranteed orientation to the Pursuit of Happiness. After World War II, through the "free" decisions of customers voting with their dollars, the pursuit of happiness evolved into the pursuit of pleasure, then the pursuit of fun.[205] Disneyfication makes it possible for the consumer to have the pleasure of consumption, recollections of infantilism, and familial togetherness all at once.

Disney's procedures could well have been directly modeled on T.S. Eliot's observation, "Humankind cannot bear too much reality." Its agreeableness is undeniable. The money it generates for those who control it is vast. Its long-term social outcome, however, is questionable. Possibly, "Disneyfication" is most successful as an instrument of control. Disney's Michael Eisner can lay claim to being the Pied Piper of consumerism. Almost single-handedly he has transformed Walt Disney's enterprise. Critic Herbert Muschamp puts his finger on Disney's mutation:

> (Walt) Disney's enchantment was America's. His images of wonder were a metaphor for a nation that, in his time, was as blessed as any magic kingdom. Then, like American moral authority, the Disney magic waned. The padded Mickeys, the bloated theme parks, the denatured wholesomeness came to seem like desperate overcompensation for curdled American innocence.[206]

When Eisner takes our children into escapist worlds less of wonder than of agreeable hallucination, can we ever get them back? Michael Parenti says that the most successful forms of tyranny are "those that insinuate themselves into the imagery of our consciousness and the fabric of our lives so as not to be perceived as tyranny."[207]

As has happened with the children of successful warriors, kings and industrialists, throughout history, the children of consumerism may well be demonstrating to us that the coupling of democracy and consumer-directed "free enterprise" has brought self-indulgent, irresponsible, frittering, and puerile decadence; and it affects a larger mass than ever before. You may have noticed that nowadays nearly everybody (except those chronically poor that our economy mandates) has the option to do as only Marie Antoinette once could: they can choose to know nothing, dress down, and play, through a whole lifetime. Many do, too.

A lament by the critic "Vroon" in *American Record Guide* of November/December 1996 is a metaphor for the attributes that consumerism encourages. In a review of *Hole in our Soul* by Martha Bayles (University of Chicago) and *The Triumph of Vulgarity* by Robert Pattison (1987), an extreme version of the quintessential consumer lies in his description of rock-n-roll:

> Man in his natural state is a selfish ranter. The vulgarian lives in the primal disorder that classical culture is designed to subdue. He goes wherever his passions take him and knows nothing of reasoned reflection. Morality is swallowed up in sensations. . . . Rock glorifies self and instinct at the expense of community and reason, and it has no social conscience.

Could this be intentional?

Is it possible that a control-obsessed caste in our own society has deliberately modeled its plans after Japan's Shogunate? When the Shoguns took over, the deposed aristocracy was encouraged to attend the long-forbidden Kabuki dramas, on the presumption that their addiction to diversions would render them ill-equipped to develop the intellectual resources or the discipline to threaten the Shoguns' control.

In our democracy, the people are our aristocracy. The lessons of the courts of Europe may apply to the American situation. In the courts of Europe the pattern was oft repeated. History excoriates the chamberlains, viziers, and courtiers who flattered and pandered to power. Their interest was not the well-being of the state but their own comfort, enrichment or advancement. Their method, history tells us, was to seize control by catering to weakness, by rendering their ruler impotent by enticing him, her or them into self-absorption, luxury, and pleasure. The consequences were disastrous every time. Now, in popular democracy, huge centralized organizations take the place of the courtiers of yore, but their methods applied to the American aristocracy, the people, are familiar. Michael Parenti points out that in the American media, "Ideological control is not formal, overt and ubiquitous, but informal, covert and implicit."[208]

In our country the public and commercial television systems have been fashioned into vehicles of thought control. The method has been the use of television as an instrument of the ideological seduction of our country's rulers, the general public. The parallels to courtiers of yore are instructive. The annals of addictions chronicle delight as a tool of control. They also point out the danger to the victim. Are these public diversions functional to others than the public themselves? They are to their creators. Thank goodness the Congress is a rotten TV producer, or the guile behind public TV's funding could be subtle, and perhaps even appealing. That would be *really* dangerous!

History would tell us that freedom is fragile. Some measure of control can return to the people if, in the realm of broadcasting, they look beneath the surface of the following statements:

"The airwaves belong to the people."

"Your contributions make it possible for you to see the fine programs you see on public television."

"Corporate support of public television is charitable."

"Ours is public television, not state television."

"We're tarts, not whores."

Chapter 27

WHAT KIND OF FUTURE ANYWAY, MR. MARX?

Public television is not an attractive target for a metaphorical corporate raider to take over and make "lean and mean". Efficiencies will have to originate from another source. From inside? Not likely. From privatization? That way, the baby goes out with the bath. The system of self-accommodating bureaucratization has had its way. In a matter of decades, without fanfare, grinding through its uncounted meetings, educational television has become another government bureaucracy, this one putting out formula television to the electorate under corporate surveillance. The hoped-for alternative to commercial TV became television by committee, television by second-guessing proposal and by Stakhanovite "peer" review process, it became timid television by annual appropriation process, frightened television politicized, desperately poor television stations scratching for some way, any way, to get an audience and get some money. Needy television stations bowing to power, elevating their winners — their fundraisers, marketers, public relations people — into program decisionmaking roles. (Imagine how benign an influence on public television programming is the participation in decisionmaking of the purveyor of the "Compost Happens" T-shirt!) We have ended up with manipulative television station executives as brokers of programs made by others, not innovative production but opportunistic acquisition specialists. That's public television.

It has been around for long enough now so that the corner offices all belong to those whom the system has encouraged. The victories have been won, the troublemakers have been exiled, the bargains have been struck, skeletons are in the closets and peace pipes have been smoked. Time has shown that good Stakhanovites in the public broadcasting system find out what the structure will allow. A lot of infighting, a lot of tribal initiation have gone into the structure the way it is. The ranks of the trustees have been winnowed. Their benefactors can now be confident that there will be no unsettling innovation, criticism or "controversy". The ten thousand faithful public TV staffers doing the government's bidding nationwide drudge without seniority, without pensions, at lower than government wages. Like the army of clerks in the Department of Agriculture or the Department of Commerce, they have no choice but to do government's bidding. Public TV initiates, like those in commercial TV, know the rules that good team players need never articulate. Whatever their articulated goals, their actions speak for themselves.

Is it a mirror to our culture? Our best hope is that it's not, but that it's a mirror of a process that can be changed.

Today, their sheer numbers make them a force. ("A bloated bureaucracy", filmmaker Frederick Weisman has called it.) President Reagan voiced a warning against just what has happened in public TV. In his final press conference, President Reagan pointed out that the underlying, inescapable primary motivation of all bureaucracy is self-perpetuation. Through this internal logic, a tribal subset of public television management has emerged. Its first priority is its own survival. Stated principles are abandoned in practice when they present an alternative to private self-interest. Implicitly, this form of "compromise" is understood by the public TV bureaucracy. It's understood by the funders, too, who exploit it for their own advantage. So, the programs that get produced for public TV are those that the public television bureaucracy now in place assesses as a guarantee of its own survival and growth. A very large bureaucracy representing a substantial vested interest can be counted on to propose and endorse a public television system that will best guarantee its own inertia.

What can viewers expect in the coming decade? They can expect the natural outcome of the Public Television Act of 1967, the power shift in noncommercial television from creative people to Congress. The workings of a Republican majority in Congress, after forty years of Democratic control, should see changes in the subjects, not the thrust, of public television programs. A cannonade of threats to the existence of public television from Republican majority leaders should be seen as simple saber rattling, its purpose to warn the public TV leadership to "shape up" and conform. The likelihood that the Congress will divest itself of its own well-funded propaganda forum is scant.

The "political correctness" pumping-up of voting blocs to feed the incumbencies of Democrats will disappear. Public TV will have to assess the agendas of an entirely new group of congressmen, and develop a strategy to flatter, cajole and pry funding out of them. Needless to say, the practice of second-guessing of congressional agendas will continue. On the basis of socio-political orientation, one can expect more imitations, more "American" whatevers, and much more use of the term "enterprise". There will be more about defining other nations as markets for American economic ideas. Neo-Darwinist animal shows should persist. As before, there will be no boat rocking allowed. It can be expected that public TV will be used to supplement the excellent "reality" coverage of C-

Span. How the fare of public TV will differ from that on commercial TV is difficult to predict, since the sponsors are the same. A domestic USIA that promotes the idea structure of whoever is behind political power and the promotion of the interests of PACs has become public TV's present and, if it is to survive as it is currently constructed, is probably public TV's future, too.

Since I first started flying to Washington in the 1950s to do CBS's service to the public as defined by the FCC, Washington has metastasized. Then, the really good restaurants were in clubs. Washington was a slow, genial, southern town. Today, it's more like the Florence of the Medicis or the Paris of Louis XIV. Ducal palaces housing lobbying enterprises vie with the Pentagon to crowd the seat of government. As in imperial ages before ours, the magnificence of the edifice signals the power of the ruler. The streets and the social gatherings are now alive with the soldiers of lordlings who vie for favor. When you arrive in Washington you need only say to your host, "What's he up to today?" and you'll get the latest on the *Roi-Soleil*, the President.

Thanks to PACs, lobbies and corporate control of information through media ownership, our government has been checkmated by industry.[209] This is no conspiracy. It's not because of malevolence, but because of duty to the imperatives of corporate structure that industry wants world hegemony. It's because of the need of occupants of elective office to be reelected, their need to have the resources of ever-larger revenues to build their own monuments, that they have sold themselves. It' s because it takes a lot of money to pay the going rates for air-time charged by the broadcasters whose empowerment is contingent on federal legislation, rates that candidates for public office must pay in the same way as any other for-profit entity. We now have the best government that money can buy. Public broadcasting is the voice of legislators caught on the horns of the dilemma of service to two masters, beholden to industry through campaign contributions and to a capricious public through the electoral process. While on the one hand promoting the industrial principles of accumulation, competitiveness, aggression, expansionism, opportunism and self-seeking, the Congress-as-instrument on the other hand defuses potential unrest by pabulum, by bread and circuses.

Those well-meaning individual contributors and volunteers who continue to support public broadcasting are compromised by their own credulity. A dwindling band, they are people of goodwill whose conscience and hope is strong enough to prompt denial of the evidence at hand. They are people who believe that the good things in life are to be shared, not simply had. Today, they represent a rearguard of an idea of civility that seems to have no place anymore. Our contention here is that these good people are wearing rose-colored glasses. "All those well-meaning people swindled by their own credulity", is the way Paul Fussell describes them in his book *BAD: The Dumbing of America* (Summit Books, 1991). He goes on to describe the phenomenon as "the manipulation of fools by knaves". People of high principle have been beguiled by the duplicity of manipulative people wearing masks of virtue. This, in public television! Would that it were not so!

Because they failed to fight for their own independence, because they turned their backs on their poverty, because they pretended, public television people have demonstrated themselves to be unworthy of the trust of these good people. That there aren't enough honorable and disinterested Americans to design, support, and work in a sound, comfortable, stable, productive community of public service television creators is a discredit to our parents, our schools, the economically well-to-do and the media who have explicitly and implicitly provided the standards of professional conduct by which we all are living today.

Chapter 28

THE BASKET CASE, WITH A SMILE

The end of the Cold War, the end of the Soviet Union were hailed by some as a victory not of the idea or the practice of democracy but of market economics. The idea of American world economic hegemony as a legitimate successor to the idea of "progress" glitters in many writings and speeches. "Globalization", American corporate economic expansionism, looks like an unstoppable force. The force of history, or at least economic history, looks as if it's "with" us. Or is it against us? Are we being caught up in another fantasy?

The ideas behind the American Revolution swept the world. France declared an end to privilege by right of birth with the simply articulated goal, "Liberty, Equality, Fraternity". Americans of those days and the decades following thought those words expressed America's national goal, too. The two revolutions were mutually supportive.

Recent years have brought to the United States the malling of America and seven-day-a-week shopping. Some foundations seem to have changed beneath our feet, while we weren't looking. For example, for *Liberté*, how does "Free Enterprise" sound? For *Egalité*, how's Neo-Darwinism's "winner-take-all and the Devil take the hindmost"? For *Fraternité*, how does "team competitiveness" sound? Or how about George Orwell's fine, "Ignorance is strength"? For "In God We Trust", how about "*Carpe Diem*"? Signals abound that our country has changed its national purpose.

A democratic people who neglect to support dissent and innovation for their own sakes, who allocate their resources exclusively to their own comfort and amusement, ape the decadent aristocrats of the societies ours was meant to supplant. The new American market priesthood sees their responsibility to anything or anybody beyond the bottom line as ending at the boundaries of family. The market has no place for selfless dedication to long-term human benefit — a guiding principle for millennia, a sustaining core of Judeo-Christian and other civilizations. When he was a cable television entrepreneur, Ted Turner pointed out the vacuum of social responsibility among America's rich on the occasion of his own donation of a billion dollars to help the unfortunate. The puniness and, more importantly, the discrimination in the kinds of support given to the idea of an independent public television by free-thinking Americans today ("viewers like you") is testimony to an irresponsibility on the part of the holders of our new wealth that separates them from *parvenus* of previous eras. To turn one's back on the openness of the society that created the conditions for one to become what one has become is a statement of thanklessness to the very community without which none of us would be here. Today's unwillingness of individuals to support a television system not beholden to special interests underlines the aptness of the 1980s term, "buccaneer".

Public television is in a sad state today in part due to the emergence of a new American power elite. Our new power elite is articulate, fit, competent, charming, attractive, seductive, well-groomed, loveless, manipulative, arrogant, callous, opportunistic, selfish and greedy. It has other things on its mind than service. Stewardship is a forgotten imperative. Articulate Americans now proudly turn their backs on the poor, the sick, the ignorant, the mad, the kind, the compassionate, the reflective, the inventive, and the wise. As individuals, our new power elite do not, for the most part support public television. Unlike Andrew Carnegie, J. P. Morgan, John D. Rockefeller, today's new rich see no connection between their incomes and any duty, responsibility or gratitude they may have to the society or the culture or the history on which they have climbed to economic preeminence. Our new rich are not stupid; it's just that, like the assumed viewer of the TV commercials they watched while growing up, they want to *have*, not to *give*. We cannot but hold the decisionmakers of public television blameworthy for their decision to ignore their part in this phenomenon or its implications. They "looked out for number one". They sacrificed their principles for their jobs.

If we are fundamentally different from all the societies that have preceded ours, US world economic hegemony may be a good idea. If we aren't different, we may do well to look back at other societies. In the past, societies ruled by competitiveness have been societies of scavengers destroyed by the cancers of opportunism and guile. We look contemptuously on Sumer and Akkad as societies of hyenas and jackals, some of them momentarily very rich. We look back to see people who took nature's gifts as their own, who cut them up into the smallest possible pieces and sold them at the highest possible price. We look back on their ruins with sorrow and pity. Assyria, Babylon, Rome. Greed, power, riches, waste, ruin.

The defined purpose of American commercial television today is to sell. An alternative to commercial television, desirable or undesirable as it may be, will only appeal to that category of humans to whom being sold things is a matter of other than primary importance. There are people, rich, poor, or in-between, who have been sold enough things to acquire a sense of diminishing returns. They are people who have an inkling or wish for a complex of human experience that gives them greater or more long-lasting satisfaction. These are people who have acquired a critical faculty despite the efforts of our public education system to engender conformism. These are the people who eschew fashion as a prepackaged commodity that only *masquerades* as the style that is worth having.

Are there any people like that left out there? Who has counted them? Well, they've been counted. In TV they're called "the people who stopped watching". They have rights too — minority rights. This is the public for which an alternative television has to be designed, a public not dominated by instinct, by selfishness, by impulse, or the call of the herd. If we are to have a national future, these are people our leadership needs to cultivate, not to neglect.

English critic A.J.P. Taylor once observed that, while the time has passed when the Great English Middle Class was defined as having at least one servant, the middle class has nonetheless continued to survive. Since they no longer have the servants, yet still survive, there must be some other common attribute, he hypothesized. The shared attribute of all members of that class, he determined, was that they are "imitators". In the 19th century they did what the Queen did (or, if not so integrated, then what Albert did). All evidence indicates that the English critic's "imitator" sobriquet applies to America as well.

When American community leaders are polled to define the issues in their communities during the past year, they invariably repeat what they've heard on the news broadcasts. (They repeat, sad to say, more of the issues carried on the larger audience broadcasts than, say, *The Lehrer News Hour*). It's understandable. Busy community leaders, like most of us, have other things to do than unearth issues. The lesson is that heeding community leaders in this context is listening to the ventriloquist's dummy. Convenient for the ventriloquist, albeit uninformative. A lesson? Watch out for the ventriloquist!

Public television stations have big publicity and public relations departments. Their purpose is to blow up pretty balloons about public TV, so the people will say "Ah!" Good middle class people, and therefore good imitators, the executives of public TV are students of the methods of presidential press secretaries, producers of commercials, and Disney.[210] They tell the public what the public would like to hear about public TV. They flatter and court their public, telling them that these "fine" programs are brought out by "viewers like you". The fawning and massaging they do are self-serving and shameless. The programs aren't fine, and they're mainly paid for by people who want the "viewers like you" to think in certain ways that are convenient for them.

Somebody at public TV knows there's something wrong. The statistics must engender discomfiture. What do they say? They show that public TV has over 200 stations (fewer than there once were) sitting in their well-staffed, multi-million dollar buildings, broadcasting over the "open air" frequencies that require a lot of electricity to reach not too many square miles. Meanwhile, all across the country, the technology of direct broadcast by satellite provides a radically cheap and efficient way to send a broadcast signal to every house in America for under a hundred dollars. That's the technology we have today. It promises to become better, more efficient and cheaper. And what about the people who get this alternative to commercial television to you? With the system we've developed, American public TV spends a billion dollars a year, one third less than the British BBC spends, and can't even approach the program production value of the BBC. (The BBC's 1991-92 spending was a little over $1.5 billion for BBC1 and BBC2 services.[21]) In America, a lot of what local public TV stations spend those billion dollars of mostly taxpayer money for is real estate, equipment and personnel. What about programs, you ask. Isn't that what television is? The billion dollars is not spent on local programs to any significant degree, and certainly not innovatively. (See the San *Francisco Chronicle/Examiner* Tom Tomorrow cartoon, "Pledge Time".*)*

Those occasional programs that make it to public TV that, in concept, proceed from a view of the public as anything other than electorate are nearly universally funded *outside* the normal public TV process. The funding of television according to the normal public TV process results in products that largely represent a view of humankind now known as "politically correct". In recognition of this lopsidedness, some decades ago the Corporation for Public Broadcasting inaugurated its Program Fund. The Program Fund was presented as an attempt to develop a quasi-independent television production funding entity under the aegis of the "non-governmental (*sic*), not-for profit, independent (*sic*) Corporation for Public Broadcasting", as it was known.

These were to be programs not born of public TV stations' courtly genuflecting toward their interpretations of the current priorities of the congressional funders. The Fund's mandate was to develop programs for the broader audience of the curious-minded. These were to be programs of a different and presumably superior kind to those being produced through the system of local station origination. The Fund represented a tacit admission that public broadcasting was not fulfilling its promise to the public to develop diverse and innovative programs, that the stations as production centers were failing the more cosmopolitan needs of the system. All this was true. The Program Fund was never very popular with stations. They saw it as taking away some of "their" money. The Program Fund's first director, the accomplished Lewis Freedman (in his youth, producer of CBS's experimental *Camera Three*), was one of television's independent minds, a pioneer of innovative programming. He lasted two years. With his resignation, the Program Fund was quickly transformed into another agency of political correctness.

What happened? One can infer that since the CPB Program Fund's source of income was the same as the public TV system's, it soon found itself subjected to the same conditional authorization pressures as the rest of public broadcasting. The Fund became a redundancy, replicating the public TV stations' role as media arm of eighty members of Congress. The Fund today has been required to devolve into a dribbler of miniscule support to ever more conventional programs about the American social issues that interest the Congress. Its annual "Open Solicitations to Producers" are "open" to programs that meet limited criteria. In about paragraph three or four of each solicitation, one may find restrictions to political correctness that identify the predilections of its funding sources. For example, the Corporation for Public Broadcasting's Station Production Solicitation with a closing date of August 1, 1995, declared among its criteria for the acceptable creative entity: "Producing teams should consider diversity: e.g., cultural, racial, ethnic, gender, geography, family configuration, age, socio-economic level." In other words, "If you're an independent television producer who's thinks there's something else to human life than political correctness, no matter how smart or experienced you are or how great your idea, don't bother to apply for a grant from us."

Here were some subjects in the works in 1993: Latino interests. Health care. AIDS. Martin Luther King. Conservative Value Systems. The Second World War. The 20th Century. Cherokees. Black Journalism. Hopi Indians. Rap. A Black Comedienne. Mexican-American Discrimination in World War II. Japanese Internment in World War II. African-American Stories. Chinese Students. Mississippi Voter Registration.[212] In 1994, the issue was "crime"; producers' approaches were given a nudge by the statement, "The siege of crime may be the price we pay for a brash, self-loving, relatively free and open society." Isn't it an uncanny coincidence how the subjects of these programs by "independent" producers stroke congressional agendas?

The elections of 1994 changed the complexion of Congress. A new wave of thought arrived with Republican majorities in both houses. Media savvy Newt Gingrich was the new House Majority leader. Gingrich quickly rattled sabers in the direction of public television. "Close it down", he threatened. Observers pointed out that Gingrich already had his own television network to broadcast his ideas, so why would he need another? As it turned out, the threats were idle. To abolish the forum for congressional discourse that is public broadcasting would be to close off a prime avenue for getting the message to the people. Public broadcasting was indeed funded by the new Congress, albeit not munificently. The real message from the new leadership to everybody involved in public television was: "Get in step, or watch out!" You can be sure the message was not lost on public television's toilers.

With Republicans now chairing the committees, the Corporation for Public Broadcasting's Program Fund, in its 1995 Program Fund Station Production Solicitation, abandoned as if overnight its Minority Primacy stance. Making the little bits of money available, they directed them to stations, with guidelines indicating that innovative talk shows would be welcome, the ancient romper-set pacifier *Mister Rogers' Neighborhood* and the issues-coming-before-Congress *The Lehrer News Hour* being examples for station producers to follow. Since everybody who knew how to do any but imitative kinds of television had long since departed from public TV, this request represents recognition of the situation as it stands. The idea of alternative television programming directed toward those needy unserved audiences characterized by sensibility, education, or intellectual curiosity has long ago vanished. Perhaps they don't vote the right way.

Could it be that the Congress believes that innovation, originality, and depth are to be found in copies of old network shows or low-budget minority and multicultural programming?[213] Obviously, innovation, originality and depth are not the issue.

Their seriousness may be measured by the level of funding made available through annual grants to public broadcasting and through government agencies. The techno-preparedness need of the Cold War was promoted by funding using federal tax money laundered through the National Science Foundation for the *NOVA* series. Not until the National Endowment for the Humanities saw the mileage it got from *The Civil War* has anything like the cost of a bridge abutment or a missile ever been offered by any agency of our government for a film idea. About as much money as Arnold Schwartzenegger makes in a minute is offered every year to a dozen or so "independent" producers. This bait (or "sop", depending on how you look at it) is to prompt budding geniuses to invent significant television programs about those select minorities defined by congressional mandate.

The Corporation for Public Broadcasting's Program Fund today supports little programs, only about issues that are "politically correct". The impact is predictable. As party dominance changes, the definition of the politically correct will follow. But whoever runs the show will call the tune. Perhaps reading them for what they are, the audiences desperate to see the resulting low-budget heartbleedings emit an inaudible clamor. (To paraphrase President Johnson, "If Lyndon Johnson were alive today, he'd turn over in his grave.")

Now that The Program Fund, too, has defaulted on its mission, it has been replaced in its intent by yet another agency that has declared as its purpose to do what once educational television, then public television, and later the Program Fund were meant to do, that is, to produce television programs free from governmental artistic control. Since about the early 1990s, it's called the Independent Television Service. You have to give them credit for trying. Once again, this agency's publicity efforts implied, caring and sensitive people who refuse to be defeated were trying to start an agency for television programs in the *public interest*.

Its initial purpose was, as stated by *Broadcasting Magazine*, to "develop shows without direct oversight by other public TV entities." How's that for acknowledgment of system failure? The Independent Television Service was brought into being in 1988 with a grant of $6 million (about the production cost of one very low-budget Hollywood "C" feature,[214] one tenth the average cost of a Hollywood feature in 1996, one-sixteenth the $95 million cost of magnificently-muscled Arnold Schwarzenegger's landmark contribution to civilization, *Terminator 2*,[215] or one thirty-third the production cost of *Titanic*), to pay for administration, production, distribution, and promotion for its first year. The language of the enabling act used the terms "independent", and "creative risk". The hope in the early days

was that somehow this largesse would be able to "save" that small part of television produced outside a corporate mantle from being totally the instrument of fealty to congressional fashion. As it turned out, by 1994, the emphasis had narrowed. Then, ITVS was
careful to direct its efforts toward a limited definition of "underserved audiences". Who
are the "underserved audiences"? The woefully neglected people of sensibility? Not this
time. Who are independents — experienced producers who have their own ideas about
shows? No.

ITVS did a replay of The Program Fund. As it turned out, perhaps predictably,
"underserved audiences" was simply a new euphemism for programs designed to give an
ego boost to a well-known select band of potentially politically influential "minority"
groups: Hispanics, Blacks, Native Americans, Eskimos and Asians. We have learned
through ITVS the meaning of the term "independent" to public TV . . . it means
"congressionally defined 'minority'". Programs by "independent producers" (minority
folk), to meet the needs of "underserved audiences", (minority folk) supported by ITVS'
staffing that heavily represents members of the approved minorities, conveys to Congress
the message of proper supineness that unlocks coffers.

Unlike Europe, the United States no longer has a living tradition of truly independent documentary (nonfiction) film and video. "Independents working out of their living rooms simply substitute freelance hell for wage slavery," writes Danny Schechter[216]. There has simply been not enough work for those independent spirits in the nonfiction film business to make a living. Instead, the nominal documentary genre is largely populated by a tortured gaggle of determined, obsessed, unfunded "producers" clamoring for attention. During recent decades, their impact has been equivalent to that of the rest of the working poor. Of no more interest to the general public than artists have been at any time, television's "independent producers", lacking the institutional protection that inspires trust in funders, are tempted, then frustrated to the point of dementia by a public broadcasting system, state controlled arts and humanities funds that smile and encourage, fund inadequately and straitjacket creative people with at best "Safe and shallow scholarly 'objectivity'[217]", and at worst simple orders. Thanks to the funding process, a fairly substantial body of independent producers denied access to the public has existed for years.

Are there real Independent Producers left? Yes. They are a group of professionals with the attributes of any profession . . . caring, imaginative, capable, reliable, makers of a product. On occasion, some are acknowledged, respected, encouraged, even engaged by the public television establishment to serve its needs.

Where do they come from? Not characterized by any accident of birth, independent producers are people of any sex, race or national origin who were trained by institutions . . . by stations, networks, and by former network personnel who have found sanctuary in university faculty. Some of these trained producers "go independent" in order to escape the yoke of servitude. They tire of producing formula programs for paying clients and funders, programs that have far less quality, imagination, or cleverness than they have learned how to do. Convinced of their expertness in their craft, often thanks to professional awards, they take their cue from the pre-revolutionary pamphleteers. They decide to be, in effect, their own publishers. These "independents" believe they have something to say based on their own life experience and the learning's of their craft. Their work is largely unsupported.

The lucky ones have rich fathers who can grubstake them. What independents lack is an institutional basis. The millions of dollars spent by broadcasting institutions to publicize their work are unavailable to an independent. Nonetheless, he is their competitor. In today's media-dominated culture, a better mousetrap is no competition for access to airtime. A producing entity like Boston's WGBH advertises itself every hour on the hour by government fiat. By sheer repetition, it becomes "known". The nationally syndicated programs and series for which it is the booking agent advertise it too. Naturally, when a large, successful institution wants media exposure, it gravitates to another large, successful institution . . . to WGBH, *NOT* to an independent.

What is a single person who knows his craft and has ideas to do? Most go into another line of work. The remainder take a leap of courage and faith. What can he or she expect? How can he or she get large organizations, institutions, or foundations to listen?

What to do after NBC writes, "We do not support the making of programs by people out-side our own company", and ABC writes "That subject is not on our agenda for this sea-son" (both of which have been written to me). First he or she must assess the obstacles. Is he or she willing to live like a Gypsy; from day-to-day Is he or she willing to live an eco-nomically erratic life? Is he or she willing to work longer hours, harder, for less pay than a truck driver, an accountant, or just about anybody else in the culture? Is he or she willing to work ceaselessly, without thought for old age, sickness or accident?

Yes? Then, is he or she willing to develop a lifetime program of relentless self-promotion? To give talks, speeches, conduct classes, write articles night after night, search for funders, and go to dinner parties with rich people to tell them about ideas? Is he or she willing to burrow through foundation and government documents in search of SOME-BODY, *anybody* who wants to say the thing the independent wants to say? To respond to Requests for Proposals with articulateness, servility, total commitment to the conceptuali-zation of whoever wrote the request, knowing that any inserted ideas based on the respon-dent's own experience, insight, knowledge or experience will be marks against the pro-posal. To essentially forget about independence in order to be "independent"? Well, that's what it means to be an "independent" television producer in the United States today.

Hundreds of meetings hosted by public television in all American cities pretended to welcome the ideas of these independents. The meetings are a sop. Funding, when forth-coming, is of a level to encourage only those ignorant of the cost of making an effective film. Today, when editing machinery alone rents for $2,300 a week, a Steadicam for that much per day, or a small film crew for the same sum, when a sound mix alone will cost $4,000, grants to filmmakers common total about $20,000.

The token moneys made available to "independent producers" would give credence to an argument that independence in American filmmaking is equated with dissidence, and dissidence is not to be encouraged except in other countries. Over the years, enough public-television-funded cheap, badly made films have now been made by "independents" (amateurs, really) to give them a bad name, which may have been the in-tention all along. For years, the Corporation for Public Broadcasting has played this Duessa game. The only players remaining now are the obsessives. A real independent pro-ducer knows better than to fall for public television's empty promises. These uncompro-mising and now desperate Seekers After Truth and Virtue, these "independents" have sim-ply been "given the runaround" by public TV. These rumpled saviors with fire in their eyes have a mission, a mission to save the misguided world through film. (A hypothetical inde-pendent producer is quoted as saying, "I'm gonna secure women's rights, I don't care how many movies it takes.") These seers were presumed to have a chance with ITVS. But to survive, to establish an adequate funding level for its own continued operation, ITVS had to conform to state policy.

Did independent producers get from ITVS the voice they have so long demanded as their democratic right? Judge for yourself. In 1992 there were over 3,000 applicants for film production grants offered by the Independent Television Service. Three million dollars were made available to underwrite 25 programs, which calculates to $125,000 thousand per program, on average. (This total for 25 programs funded is *one tenth* of the average cost of *one* Hollywood film [*The Economist*, 10/22-28/94]. In 1992, *each* episode of *Cheers* went for $3 million, *NYPD Blue*, $2 million, *Law & Order* $1.2 million. In 1997, commercial time on one episode of the hep (not hip) urban series *Seinfeld* cost sponsors a *million dollars a minute*.[218] In 1998, NBC anted up $13 million per episode for the formula medical thriller *EMR* — the cost of *one EMR* show was enough to produce *one hundred* "independent" documentaries. In 1994, Kevin Costner was chided for going over $120 million for a feature film; *Titanic* cost $200 million, just so you'll have a standard of comparison.) You may ask why "the system" we live in and rejoice in can offer talented, creative production people (whose intelligence and imagination are colored by altruism) only ten percent or less of what the commercial people get for imitations, and why any self-respecting person would take it. The reason they take it is that if they want to do what they know is best, if they want to practice their craft without pandering, they have no alternative.

Now, you may ask, for just what potential enduring contributions to the literature of human experience were these munificent gifts from the Independent Television Service given? Fourteen of the 25 selected programs (surprise, surprise) — more than half — are about potentially politically powerful American minority groups, (five are about Asian-Americans, three about Blacks, two about native Americans, two about older Americans, three about "Latinas and Latinos", one about Hawaiians, one about Gays), others are about the environment and abortion — two "hot" political issues. Political correctness, it appears, is hydra-headed; lop off one and more appear.

Six of the 25 programs funded by the Independent Television Service may have public interest outside the sphere of political correctness. They include David Collier's inquiry into love, work, family and money ($34,140), Faith Hubley's animated short about the faces of time ($77,375), Ruth Payser's animated short about a woman who trips and falls into a dream ($30,250), Lynn Smith's animation of Carl Sandburg's *Arithmetic* ($37,512), Edin Veldez' reassessment of Columbus' discovery of the New World ($197,955 — patriotic subject matter can jawbone a better level of funding), and Clay Walker's film abut the process of creating political street art ($92,155 — a little more than the others got, for politics). It's wonderful the resources the United States is willing to commit to the pursuit of disinterested innovativeness! A sum equal to the cost of one episode of a hit TV show.

This is what we've gotten as the product of years of work by people willing to sacrifice for the deeply American desire for a society and a television free of bribery or coercion. As you can tell, yet another well-meaning, piping move toward independent noncommercial television in the USA emerged less free than it might be. As in the past, the influences from commerce and government have shown themselves to be unclear as to where their personal self-interest and the public interest diverge.

One suggestion from within public television about how to get out of the chains of fealty to legislator/producers and get back to its original purposes is to try CABLE. A project called Horizons TV plans to use the public access provisions of cable franchises to provide a forum for "thinkers, authors, scientists, artists and teachers". The Public Broadcasting Service and the Boston and New York public TV stations are cooperating in Horizons TV. There will be no government funding. It will be a "financially independent, self-sustaining nonprofit enterprise",[219] in other words, "cheap". One may expect programs of college, university or local cable TV originated lectures. (My *Space, Life and the Moon*, 1962, for CBS from the University of Florida, a bottom-of-the-barrel "public affairs" FCC pacifier piece could well be a model.) It looks like a new idea for talk shows that nobody will watch, just like the ones that killed educational TV forty years ago.

Here's cable, that other one-time great hope for innovative community programming that has instead developed into a middleman, controlling public access and charging a markup. Public television wants to get into *that*? Why? So that that vast community of articulate people who don't serve the government's definition of its interests will have television access to the public. What an indictment of public TV!

Inference has led to the conclusion that since there's nobody at public TV who knows how to make programs anymore, and now that public television is simply a prospering tribe of fundraisers, brokers, promoters, public relations people, auction staff, mail-order storekeepers, marketers and accountants supervising some re-edits and a journalist or two, why not? Well, getting into the cable access business and making it look like a good thing should provide work for the bureaucrats in public TV, doing what they know how to do best. The outcome — a jobs program to replay past failures.

Another alternative getting attention in Congress nowadays is the folding of public broadcasting into the market system. The Public Broadcasting Self-Sufficiency Act of 1996, proposed by Congressman Jack Field (R, TX) on which hearings were held in February 1996 would allow sponsorship of public television programs. It would allow the sale of public broadcasting channels to commercial stations. It would privatize the Corporation for Public Broadcasting. Testimony at the hearing was given by employees of public broadcasting only. As could be expected, their plea was for maintenance of the status quo.

The House bill's avowed purpose is "to ensure the financial self-sufficiency of public broadcasting", a euphemism for "going commercial". Its provisions tactfully state its goal. HR 2979 would "not prohibit a public broadcasting station from . . . accepting remuneration for broadcasting." It would allow logos, slogans, and calls to action from sponsors (not to mention hints about show content over lunch) for which stations "may receive compensation".

The House bill's revised Corporation for Public Broadcasting policy would be made by a board selected on the basis of their political and commercial credentials. Six board members may be of the same political party (ensuring political partisanship as a key component of decisionmaking), one is to be from investment management, one from corporate finance, one from telecommunications, one from education (a fundraiser?) and one from public broadcasting (a marketing vice-president?). It appears that they may well be grooming the Corporation for Public Broadcasting to become a business.

Restrictions on broadcasting in the proposed legislation include the following vapors: It must "advance education, support culture, and foster citizenship". It must promote "creative and diverse programming of high quality and excellence". It must reflect "cultural diversity", serve "underserved audiences", and promote "editorial integrity and independence".

Sounds good, doesn't it? But let's look at the loopholes. Television professionals and educators agree that everybody learns from television. It's *all* educational. The issue is *what* they learn. The loophole is: whose definition of education is to be advanced? No clue given.

Next: "support culture". Again, whose definition? High culture or low culture? (take any bets?)

"Foster citizenship." That's what public broadcasting does already, if you define citizenship as promotions about people in politics and what they think the public should know (see Chapter 22). Public television's failure to practice in terms of the goal of "creative and diverse programming of high quality and excellence", a phrase that deserves to be exhumed from its inoperative status of the last thirty years, is the subject of this book. The question is, according to what standards of creativity, diversity, high quality and excellence do we operate. . . Mickey Mouse's? The meaning of "underserved audiences" and "cultural diversity" is dealt with elsewhere. And as we have mentioned, the history of editorial integrity and independence have been compromised by the prohibition of dissent as "controversial" and therefore unsupportable by those who authorize funding for public broadcasting. A guarantee of editorial integrity and independence would indeed be a step forward in public, as in commercial broadcasting.

The "privatization" of public television would snuff out the last broadcasting agency free from temptation to mind control by the institutions of commerce and those beholden to them. Commercialization of public broadcasting will simply make sure that *all* television channels in the United States promote profit-inducing public credulity, ahistoricism, anti-intellectuality, capriciousness, self-absorption, impulsiveness, acquisitiveness, competitiveness, and infantilization, instead of having, as we have now in a limited way, a single possible exception. Understandably, the agencies that profit from the nearly universal consumerist thought-control would find comfort in the extinction of any potential vehicle for any kind of criticism, even one so backward and niggardly funded as American public television.

The privatization fad may take all before it. Airlines are (or were until very recently) crowded, dirty, insecure, lacking in amenities, and profitable. Corporatized medical care is working toward reduction of services and the exclusion of the poor; and it is profitable. We may look forward to privatized public schools, resulting in job training for the more fortunate and no education at all for poor children, through the voucher system. The privatization of science has led to a decline in pure research. We know that symphonic and chamber music, poetry, speculative thought, and art that doesn't feed publicity organs are losers, and are headed for the dustbin. (The current president of Yale University, a place once dedicated to the disinterested intellectual inquiry that represents the most exalted enterprise of our species, is an *economist* of all things). Toll roads are staging a comeback. In the interest of logical consistency, should we not institute privatization of church property, the renascence of the dowry system for marriages, entry fees for state and local parks and libraries, prostitution for the children of women without skills who have exhausted their welfare eligibility, prisoners in privately owned prisons as unpaid labor?

Thirty years of evidence show embarrassingly limited success for the community fundraising efforts of public broadcasting stations. Cities large and small, universities and states plus dedicated local citizenry, have provided ample evidence that no locality can muster the conviction to voluntarily contribute enough money to keep a nonprofit TV station open, let alone one producing more than rudimentary television.

What the Congressmen are really saying when they say "self-supporting" is "Public stations, go commercial!" As viewers can see by the increase in the length and pictorial embellishments of commercials on public television, the privatization of public TV is underway.

Public television's commercialization will cure a lot of headaches. Lobbyists will be able to use public TV to support the public promulgation of the private tastes they share with key members of Congress. And most conveniently for both the members of Congress and the government contractors and image polishers who sponsor it, an advertiser-open public broadcasting system will guarantee that dissent will continue to have no avenue to reach the general public.

Congressional TV's future may be in doubt, however. Somebody may point out that Congress itself may no longer have so strong a need for public TV. They have another outlet to the public, one that allows them more direct access in terms habitual and congenial. That outlet is cable TV's ably produced C-Span. C-Span lets a Congressman be both producer and performer, not merely producer as with public TV. C-Span lets them talk, wave and shout. C-Span lets them have their faces on camera, with no distractions, no argument, no controlling interviewer, no foolish plot or story. Unlike public TV, no pretense is required, either.

C-Span adds a dimension to the *Lehrer News Hour*. More than just the follower of the events of the day, its audience is the public affairs junky. C-span's limitation is that the small audience of a free-to-choose public that the all-talking-heads C-Span attracts will eventually demonstrate the continued desirability of a television production entity as a more alluring vehicle for the wider promulgation of the ideas cherished by our lawmakers.

What Congress should rethink is not the elimination of public TV but the release of its usurpation — the restoration of public TV from Congressional imprisonment to its rightful place as an alternative television for a free people.

Chapter 29

SURVEY THE TERRITORY, DEVISE A METHOD

T he structure of American television established by legislation governing commerce and broadcasting has established the mission of commercial broadcasting as the exploration, discovery and intensification of the proclivities, tendencies, likes and dislikes of that select portion of the population that is quick to buy. A preeminent activity of commercial broadcasting has been the enhancement of both commercial and governmental revenues. Any social consequences of the mutual reinforcement of the economic interests of government and commercial broadcasting are operationally irrelevant.

The cause of what Stephen Metcalf has termed "TV's relentless marketing juggernaut"[220] is not a conspiracy between government and commerce, but a confluence of perceived self-interest. Even though large companies like General Electric pay little or no federal taxes, their suppliers, employees and customers do. Therefore, the better General Electric does, the more money from tax revenues is available for members of governing bodies to spend. The encouragement of corporate growth by elected representatives may have at least as much to do with their own vision of the legacy of their choices as to how to spend revenues as it has to do with your well-being. (An upsurge in congressional resignations in the 1990s may well have been the result of Ronald Reagan's having committed present and future revenues, depriving his successors of a significant means toward achieving immortality.) Because of these common proclivities in both government and commerce, if anything is to be done to ensure that television proceeds as a public service, their predilections must be factored in.

The power of public television's totemic significance, cultivated by commerce and government, has overcome the evidence of its failure. Its track record notwithstanding, public television has been for decades the media sacred cow of the degree-certified American middle class. But their loyalty to our state television is not loyalty to the state. The loyalty many have to public TV is loyalty to hope, to possibility, to what used to be known as "a cultivated populace", to civilization. It is loyalty to a dream. It is symbolic of the yearnings of the schooled among our population. The loyalty of public television supporters, persisting through public television's obvious ineptitude, shows how deep is the need. These yearnings persist despite the evidence that the hopes, the confidence of the American middle class are violated in practice by "their" public TV.

What are the yearnings that have been transferred to the idea of public television? What is it that the meager and insufficient contributions are supporting? What is this inchoate, this luminous, this trusting hope?

What I see, from my decades of observation, is this. A primary attraction is to the idea of a media entity that can't be bought and sold. This is the core of the difference between public and commercial TV that the public desires. The American middle class wants to bond to a television, to *something* not ruled by the cash register. They want a television that is hopeful, informative, funny, creative — a TV that is "clean". The middle class longs for a television that affirms beloved currents of our civilization's history. They crave a television that somehow outmaneuvers the dominant trend of our times, the "big store" most of us occupy from 9:00 to 5:00. And for decades this media entity represented a hope for "something better" held by people whose economic lives are defined by buying and selling.

Many astute people perforce allow themselves to be defined by the currents of their times. Many people compromise for "success". They "get along by going along". It's been that way forever. They may be mall developers, media moguls, retail chain operators. But deep down inside, people crave an American media entity that is disinterested . . . a media entity that is dispassionate . . . a media entity that can be a playing field for intelligence and creativity. What the middle class seems to want is a secular media "church", where purity, honor, integrity, joy and inspiration serve a search after meaning and truth that can be a beacon into the unknown future. Is that a bad thing? No. Is it impossible? No.

Is a disinterested television entity wrong because the middle class wants it? Is it elitist because it doesn't represent the desires of the lowest common denominator? Is it to be rejected because of the cynicism of "owners" that affirms value only in what comes from the commerce that funds media manipulation and the voting blocs that respond to media manipulation?

The US Congress' 1967 takeover of educational television as "public television" can be looked on in retrospect as a *coup d'état.* Did educational TV really need a government bailout, or was it an opportunistic device of legislators to get themselves a domestic USIA? Was federal funding of public television simply a device to control a communications vehicle for the transmission of Sanctified Truths About Our Nation . . . that is, propaganda? For starters, we might ask ourselves why we need state television at all. We didn't ask for it. "Educational Television" simply collapsed into "public television". As citizens and taxpayers, Americans have a right to question the efficacy of their alternative TV. They have a right to make demands of it.

A 1997 statement by Carolynn Reid-Wallace, Senior Vice President of Education and Programming of the Corporation for Public Broadcasting, reiterates the early goals of public television. "CPB-funded initiatives must continue to provide an alternative . . . a forum in which creative geniuses can produce works that lift our disconsolate spirits, move us to right what is wrong, prompt us to rejoice in the best and noblest of our past and encourage us to embrace the myriad possibilities of a future" (and here she throws the sop) "that promises to expand and enrich *the mainstream* (italics mine) of our nation's life and culture."[221] Ms. Reid-Wallace's use of "expand" and "enrich" is pointed . . . happily she does not use the term "reflect". Without "the mainstream of", hers would make a desirable and workable statement of objectives for public television.

After forty years of proving itself, some unasked questions need to be asked of noncommercial television, in the interest of our society. Such as: Has public television functioned as an alternative to supplement or complement commercial television in the interest of a civilized society? Has it addressed unmet needs of our people? Has it been creative?

A test of aptness could include these questions: Did public TV shed light on the implications of the unprecedented national debt to the 1980s and 1990s? Did public TV shed light on the looting of our financial system that came from deregulation and government guarantees for Savings and Loans? Did public TV draw our attention to the flight of American industry? Did public TV point out, or question, the weakness and vulnerability of the Soviet Union? Did public TV shed light on the causes of violence in the United States? The causes of narcotic addiction? The dangers of overpopulation? The robotization of work? The usurpation of middle management jobs by computer programs? Consumerism's hogging of nonrenewable resources? The destruction of community? The purposelessness of the lives of our children? The incursions on privacy? The trivialization of American experience? The "dumping" of the mentally ill? The neglect of the poor? The hardening of our hearts? The atrophy of public education? The disappearance of productive work for the poor? The widening gap between rich and poor? The internationalizaton of American business? Did public TV use drama to suggest models for the future? Did it develop alternative television forms? Or did it whitewash Washington careerism and fundraise through nostalgia for the elderly?

We have to ask ourselves if we really want state television as an alternative, or a reversion to vending machine television. If the answer is "neither", we should dump public TV. If we want an alternative, then we should go about wresting control from the state.

How? What steps should we take? It really makes sense to get rid of the antiquated technology, yes, and drones doing busy work in the stations. How can we?

Past recommendations may be instructive. More than two decades ago the Carnegie Commission on the Future of Public Broadcasting issued a report called "The Public

Trust". Repetition of some of its observations and recommendations would be appropriate today. Behind their 1979 recommendations, the commission said, was a desire to *"create a safe place for nurturing creative activity"*.

Carnegie didn't mean creative marketing and fundraising activity, or brokering ready-mades from abroad, or congressionally mandated programs, or retail shops, they meant and said, "capability to produce programs of excellence, diversity and substance" through public television stations' spending "the bulk of their . . . resources on programming". The history of public broadcasting up to that time, they stated, showed "no serious, transcending effort to construct in public broadcasting the conditions for sustaining creative (sic) work". Did the stations, did the CPB, did PBS, did the Congress of the United States pay attention? Look around and see.

The stations structured themselves to make any instrumentation of Carnegie Commission recommendations impossible. Stations restructured themselves on the corporate model, defining their creative people as "workers". Low pay, small benefits, and job insecurity established creative people as expendable. The stations' revolving-door system of "project contract" or piecework employment of creative people assured their docility. Attempts by creative people to gain some say in programming through unionization were rebuffed. The Carnegie Commission predicted, accurately, that creative activity would "become a casualty of the many other institutional priorities of this complex enterprise". "Programming excellence" they continue, "requires a tradition and a structural framework hospitable to creative endeavor." The stations, they found, "are inappropriate agents for national leadership in public telecommunications, they are too diverse, occasionally timid." And more: *"To anyone possessing even the most rudimentary knowledge of the arrangements in other communication arts that have stimulated original achievement, the structures and procedures of public broadcasting seem almost consciously designed to block such achievement . . . the individual creator remains, in the eyes of this medium, The Enemy"* (italics mine). True in 1979, truer now.

The Carnegie Commission really hit the nail on the head — and what good did it do? Absolutely none. Despite the cautions and recommendations of the Carnegie Commission on the Future of Public Broadcasting, we now see a billion dollars a year supporting 10,000 workers seriously involved in not making waves, and all of this with the enthusiastic support of the people supplying the billion. That is a mountain that's hard to move.

Chapter 30
TV AS ART

Art is not ornament. Though it may include the exquisite, art is not by definition "nice". When a significant work of art is new, it is *always* controversial. When new, *all* art is dissent. It "stops our ordinary patterns of knowing and replaces them with disturbing queries", writes Wayne Koestenbaum in *The New York Times Magazine*. He calls art "The only individualism the world has known." A primary civilizing force, it is a method whereby the uncorrupted hold up a vision of truth to the rest of us. Risk and experimentation are inherent in the production of all art. That vision represented by creativity in the arts may be indictment, as so much of our art is today, or an image of possible perfection. Either way, the role of art in all of history has been to subvert entrenched interests when they attempt to ossify the conditions of the authority of privilege. Because any work of art is unique, it inherently represents a view not expressed by any but the artist; it is by its very nature a denial of consensus. Art represents a priority of the individual vision over the consensus that underlies representative democracy. The consensus that is essential to democratic governance and the uniqueness that is a work of art represent different paths. Each is an essential component to contemporary civilization. Each route may illuminate the other. The integrity of each demands that it support the other . . . but the relationship is equivocal. The very concept of a "National Endowment for the Arts" in a representative democracy may therefore be a contradiction.

Television is an art form. Nobody in government finds it opportune to publicly admit television's significance as a cause, as a religion, as role model, as art form. That would put television in a category with the subjects of current controversy at the National Endowment for the Arts. These are subjects that essentially question the presumptions of the status quo, always looked upon by those who profit from the status quo as being of dubious merit. Someday in the future a spokesman for humanity will be heard, because reason ultimately prevails, telling us that government/corporate mucking around in the arts is regressive tyranny.

Government/corporate mucking around in noncommercial television is mucking around in an art form, an attempt to create an Official Truth. Attempts to create state truth have been made more than once in the 20th century, to the ultimate discredit of their perpetrators. "Art and politics are two different things. One has nothing to do with the other", said the noted documentary filmmaker Leni Reifenstahl at age 70. "Official truth" and art may be incompatible. Iris Murdoch wrote, "Serious art is a continuous working of meaning in the light of the *discovery* (italics mine) of some truth." As it is with the National Endowment for the Arts, the present-day linking of funding for public TV with the ideological conformity that arises from current procedures in the instrumentation of democracy is both a tyranny and a denial to creative people in this medium of their first amendment rights. We in this country will endure this kind of tyranny for a long time . . . until it's pointed out to us. I'm pointing it out.

Most entities of communication in our country, including public television, are directed and operated by people whose vision is determined by their definition of self-interest. The short-term interest of both consumer industry and government discourage freethinking, encourage docile conformity, and if not obedience, then unreflective acquiescence, or as in the extreme case of the Disney product and its imitations, infantile regression.

Manipulators on every level of commerce and government do not see their short-term interest served by the encouragement of independent thought. The consequences have been among other things, a paralysis of public debate. "We've tended to trivialize issues to the point where meaningful debate has become almost impossible", declared Rep. Mickey Edwards of Oklahoma.[222]

SUPPORT REVOLUTION

What should be done? Here's a few suggestions.
1. Recognize that the now primitive technology of local broadcasting has been superseded by satellite and cable, cassette and videodisc delivery.
2. Face the fact that local public stations are a failure, that they produce little or nothing that justifies their existence as local; even their sensationalism is trivial. Shut them down.
3. Develop a single National Alternative Television Production Center to produce and distribute programs to the nation via satellite, cable, videotape and videodisc.
4. Involve creative people in significant roles in its operation.
5. Guarantee its independence. Insulate its funding through a trust fund. If there is to be a government connection of any kind, let it be through a National Endowment for the Arts that is itself guaranteed freedom from ideological control. Go back to "Go".

Who will do this? Grassroots voluntarism is probably the only course open to caring Americans who want an alternative television. A once-free, creative public television has become a puppet of powerful agents of what Alfred Kazin has termed "a society moved so much by greed and a politics incapable of minimum sincerity."[223] Self-interest as defined by both commerce and government has shown itself to be inimical to the health of any media vehicle for a disinterested free marketplace of ideas. We exist in a time in which government is conducted largely by special interests and pressure groups. If people really want what they say they want from noncommercial television, they'll have to form a pressure group to get it. A coalition of groups like Citizens for Independent Broadcasting, the Children's Defense Fund, the National Education Association, The Association of College and University Presidents, The Association of University Women, The Association of public television Producers, The Association of Learned Societies, The American Philosophical Society, Mensa, and perhaps hundreds of other **groups dedicated to the general welfare can and must pressure the government to give up its stranglehold on public television.**

Chapter 31

LET'S TRY EDUCATION, FOR A CHANGE!

Americans hate "education". Their dislike is a tribute to the soundness of their instinctive intelligence. The "educational" institutions we've brought into being force us to hate the training we get that masquerades as education. Real education has to do with the process of learning, a kinetic process of glorious discovery, a fervent revelation of hitherto unknown relationships between oneself and some element of the profound reality that is the world we live in. Learning is a celebratory event that can be repeated infinitely throughout a lifetime. People committed to it know it beats all other thrills. No chemical can touch it.

The education the United States committed itself to in the 19th century was derived from Cicero and Cardinal John Henry Newman. It defined learning as divorced from "necessary cares", dedicated to the pursuit of knowledge for its own sake, the "high protecting power of all knowledge and science, of fact and principle, of inquiry and discovery, of experiment and speculation".

For over a century in the United States the idea of free public education amounted to a hallowed principle. It came into being because of bitter experience. The idea of free public education was a logical extension of democracy as an alternative to hereditary monarchy. Application of the scientific method to analysis of human genetics showed that socioeconomic status of parents is no predictor of a child's competence. Self-evidently, the well-being of the larger society demanded that all able children be given the greatest possible opportunity to learn.

Now it's pointed to as a wormy apple. If you look at the pointers, you may find among them some whose concern is for the continuation of their privilege, who would safeguard it from attack from the next generation. You may find those who simply want to institutionalize the conditions of their own rank and that of their descendents. To the reasonable among them it must be proven that they, too, are the beneficiaries of democratic benignity. The others must be either circumvented or prohibited from doing harm to fragile children.

American public education today is so remote from learning as to leave most of its participants virtually untouched. The methodology of our community-based public school system is hostile to its educators and to the community interest. In the public education system, visionary young teachers become dried-up and embittered by a system that is antipathetic to independent thought and that discourages the development in children of imagination and the power to reason for themselves. Smart students become angry, obstreperous, hostile, vengeful, and passive. The well-to-do pull their children out. They're right to do so, because they're being "had".

What's the cause? Is free public education a bad idea? No. Is local decisionmaking? Yes. Localism is a flawed concept. It pretends to offer an alternative to the difficulties and complexities of cosmopolitanism.

In the post-Soviet era, the tendency has been stronger than ever to turn American education into training. In England, in 1993,the Secretary of Education was succeeded by the former Secretary of *Employment!* The articulate *Economist* magazine has endorsed the conversion of American higher education to the production of Stakhanovites for the "knowledge economy" (October 4, 1997). Education authorities in the state of Oregon have just about come to the conclusion that they might as well accept the trend of our history. . . all high schools in the state will be vocational schools.[224] Atlanta's Rich's Department Store, as well as Sears, Roebuck & Co., Burger King, UAL Corp, and Baxter International, have entered the education arena by calling a spade a spade, and opening their own elementary schools.[225] An outsider may speculate whether an enterprise whose holy mission is monetary rewards for its owners can see an advantage in encouraging independent thinking? Or might it be rather to train people to lead lives directed toward the schoolmasters' corporate interests? Wanna bet?

Educator and MacArthur "genius" award winner Stephen H. Schneider has declared that "The US education system overall is set up to package information and to process people to be plastic cogs in the economic engine".[226] The vocationalization of American education plays into the hand of powers unsure of the reasonableness of their control. Those who fear the bright light of thoughtful inquiry have always had reason to fear knowledge and thought. Their power over educational policy in America is also a national disaster.

Democracy is education's beneficiary. Democracy may be education's strongest reason for being. The training that passes for education in America is the gelding of human potential.

Children hate the very word "education" because it speaks to them of imprisonment, drudgery, *ennui*. They quickly learn from school and TV that the real world is to be found in sports, where you give your all to obey rules that somebody else made and that you never question, where you're admired for winning, whatever it is that you win or however you do it. Our children learned to hate the term "educational television", too. It spoke of technological backwardness and poverty, naturally abjured by right-thinking postwar technocrats young and old.

Distracted by the jousting of interest groups, most of our country has forgotten the meaning of education. Only for the power elite, in places like MIT — that Valhalla of the technology that lies behind both the avalanche of consumer products and the armature of our imperial posture — can we find a recollection of education's purposes. MIT's Prof. Mikic (quoted in the *World Monitor*'s September 1991 article "MIT, Life on the Infinite Corridor"), succinctly described what our tax-supported educational system has discarded but which thankfully is remembered at MIT. "It doesn't really matter what you study here", he says, "We teach you to THINK . . . *Then you can do whatever you want*" (italics mine). *That* is learning, the friend of the free.

There seems to be an endemic need for our leadership to validate its testosterone to the public by declarations of periodic wars. Well, there are still wars to be fought. The greatest among them was and is the war against the profound ignorance that is historic to the human condition. As described by Renato Rosaldo, Professor of Anthropology at Stanford University (*The New York Times*, December 9, 1990, E5), the "Western cultural tradition (is) rooted in a commitment to rational inquiry . . . converging century by century on the truth." A first step, in the words of *The New York Times*' Leslie Gelb, is "to know what we do not know". A momentary alteration of this historic problem is more apparent than real. We appear to have entered an era when economic interests have created a climate for children where ignorance appears as no obstacle to fulfillment. Teachers today unite in the complaint that many, sometimes most, of their students are utterly indifferent to learning.

Students seem to concur with Lady Bracknell in Oscar Wilde's parody of leisured English life, *The Importance of Being Ernest*, "Ignorance is like a delicate, exotic fruit . . . touch it and the bloom is off!" Students today define instinctuality as natural, define natural as good. Their conduct demonstrates their belief that they themselves can be "noble savages", that learning tampers with the purity of natural ignorance. How did Rousseau sink so low?

Sony's president Norio Ohga has described what's left of America's educational system as "Collapsing". There are similarities and perhaps connections between the fate of our public education and public television. The causes may be inherent in the way we structure our information/education organizations. We are hung up on their being democratic and capitalistic. Public education power in the United States is locally centered. Public education is placed by law and tradition in the hands of local boards of education. Members of local boards of education are people whose concerns are by design parochial. The end result is the opposite of the development of observational, critical, reasoning powers. Free public education in the United States is torpedoed by local education agencies, whose members correctly see an educated public as a threat to their own preeminence. Their actions demonstrate that they know, as Gore Vidal observed, "The only thing a totalitarian ruler must always keep from his slaves [is] knowledge."[227]

The hand that pushed the pushcart now rules the world. America's educational disaster may be a concomitant of our commitment to consumerist economics as a driving force. During the last decades, we have watched our country move toward a "two tier" society. This is described as "rich and poor". It may be more accurate to describe it as "exploiters and exploited", as "manipulators and manipulated," as "plunderers and plundered". It is a delicate balance. The manipulators rejoice in their control, their power, their riches, while the manipulated play in their sandbox with ever new titillations. However described, the structure of the economic polarization we have created among ourselves discourages wisdom, that is, a knowledge or insight into the greater context of the immediate enterprise, in either the users or the used. It is to the perceived interest of manipulators in large organizations that their colleagues, too, be untroubled by the larger issues of human purpose. It is to the perceived economic interest of manipulators, also, that the manipulated be kept as gullible and as impulsive (that is, as childlike) as possible. *Ergo*, keep them stupid. *Don't* educate them. The economic imperative is marshaled against all education in America. The economic imperative countenances only training. American public education, today, is un-American.

"AD COIN ROLLS TO YOUTH", trumpets *Variety*.[228] My observation is that consumerist marketers targeting the "youth market" encourage youngsters to follow their instinctual appetites. Simplistic commercials validate the gullibility of the viewer. In a certain TV commercial, one could watch animated raisins and nuts rush unreasoningly about a bowl; in another, cereal bowls fly to the ceiling in refusal of the competitor's product. What conceivably has this to do with nutrition, satisfaction, or breakfast? The commercial is repeated because it sells the food. The unreflective, many of them young, are captured by movement, personification, colors, music, fun. Another commercial begins with a close shot of a clean-cut Anglo-Saxon man. He declares, "I'm not a doctor, but I play one on TV", and then proceeds to prescribe a medication! Would *you* buy a medicine prescribed by a paid *actor*? Probably not. In this commercial, an admittedly false image of the respectability of the science of medicine is layered on the presumed attraction of TV celebrity. And it works! The gullible audience doesn't bother to go beyond image. Commercials such as these aren't for you. They are, however, products of astute insight into the workings of the impulsive mind. In the interest of commerce, suggestible people are wooed, supported, encouraged toward a state of unreflective spontaneity that ever since the sacking of the Roman Empire has been defined as barbarism. Barbarism in this context is not only allowed, but also actively encouraged. It's good for business.

This foolishness would seem to be a private matter. One's choice of cereal would seem to be nobody else's business. The problem is that habits of mind are developed through approved conduct. Conduct approved by the Big Friendly Food Company, however, may be disastrous when applied to the exigencies of a human life. What is called "lack of discipline" in teenagers is simply conformity to the teachings of the TV commercial. A statement of irresponsible self-absorption, implicit in every commercial, is: "What you want now you have a right to. You deserve satisfaction of desire. The structure of our society ("we") exists to see to it that you get what you want now . . . at practically no cost." Parents, teachers and legislators know that children are fed this message over a lifetime and yet they are still alarmed that the children then engage in antisocial behavior. They could use some help themselves toward understanding behavior pattern formation.

Currently operative economic theory justifies the manipulation of the uncritical on the basis of the economic result. Money is only useful when it is in circulation. Two-thirds of our Gross Domestic Product comes from consumer goods. Children consume. Non-economic factors stand outside these calculations. The economists view and the sponsors' view go no farther. This compartmentalization of professional, academic and legislative activities acts as a barrier both to understanding and to remedial action. We lack a conceptual framework to validate the abundant evidence that TV influences behavior, often in an antisocial way.

As humans, our "puppy" consumer children move on to an adulthood characterized by empty consumption. They consign themselves to the ash-heap of civilization, while serving a momentarily thriving economy. That these victims harm not only themselves but their victimizers is attested to by the privatization, the security police, the walled communities newly found necessary by members of "the dominant culture". The dissoluteness, vagrancy, and lawlessness, the spiritual and moral degeneracy and disease that some of our children grow into cause outrage in many in the mercantile class. The victims are then excoriated and blamed. Instead they should be accepted as the natural consequence of the struggle of the fittest to accumulate.

Signs abound that we are moving into a society that opts to deny whatever in the body of human history is momentarily inconvenient. We look about ourselves and see a consumer culture fixated on the present moment only. Here everything that is not expressly forbidden is allowed "The rule of law", they call it. The law sets minimum standards, which in practice become maximum standards. In this emerging culture, technology serves industrial, corporate and government growth. Education, as defined in an OECD study, is to become "not so much a moral or cultural force, more of an incubator of new industries in a technology-dominated economy". The price we pay is a denial of history. What we build is a society of ants. **The internal logic of a society of consumerist economic determinism is taking us back to a civilization of the level of Hammurabi's Babylon, with microchips. Is this what we want?** If you examine the behaviors of economic activists among us, this is what you find.

Chapter 32
A MEDITATION FOR LEGISLATORS

The governance of a people is a highly specialized craft. The fundamental purpose of American government is, as was the purpose of all its predecessors, to secure the well-being of the governed. Governing requires a lifetime of knowledge, study and application. Its practice requires deftness and skill. In our democracy, voters return those representatives to office who seem to excel in their craft, who represent the interests of the voters as they see them. A primary challenge to governance, too often unmet, is for legislators to legislate in the interest of others who may be more intelligent, more knowledgeable, more sophisticated, more creative, subtler, more sensitive than they.

To act in the interest of somebody more intelligent than yourself is among the most difficult assignments of teachers, parents and legislators. How do you do it? The methods of the MacArthur Foundation might well be applied to congressional judgments about public television. History would look kindly on it. This is what "nobility" has always meant.

Our government's decision to support an alternative to commercial television appeared at one time to be consistent with the public welfare as a prime goal of government. At the birth of public television, President Lyndon Johnson stated a warning (in his message to Congress of February 28, 1967). He said, "Non-commercial television and radio in America, even though supported by federal funds, must be absolutely free from any federal government interference over programming." Events have proven his warning to be well-taken. Today's legislators are pampered by industry. Legislators use public office, PACs and taxpayer's money to bribe their constituencies for votes. The *hubris* of a pampered and indulged governing class has led them to, in the words of Yale Historian George W. Pierson,[230] "Define the public interest as your own and you can usurp anything you choose to usurp", including a public television particularly designed to be divorced from your influence. In practice, the operations of Murphy's law ("Whatever can happen, will happen") have produced what was probably an outcome too bizarre to be contemplated in the medium's infancy, *two American television systems, both serving the economic interests of the mercantile class, one of them at the same time serving the career objectives of legislators.*

All is not well with American television. As part of any forthcoming evaluation of our present and future, Americans will have to come to terms with our television as part of what political scientist Andrew Hacker has called "A modern world disfigured by commerce, competition and technological arrogance."[231] Over the long haul, change is inevitable. Critic Daniel Singer has put it this way: "The commercial juggernaut of cultural conformity (through mass culture) codifies our desires, stifles our dreams, shrinks rather than widens our consciousness."

An ambitious media professional today needs only to follow a simple formula to job advancement. The broader the hints at pornographic intent, the greater the sales. Thus is chosen the path of mass-market culture, made inevitable by the imperative not simply of profit to the investor, but of *ever-increased* profit.[232]

The slow, subtle and evidently inevitable denigration of human sensibility caused by "culture treated as a commodity" requires that we undertake "the painful search for a world in which artistic creation will no longer be dominated by the tyranny of the market but will not be subjected to the dictatorship of the state either."[233]

In 1938, E.B. White wrote, "I believe television is going to be the test of the modern world . . . we shall stand or fall by television." Time has proven that he was in some measure correct. We have all witnessed in the short term the fall of the despotic empire called the Soviet Union, in the long term the development in the United States of a nation of aggressive and calculating Sybarites. Neither of these events perhaps would have happened without television. Television has demonstrated its power to move, to persuade, to inform. Anybody who has the power has a responsibility to see that this potent instrument serves the general good. "The effect of television is, in fact, frequently compared to that of the atom bomb."[234]

Jim Robertson, in *Televisionaries,*[235] declares, "The potential of these broadcast media is so great, it's as if it were medicine, let's say. Here are tubes capable of carrying life-saving blood. Instead there's a mixture of beer and Clorox and all kinds of dangerous drugs . . . The perversion is almost too unimaginable. It's as if we designed fine instruments for operating on the brain and here are these guys standing around slicing bread or chopping leather with them."

Or Raymond Hurlburt of the South Carolina ETV Commission: "Television is the most dangerous instrument that has ever been devised by man . . . If Mussolini had had this same instrument, he could have made warriors out of babies. We have been derelict, restraining television from doing what it ought to have been doing."

Professor Brandon Centerwall, an epidemiologist at the University of Washington, says that "The evidence indicates that if, hypothetically, television technology had never been developed there would today be 10,000 fewer homicides each year in the United States, 70,000 fewer rapes and 700,000 fewer injurious assaults. Violent crime would be half what it is."[236]

The Congress of the untied states has gotten us into this terrible bind. First it declared the airwaves to belong to the people. Then it declared that they would be leased as an advertising medium. The poor and the ignorant in the emerging two-tier society learned the delights of acquisitiveness and vengefulness from the commercials and the violence on their more or less constant companion, "the tube". These students of what has been called "the world's worst educational system",[237] the School of TV, have shown themselves to be apt pupils.

Disagreeable as it may be for those who profit from it to admit, the fallout from prioritizing use of the airwaves with first preference given to profit and power has led and will lead to social consequences nothing short of disastrous. "Monkey see, monkey do". Look around. The evidence is overwhelming. Our once tranquil country is now beset by brigands, that army of frustrated and enraged people who are barred from the consumerist Valhalla. These thwarted folk act out the lessons of TV. They try to take a pill, to dull the pain by turning away to narcosis, or they adopt the aggressive competitive, exploitative, and predatory approach they see in the TV heroics and among barons of industry . . . they just do it on the street.[238] An editorial in *The Nation* made this point:

> What about the millions condemned to joblessness or wages of hunger? For them, advertising doesn't stimulate demand, it provokes violence. By snatching the things that make people feel real, every mugger tries to become like his victim. TV gives full service: Not only does it teach people to confuse the quality of life with the quantity of things, it offers daily audio-visual courses on violence, with video games for supplementary study. Crime is the biggest thing ever to hit the small screen. *Strike before they strike you*, warn the electronic toys. *You are alone. You alone can be trusted.* Exploding cars, people blown away: *you too can kill.*
>
> This *fin de siècle* world, which invites everyone to the banquet but slams the door in the face of the majority . . . there are no peoples, only markets; no citizens, only consumers; no nations, only companies; no cities, only agglomerations; no human relations, only commercial competition.[239]

And what do we do about it? Blame the victims. Since this underclass doesn't vote, legislatures make no effort even to understand the motivation of people who are simply trying to "get theirs" in ways TV demonstrates to them.[240] Legislators, with no fear of losing their jobs to this disruptive but nonvoting class, put them in jail and charge the rest of us the bill ($25 billion a year was the 1995 count). While the malefactors are in jail, their fatherless kids learn from their electronic "nannies" about approved self-indulgence and problem solving through violence. Television is not unique in its anti-social curriculum . . .

the October 25, 1993 issue of *Variety*, as a random example, carried thirteen full page ads for upcoming films that featured guns. One writer calculated that if the proportion of characters murdered in one night of network TV carried through our population, everybody would be dead in 50 days. An entertainment arcade adjoining Denny's restaurant in Fontana, California, in 1993 included a drive-by shooting arcade game, replaced in 1994 by a highway hot-pursuit shooting arcade game. The kids grow up. Then they act out according to the strategies they've learned from games and fiction. This is the way it is. It's also the way it has been for centuries: read the Bible. Read Henry James. Read Jane Austen. Monkey see, monkey do. It's all there.

"The average person learns from his own experience", complained Socrates. For more people than many of us would like to admit today, television *is* their own experience. "People Learn from Television", sloganed a campaign of the Public Broadcasting Service. People today learn much the same as earlier generations learned from fireside storytelling, from the church, from nursery rhymes, from gossip, from bas reliefs, from painting and sculpture, from literature, then from films.

"A good many Americans are still embarked on a campaign to live out their life vision as it has been shaped by mass culture" writes Neal Gabler in *The New York Times*.[241] Critic Susan Sontag describes her own childhood movie experiences thus: "From a weekly visit to the cinema . . . you learned (or tried to learn) how to walk, to smoke, to kiss, to fight, to grieve. Movies gave you tips about how to be attractive. Example: it looks good to wear a raincoat even when it isn't raining."[242] I learned from the *Three Little Pigs*, *Li'l Abner*, *Jack Armstrong*, *Aesop's Fables*, from Chaucer, Henry James, from sermons. These were simply my environment. How could I help but learn from them?

Why should exposure to television be different? Television viewers see and thereby learn violence as a method for settling disputes, resolving dilemmas, getting what you want, and violence as fun. (In the film *Thelma and Louise*, a character administers a drubbing to a marauder. "Where did you learn that?" asks the other in wonderment. "On TV", is the reply.) They learn ahistoricism. They learn that the good life is the gratification of desire, that sensuality and impulse are approved. They learn to consume both products and ideas. They learn these things because that's what's there, in television. The phrase "As seen on TV" is an authentication that corroborates inarticulate truth. Why shouldn't viewers take what they can from it?

Since people are not and cannot be a controlled study group, many of the assertions you find here are not scientifically demonstrable. That's one of the weaknesses of social science. Notwithstanding, mountains of evidence surround us all. I say here that there is sufficient precedent among other forms of communication to validate the assertion that much of the dissolution of our social fabric, the pollution of our environment, and metastasizing violence is a natural human response to the stimuli offered by commercial TV. From commercial television, small children learn about consumer products. They learn about lifestyles. (The terms "Ozzie and Harriet", and "Leave it to Beaver", now in common parlance, takes it for granted that a television series did provide a recognized role model of middle-class family-centered, consumerist *zeitgeist*. Remember?)

In any organ of information supported by advertising, the connection is seldom made about the role of television in determining the thought patterns of the poor. Poor households have limited choice. The TV set is sitter for infants, children and adults alike. But a child is a sentient, growing, learning entity. The television set provides visual and auditory stimulus to hold the attention of an infant, freeing the parent. But though informant, the TV set isn't Mother. As it rivets the attention of the infant, the TV set withholds from the infant the bodily warmth and soothing tactile stimulus, the humming, singing, stroking enjoyed by infants elsewhere throughout the mammalian spectrum. The TV set is a loveless nanny, a loveless "mother" to the child. In the same way as a child picks up cues for a lifetime from its nanny, it learns what the world is like from the days and years of bait without fulfillment that it finds while parked in front of a television set.

With our changing economy, the poor are now joined by members of the middle class; two working parents today are able to be parents to their children to about the same degree as poor parents. The deprivations formerly suffered by poor children as an outcome of TV-as-nanny are now extended to the middle class. A cover story in *Business Week* observed, "busy parents no longer act as filters between their kids and the outside world."[243] Says *The New York Times*,[244] "The family is the place where good values should be taught. But because of economic pressures, both parents are working just to provide necessities, and people have less time to inculcate values. So people see TV, movies and other kids inculcating values, and they're the wrong values." *New York Times* television critic John O'Connor notes that "By the time he or she sets foot in a kindergarten classroom, a child is likely to have spent more than 4,000 hours in front of what amounts to an electronic preschool."[245]

As it becomes capable of increased understanding, what does the child learn from the TV sitter? It learns what the world is like. . . or, more accurately, how the world is fictionalized by the people who construct TV programs as inducements to be presented to potential buyers of their sponsor's products. From commercials, the baby learns that there are all sorts of good things out there to gratify ones' wishes. "The message coming out of the TV screen is now exactly the same as the message coming out of the other means of mass communication in America: '*Enrichissez-vous*'" said Benjamin J. Stein.[246] While learning this, the child also learns that the gratification of its own wishes is a good thing, and will bring smiles to its life. It learns from the soap operas that seduction is important, that men have jobs that they seldom work at, that one's emotional life is supremely important. The growing child learns from game shows that Winning Big is a good thing, that ordinary people can be somebody and gain the applause of their peers if they can Win Big. It learns from police and Western shows that life's dilemmas can be solved with an act of violence. It learns from news programs that the supreme authority of the world's richest, best country solves its dilemmas with violence. It learns from all shows that it's winning, it's Getting the Gold that counts. Says *Business Week*, it learns that "Little exists without a sales pitch attached and that self-worth is something you buy at a shopping mall."[247]

A character in the 1994 film *True Lies*, itself an exercise in comic-book mayhem, declares to the character played by Arnold Schwartzenegger regarding an unruly daughter, "You're not her parents anymore. Her parents are Axel Rose and Madonna. The five minutes a day you spend with her can't compete with that constant bombardment. You're outgunned, Daddy-O!"

The carry-over from leisure and childhood activities to adult action is the explanation for 19th century English emphasis on training in tennis, cricket, baseball, football and the 19th century English novel. Queen Victoria knew that "small acts, when multiplied by millions of people, can transform the world.[248] She made civility and manners into national priorities. It has been understood since biblical times that people, particularly children, model their conduct on fictional models. The parables of Jesus, Aesop's fables, Grimms' fairytales — throughout history all were universally understood to present models of conduct that would be imitated by readers. My parents shared a set of manners and beliefs gained in the common reading of *Gulliver's Travels*, *Pilgrim's Progress*, *War and Peace*, *Alice in Wonderland*, the novels of Austen, Dickens, Thackeray, and Henry James, and the plays of George Bernard Shaw. Their reading was encouraged, prompted, demanded by the educational system, by peer pressure, by a motivation toward transcendence. Queen Victoria and her Parliament knew that *people imitate the signals around them*. Victoria's parliament, the British aristocracy and "establishment" put into place a system of "correct" behavior that policed the actions of the populace. Nowadays, the leftovers of 19th century Anglo-Saxon culture, the people who weren't brought up by TV, who imitate mum and dad instead of S&V, people who have jobs and are raising a family and drive a car, today see fit to build walls around "communities" that are simply dormitories; they install alarms in their houses, and carry guns. They've watched their happy, safe, agrarian country become an armed camp. Thank you, consumerism, thank you TV, and thank you legislatures.

It's difficult to be a legislator in a democracy. While thinking about your own future, you have to work for the people and you try to be wise. Sometimes the three are incompatible. It's hard to know what to do. Nobody is ever satisfied. The solution is simple, though its execution is not. The goal to be pursued if the promise of democracy is to be approach is that our "Solons" should know *everything*. They should be selected on the basis of their wisdom. They can't be, of course. But it's their duty anyway to get as close to omniscience as they can. How? By what method? The one that works. Call in the experts. Delegate. Listen.

Public television, Congress' domestic USIA, is a flop. The Congressional Broadcasting System produces television programs out of Philistinism. Viewership is declining.[249]

What to do? Here's a radical new idea for American legislatures. Rediscover the goal of public television as a broad alternative. "I saw noncommercial radio and television in the role of helping us define our culture and our values in a useful way, a role the networks had rejected" wrote Prof. Harry J. Skornia of the University of Illinois in 1991.[250] If you as a legislator want to give public TV a chance to survive, enrich the matrix. However uncomfortable this may be, support people with ideas. Don't treat them as dissidents. Support people who think. Support intellectuals and artists. Give them power. Why? Because we need them. Where are politicians to get their ideas if not from people who earn a living by thinking? That's the way it's always been. Don't count their numbers. Intellectuals are too small a minority in any culture to constitute a voting bloc. For this reason, in our democracy that often succumbs to the temptation to politicize everything, intellectuals are an endangered species. They have no acknowledged place in our political life ("a marginalized minority", James Atlas of *The New York Times* calls them[251]) because their numbers deprive them of political power.

Politicians, however, neglect our intellectuals at their peril. People who think represent the central differentiation of our species from animals. The others, the people who plan and act (a preferred activity of most attorneys and politicians) must have somebody else to do their reflective thinking for them. The world is as good a place as it is only because of reflective thought, only because of reason coupled with inspiration and intuition. Politicians who attempt to direct this highest of human functions toward the goals they have selected pervert the very soul of society. Hard as it may be to find them, our politicians can save our country by encouraging and allowing the tiny minority who *think*. The encouragement of sageness as a matter of government policy by the emperors of dynastic China aided a society's survival for millennia. The philosophers of the Greece of the Eighth century BC provided a moral and intellectual basis for the civilizations of Europe into the 20th century. Our celebrity billionaires can hardly be counted on to leave such a legacy.

Universal literacy has given many people an opportunity to have an education. Our nation has proven the worth of a concept that recognizes that human potential is classless in origin. A doubtful legacy of literacy is that it has given communications skills to once-mute savages. The localisms of television's Joan Rivers, the Beavises and Buttheads, the vicious and stupid are foisted on us all by those now awakened from centuries of deserved oblivion and raised to worshipful status by the goddess of retail sales.

Our common commercial culture has strayed from guidance, from thought, reason, tradition, a sense that anybody who ever lived has much of significance to contribute to the working out of issues that confront us today. Look again at *Variety*, October 25, 1993. At the top of a page featuring a kinetic figure wearing day-glo strapped leather and long-johns, with his assistant in skeleton costume, haranguing an audience of shadows, the come-on for the film *Rave* declares "There are no limits, no values and absolutely no rules." This is how mass culture sells itself.

For many consumers and a surprising number of our educated youth, this escapist blurb qualifies as philosophical statement, a guiding principles of our present and future. Consumerism's interior contradictions promise a society of churls ruled by a society of knaves. The entertainment industry aggressively pursues the goal of churl-infantilization. As will inevitably be proven, the sellers' implied "philosophy" is a short-range self-serving sham. However often we may be told by merchants that the experience they promise us is utterly unique, utterly unprecedented and therefore utterly desirable, we're each not essentially different from our predecessors of the last hundreds and even thousands of years.

Is there a way out of the pit we've dug for ourselves? Well, here are some first steps as far as public television is concerned:

1. Legislators should recognize that the need for alternatives to consumerism is imperative. They should immunize themselves to the blandishments of their public television hirelings, their own constituencies, their PACs. They should short-circuit the powermongers who would use public television as a tool to their own ends. The duty of legislators is to the governed.

2. Legislators should step over public television's in-house puppy dogs conniving to please with an eye on the next morsel. These should be eyed with skepticism.

3. Legislators should be very careful of attractive powermongers, dazzling manipulators, the selfish smiler and the greedy donor — just the kinds who gravitate to legislators.

4. For its own sake, our democratic system must develop a method to provide the "no strings" financing of systems tolerant of dissent long ago recommended by the Carnegie Commission.

5. Congress should be required to trust experts, and to entrust public television to them. Not artists themselves, the holders of the purse strings must recognize that television is an art form with a role of acute responsibility in our culture, and that its full importance may be outside their ken. ("Art and politics are two different things. One has nothing to do with the other.")[252] By statute, Congress should establish a requirement that significant numbers of creative Americans be included among the membership on the local, state and national decisionmaking boards of Public Television. This was the 1979 recommendation of the Carnegie Commission on the Future of public television.[253] Implementation is long overdue. Give a chance to give diversity to public television policy to decisionmakers who are selected from among the likes of John Updike, Joyce Carol Oates, Kurt Vonnegut, William Kennedy, Lewis H. Lapham, Gore Vidal, Todd Gitlin, George Steiner, Tom Wolfe, Philip Roth, Neil Simon, David Foste Wallace, Edward Albee, Tom Stoppard, Sam Shepard, Tony Kushner, Wendy Wasserstein, Saul Bellow, Saul Steinberg, Gary Trudeau, Gary Wills, David Mamet, Robert Motherwell, Toni Morrison, Gina Bereriault, Maurice Sendak, Isaac Stern, Stan Wojewodski, Robert Stone, Thomas Pynchon, Don De Lillo, Michael Yeargan, George C. Wolfe etc. Require legislatures to allow free speech to others than themselves, to give creative communications adepts a chance to apply their

insights to public television. Because in the final analysis, TV is an art form.

6. Our legislators should follow the way pointed by former President G.H.W. Bush, who once declared, "Democracy brings the undeniable value of thoughtful dissent" (January 29, 1991). Only long-term, no-strings financing of an alternative to commercial television can protect its viewers from the preachers who want to spread their truth, the tub-thumpers who use it in furtherance of demagoguery, the powerful who wish to secure their power, and the well-meaning administrators who can't distinguish public television from a pulpit, a book or a radio. **To allow freedom of speech is the only way legislators can serve the public through television. This is the only way they can protect** *themselves.*

Chapter 33

A MANIFESTO

The proper institutional model for a public service television entity is not government. It's not business either . . . or a newspaper . . . or a magazine. Instead, the developmental model for a viable alternative to commercial television is a marriage between the organizing concepts of university and the *atelier*. Television, the child of theater, demands trained and intelligent people in policy roles as well as in the field. It demands people who "think" with images in time. It demands people in leadership positions in whom imagination is a strong and vital force. It demands people who understand nuance. It demands leaders who know their theatrical history back to Aristotle and Sophocles.

It demands a willingness to risk. It demands a mission of sufficient clarity and precision to withstand public clamor.

It must be protected.

If a television entity that conforms to our heritage and to the principles of our Constitution is to be brought into being with the power system now in place, provision for these people must be legislated by a Congress of the United States that recognizes its interest as well as its mandate as served by the yielding of some usurped power so that the legislature may act as a facilitator for the functions of democracy as part of the structure of positions of leadership. A model for a proper goal for noncommercial broadcasting in the United States may be found in the opening pages of the magazine *Foreign Affairs*. It reads,

> The articles in *Foreign Affairs* do not represent any consensus of beliefs. We do not expect that readers will sympathize with all the sentiments they find here, for some of our writers will flatly disagree with others, but we hold that while keeping clear of mere vagaries, *Foreign Affairs* can do more to inform American public opinion by a broad hospitality to divergent ideas than it can by identifying itself with one school. We do not accept responsibility for the views expressed in any

article, signed or unsigned, that appears in these pages. What we do accept is the responsibility for giving them a chance to appear.

A statement like this, which has guided one of America's most respected publications, if altered to suit a broadcasting entity, would be a worthy sign-on to the broadcast day, a worthy component of a revised legislative mandate for public broadcasting.

The annual authorization and appropriations process of the federal government, which supports public television to the tune of $200 million a year, establishes mortal constraints on creativity. The process guarantees that the subject matter of America's production for public television is determined by a phalanx of two polarized groups of career-building attorneys, both heavily committed to political power. These are the oligarchy whose agreement determines what is fitting to be made in America to be seen by viewers of public TV. Such practice is a denial of the pluralism that is a foundation stone of the concept of a democratic society. If reason is insufficient motivational force for a change in the current system, the Congress may be prodded by court charges of usurpation of power and denial of First Amendment rights to public broadcasting through the annual authorization process.

A study of parallels between artists of the early Renaissance and today can help to form a new and better structure for alternative television. The Sistine Chapel would have cost too much for Michelangelo to build or adorn . . . Pope Sixtus had to pay the cost. A market system that relies on an artist's willingness to dedicate a lifetime to self-promotion will exclude many valuable contributors. We must recognize that artists today are in need of institutional help. Television programs are expensive. As "independent" filmmakers can attest, film and video production is not a cottage industry . . . the artist can't afford to make them, on his own.

People who are accomplished practitioners of one discipline are often not so good at another. Patterns of history demonstrate that the bureaucratic mind has trouble grasping art. Whenever it tries to support the arts, it gets into trouble. An understanding of the arts requires a particular combination of experience, education, training sensibility and intuition. Few have all of these. Among the few who have them, few care to run for public office. Few are content to manage an enterprise. But they exist. Arts organizations, theaters, symphonies, opera companies all over America benefit from the talents of people who have an instinct for the arts and administration. These people should be a prime resource for the support and staffing of public TV in the United States.

Some bureaucratic adepts who lack one or more of these attributes nonetheless have again and again been given or have given themselves the authority to make cultural decisions. Some of these people have sought out for themselves roles in decisionmaking for public television. They do this for reasons other than an instinct for the arts. They do it for "status". Knowing that the learned and the accomplished always have done so, they try to support "the arts", too. What has emerged has too often been support for caprice, faddism, incompetence, egomania, careerism, hoodwinking, or at best simple reliability.[255] The critical press and knowledgeable people have been quick to point out to bureaucrats that ineptitude in decisionmaking regarding fields of human achievement not their own is a public waste. Historically, the bureaucratic response has been one of petulance, simply to confess to being out of their depth by cutting out support for anything that smacks of originality or real seriousness. In public television, The US Congress through their agency the FCC snuffed out originality with a declaration that they cannot authorize support for anything "controversial" (code for "original", "taboo", or critical of the status quo). Thus the process of American representative democracy stilled the engine of culture-through-broadcasting.

A strategy of opposition to originality or insight that encourages and rewards the tame and conventional is a poor strategy for long-term survival. Former *New York Times* Editor Max Frankel has written, "The true pollution of the media environment comes when the editors, publishers and producers of serious content are *constantly* on notice that they will be financially damaged if they dare to shock a few readers or serve up "controversy".[256] Something inside us seems to know that our process is wrong. Cultural decisions made by a cabal of legislators and managers, as today in state and national arts programs, provide a small living for a few wannabe's, *pasticheurs*, careerists, posturers, grandstanders, opportunists, and lunatic fringe who choose to present themselves as artists, and for well-meaning managers who maintain the edifices of their folly. The result is that almost no art is produced in the USA.

In a proper *atelier*, though, the people running the show have extensive training in the subject. Historically, systems of patronage allowed promising individuals to be spared common drudgery in the interest of greater human benefit. Plato was able to learn under Socrates, Beethoven was able to learn under Haydn, da Vinci worked for the accomplished Verrocchio. None had to apprentice as a cashier in a store or a groom in a stable to stay alive.

To remedy the stasis represented by the swamp of contemporary public television, I here propose that people who lack expertise in the arts of history, literature, theater and the fine arts be forbidden to make policy and production decisions in public television. I propose that American public television be structured so that the managers and accountants stick to managing and accounting, and that others make decisions about the content of noncommercial television.

I propose that public television be regarded as an art form, and that its alliance with disinterested centers of learning be renewed.[257] I propose that American public television be centered in *one* institution, an institution of higher learning with distinguished departments of literature, drama, international affairs, history and philosophy. I propose that this new alternative television be acknowledged as an atelier, a community of principled reflective and creative people supported for its originality, creativity, and reasoned dissent.

But then the TV people will go hog wild, won't they? Producers'll do "awful" programs that the people "shouldn't" be allowed to see. Allowed by whom? The Pope? The king? Jesse Helms? By what right? Parochial school education that doesn't "allow" children to know about sin, produces sinners. We've all seen that. Doesn't democracy encourage a "free marketplace of thought"?[258] "I disagree with what you say, but I'll fight to the death that you may have the right to say it", was the declaration of an American patriot. Thought control is just what we don't need in the United States.

Access TV is already beginning to demonstrate a diversity of American thought hidden for a generation. A television that presents an alternative to the pied piper of consumerism would be medicine for our culture. As originally conceived, educational television might have become the voice of a loyal opposition, a creator of alternative visions of a future. Instead, as we have seen, through the carrot and the stick what was envisioned as alternative television has been made into no alternative at all, just another hired voice. Because of its organizational structure, American public television is beholden to the campaign contributors of the federal legislature. The legislature is now through the power of the purse the *de facto* programmer of public TV. Thanks to its indebtedness, the legislature cannot find in its being the conviction, the unity or coherence of purpose to risk short-term benefit in order to pursue the public interest.

America's now dominant entrepreneurial aristocracy is in greater need than ever of at the very least a "court jester", an independent objective critic, or, at most, some who will assume the role of "the conscience of humanity". For decades, in England, this role has been that of the BBC. The British Department of National Heritage points out in its 1992 document, *The Future of the BBC*, "It has been an essential feature of public service broadcasting in this country that decisions about programmes have been taken by broadcasters or broadcasting authorities, not by the Government or other interest groups". The United States has that broadcasting need today.

Through simple denial of options, public television has been lured into bondage by the skills of minions of the corporate value system, by the middlebrow taste of its courtiers and by political expediency. Public television's fatuousness is simply symptomatic that the politico-economic interests that have assumed control of it have not only run out of things to say, they disallow dissidence. If we are to advance, we must demand an alternative TV that goes beyond the politico-economic dominance that places the kinds of narrow limits on human possibility that we see in public television. We must demand that our excellent politico-economic system work to the advantage of our democracy, not the reverse. We must take a truly conservative vision in our alternative television service, looking back to that broad range of human concerns that occupied humankind prior to the industrial revolution, forward to the possibility of improvement of *all* human life that was the original goal of that industrial revolution. American democracy's *post-industrial* survival may depend on a reaffirmation of our *pre-industrial* goals.

The British Department of National Heritage document cited earlier states that "audiences should take priority over other possible interests . . . the broadcasters, advertisers, shareholders or political parties." If we are to have an alternative television in this country, we must develop a structure to assure that our own broadcasting can do the same. An alternative television still offers the opportunity for an expanded "fourth estate", a locus for voices other than those who now control the public airwaves to speak for *their* interpretation of the public weal. Alternative television offers the opportunity of a forum, one which will "galvanize the spirit and engage the intelligence" (in Jonathan Miller's phrase) through the devices of fiction and nonfiction, by visual expression, by speech.

American television viewers today have a choice between only two televisions, one a television system that defines them as consumers and one that defines them as voters. What I propose here is a third option, a profoundly conservative television, one that defines television viewers as people capable of reflective thought.

It is one that looks upon societies that define themselves by their economics as an experiment whose outcome is unpredictable. (One has recently failed rather spectacularly.) I propose an alternative television with a clear mission statement of public interest that frees it from subjugation to economic or political expediency. It is a television born of a marriage between the academy and the theater, presupposing definitions of human excellence that transcend and precede economics and politics. It looks upon an important goal of American democracy as derived from the French Revolution, "Liberty, equality, fraternity", a society in which all persons are valuable, a meritocracy in which opportunity is extended to all persons. Its cornerstone is Trevelyan's dictum, "Disinterested intellectual curiosity is the lifeblood of real civilization." It is a vision that looks upon the society we should work toward as one where no person is encouraged to exploit another for his own advantage, a society where each person is the support of the others, a society where a poor person is not a nonperson. It is a vision of an America with a future connected with its past.

The United States must rediscover freedom of expression. Why should only an alliance of legislators and consumer products manufacturers have total control of content of the most pervasive communications medium ever invented? How little confidence some of us have in our fellows, or our system, that we set ourselves up as the gatekeepers of another's righteousness. Western history, and oriental history, and presumably histories that multiculturalism has yet to reveal to us show that valid social criticism has more often than not been labeled as "unrighteous". If the system we've put our faith in is any good, people will reject the bad and select the good (if they're allowed to). That's what democracy means, isn't it? If democracy can't handle dissent, then the system isn't any good.

Our democracy will never be a democracy unless we the citizenry trust the citizenry. Our democracy will never be a democracy unless the citizens understand and participate in the idea and the practice of diversity. In television, that means a retreat in the minds of audiences and legislators from the idea of the desirability of prescription and proscription. Anarchy? Maybe, to some. Compulsives too, must recognize the rights of others. If we are to be a free and democratic society, we must recognize that the people have a right to see garbage. People have a right to show people garbage. We will only have a real citizenry if people are (1) allowed the option of discrimination, (2) allowed to develop in themselves the tools of discrimination. Then they'll know what to reject. We'll never need to fear demagogues and manipulators if we have a population that thinks for itself. Saying "yech" is an American right. There is today one kind of television we can say "yech" to . . . it's called commercial television. There should be other television we can say "yech" to.

Former presidents Bush and Clinton have both spoken of the desirability of a sense of "stewardship" . . . it is a word not in general currency. "Stewardship" has to do with a person's sense of responsibility to something aside from himself, his immediate family, his own church congregation. Derived from the once aristocratic concept of *noblesse oblige*, it translates well into our democracy. In democratic terms the idea of stewardship states that anybody who possesses a knowledge or an excellence of any kind will aid the society by sharing. It implies duty. It honors selflessness. It denies the "Race to the swift, the devil take the hindmost" motivation of the buccaneer yuppie generation whose fallen house of cards brought shame on them and others. Quite the reverse, it affirms the value of every member of the group. Deeply conservative, it affirms the tradition of our forebears, also capitalist "winners" like Andrew Carnegie who in a gesture eloquent with sense of self, with humility and with compassion, gave public libraries so that the curious whatever their origins or economic status could avail themselves of what wisdom Western civilization had accumulated, so that immigrants could become more knowledgeable than their benefactor.

Stewardship is a concept that could inform a new and revised public television. Based on the concept of the brotherhood of man, it prescribes that anybody who has anything that another doesn't that is valuable should reach out to the other to help him or her to also have it. A dedication to the idea of stewardship should be a condition of employment in public TV, from top to bottom. To the economy it represents not a penny's additional cost. As a nation we must have it, if we are to continue to be agents of human progress. To save public television, *bring in the stewards.*

Yes, stewards of public TV should be paid. An occasionally articulated prejudice of our country is that people doing benign things get satisfaction from their work, and should therefore be content to live otherwise impoverished lives. This attitude is one among those that justify our harassment of members of the teaching profession. This prejudice is simply an ugly denial of benefit to productive and useful members of the society. Why should only the compromised, the greedy, the manipulative and the exploitative be allowed the freedom of decisionmaking that is a goal of American life? Why should only the Ivan Boeskys, the Michael Milkens, the T. Boone Pickens, the Carl Icahns be able to see the Mona Lisa, have lunch on the Piazza San Marco, send their children to a school that isn't a zoo, sleep in a quiet room?

Television is a new art form. Its exploration of the possibilities offered by its very being is its critical act of leadership. In both commercial and public television today, as I have pointed out, the possibility of leadership by people of vision has been undercut because of imperatives of secondary importance generated by organizational structure and financing.

With organizational restructuring, the public television system's billion dollars a year, if spent from a single production and distribution center, would give viewers a complete three cycle season of prime evening time filled with brand new programs with budgets matching the $850,000 per half-hour of *Golden Girls* (though a bit less than the $3,000,000 per episode production cost of *Cheers*[259]) and would leave $300 million dollars for daytime programming and administration! Direct broadcast from satellite into your home is technically feasible. If its costs approach those of satellite broadcast today, they will be practically nothing. Technically, the lion's share of public television money could therefore be spent on *programs*, not on buildings, machines, transmitters, and their custodians. At least technically, the not-too-distant future seems to hold the promise, once again for an alternative television service. Once again we have to ask an old question: Is there a way to a genuinely contributing noncommercial television service?

The British have shown us one way. The essays of Kenneth Clark and James Burke are as important as television models as are their immaculately produced fiction. With the concept of the *auteur* film, the French have led. We shouldn't be too proud, too blind, too afraid to imitate the approach that has led to their success. **Essential components are a committed, stable creative community irreverent toward established institutions, possessing a sense of comradeship, knowledge of the cultural artifacts of the past, a vision of a future endowed with wisdom, with taste and sometimes even beauty.** These can best be fostered in a collegial organizational structure, perhaps on the model of employee involvement, participative management, trust and the Golden Rule brought to Japan and the Ford Motor Company by the late W. Edwards Deming.[260]

Chapter 34

STILL HOPE FOR REASON

In their book *Down the Tube, an Inside Account of the Failure of American Television,*[261] Baker and Dessart define state television in a way that includes our own public TV. They write, "Government operated systems fulfill the ideological purpose of controlling the flow of information in what the government considers the best interest of the people." American legislative process applied to the allocation of funds for noncommercial broadcasting has allowed currency to only those human insights validated by the political process. The US federal legislature has used its power of authorization to create a television vehicle for the transmission to the public of the thought it favors. Congress was never authorized to do that. The subjecting of television to legislative gatekeeping has built a body of product that amounts to a curtailment of free expression. The structure of congressional authorization and appropriation of public revenues denies the possibility of art to the art form that is television. The structure of noncommercial television in the United States today allows tyranny. And it gets it!

America is not a creative desert, even though it may look it on public TV. The people are here; they're just not used. The producers of *The Great American Dream Machine*, NPR's witty Susan Stamberg and Robert Krulwich are among the proud products of public broadcasting. They have been elbowed away. I've seen more than enough budding American talent while making films with children, while watching intelligent and creative people pass through commercial and public television on their ways to more secure and productive lives.[262] Where in the Congress, in the foundations, in the membership of the promulgators of public television are we to find attributes such as these? A grateful American public has seen images like these of another country brought into our living rooms because of a Yankee tradesman's bargain. The brokering of British TV has given Americans a TV taste of wit, style and intellectual complexity. Can you imagine what it would be like if something of the sort could be done here? What health might it bring to our culture if Americans were to see sport made of American business, marketing sent up or down? Sport made of generals, NATO, the Federal Reserve, leveraged buyouts, or goods overconsumption?

Sources of material abound. A starting list of possible subjects was given by President Vaclav Havel in a 1999 address:[263] 1. The dictatorship of money, of profit, of constant economic growth. 2. The plundering of the earth without regard for what will be left in a few decades. 3. The materialistic obsessions of this world. 4. The flourishing of selfishness. 5. The need to evade personal responsibility. 6.The alienation caused by the sheer size of modern institutions. Other program themes like "Pitfalls of Prosperity, What Happens to Rich People?", "Can We Afford Our Rich?" "Hegel wins! The Triumph of Economic Determinism", "Selfish America", "Where will Transnationals Take Us?", "American Losers", "Living on Social Security", "Competition vs Cooperation", "Keeping Unemployment Up", "Games of Chance", "Sport: Training Ground for the Footsoldiers of Commerce", "Trivialization and Its Impact on Culture", "The Assassination of Excellence", "The Decline of Art, Literature and Philosophy (And the Rise of Politics, Economics and Entertainment)", "Powerlust and its Consequences", "The Iconoclasts", "The Dissenters", "Sponsoring a Congressman", "Hedonism", or almost any of the titles of Mustich and Goulder's "A Common Reader" catalogue. Why not a series for children on the lessons stories tell? Do our people need guidance toward human responsibility more than they need one more highway overpass, or not? What about "How to Become a Decisionmaker"? What about Ralph Nader's catalog of "unmentionables": corporate welfare, reckless deregulation, corporate crime, corporate buying of politicians, multinational corporate erosion of our national sovereignty, corporate munitions trade, corporatist education, corporate dominated media and corporate environmental destruction?[264] The list of provocative and important subjects currently forbidden to public television is substantial. When will we be a country confident enough to acknowledge dilemma? Never? Certainly unpopular ideas can't be disallowed just because they may be untrue . . . so were the benignity of atomic power, the threat of Soviet military power and the potential disaster of Quemoy and Matsu.

Respect for the public intelligence requires that various voices be heard. A good, true and honest entity need never fear — virtue is invulnerable to slander. The public mind, like the individual mind, will never be equipped to make realistic judgments as long as it is denied the opportunity to evaluate truth or falsity for itself.

What American television needs was succinctly stated in an advertisement for Adelphi University of Garden City, New York in *Harper's Magazine* of February 1994. The ad said, "In a competitive and turbulent global environment, the idea of expertise must include such old-fashioned attributes as versatility, imagination, reliability and inventiveness." These are provided by an education, defined by Adelphi as a "commitment to ideas, to the acquisition of knowledge, to the development of critical intelligence, and to the willingness to ask fundamental questions and derive unsettling answers", with this aim: "To illuminate the central problems and explore the fundamental controversies of our age and its endlessly refined information." They then ask, "Does everybody need an education this good and this radical? We say "no, everybody doesn't . . . only your Congressman, your doctor, your lawyer, your business partner, your accountant, your daughter, your son, yourself."

When educational TV was first invented, Pennsylvania's Senator Hugh Scott said, "I want to see things I disagree with. I want to see programs I hate. I want a television that will stimulate me to think things through, to reexamine my own positions." Senator Scott knew what free thought is about. He was on the right track. Audiences should have the opportunity to experience the Congrevian waspishness of a William F. Buckley, Jr.[265] as he tries to persuade the world he deigns to view as through a lorgnette to arrange itself to suit the dynastic interests of the Buckleys and the Bozells. Audiences should be allowed to examine the case of the "fringe" economist Larry Abraham, who offers the hypothesis that those distinguished bodies of decisionmakers known as the "Roundtable", the "Bilderburgers", the "Trilateral Commission", the "Council on Foreign Relations", the "Group of Seven (or Eight)", these groups that formulate and execute policy for the federal government in areas too cerebral to be offered to the electorate, are mere devices for world political control through world financial control.[266]

Why are these areas not offered to the electorate? Because somebody might get the wrong idea? *What* wrong idea?

"Controversial" television programming is a public right. A policy that bans controversy explicitly excludes any insights not previously validated by governmental processes. Its denial to the people implies an unwarranted assumption of blanket public ignorance, and of the right of government to tell others what to think. For individuals as they contemplate the concepts that motivate our society, and for collective entities representing groups, it's intellectually stimulating to have experiences of disagreement. We have been a strong and a free people. If we are taught to think, we need not fear gullibility. A free marketplace of thought is our individual right. Humanity is invulnerable to bad ideas over the long haul. We can handle silly people, wrong people, misguided people on our TV. Let them speak out. We should all want that, and we should get it!

Because of the state we've allowed ourselves to get into, if we do want it, we'll have to stage a revolution. We'll have to rearrange our broadcasting system, restoring those needed line officers, the marketeers, fundraisers and publicists once again to positions of circumscribed responsibility. We'll have to think again about a public television service that is nonpoliticized, where creative people have creative control. Only then may we partake of the attitudes of other civilized nations like France, whose onetime Minister of Culture Jack Lang stated, "Films and other cultural works are not like common goods. Each work is in itself rare, fragile and precious, and merits attention and protection. They should not be treated in a commercial negotiation in the same way as soap."[267] We'll have to think of public service, of stewardship, of media professionals who see themselves as humble facilitators in the unfolding drama of our history, as givers rather than takers. We'll have to think about limiting the role of government in what is, after all, an art form. We'll have to risk a degree of self-determination among our broadcasters. We'll have to change some attitudes, too . . . to allow dissent, to allow unpopular views, to allow small voices to be heard speaking to small numbers. A free people's television should offer options, options that a free people may turn on or turn off.

The issues that have dogged public television are important issues of our culture. Is buying and selling things the best we can ask of ourselves? Do we believe neo-Darwinism to be a true explanation of societal evolution? Do we believe that if we manipulate one another, exploit one another, work in hierarchical authoritarian environments, we will make any kind of future for our successors? If societal evolution is essentially a cooperative venture rather than a competitive one, institutional changes are in order.

Guided by the US Congress, the practitioners of public television have chosen opportunism over principle. Public television has compromised itself into disutility. It can no longer call itself an alternative. It is now simply a mouthpiece for a club, a club that has a set of priorities and interests that represent a limited segment of common humanity, a club that has an agenda that represents one interpretation of the general well-being. This club is conveniently known as "Washington" and includes the interests and powers that represent the money and significant voting blocs Washington is beholden to. This club is neither the highest and best among us, nor is it the public.

With recent technological advances, with videocassette distribution to homes by mail, with fiber optics, with Direct Broadcast Satellite capability, with the options offered by the Communications Act of 1996, a new alternative television service like the one dreamed of by the Ford Foundation could still have a chance. Its development would take a small revolution at Congress and the FCC. To unseat the US Congress from its determination to make public television into an endless civics course would demand a concerted citizen effort directed toward the retrenchment of government power over public television. It would require long-term no-strings financing, which would require key congressional committee members to give up their role as Executive Producer of the domestic US Information Agency. Congress would have to relinquish its role as arbiter of the cultural and intellectual life of the United States. It would require a restructuring to allow a renewed partnership between the national legislature and advanced centers of thought. It would change its emphasis from *control* to *support*. If history is any guide, the devolution of power from any agency requires a concerted effort, a willingness to tolerate ugliness . . . it requires militancy. Control of public TV may have to be wrested from Congress. Citizens themselves may have to organize in the interest of Alternative Television.

"Since the earliest days of American radio, reasonably assured stable, politically insulated financing has been a central issue in public broadcasting, perhaps *the* central issue."[268] A non-congressionally supervised public TV would recognize that creativity in television is too costly, too fragile and too rare to flourish in every city and town. National and international in focus, it would give localism back to cable. This would entail requiring cable stations to do the local public access they promised to the communities they serve. It would require the closing of those 385 retransmitting antennas of the public television sinecure fed by satellite signals. With the proceeds an alternative television center could be established, just one center, *not* in Washington DC, where people can gather to make programs.

This Creative Center could be staffed by people who can define their public as more than electorate or customer. The only requirement for employment for production personnel and policymakers alike in Alternative Television should be a proven background through undergraduate and graduate study that includes the history and practice of theater, literature, and the visual arts from ancient times to the present. *American Playhouse* would then stand a chance to become not an agent of political correctness, "an outlet for voices not often heard on television, *particularly those of ethnic minorities*"[269] (italics mine), but a vehicle and perhaps even an engine of human creativity.

Television *is* theater. Television *is* literature. Television *is* an art form. Therein lies television's destiny. Our television today is a greater or lesser part of a noble and enlightening tradition that has had a civilizing place in all societies. American television should be given the chance to be *good* theater.

American television is a prime locus of our aspirations. In our television the nation finds our definition of excellence. If our national and personal aspirations are simply everyday, if they are merely the encouragement of national loyalties or the possession of toys and nostrums, so be it. Then American television should remain simply a tool of merchants and lawyers. This, however, is a denial of the history of the noble experiment that is our country, and the hopes of our ancestors.

Public television is more than thirty years old. It has a record we can now examine. This is the time to start thinking about the results America is getting for the billion dollars a year spent in public broadcasting. It's time for us to think once more about a phoenix alternative TV, a reincarnation of a good old dream out of the ashes of a fatally compromised state propaganda service.

Chapter 35

TV AND THE NATIONAL DESTINY: MOVE ASIDE, CONSUMERISM; MOVE ASIDE, GDP

W e have a past to live up to. Once, America was a dream. "A city set on a hill", Massachusetts Bay Colony Governor John Winthrop called it in 1630. Learnings derived from successes and failures across the vast panoply of human history and applied to a democracy were components of "The Great Experiment". From the riches of history, a definition of societal virtue derived from the thought of Periclean Athens, plus the concept of a secular society served by reason that came from the enlightenment, and other precedents gave us tools to use in pursuit of our ancestors' goals. Christianity as ethics offered the concept of the brotherhood of all humans. The works of centuries of artists, thinkers and scholars were thought to be a basis whereby the living may have the tools to build the better society envisioned by their parents. America was for centuries understood to be a common enterprise where people could learn from the mistakes of the past, where each member could have a part in building a better place for all. Our ancestors killed so their descendents might have the chance to develop a fair and equable society.

Noncommercial television arose from that tradition. Was it a mere spasm of a centuries' old dream that was dying? Public television's history appears to demonstrate the ebbing strength of the idea of democracy as an ennobling force. Two outstanding historical factors contributed in large measure to the abandonment of the dreams of our ancestors. War was one. Starting in 1941, the United States became an arsenal. This left no place for the Arcadian ideal. The Cold War with the Soviet Union during the forty years following World War II and the caste enriched by the Cold War made preparation for war into an American habit. Added to this, the rise of consumerism as a late phase of industrialization guided people's attention away from the ideal of domestic tranquility that was a building stone of the US Constitution.

In 1989 the Soviet Union imploded. At the same time, a technical innovation cata-pulted the industrial revolution ahead as a means for the elimination of drudgery. It was the computer. A computer program can now perform the corporate functions once as-signed to middle management. When we become accustomed to middle class job loss (as we became accustomed to craftsperson job loss in the 19th century), we will see that those with imagination are now free to pursue more interesting activities. Our uses of technol-ogy have created the conditions to liberate America from preparation for wars of survival, and from the drudgery of keeping track of goods production and distribution.

The abolition of history was an unforeseen outcome of the triumph of marketing. But it is not a necessary outcome. Educational television was invented to be an agency outside commerce directed toward uses of democracy as a civilizing force. It could still be, if a sig-nificant body of Americans had the will. An alternative television defined as an artistic medium could still provide a matrix for constructive criticism and recommendation for application to the outstanding anomalies of our cultural being. Public television, even as it stands today, could form a substructure for a public forum that integrates current diver-sity into the historic matrix. All it would take is a small revolution. Some of the basic is-sues are well known. Others may be defined. These can be counted among the last half-century's cultural changes eroding the Great Experiment:

1. Since the recovery from the Great Depression and our victory in World War II, many among us have little by little adopted "business ethics" as our national creed. Since World War II, *Carpe Diem* and "The race goes to the swift, the devil take the hindmost" describe what some Americans have done with our legacy.

2. Our ancestors killed so their descendents would have a chance to develop their capacities to the utmost. Instead, the schools are empty, the homeless shelters are full, onetime seats of the higher learning now teach job skills.

3. Since World War II, the United States has focused its educational efforts toward warfare, and commerce with the globalization of consumerism. The first led us toward bankruptcy; the second leads us toward a decadent barbarism.

4. We trivialize the sacrifices of our forebears. By mid-century, this trivialization had been amply demonstrated in the American media. Into this context noncommercial televi-sion was born. Noncommercial television was meant to be an agency affirming goals un-met by the market sector. It was meant to be an agency for a reaffirmation of historic American principles. It was meant to offer options to the American people other than the recreation of Nineveh. That's why it was noncommercial. But over time, partly thanks to the sanctification of the idea of privatization, noncommercial television has been neutered into the voice of the noncontroversial status quo, with the consent and participation of business, government, and the educated elite.

I too was a participant in this transformation.

During and after The Cold War, institutions dedicated to helping the government pass laws serving special interests multiplied. If there was profligacy in government, it was not in the administration of government programs. The government itself was studiously kept "in its place". My own experience as a delegate to government funded activities showed me that the quality of remuneration, facilities and amenities allowed those working for the government were of a character historically reserved for mendicants. I discovered that there are drab, depressing, second-rate motel chains dedicated almost exclusively to providing sleeping facilities for itinerant government employees.

But under the cover of the Cold War, the money brought by associations and foundations to support their missionary efforts drove Washington's rents higher, and made rich men of law partners. Today the District of Columbia has the highest per capita income of any city in America. Those incomes are not paid to government workers. Instead, they are paid to people to tell the electorate's representatives how to legislate in their interest . . . the tobacco industry alone supports 192 lobbyists, one for every three members of Congress.[270] The restaurants are now superb, the sleek headquarters buildings of the "American Council of (Whoozit)" or the "National Association for (Whatsit)" are the landscape of Washington. The evidence of a walk through downtown DC calls out to any sophisticated person that the wags are right to say, "We have the best government money can buy." Washington today is where those people whom a distracted electorate places in office are reasoned with, petitioned, cajoled, pressured, flattered, bribed, wine-and-dined, and appointed to boards and trusteeships. The result? "The man who pays the piper calls the tune" — in Federal City, too.

Commercial broadcasting, through the lobbying efforts of the National Association of Broadcasters has had a profound influence on the electoral process. Commercial television's uncompromising pursuit of corporate self-interest through the sale of airtime to candidates for public office renders it an accomplice in the venalization of the democratic process.

To politicians, the electorate's greatest vulnerability is its susceptibility to manipulation through flattery and bribery. The electorate's legislators, having fewer illusions, have no need themselves for the former. Bribery is another matter. The bribes, also known as campaign contributions, must be taken by legislators who want to win elections. The moneys are then passed on to and happily received by agencies licensed by the legislators to sell them television time. A sponsor willing to spend millions on TV commercials can only rejoice in a process that allows him to pay less than the rate he pays for commercials to get legislation passed that is favorable to his enterprise. Q.E.D., through private sources presidential candidate Texas Governor George Bush could raise all the capital he need to buy the TV ads and air time that have been demonstrated to be critical to electoral victory. An emerging public perception is that in The United States the law is for sale to the highest bidder.

Today's public television was originally designed to escape the enchainment of intellectual and artistic life to the service of commerce. Subordinate to the interests of government, like government itself, public television has almost imperceptibly become a servant of commerce. The erosion of public television as an alternative to commercial television is symptomatic. Its history reflects a behavior pattern in the American political/industrial/ commercial leadership class. Whether cause or effect, that class now elects to choose opportunism over principle. A force beyond their control has caused elected officials during the consumerist phase of industrial capitalism to neglect its implicit social contract to serve the long-term needs of the population as a whole. The evasion of the ideas that prompted public television is symptomatic of a late 20th century usurpation by an ahistorical political opportunism and market economics of the role of cultural arbiter that in other centuries was held by persons learned in religion, philosophy, the fine arts and literature.

Today our own American radical economic determinism, wearing the silk suit of "monetarism" or "conservatism", demands that we face a national future in which we simply gobble up the earth, without a vision of challenges to be met and without a plan for meeting them. Czechoslovakia's President Vaclav Havel has shed a light on our practices that is cause for reflection:

> Contemporary America is an almost symbolic concentration of all the best and the worst of our civilization. On the one hand, there are its profound commitments to enhancing civil liberty and to maintaining the strength of its democratic institutions, and the fantastic developments in science and technology which have contributed so much to our well-being; on the other, there is the blind worship of perpetual economic growth and consumption, regardless of their destructive impact on the environment, or how subject they are to the dictates of materialism and consumerism, or how they, through the omnipresence of television and advertising, promote uniformity and banality instead of a respect for human uniqueness.[271]

Mounting evidence compels us to acknowledge, however unwillingly, that commercial television has been a formative influence of immense power over the character of American life. The quite demonstrable fact that billions of dollars worth of goods do move from the shelves as a direct result of advertising on TV qualifies as proof of the argument that TV makes things happen.[272] Another sponsor strategy with ample proof of television's power to influence behavior was the 1997-1978 investments of $275 million for political issue advocacy commercials[273] by those who stood to benefit. Events proved this to be money well spent. That sponsors and broadcasters alike deny that television causes anything to happen but product purchase is a smokescreen strategy for the avoidance of lawsuits like those that nearly crippled the tobacco industry. Behaviors recorded on police blotters simply provide another kind of evidence, but their causes being both difficult to prove and unwelcome of acknowledgement does not negate their possible reality.

None of this happened overnight. Back in 1963, critic John Horn wrote about the influence of television in Black households: "Television is a fifth column bringing into Negro homes White nonsense, White violence, White affluence, White materialism, White indifference to fellow Americans of color. To all human beings television is a continuous assault on the heart, the mind and the spirit. To Negroes, as to all racial minorities, it is a major alienating force."[274] Mr. Horn's prescient 1963 statements apply not only to minorities. The baby who has learned during the first five years in the company of the TV sitter moves into the larger world and acts out its learnings. That children with little other upbringing than TV believe in and act according to *enrichissez-vous* with a gun should come as no surprise.

"The combination of 400 ads a day creates in children a combination of narcissism, entitlement and dissatisfaction," writes Mary Pipher in her bestseller about family life, *The Shelter of Each Other*. These children become adults. The gimme-grab fellow citizens whom we excoriate and imprison can be seen as simply apt students of the TV school. The growing frustration and rage that young people feel when their ignorance and poverty thwart access to the goodies of TV's Consumerist Paradise has a predictable outcome. Animal trainers know that tempt-and-thwart can drive a dog to viciousness. Why, then, are middle class people surprised at the lack of social awareness, the self-absorption, the violence, the graffiti, the drive-by shootings that declare, "look, I am!" The child has learned from television.

It's convenient for those whose narrowly self-defined interests are being served by television as now structured in the United States to assert, correctly, that it is next to impossible to scientifically demonstrate a causal relationship between television and the antisocial crime, greed, selfishness, the acting out of frustration and anger, the violence, impulsiveness, irresponsibility that seem to be its correlative.

Of course, we know intuitively that the correlation exists. A 1995 *New York Times* Poll found that "Many Americans say they believe there is a direct connection between the fictional world young people are exposed to and the way they behave in real life."[275] Can we not extrapolate from the demonstrable cause and effect of a television commercial and product sales that television causes people to model their actions on behaviors suggested on the tube? Jim Squires, former editor of the *Chicago Tribune*, asks, "What is the mystery then about a society that has the manners of a rock band, the morals of a soap opera, the decisionmaking ability of the Simpsons and wants to pay for government with Visa and American Express?" They get their learning from the tube.

It happens to be convenient for a lot of people to deny any connection between television and social malaise, or when it is made, to ignore it. Way back in 1965, the Dodd Committee of Congress in their interim report declared, "It is clear that television, whose impact on the public mind is equal to or greater than that of any other medium, is a factor in molding the character, attitudes and behavior patterns of America's young people. Further, it is the subcommittee's view that the excessive amount of televised crime, violence and brutality can and does contribute to the development of attitudes and actions in many young people which pave the way for delinquent behavior." That was in 1965.

Dr. James Gilligan's 1996 book *Violence* is the product of the author's ten years as psychologist in a maximum-security correctional institution. His conclusion: essentially, the cause of violence is violence. To attempt to discriminate about whether causative violence is "fiction", "news", the defense budget, TV or family life, or a combination, is to evade the point.

In 1991 representatives of The American Academy of Pediatrics, the national PTA, the national Coalition of Television Violence and the American Psychological Association joined in support of legislation sponsored by Sen. Paul Simon and Rep. Dan Glickman to exempt the television networks from antitrust laws for three years . . . a government bribe so television might develop a plan to limit program violence. In 26 years, a step was taken. In 1993, Rep. Ron Wyden (D-Ore.) pointed to a "tidal wave of violence, murder and bloodshed" during the May ratings sweeps. Could it be that the billions of dollars of people's income that comes directly and indirectly from television is related in some way to the development of a stratum of society that seems bent on the destruction of itself and others? It is undeniably evident that the *monkey see, monkey do* cause and effect relationship brings in the swag that builds the commercial-TV makers' islands of civility in Newport Beach, Bel Air, Greenwich and Martha's Vineyard. "Decades of second-rate television have habituated Americans to seeing conflict and violence rather than wit and wisdom as the solution to all problems", writes *US News & World Report's* Mortimer B. Zuckerman.[276] "The cause and effect relationship to TV programs that is the acting out of the gun as solution to problems on the streets of America is the same *monkey see, monkey do.* How can those who profit from it in one case deny it in another so similar? Easily. The tobacco companies did it for decades: (1) Point with pride to the Gross Domestic Product. (2) Scapegoat. (3) Blame the victims. (4) Put the malefactors in jail. (5) Turn your back.

Someday, somebody is going to have to face the dilemma that the price our society pays for the incomes of some of us may be a threat to the viability of our culture. Prison construction can't keep up with the proliferation of lawbreakers. In 1993, 300,000 American schoolchildren took firearms to school each day. A resentful underclass takes up arms and sets fire to our cities. Time will tell if we can be honest with ourselves and face the possibility that the social harm done by TV violence is a price we pay for effective marketing strategies. Time will tell if those who live inside walled enclaves will be willing to acknowledge some responsibility for creating the desperados who threaten them.

Our inability to demonstrate television as a cause of harm to individuals and groups in a way that is provable according to currently accepted criteria of proof simply indicates the coarseness of the standards we elect to apply. We know in our *bones*, as the manufacturers of the consumer products sold on TV know in their balance sheets, that TV is enormously significant in American life. Maybe it's time to recognize TV as a force that causes people to behave the way they do are in our country today, and will tomorrow.

As it presents itself, America's current leadership class is differentiated from earlier leadership classes by an increased focus on the behaviors of competitiveness and acquisi-tiveness, mitigated by the highly selective application of "family values". ("Family values" is code for "Take care of your own and to Hell with everybody else.") In the decade of the 1980s, this class created the impression that it intends to exploit an economic structure of incentives leading to a two-tier society, a society of winners and losers, the users and the used.

The results are as predictable as a laboratory demonstration. In the words of Repre-sentative Markey (D-MA), "The nitro meets the glycerin." In practice, the losers have also been imbued with the values of competitiveness and acquisitiveness. But deprived of a means of realization, the losers, instead of giving up, try to redress the self-evident imbal-ance by a method they have learned from the world as it comes to them. Good students, they achieve or attempt to achieve the goals of the dominant culture by means they see on TV. They become highwaymen

The poet T.S. Eliot found it necessary to point out, as philosophers have done for centuries, that "Our means *are* our ends." Functional Leninists among us, those who be-lieve that "the ends justify the means", have hidden behind the GDP, smiling on any activi-ties that keep the cash registers jingling. All of television, commercial and noncommercial, has drifted into a state of irresponsibility, hiding behind "the bottom line".

Industrial capitalism in America was adapted from the English model. Nineteenth-century American theoreticians anticipated wrenching social turmoil in the conversion from hereditary authoritarian agrarianism to the authoritarian industrial capitalism of self-defined leaders. Then, the promise of "vulgar" industrial capitalism to provide a decent standard of living, shelter and food for all people made it seem worth the sacrifice. Through industrial capitalism, the interests of democracy, it seemed, would be met. Will-ingly, Americans undertook the transformation of their society.

Generations of struggling Americans knowingly compromised the present in the interest of a better future society to be characterized by fairness and equity. It didn't occur to most parents who taught their children sacrifice in the interest of the common good that the goal of basic equity in the distribution of the plenty made possible by industrial capitalism would be abandoned as a matter of policy. It didn't occur to the children who accepted the sacrifice of working in the mills that the producers of goods would become manipulators of their customers' desires. It didn't occur to the children brought up on civ-ics courses that the poor and the lower middle class in our democracy would be held hos-tage to the producers of consumer goods. It didn't occur to the average American that in-dustrial might manipulate elected officials to allow a substantial body of its workers to be moved toward penury. It didn't occur to people that the government would be the facilita-tor of a society of well-dressed peddlers characterized by competitiveness, clawing ambi-tion, road rage. How could it ever occur to a believer in American democracy that the lead-ership of his country would adopt economics as its creed, encouraging ignorance and poverty to sustain a pool of low wage working class employees to produce low priced consumer goods for the gratification of middle class impulse, investor returns, and tax revenue?

Consumerism has succeeded beyond its inventors' wildest dreams. The late, decadent phase of the process of industrialization, consumerism is the *de facto* American philosophy of life for more than just those addicts who sport "shop 'til you drop" bumper stickers. *The New York Times Magazine* of April 17, 1994 contains a confession by a young man dying of AIDS, in which he wrote, "Instead of letting go, we became acquisitive, stealing all the things we'd never owned: a blender, toaster, coffee grinder, new shoes, black baggy Levis . . . Ours was a typical American response." How many more thieves does he speak for? The 17 year old who kidnapped school teacher Kathleen Weinstein in New Jersey and murdered her because he "wanted her car"? Who could have predicted that a Judeo-Christian tradition of prudence, restraint and self-denial taught by America's one-time WASP leadership would vanish from public view? Who would have predicted a universal acceptance of a radical new idea that flew in the face of the teachings of all of the world's great religions, prominent among them not only Christianity but also the one founded in the Deer Park at Benares by Gautama Buddha? Gautama's religion established each person's life goal as "the extinction of desire", the precise antithesis of consumerism.

The 14th century Christian poet Dante Alighieri, in his "Inferno", consigned the symbol of unquenchable desire, Francesca Da Rimini, to be buffeted through the air by winds for all eternity in one of the levels of Hell. Impelled by desire, she was forever denied peace, tranquility or contentment.

Christianity, America's former religion, deplored "moneychangers in the temple". Twenty-five hundred years ago, Confucius declared, "It is shameful to make gain your sole object." In a revision of the lessons of history, today the moneychangers *are* the temple. Television and advertising are acolytes, two of the instruments used to fan the flames of desire. One result has been what *The New York Times*' critic Herbert Muschamp has described as "the apocalyptic wastefulness of consumer society". Philosopher George Santayana observed that those who are ignorant of history will only relive it. The 20th century saw American media put the lessons of history behind itself.

The consequences of the redeification of Mammon, one may fairly predict, will be as they always have been. Future generations will not kindly remember a chronically self-absorbed people who pillaged the earth so they could change their minds at will about the shape of their garments, their mode of transport or the chairs they sit in. And who is to say that the crumbling of civility in our society doesn't point to the conclusion that our 90-year-old experiment in consumerism may be a pathology?[278]

Commercial radio and commercial television, in doing as they are chartered to do, have promoted any ideas that foster their own economic interest. It is they who have been the educators of the poor and the ignorant. The consumerism they promulgate is an assiduous cultivation of impulse gratification and insecurity.

Commercial music's illusion of libidinal empowerment is only one prominent symptom. Our countrymen's epidemic selfishness, crime, violence, suicide, and alienation may well be in part a natural consequence of consumerist-sanctioned self-absorption's concomitant misanthropy, fear and hatred.

Consumerism's tunnel-vision has caused a one-time somewhat homogeneous democratic society to divide into four camps, the rich, the poor, the imprisoned and a tiny minority of what Vaclav Havel has pointed out developed in the communist east, "A stratum of educated people aware that the system, should it continue, would eventually destroy us both morally as individuals and professionally as artists, scholars and intellectuals."[279] And where is this stratum in America today? They are an underground. Not hired, not published, anonymous, unheralded. Even the education system, higher and lower, has been taken from them.

Is marketing, consumerism's active voice, a destructive force? Is the rampant misanthropy of the films *Mad Max, Blade Runner, The Truman Show,*[280] *American Beauty* a realistic projection of an epidemic consumerist psyche in a high-tech matrix? Is Russia's Alexander Solzhenitsyn on the mark when he points with alarm at "the self-indulgent and squalid popular mass culture"?[281] Was former US National Security Advisor Zbigniew Brzezinski on the mark when he pointed with alarm at "the self-indulgent advanced nations (who) have their minds fixated on the instant gratification of their desires and appetites: material, sensual and sexual"?[282] Was it accurate of Czech President Vaclav Havel to describe a future "global dictatorship of advertisement, consumerism and blood-and-thunder stories on TV"?[283] Maybe.

The flaws in our television are both causative and symptomatic. The economic theories of John Maynard Keynes held that money should be kept in circulation. As a sanctioned means to this end, the guileful stake out and massage the gullible and the impulsive for profit. As economics, the practice works pretty well. As social theory, its long-term outcome promises to be environmentally and socially ruinous. The consequence of the ahistoricism of economics is a vast enhancement of the power of manipulative people and a smoldering resentment on the part of the legions that are beginning to believe they're being "had".

As we look about us, even in our arts and architecture, we see a culture drifting into a "post modern" state of trivialization and narcosis. We reap the benefits and the costs of a historical vision dominated by the economic hypothesis known as "economic determinism" described by Hegel, the philosopher who inspired Karl Marx. The radical hypothesis of Karl Marx, as put by Sir Isaiah Berlin in his introduction to *Karl Marx, His Life and Environment*[284] was, at its most simple, his "emphasis upon the primacy of economic factors in determining human behaviour."

Macaulay's idea that material progress would be the ally of moral progress is denied endlessly by our daily press. Philosopher and essayist Octavio Paz has observed, "The market is highly efficient, but it has no goal; its sole purpose is to produce more in order to consume more.[285] Why, then, should not "Some American actions ignore democracy altogether and simply make a corner of the world safe for United Fruit"?[286]

Beyond attempts to land a man on Mars, the only major, long range national goal that former President Bush and his successor publicly advanced is a version of what was once called "economic imperialism", to make over the rest of the world in the image of to-day's economic fashion. The US Department of Defense in early 1992 recommended that we maintain an unchallengeable military force to guarantee our "interests" worldwide. Of course, "interests" means *economic* interests. President Bush I's successor placed a sign in his office saying, "It's the economy, stupid!" Perhaps we might again look to the philosopher Karl Marx, who held that the proper goal of human governance is not economic prosperity, but instead, a *freedom* (sic) available to all through the conquest of drudgery.

The 1997 return of Labor to power in England was described thus: "The eighteen years of Thatcherism and post-Thatcherism, with their vulgar gospel of selfish individualism, brought the British public to a point at which they could no longer live with their own self-dislike."[287] No such revulsion in the United States! Here there's more rejoicing than ever in the principles of Thatcherism. Our nation seems to have forgotten its historic mission, stated in the words of poet F.D. Reeve: "putting human relations and human welfare at the center of our social purpose."[288]

Economic determinism has declared a mass of American citizens to be non-persons. Called "The Poor", and "The Homeless", these nameless losers represent a positive force in current economic thinking. As needy job-seekers ready to replace jobholders, they keep workers' wages down, and consequently keep the prices of raw materials down for manu-facturers. They keep prices of finished goods down for the middle class (including legisla-tors). They keep inflation down. An entire class of people numbering millions is perma-nently denied the benefits of industrialization by monetary policy. The benefits are not universal. What may be good economic policy may be social poison. Economic policy per-manently denies to millions of Americans, "the poor", "the homeless", " the unemployed" the wherewithal to even hope to develop themselves humanely, to learn, to experience, to become productive in any way but as an instrument of somebody else's plan. In the Ameri-can "big store", they are lepers. The worst part is that official economic policy demands encouragement of conditions leading to their failure.

But a "good thing" for current economic policy may be a bad thing for our collective future. A side effect of our nation's revolutionary adoption of economic determinism as its creed has been a disastrous epidemic of drug use. William M. Adler has written, "Until there are more attractive and practical options for young people mired in urban and rural ghettos, until their life prospects amount to more than serving or cleaning up after other people, gang membership and selling drugs will continue to be rational career choices."[289]

Drug use is a poultice, a way of denying the pain of existence, like alcoholism, video games, superbowls, high fashion, Disney, golf, a big Mercedes, or a luxurious apartment. The search for narcosis represents the acting out of a systemic critique that crosses class boundaries. Its cause is the fact that the poor among us see their lives as hopeless, the rich as pointless. In this sense, drug use is merely an acted-out criticism of economic determinism. The middle class, unreflective, uncompassionate and afraid, blames the victims. So far, they have removed 1,400,000 people from their world for violation of drug or alcohol laws.[290] This is serious.

Without the promise of war, with the efficiencies brought by computerization, the American merchant class careens ahead. The apparent demise of the Soviet Union has opened a tempting vision of world domination for American commerce — which would be fine if CEOs were infallible, if their vision of humanity were the best that has ever been, or if their methods were not replicable by non-Americans. Unfortunately, the merchant class in its relentless pursuit of its own short-term objectives finds its interests served by using the communications industry to create a benign picture of a profligate usurpation of the planet's resources, ahistoricism, the promotion of hierarchical authoritarianism, opportunism, greed, exploitativeness, manipulativeness, callousness to any and all outside its immediate sphere, the development of a two-class society in which the underclass is depraved into a choice among trivial consumerism, resignation, poverty or violence. The inward-directed post-modern skyscrapers of New York, the walled communities of Florida and California, the diversions of private jets and celebrity dinner parties can't keep out these truths for long.

* * *

The question, "is market value the sole criterion of social value?" is an open one. If answered affirmatively, it declares public television or any alternative television to be unnecessary, even wrong. If market value is the sole criterion of all social value, public television should be dismantled immediately. If market value is the sole criterion of all social value, the public needn't vote either, it need just allow a free hand to Political Action Committees. If, however there are important components of human experience that exist outside the market, there is a place for an alternative. If there are important components of human experience that exist outside the market, institutions of communication should not be dominated by people, however clever, whose lives are directly or indirectly dominated by the market. In either case, American legislators are not equipped to decide on what Americans should see on TV. This is a decision the culture has to make *for* its servants. The servants of the culture are industry and government.

There is much for us to do in the 21st century. The ancient questions — "Where do we come from?" "Why are we here?" "What is the destiny of our species?" "What is the nature and meaning of reality?" "What is the good and what is the good life?" "Can we create a community that asserts the brotherhood of man?" "Can we provide for those who pursue virtue?" "Can we foster imagination and creativity?" — are questions that philosophers and artists of the past, present and future have always and will always address. These are questions for which an art form like television is an appropriate vehicle.

An alternative to today's public television, to commercial television, an alternative television with an open agenda can give America a voice that speaks with the diversity of opinion, the diversity of ways of thinking that societies have always called The Arts.

By its founders, ours was meant to be an open society. As a nation we were once committed to fight for that openness. As trustees of our own legacy, we must see to it that human issues and human possibilities aside from those of politics and economics have a place in mass communications. We must develop a television that sees itself as part of the continuum of human development, that has a regard for the planetary history of which we are a part, a television that helps us to see the present as an instant in the continuum of past and future that we all make together.

Television has become a powerful force in America. It is a significant component of our literature, our history, our daily lives. Japan annually spends $32 per person on non-commercial television. Canada spends $31 per person. Great Britain spends $38 per person. In America, we spend far less, only $1.09 per person per year on public television. Some measures have been proposed (1997) in Congress that may establish a trust fund for public television. A trust fund, it is said, would insulate noncommercial television from the control of politicians.

The establishment of a trust fund to support an independent noncommercial television entity in America is a good old idea. It was recommended by the Carnegie Commission decades ago. The Oversight Plan for the House Committee on Commerce of the 105th Congress predicted in 1997 that among the Telecommunications, Trade and Consumer Protection issues to come under its oversight would be to "investigate to what extent federal funding is necessary for the continued survival of CPB." An investigation that would wrest this instrument of thought control from Washington is long overdue. As the legislation makes its way through Congress, the thoughtful public should intervene in the interest of television as the literature of our times. It should watch the wording of the legislation carefully for loopholes like those in the Public Television Act of 1967.

As proposed, the trust fund would allow the income from $1 billion to be available for public television. (At 6%, that would guarantee public television "no strings" funding of $60 million a year, which is unthreateningly just the equivalent of the cost of production and promotion for *one* average Hollywood film in 1996). We must recognize its place in the matrix of human history, commercial and noncommercial media, entertainment, education and information, American and foreign, present and past; but this proposal should be welcomed. It's a start.

Picture Credits

Endnotes

1. A character in Voltaire's picaresque novella *Candide*, Pangloss was a send-up of theists who believed that since God is good, the world he made has to be good, "the best of all possible worlds". Pangloss endured a multitude of misadventures, each more grievous than its predecessor.

2. Charlie Chaplin's film *Monsieur Verdoux*, in which the protagonist followed "business ethics" in his personal life and "personal ethics" in his business life, is a wry satire most notable for its absence from today's screens.

3. Home Base Expo, Clairemont Mesa, San Diego, CA 1996.

4. See "A Stifling of Artistic Freedom Persists", on Chinese Communism, by Sheila Melvin, *The New York Times*, Section 2, September 26, 1999.

5. See Chapter 25.

6. As quoted in "Misfortune in Shanghai", by Jonathan Mrisky, *New York Review*, November 4, 1999, p. 12.

7. "The Hope for China", Fung Lizhi and Perry Link, *New York Review*, October 17, 1996.

8. Samuel Taylor Coleridge, *Essay on the Imagination*.

9. *The Nation*, June 3, 1996, p. 28.

10. Cairo's largest bazaar is characterized more strongly by the hectoring of merchants and their hirelings than by the quality of their merchandise.

11. As quoted in *Investment in Innovation* by Paul Woodring, Little Brown & Co., 1970.

12. From "The Vision of Leonardo", by Prof. Henri Zerner of Harvard University, *New York Review of Books*, September 25, 1997.

13. *Ibid.*

14. See "The Fabulous La Fontaine", *The New York Review of Books*, December 18, 1997.

15. Senator Helms vs Robert Mapplethorpe, 1991.

16. November 9, 1997, p. 14.

17. "Washington's Stake in the Arts", April 12, 1998, Section 2 p. 1.

18. June 28, 1998, p. 32.

19. "A cliché dear to left-wing critics, although no less true for being a cliché", he continues in *The New York Review of Books*, "The Fabulous La Fontaine", *op. cit.*, p. 39.

20. "The Unsparing Vision of Don DeLillo", in *Harper's Magazine*, November 1997, p. 73.

21. Conversation in a New York production meeting.

22. See the telephone company building across New Haven Green from the Yale School of Architecture, where Philip Johnson once lectured.

23. In *Modern Maturity*, October-November 1992.

24. The term is Oswald Spengler's, used in *The Decline of the West*. Freely translated, it means

"world feeling".

25. *The Economist*, October 10-16, 1992, p. 22.

26. "Elected Bodies With Hardly a Cultured Bone", July 26, 1998, Section 2, p. 1.

27. *Extending Choice, The BBC's Role in the New Broadcasting Age*, 1993.

28. "Televiolence", *Washington Monthly*, June 1998, p. 52.

29. "Our Hollow Hegemony", *The New York Times Magazine*, November 1, 1998, p.47.

30. *Mayhem: Violence as Public Entertainment*, Addison Wesley 1998.

31. *Ibid.*

32. *Violence*, p. 5. New York: Grosset/Putnam, 1996.

33. *Los Angeles Times*, February 26, 1994, F10.

34. See also *The New York Times*, May 9, 1999, p. 23. "Hundreds of studies done at the nation's top universities in the last three decades have come to the same conclusion: that there is at least some demonstrable link between watching violent acts in movies or television shows and acting aggressively in life."

35. In "Putting the Media on the Couch", *The Journal of the California Alliance for the Mentally Ill*, Volume 4, Number 1.

36. June 8-14 1996, p. 23, under the heading, "Violent and irrational — and that's just the policy."

37. "Many Researchers Say Link Is Already Clear on Media and Youth Violence", Lawrie Mifflin, *The New York Times*, May 9, 1999, p. 23.

38. *Variety*, July 12, 1993, p.56.

39. From "A New Prescription", Joseph A. Califano Jr. *The Washington Monthly*, October, 1998.

40. Even though the Congress was known then as a "club", the term didn't yet carry connotations of self-selection to alternate speciehood as, say, President Bush's Yale secret society membership always has done.

41. *The New York Times*, December 13, 1992, p. H31.

42. Selected by Wendy Wasserstein in *The New York Times Magazine*, April 19, 1999, as the "best clown of the twentieth century".

43. *The New York Times*, January 10, 1993.

44. As recently as 1991, *Variety* quoted John Miller, executive Vice President of advertising-promotion for NBC Entertainment, saying "We scheduled two of the best game shows on the air in *Wheel of Fortune* and *Concentration*, but they skewed too old — advertisers weren't rushing in to buy them". (*Variety*, August 19, 1991.)

44. "Niche" marketing on the next level has developed a two-fold thrust: 1. "Since they're not served, we can give them a second-rate product and charge a significant markup" (prosthetic devices, diabetic chocolates are examples), or 2. "We'll provide an excellent product that mass merchandising can't match, and give ourselves a huge markup", (Neiman Marcus, *et al.*). Either method contributes generously to the providers' own enrichment.

45. Broadcast journalist and Neiman Fellow in Journalism, author of *The More You Watch, the Less You Know*, New York: Seven Stories Press.

46. Arnold Shapiro, "The Guru of TV Docudrama" (*The Christian Science Monitor*, Thursday April 18, 1991) declares, "The majority of people watch television the majority of time to escape their personal woes, to be entertained and as somewhat of a narcotic, a desensitizer . . .

That's why you see what you see on television."

47. A Creators Syndicate cartoon by Doug Mariette of the week of April 24, 1994 depicts Rose-anne Barr and Tom Arnold alongside "paramecia" and "amoebas" under the collective head-ing "Lower Life Forms". A "boorish", "Rabelaisian backlot brat", writes Maureen Dowd (op-ed page, *The New York Times*, September 3, 1993.

48. *Variety*, April 26, 1993.

49. "Racing fans, a third of whom are women, are more likely to buy sponsors' products than fans of any other sport." *Fortune*, March 31, 1997, p. 38.

50. From "Sex and Violence on TV", *U.S. News & World Report*, September 11, 1995.

51. "Racing fans. . . ", *Fortune, op. cit.*

52. The success of this strategy may be noted in Juliet B. Schor's *The Overspent American*. "My research shows that the more TV a person watches the more he or she spends." Basic Books, 1998.

53. A comment that supports this contention comes from Kalle Lasn, co-editor of *Adbusters*, the quarterly magazine of the Canadian Media Foundation: "North America is currently domi-nated by product pushers whose ads promote consumerism and a lifestyle that is destroy-ing the planet."

54. From "The US and The World: An Interview with George Kennan", Michael Ullman, *The New York Review of Books*, August 12, 1999, p. 6.

55. "Sex and Violence on TV", *U.S. News & World Report, op. cit.*

56. "To Serve the Public Interest", Syracuse University, 1979.

57. Paul Woodring, *Investment in Innovation*, Little Brown & Co., 1970.

58. Its purpose, "experiments and new developments in education." *Annual Report*, lj951-52 p. 7.

59. Alvin C. Eurich, *Reforming American Education*, New York: Harper & Row, 1969, p. 15.

60. And is therefore what committees and bureaucrats could deal with in lieu of substantive considerations. So they did.

61. Earl Shorris writes, in *A Nation of Salesmen* (New York: W.W. Norton), "Homo vendens *can-not make judgments. He operates on the principle that all value is exchange value and, as such, is set by the market, no one and nothing else. Neither the utility of the thing nor its other intrinsic qualities (beauty, du-rability, happiness, economy, healthfulness, and so on) can change the judgment of the market. Condemned to endless and ever-changing tolerance,* Homo vendens *lives in a world in which all products and all acts have been emptied of content.*" Abridgement, *Harper's*, October 1994, p. 46.

62. "Shopping has become a competitive sport," says *Business Week*, June 30, 1997, p. 65.

63. "The Visible Hand", *The Economist*, September 1997, p. 17.

64. Joyce Carol Oates in the *New York Review*, September 1, 1996.

65. *Harpers Magazine*, April 1997, p. 8.

66. Earl Shorris, *op. cit.*, p. 49.

67. Anne W. Branscomb, Aspen Institute Program on Communications and Society, 1975.

68. From Jonathan Rae, contributing editor, *The Washington Monthly*.

69. See: T. S. Eliot, *The Cocktail Party*.

70. "Architecture View", *The New York Times*, December 13, 1992, Section 2, p. 34.

71. See: "The Man Without Qualities", planning for "The Austrian Year".

72. Annual Report, 1957.

73. "This practice obviously contravenes the spirit of the prohibition against commercial uses of the station," Anne W. Branscomb, Aspen Institute Program on Communications and Society, 1975.

74. *Harper's*, April 1992, p. 10.

75. In his book *BAD, The Dumbing of America* (Summit Books, 1991), Paul Fussell describes this kind of situation as a common phenomenon: "The manipulation of fools by knaves," a tragedy of "all those well-meaning people swindled by their own credulity."

76. *Variety*, April 21, 1982.

77. "The Case for a New Domestic Order", *The New York Review of Books*, November 21, 1991.

78. The phrase is Lester Thurow's, of MIT.

79. "Chronicle of a death foretold", *The Economist* August 1, 1992, p. 50.

80. "I Know Why the Caged Bird Cannot Read", *Harpers Magazine*, September 1999, p. 83.

81. See William Butler, *The Way of All Flesh*. Or, Punk Rock singer Exene Cervenkova, who sings of "The Nothing Generation" and says that the goal of the corporation is "the unrelenting homogenization of the world", according to the article "Waging war on the environment and the human soul", *Los Angeles Times*, May 31, 1997, F10.

82. The other is inequities caused by the system of local financing. *Los Angeles Times*, February 2, 1997, p. M3.

83. Joyce Carol Oates in *The New York Times Book Review*, September 1, 1996, p. 11.

84. From *The Key of Liberty: The Life and Democratic Writings of William Manning*, "A Laborer", 1147-1814, Harvard University Press.

85. From "The L-Word", *The New York Review*, September 24, 1998.

86. According to *The Economist*, January 25, 1992, p. 71, the final cost of each B2 Stealth bomber "will be a ridiculous $2 billion per bomber".

87. ABC News reported (April 1997) that the navy is willing to commit the taxpayers to between $80 and $100 million for *each* F22 killing machine.

88. "American society exists to service the needs of the economy, not the other way around." Edward Luttwak, *London Review of Books*, November 2, 1995. "The commonplace that we have arrived at some sort of corporate utopia, that business has somehow supplanted civil society, is a commonplace of High Corporate Baroque," Thomas Frank in *The Nation*, December 30, 1996, p. 9.

89. The term coined by Theda Skocpol, Professor of Government and Sociology, Harvard University.

90. Term prominent in the promotion of Ronald Reagan for the presidency.

91. *Time Magazine*, October 18, 1971.

92. *Harper's*, June 1992, p. 10.

93. *The New York Times*, December 9, 1990, E5.

94. *Governing with the News*, University of Chicago, 1997.

95. *Cf* Mozart's *The Magic Flute*. Sarastro, high priest of Isis, was the embodiment of the idea of wisdom gained from education and experience.

96. One-time board chair Sonia Landau was noted by *Variety* for her controlling actions. "Sonia concocts all the plots. . .", they quoted, she "holds sway over the Republican majority on the board." (1986)

97. From *Current*, June 11-25, 1985.

98. During the heat of the Paris Commune, a citizen could assure the decapitation of a person

by pointing to him and shouting "aristocrat". A *lettre de cachet*, a written accusation of that nature, had the same effect.

99. Used prior to the French Revolution to consign dissenters to the Bastille for indefinite periods without trial.

100. A policy statement printed at the end of each table of contents boasts that "The articles in Foreign Affairs do not represent any consensus of beliefs . . . [FA] can do more to inform American public opinion by a broad hospitality to divergent ideas than it can by identifying itself with one school. . . ."

101. Nicholas Johnson, *How to Talk Back to Your Television Set*. Boston: Little Brown & Co., 1970.

102. Prof. Owen Fiss of Yale Law School, *The Nation*, July 21, 1997 p. 14.

103. Floyd Abrams, visiting professor at Columbia Graduate School of Journalism, quoted in *The Nation*, July 21, 1997, p. 13.

104. June 27, 1985, A23.

105. The phrase is Oswald Spengler's, and is a key to his reasoning in *The Decline of the West*.

106. "Modern Victorians", in *Harper's Magazine*, July 1995.

107. My memo dated May 28, 1975 to WGBH's then newly-appointed Vice President Michael Rice asked, "Since an officer class called 'management' seems to be appearing, is it to be assumed that there is a laboring or footsoldier class? Is the model for administrative structure at WGBH properly an industrial one?"

108. Perhaps had public TV instead mounted Donizetti's *Elixer of Love*, they may have seen portents of their own future. In this opera, the "peripatetic quack" Dr. Dulcamara peddles a false potion that not only actually sometimes prompts the results he predicts, but even persuades Dulcamara himself of its magical powers.

109. *Variety*, September 10, 1990.

110. Joan Ganz Cooney's 1967 proposal for *Sesame Street* had pointed out that effective television had costs, and that if children's television was to be effective, it must be able to compete with the flair, style and complexity, the "production value" of commercial television. The argument still holds.

111. "One of the unfortunate byproducts of the growth of the Federal role has been a tendency for many nonprofit organizations to focus as much on what concerns Washington as on their own contributors and clients." Leslie Lenkowsky, President of Institute for Educational Affairs, in *The New York Times*, November 12, 1986.

112. *The Nation*, June 3, 1996, p. 16.

113. From "Moral Economics", *The Washington Monthly*, September 1998, p. 42.

114. "Socially, the merchant class was placed below the peasantry", C. P. Fitzgerald, *History of China*, p. 95. Horizon, 1969.

115. *Ibid.*, p. 16.

116. Vicki Goldberg's feature piece, "Testing the limits in a Culture of Excess", in *The New York Times*, Section 2 (Arts & Leisure), p. 1, October 29, 1995.

117. Louis Menand, Professor of English, Graduate Center of the City University of New York.

118. *New York Times Book Review*, December 1, 1996, p. 13.

119. Released in 1982.

120. "Hindemith and Mozart", *The Nation* June 3, 1996, p.44.

121. In Chaucer's *Troilus and Cressida*, Pandarus "arranged" the lovely Cressida for Troilus.

122. S. L. Harrison, *Washington Monthly*, January 1986. Harrison was Director of Corporate Communications for the Corporation for Public Broadcasting in the early 1980s.

123. *Public Service Broadcasting*, Robert K Avery, Ed. "The British Approach", p. 5.

124. *Time Magazine*, October 18, 1971.

125. This 1975 warning was apparently taken as advice: "Public broadcasting is unlikely to obtain funding unless it strives . . . to air the various views of the politically influential officials who control whatever public funds are being made available." Anne W. Branscomb, paper from Aspen Institute Conference on Public Broadcasting.

126. *The New York Times*, October 27, 1991, p E 15.

127. This apt phrase was used by writer Francine Prose to describe conditions of oppression in a rural New York public school. "Outer City Blues", *The New York Times Magazine*, April 21, 1996, p. 68.

128. Universal Press Syndicate, March 4, 1999.

129. *Op. cit.*, p. 52.

130. *The New York Review*, November 5, 1992.

131. *About Television*, Harper & Row, 1972.

132. "Frivolity and Unction", *Air Guitar: Essays on Art & Democracy*. Los Angeles: Art Issues Press, 1997.

133. *The New York Times*, January 31, 1993.

134. I asked a friend, "Who won the Super Bowl this year?" "Same one . . . Budweiser", he answered.

135. "Coming to a Speedway Near You", *Fortune*, March 31, 1997, p. 38.

136. As quoted in Molly O'Neill's "Take Me Out to the Snack Bar", *The New York Times*, Week in Review, March 31, 1996.

137. From "Sex and Violence on TV", *U.S. News & World Report, ibid.*

138. *Entertainment Weekly*, September 19, 1997, p. 26.

139. "Will Whizbang News Work?", *Variety*, February 22, 1993.

140. Harvard University, Kennedy School of Government.

141. *Extra!* May/June 1994, p. 17.

142. *The More You Watch, the Less You Know*, p. 186. New York: Seven Stories Press, 1997.

143. *World Monitor*, November 1990, p. 26.

144. "To Whom It May Concern", *New York Times Magazine*, January 18, 1998, p. 14.

145. *Harper's*, June 1992, p. 42.

146. "Scribes Say Network Wimps Crimp Their Style", *Variety*, July 1, 1991. Former FCC Commissioner Nicholas Johnson, in his volume *How to Talk Back To Your Television Set (op. cit.)* selects a cause: "Network television programming follows the classic pattern of oligopoly behavior, restricted choice, elaborate corporate strategies and reliance on 'the tried and true'".

147. "Whose documentaries are one of American public television's proudest achievements", *The New York Times*, September 2, 1990 H23.

148. *Newsweek*, December 24, 1990 p, 51.

149. In an unintentionally whimsical "Producer's Guide to Public Television, Who Funds PTV?" the Corporation for Public Broadcasting lists a number of funded agencies as funders, as if the National Endowment for the Humanities got its money from the National Endowment for the Humanities, and not from exactly the same source as the Corporation for Public Broadcasting or many of the other agencies included in this diversionary listing.

150. Ian Baruma in *The New York Review*, March 25, 1993.

151. *The Economist*, August 21-27 1999, p. 41.

152. Quoted in *The New York Times*, Sunday July 8, 1990.

153. Wednesday, September 18, 1991.

154. "An earnest effort that failed was in bringing in younger authors, creative writers and artists into the (Carnegie Commission) project to assist in developing a feeling for the potential of educational broadcasting and the expression of that feeling. This was an area which the staff struggled with, but they were never completely successful, in Goldin's view (Hyman Goldin, associate professor of Communications, Boston University and Executive Secretary Carnegie Commission o Educational Television) in getting anyone who could expound that view with sufficient imagination and clarity to be helpful." From *An Historical-Analytical Study of the Legislative and Political Origins of the Public Broadcasting Act of 1967*. Dissertation, John Edward Burke, BA, MFA, The Ohio State University, 1971.

155. Susan Stamberg, one-time editor, became the leading light of NPR's *All things Considered*. She brought savvy New York irreverence, wit and wry detached humor to observations of the American scene. Robert Krulwich's radio pieces recalled a standard for style in humanistic journalism once set by CBS news. Only the obscurity of NPR allowed the development of Krulwich's exceptional talent. His venture into television, with *Edge*, a WNET-BBC co-production, followed his ingenious, responsible and compassionate radio tradition. An *Edge* piece on Cowboy Poetry is a small masterpiece. The magic of both Stamberg and Krulwich has been replaced on *All Things Considered* by an earnest and humorless factualism on the Soviet model. Stamberg is writing books Krulwich is at ABC News.

156. "SIGNALS". WGBH Educational Foundation, PO Box 64428, St. Paul, MN 55164-0428, 47 pp.

157. "WIRELESS". Minnesota Public Radio, PO Box 64454, St. Paul, MN 55164-0454.

158. Richard Russell, in his conservative *Dow Theory Letters*, declares, "It's still a mad, mad world. And it's still run by money, greed and the will to power" (April 3, 1991).

159. "P.C. On the Grill", Barbara Gruzzuti Harrison, in *Harper's*, June 1992.

160. Gardening is one of my avocations. An ancient tradition, I see the garden as a metaphor for human society. In a garden, the population characterized by competitiveness and aggressiveness is known as "weeds". What is most cherished is hybridized, fragile, difficult to grow, and requires careful cultivation.

161. "We are just not creative artists. We are journalists." Quoted from a statement by Jack Freeman, NBC Nightly News writer in "Are NBC News Writers Professionals? In Lawsuit, Writers Decline Honor", *The New York Times*, July 14, 1991, p. 12.

162. David L. Altheide, *Media Power*, Sage Library of Social Research, 1985, p. 120.

163. An example: "Richard Mellon Scaife . . . and $200 million of his money . . . is the man behind the conservative revolution", from "The Man Behind the Curtain", by Nurity C. Aizenman, *The Washington Monthly*, July-August 1997.

164. "The availability of funding from corporate sources naturally determines the direction of programming choices." Anne W. Branscomb, paper delivered to Aspen Institute Program on Communications and Society, 1975.

165. Alexander Cockburn in *The Nation*, December 9, 1996, p. 10.

166. From Stephen Bach's *Final Cut, Dreams and Disaster in the Making of Heaven's Gate*, p. 76.

167. "The news will surprise some of its members, but no one appointed the Congress of the United States as God", *The Economist* tardily remarked, March 29, 1997, p. 17.

168. "Mobil News That's Fit to Print", *The Nation*, January 27, 1979.

169. Leach, William, *Land of Desire*, Pantheon, 1993, p. 11.

170. "Sponsors Call the Shots on Public TV", November 13, 1985, p. 93.

171. *Washington Monthly*, January 1986.

172. A "Fortune Fifty" agricultural processing company called "America's biggest Welfare Recipient". "At least 43 percent of ADM's annual profits are from markets that would be virtually nonexistent without government subsidies or protections." From Bovard: *Shakedown, How the Government Screws You from A to Z* (New York: Viking, 1995).

173. *Variety*, June 1, 1992.

174. "Law of Wild Prevails in Washington", *The New York Times*, December 19, 1993, p. 15.

175. Act II, Scene II.

176. Op-ed piece, "Kafka on Madison", by Maureen Dowd, April 20, 1996.

177. *The Nation*, March 18, 1963.

178. "The Information Tyranny", *The New York Times Magazine*, June 13, 1999.

179. *Electronic Media*, March 13, 1989.

180. "The More You Watch, the Less You Know", *op. cit.*

181. *The Nation*, December 4, 1995.

182. See GE Annual Report photos.

183. *Extra*, November/December 1994.

184. Nicholas Johnson, *How to Talk Back to Your Television Set. Op. cit.*, p. 53.

185. *Ibid.*, p. 57, and pp 52-53. Or, note *Variety*'s David Kissinger (March 2, 1992), "Part of the attractions of owning a major web would be its news division and the access to Washington power brokers that affords."

186. "Kent Sent Packing", August 24, 1992, p. 82.

187. *AARP Bulletin*, March 1996.

188. "Corporate censors keep from your TV screen the full range of needs, tastes and interests of the American People." Former FCC member Nicholas Johnson, *op. cit.*, p. 95.
    "When we use TV we're not using it to support First Amendment rights or artistic freedoms, we're using it because it's a good business decision for our client, and nobody wants the result of a business decision to be loss of customers", Betsy Frank of Saatchi & Saatchi, *The New York Times*, December 8, 1991, p. H31.

189. American advertisers do not hesitate to censor media materials they find offensive. The Ford Motor Company withheld advertising from *The New Yorker* for six months in 1996 because it objected to the content of an article; Titleist and Foot Joy withheld $1 million from *Sports Illustrated* in 1997 for the same reason, according to former *New York Times* editor Max Frankel (*New York Times Magazine*, June 1, 1997, p. 24).

190. See Michael Ignatieff's review of Samuel P. Huntington's *The Clash of Civilizations and the Remaking of World Order*, in *The New York Times Book Review*, December 1, 1996.

191. A convenient if not universally accepted criterion . . . in the words of one of the century's significant intelligences, Sir Isaiah Berlin: "Verifiability is not the only, or indeed the most plausible, criterion of knowledge or beliefs or hypotheses" (from Berlin's essay, "The Purpose Justifies the Ways", reprinted in *The New York Review of Books*, May 14, 1998, p. 54).

192. Composer John Adams in *Stereophile*, April 1997: "I think there's a general anti-intellectual streak in American life. It's always been there, but it's disturbingly strong right now."

193. From "A Composer's Lament: the Music Goes Soft", *The New York Times*, July 12, 1998, p. 27.

194. The term is George Will's.

195. Orlando, Florida, June 8-11, 1991. Organized by The Corporation for Public Broadcasting, System EEO Support, Television Program Fund, with support from The Public Broadcasting Service.

196. The Independent Television Service, designed to promote access to television by outsiders, defines those outsiders not in terms of noncommercial, artistic or nonpolitical acceptability, but in what amounts to the definition of bigotry: it defines them in terms of an accident of birth. Membership application forms include a checklist for applicants to indicate their membership in "Asian American, Black/African American, Latino/Hispanic, Native American/Alaskan Native, Pacific Island American, or White/European American" groups, plus "male" or "female". The categorization of creative people in this way is an insult to them and to their craft. It guarantees a response only by opportunists and "losers". Its results will damage their cause.

197. In his *Dow Theory Letters*, Richard Russell ascribes one cause of public pessimism to "a Congress that is seen to be corrupt, self-serving and interested first and foremost in getting re-elected" (March 4, 1992).

198. *The New York Times Book Review*, February 23, 1992, p. 3.

199. Editorial, October 31, 1992.

200. *Extending Choice, The BBC's Role in the New Broadcasting Age*, 1993.

201. *The Charterhouse of Parma*, Chapter 1, Richard Howard's translation.

202. Baker & Dessart, *Down the Tube*, p. 123. Basic Books, 1998.

203. Scribner, New York.

204. In his foreword to Danny Schechter's *The More You Watch the Less You Know, op. cit.*

205. An evolution pointed out by literary critic Clifton Fadiman, on CBS's *The Year Gone By*, of 1957, on which I was production assistant.

206. *The New York Times, op. cit.*

207. Michael Parenti, *Inventing Reality, the Politics of the Mass Media*. New York: St. Martins Press, 1986.

208. *Ibid.*, p. 234.

209. The $30,000 a year that Oracle pays former congressman Jack Kemp as a board member is surely not due to his ability to contribute to software development. Added to his fees from American Insurance Group, Inc., Carso, Inc., Everen Capital Corp. and The Sports Authority, Inc., it should help to pay for his efforts in Washington quarters to secure special attention to the pursuit of their corporate interests.

210. On their own turf, the Music Center of Los Angeles County honored "Legendary (sic) Hol-

lywood Publicist" Henry C. Rogers, inflator of balloons about Gene Kelly, Paul Newman, Charlton Heston, and Jack Valenti.

211. *The Economist*, November 28, 1992.

212. From "Programming Profile, Corporation for Public Broadcasting", July 1993.

213. In 1993, the Corporation for Public Broadcasting announced the subjects of its Program Fund awards. Of 37 awards, 15 were for "minority" programming. For the rest of us, two were about disabled people, and one features a politically-prominent conservative on the subject of "values".

214. *Variety*, January 6, 1992, p. 5.

215. *Ibid.*

216. *The More You Watch the Less You Know, op. cit.*

217. Richard Taruskin, Professor of Music, University of California Berkeley, quoted in *The New York Times*, January 27, 1991.

218. *The Economist*, June 7, 1997, p. 64.

219. According to an AP dispatch quoted in *The Christian Science Monitor* of May 25, 1993.

220. *The Washington Monthly*, June 1998.

221. "American Voices, Essays on Public Television Programming", Corporation for Public Broadcasting, 1997 Introduction, p. v.

222. *The New York Times*, March 17, 1990, p. 1.

223. "Missing Murray Kempton", *The New York Times Book Review*, November 30, 1997, p. 35.

224. *The New York Times*, June, 1991.

225. *The Wall Street Journal*, April 18, 1991.

226. *World Monitor*, April 1993.

227. *The New York Times Book Review*, July 4, 1993.

228. December 27, 1993, p. 33.

229. Universal Press Syndicate, from the Pueblo Colorado *Chieftain*, March 5, 1999.

230. Quoted in "Quarrels With Providence", by Lewis Lapham, *Yale Alumni Magazine*, Tercentennial Edition, March, 2001, p. 48.

231. "Diversity and its Dangers", *The New York Review of Books*, October 7, 1993.

232. An example is the downward progress of S. I. Newhouse's once distinguished magazine empire, Condé Nast (Alex Kuczynski's "The Truman Show", *The New York Times Magazine*, Sunday August 1, 1999 p. 32).

233. "Letter from Europe", *The Nation*, January 17, 1994.

234. Quoted in "Quarrels With Providence", by Lewis Lapham, *Yale Alumni Magazine*, Tercentennial Edition, March, 2001, p. 48.

235. John F. White, President of National Educational TV and Radio Center, in a speech to the Harvard University School of Business Administration, August 2, 1963.

236. Tabby House Books, 1993.

237. Quoted from *The Public Interest*, Spring 1993, by Irving Kristol in *The Wall Street Journal*, May 31, 1994.

238. "To counter their feelings of powerlessness, inner-city kids have filled their imaginations with the sanitized mayhem and heavily armed heroics of *The Terminator* and *Die Hard*. In turn this mainstream imagery has become the most important source of legitimacy for mas-

culine identity based on sexual conquest and violence." Carl Husemoller Nightingale, *The New York Times* Op-Ed, December 5, 1993.

239. *The Nation*, Editorial, January 1, 1996 p. 4.

240. "Wheredjalernat?" queries a character in the film *Thelma and Louise*, in awe after witnessing her companion demolish a person who had been obstructing her will. "Onteevee", is the matter-of-fact reply.

241. "Molding Our Lives in the Image of Movies", October 25, 1998.

242. "The Decay of Cinema", by Susan Sontag, in *New York Times Magazine*, February 25, 1996.

243. *Business Week*, June 30, 1997, p. 54.

244. "Americans Despair of Pop Culture", August 20, 1995.

245. December 13, 1992, p. H31.

246. *The Washington Post*, October 17, 1984, as quoted in *Make Believe Media*, by Michael Parenti, New York: St. Martins Press, 1992.

247. From "Hey Kid, Buy This!", June 30, 1997.

248. From *You Can't be Neutral on a Moving Train*, Howard Zinn, Beacon 1994.

249. Frank Rich, Op-Ed in *The New York Times*, April 17, 1994 p. 17.

250. *Illinois Quarterly*, Winter 1991, Volume 3, Issue 1 p. 39.

251. March 29, 1992 p. E3.

252. Leni Reifenstahl, Hitler's filmmaker, the power of whose works transcends ideology.

253. "Set up procedures that respect the artists, writers, producers and directors who make the programs, and include as decisionmakers the outstanding members of the creative community itself." *A Public Trust*, p. 167.

254. From a review of the opening exhibition of the refurbished Palazzo Farnese in Piacenza, by Gianfranco Malafarina, *FMR*, October - November 1997.

255. Students may look to the New York art market, the exhibitions of the Whitney Museum, and the Ford Foundation's support of the arts for ample demonstration of this assertion.

256. "Pollution Alert", *New York Times Magazine*.

257. In a speech given at Columbia University's bicentennial observation one of the century's foremost intelligences, J. Robert Oppenheimer advised institutionalization of an alliance between the artist and the university, to "protect him from the tyranny of man's communication and professional promotion".

258. Morris Ernst's phrase.

259. *Variety*, February 10 1992, p. 21.

260. See article on retired Ford Motor Co. President Donald E. Petersen, in *World Monitor*, October 1991.

261. Basic Books, 1998.

262. Mel Ferber and Bob Guinette from CBS, Rick Hauser and Henry Morgenthau from WGBH.

263. On acceptance of the First Decade Prize from the Polish daily *Gazeta Wyborcza*, reprinted in *The New York Review of Books* under the title "Paying Back the West", September 23, 1999 p. 54ff.

264. *The New York Times*, September 1, 1991

265. Actor Dustin Hoffman, who used Buckley as a model for the pirate "Hook", was quoted as saying of Buckley, "There's something scary there." Perhaps this is what he sees.

266. Larry Abraham, *Insider Report.*

267. *Variety*, April 1992.

268. *The History of Public Broadcasting*, Witherspoon & Kovitz, p. 47.

269. From a promotional flyer, Museum of Television & Radio, November 1992.

270. "The States Spring a Surprise", *The Economist*, November 21, 1998, p. 27.

271. From his Fulbright prize address, October 3, 1997.

272. "Among social scientists, there is a broad consensus that there is at least an indirect relationship between popular culture and behavior. Otherwise, how can television executives make the case to advertisers that buying air time will boost their sales?" "Americans Despair of Pop Culture", in *The New York Times*, August 20, 1995, section 2.

273. AARP, *Critics question TV advocacy ads*, October 1999, p. 3

274. *The Nation*, March 18, 1963.

275. "Americans Despair of Popular Culture", *The New York Times*, August 20, 1995, section 2.

276. "Among social scientists, there is a broad consensus that there is at least an indirect relationship between popular culture and behavior. Otherwise, how can television executives make the case to advertisers that buying air time will boost their sales?" "Americans Despair of Pop Culture", in *The New York Times*, August 20, 1995.

277. Editorial, *U.S. News & World Report*, June 12, 1995, p. 94.

278. "Societies driven by the need to accumulate capital, and subjected to the pressures of the market, suffer from severe deformations including the alienated consciousness induced by extensive commercialization, the deformation of individual character caused by the over-division of labor, and the socially harmful bias toward self-directed rather than other-directed values." Robert Heilbroner, in *The Nation*, September 27, 1993.

279. From a letter published in *The New York Review of Books*, February 17, 1994.

280. "Homogenized consciousness revamping the world into an insidious consumer mirage", *Entertainment Magazine*, December 25, 1998.

281. Quoted in *The Economist*, July 31, 1993, p. 79.

282. *Out of Control*, Zbigniew Brzezinski, New York: Scribners, 1993.

283. *New York Review*, June 22, 1995.

284. Oxford University Press, 1939.

285. As described in "America's Burden", by Judith Miller, *The New York Times* Week in Review, December 8, 1991, p. 1.

286. *The New York Times* Week in Review, Sunday February 18, 1996.

287. Neal Ascherson, in *The New York Review of Books*, January 15, 1998.

288. "What's the Matter with Poetry?", in *The Nation*, August 24, 1993, p. 711.

289. "Land of Opportunity, One Family's Quest for the American Dream in the Age of Crack", *The Atlantic Monthly.*

290. Joseph A. Califano Jr., *op. cit.*, p. 9.

Index

Printed in the United States
3920